Zimbabwe's New Diaspora

STUDIES IN FORCED MIGRATION

General Editor: Roger Zetter, Refugee Studies Centre, University of Oxford

Zimbabwe's New Diaspora

DISPLACEMENT AND THE CULTURAL POLITICS OF SURVIVAL

Edited by
JoAnn McGregor and Ranka Primorac

Berghahn Books
New York • Oxford

Berghahn Books
www.berghahnbooks.com

©2010 JoAnn McGregor and Ranka Primorac

Library of Congress Cataloging-in-Publication Data

Zimbabwe's new diaspora: displacement and the cultural politics of
survival / edited by JoAnn McGregor and Ranka Primorac.
    p. cm. -- (Studies in forced migration ; v. 31)
Includes bibliographical references and index.
ISBN 978-1-84545-658-0 (hardback : alk. paper)
1. Zimbabweans--Foreign countries--Politics and government. 2. Forced
migration--Zimbabwe. I. McGregor, JoAnn. II. Primorac, Ranka.
DT2913.15.Z56 2010
325--dc22

                    2010018161

British Library Cataloguing in Publication Data

A catalogue record for this book is available from the British Library

Printed in the United States on acid-free paper.

ISBN: 978–1–84545–658–0 (hardback)

Contents

Editors' Preface and Acknowledgements

This volume had its origins in papers presented at a Britain Zimbabwe Society (BZS) research day, *Displacement and Survival: Zimbabwe's New Diaspora*. We would like to thank the African Studies Association (UK) and St. Antony's College, Oxford, for the support they provided for that event, which enabled us to bring over James Muzondidya from the Human Sciences Research Council in South Africa. The day was a memorable occasion, indicative of the changing character of the Society's annual research days in recent years, which have been enlivened by the growing number of Zimbabwean intellectuals based in the UK.

The BZS, which was formed in 1981, is a friendly society independent of governments of either country. It has promoted exchanges between Zimbabwean and British people, civil society organisations and academics, aiming to encourage open discussion and debate about Zimbabwe, within an overall framework of support for human rights and democracy, and a more just and equitable world order. In the light of these goals and the unfolding crisis and deteriorating relationship between Zimbabwean and British governments since 2000, the society has reoriented some of its activities, and has become engaged with the issue of Zimbabwean asylum seekers' rights in the UK and supporting challenges to deportations. This volume reflects on the period of protracted crisis from 2000, but the BZS looks forward to a new era in Zimbabwe oriented around reconstruction, rights and democracy rather than displacement and exodus.

We would like to thank the BZS for electing us to serve as executive members at various junctures, and for the knowledge and experience that key members have shared with us. Many people have provided direct support and encouragement in the writing of this volume, have commented on draft chapters or have helped indirectly in furthering our understanding of Zimbabwean politics and society. Particular thanks are owed to BZS President Terence Ranger and the current Chair, Knox Chitiyo, Jocelyn Alexander and Stephen Chan, and to the many BZS members who made thoughtful interventions in the course of the BZS research day.

Introduction

The Making of Zimbabwe's New Diaspora

JoAnn McGregor [1]

It is noon on Friday 11 July 2008 in St Margaret's Church, Westminster Abbey, London, where there is a service of prayer to 'Restore Zimbabwe' led by the Most Reverend and Right Honourable Dr John Sentamu, Archbishop of York. The church is full to bursting with Zimbabweans, some wearing the regalia of the Zimbabwean political opposition, the Movement for Democratic Change (MDC), others sporting t-shirts from the Trades Union Congress (TUC) sponsored London campaign for migrants' rights, 'Strangers into Citizens'. Eminent British political figures file into the building, among them Minister for Africa, Lord Malloch-Brown and members of the All Parliamentary Committee on Zimbabwe. As the London Zimbabwe choir begins to sing, the music sets the tone for a moving occasion and the congregation stands to join in, clapping, dancing and ululating. In the early part of the service 'Zimbabwean voices' – asylum seekers without papers-stand bravely in front of the congregation and television cameras to speak emotionally of the difficulties of life in the UK without rights to work, study or use their skills. Among them are a policeman, an accountant, an engineer, a banker and a business woman separated from her children for eight years. Following each voice, the congregation sing the interlude *'Jesu Tawa Pano'* [Jesus, We Are Here], and prayers are said for all Zimbabweans at home and abroad – for the victims of violence and the perpetrators, those who fled and those who remain, those who are hungry or destitute, detained or bereaved, and for peace, unity and love to descend. Later Sentamu uses the Address to make a direct appeal to the British Government – for Zimbabweans in Britain to be granted permission to work and for Security Council intervention in Zimbabwe. He begins by invoking Joshua Nkomo's words at the funeral of Lookout Masuku (an ex-Zipra guerrilla and commander in the Zimbabwe National Army, who died in 1986 after four year's illegitimate detention for treason during the Matabeleland conflict): 'We cannot blame colonialism and imperialism for this tragedy. We who fought against these things now practice them. We are enveloped in the politics of hate. What Zimbabwe fought for was peace, progress, love, respect, justice, equality, not the opposite'. Gordon Brown's move to suspend deportations to Zimbabwe was an honourable first step, Sentamu reasons, but Britain must now grant temporary leave to remain: this is a matter of justice for Zimbabweans and also common sense, as it will foster the skills necessary for reconstruction and will allow Zimbabweans to contribute to British society through work and taxes. No Zimbabwean should be in detention or destitute on the streets of Britain. More ululation, and the service closes with the Zimbabwean national anthem. As the congregation leaves the church, people are ushered over the road to a rally in Parliament Square, where they cheer 'we want to work and pay tax', and from there, Sentamu leads the crowd on to the Home Office to hand over a letter in person.

This event was testimony to the unique embeddedness of Zimbabweans in Britain and to the opportunities it has provided to mobilise for rights in the UK and to engage in 'long distance' politics (Anderson 1992; Østergaard-Nielsen 2003) through lobbying and campaigning to transform the Zimbabwe situation. The exceptional place Zimbabwe occupies in the British public sphere has been produced through the legacies of Rhodesian settler colonialism and the struggle for national liberation, and this 'presence of the past' is reflected in today's diasporic claims and transnational engagements (Waldinger 2006 cited in Dumont 2008: 794). The special relationship between the two countries helps to explain why events in Zimbabwe make headline news in Britain for days on end, and why moves to resume deportations can spark protest not only from Zimbabweans themselves, the churches and groups promoting migrants' rights, but also from members of the Conservative Party, the House of Lords and the xenophobic right wing tabloid, *The Daily Mail*. Friends of Zimbabwe include members of both conservative and liberal establishments in Britain – those with connections to Rhodesia through farms and other investments (and their friends and relatives), as well as those involved in the solidarity movement against white minority rule or postcolonial NGO networks. While this special relationship certainly provided unusual access to the corridors of power in Britain, it also produced contradictions, as British criticism of Mugabe's ruling Zanu(PF) party and support for the MDC contributed to the crisis in Zimbabwe, and was used skilfully by

Mugabe to build support from other African heads of state through a shared anti-imperialism (Phimister and Raftopulous 2004). Moreover, the concessions won through legal challenges to deportations, though significant in allowing many Zimbabweans to stay in Britain, have also been temporary and limited, such that those lacking papers or trapped in an eroded asylum system have remained insecure without basic rights.

As former colonial power, Britain has been particularly important among 'western' destinations for Zimbabweans in the extraordinary exodus since 2000, which has involved as much as a quarter of Zimbabwe's population, or 3 million people (Chetsanga and Muchenje 2003); the UK Home Office estimates a population of 200,000 Zimbabweans in Britain (Pasura 2006). But Britain is only one of many countries of settlement beyond the southern African region, as Zimbabweans are now scattered throughout Europe, the USA and Canada, Australia and New Zealand. These migrants are drawn predominantly from Zimbabwe's elite and middle classes. They have been formed from those who could afford the long distance flights, and had the professional qualifications or contacts necessary to make the journey. The distance from home and this elite social base have helped to foster diasporic communities and transnational connections that differ from those within the southern African region.

Within southern Africa, South Africa has been by far the most important destination for labour migrants, professionals, refugees and circulating traders, though Zimbabweans are also numerous in other SADC countries. In South Africa, Zimbabweans also have a particular embeddedness, shaped by shared histories of struggle against white minority rule, more than a century of labour migrancy, close integration across a common border as well as a multitude of older, precolonial connections and some shared languages. This too has created particular opportunities for claims to rights *in situ* and for long distance politics. Zimbabweans in South Africa likewise make headline news, not only because of the sheer scale of the movement, but also because the crisis in Zimbabwe became a political crisis for the South African government, the ANC, SADC and the region as a whole (Raftopoulos 2008). But for Zimbabweans in South Africa too, close embeddedness has produced frustrations and insecurities alongside opportunities. South African premier Thabo Mbeki's support for Mugabe and Zanu (PF) between 2000 and 2008, and his denial of crisis conditions in Zimbabwe worked not only to delay a political solution, but also to undermine displaced Zimbabweans' claims to protection and assistance (Phimister and Raftopoulos 2004, Sisulu et al. 2007, Kriger this volume). Zimbabweans in South Africa can draw on a range of networks to mount political challenges, build solidarity networks, make claims to citizenship or historical belonging. But they have also been subject to exclusionary state policies hinging on detention and deportation in an environment of intense popular xenophobia. A temporary protection arrangement was announced by the South African government only belatedly, in 2009 (Kriger and Rutherford, this volume).

This volume explores the emergence and dynamics of these new Zimbabwe diaspora communities in South Africa and Britain from 2000. It brings together some of the first empirical research conducted on Zimbabweans displaced beyond national borders in these two locations and explores the development of diasporic identities and political claims, and the social networks created in the struggle to survive, support family and meet socio-economic aspirations. The book shows how the Zimbabwean case can be illuminating for the broader literatures on diaspora and transnationalism, particularly debates over 'new African diasporas' (Koser 2003) – formed by movements beyond national borders in a postcolonial context. It also aims to highlight the commonalities, contrasts and connections between diaspora communities in proximate countries within the region and those who live in the West. Diasporic identities are, of course, intimately shaped both by the politics of receiving countries and by unfolding events back home. Yet this volume does not aim to provide a detailed investigation of the political economy of displacement and survival inside Zimbabwe from 2000, which is explored in other forthcoming collections (see Crush and Tevera forthcoming; Hammar et al. forthcoming). The focus here is rather on the perspectives and circumstances of those Zimbabweans living outside Zimbabwe's borders. For some, who are able to circulate back and forth, relationships with home are based on direct contact, but others depend on texts, emails and diasporic websites, whose role is explored in this volume.

The title – *Zimbabwe's New Diaspora* – reflects this perspective of Zimbabweans living beyond national borders, though not all Zimbabweans outside their country conceive of themselves as diasporans, for reasons illuminated below. Indeed, shedding light on how, to what ends and under what circumstances diasporic identities have been taken up is one of the aims of the book. Using the prefix 'new' emphasises the unprecedented dispersal of Zimbabweans over the last decade, and differentiates recent movements from the previous displacements that have so profoundly shaped Zimbabwean history. These past migrations include colonial histories of African labour migrancy within the region implicated in earlier transnational worker, Africanist and religious movements, the mobility of white settlers that shaped Rhodesian nationalism and its demise, the unsettled histories of town and countryside shaped by eviction, segregation and rural/urban circulation or the mass displacements within and beyond borders produced by the liberation war. Though the book focuses on recent events, the echoes and legacies of these earlier episodes of movement are present in the contributions, not just as a passive backdrop, but as a fabric of understanding and a resource of connections that are used to make claims today. The volume is empirically grounded and places strong emphasis on history and politics, highlighting the shaping and constraining influence of state policies and the law. The contributors echo other commentators who have argued that states and borders continue to matter profoundly in today's migrations and transnational engagements (Koopmans and Statham 2001, Turner 2008). But the collection also retains an emphasis on human agency and creativity, conveyed through its focus on the 'cultural politics' of survival in new locations. Zimbabweans beyond national borders are profoundly affected by the state policies of host- and homeland, but they have manoeuvred within and around these constraints, and have tried to influence the circumstances of displacement to their own ends, both through political claims-making and a broader range of social and cultural initiative that has been crucial in making ends meet, creating a sense of belonging in new places as well as perpetuating attachments to home.

Although the new Zimbabwean diaspora has been shaped by some of the specificities of the nature of the crisis at home and historical relationships between sending and hosting states, it has also been shaped by broader global, political, economic and cultural trends that all migrants in the world today have to navigate. These include the reconfiguration of borders and citizenship in an era of restrictionism and securitisation; the development of globalised labour markets in skilled and unskilled labour, the rolling out of neo-liberal economic policies and effects of global economic recession, the rise of new technologies of communication, the expansion of transnational religious movements and globalised discourses on human rights. This means that the collection addresses debates that go beyond the particularities of the Zimbabwean case, and by spelling out insights from the experiences of Zimbabweans recently forced beyond national borders throws further light on broader theoretical debates about transnational engagements, the making and unmaking of diasporic identities, about displacement, migration and asylum in the world today.

Diasporic Identities and Shaping Contexts

It would be conventional to begin an introductory discussion such as this by defining terms. What does 'diaspora' mean? The word has long escaped its grounding in Jewish history and has been used in so many different ways and contexts that some commentators feel it risks losing its meaning (Clifford 1997). How, the discussion might have continued, does the idea of diaspora relate to that of transnationalism? (Vertovec and Cohen 1999; Werbner 2000; Levitt and Jaworsky 2001), and how has it been operationalised recently by governments and policy-makers

(Mercer et al. 2008)? But this book enters these debates through a different route, as it begins by asking how the idea of diaspora has been taken up by Zimbabweans themselves. As Turner and others have elaborated, 'the term [diaspora] is moving rapidly from academics to policy-makers and to migrant groups themselves who use the term to claim recognition' (Turner 2008: 746; cf. Kleist 2007; Axel 2004). The Zimbabweans living beyond national borders who are the subject of this book are testimony to this trend, as the idea of a community of 'diasporans' (*madiaspora* in Shona, or *amadiaspora* in Ndebele) has entered popular discourse since 2000, both as a self identification and ascribed label. There has been a rapid proliferation of specifically diasporic political campaigns and a mushrooming of formal and informal diasporic associations fulfilling a range of social, emotional, religious and other needs. This is a novel development as the 1970s generation of Zimbabwean political exiles and students who moved to other African countries and Britain during the protracted struggle for independence did not use the term diaspora to describe themselves or their relationship with home. In this context, it becomes less important to discuss how well this particular new diaspora fits academic definitions than to explore how the term has been given political and cultural salience, by whom and what the implications might be.

Diaspora communities should not be understood as reified groups with a fixed essence, but as the outcome of historical, political and cultural processes through which ideas of belonging come to be defined primarily in terms of attachment to a distant homeland and shared national imaginaries. This is important in the context of a literature where some leading authors continue to deploy the term in an essentialised manner as 'neither invented not imagined' (Sheffer 2003: 7) so that it can retain the overtones of a racialised epithet notwithstanding efforts to appropriate it to an inclusive cosmopolitanism. As Turner (2008) argues, the term diaspora is more appropriately used as an adjective than a noun, though Zimbabwean discourse goes against this view, as writers tend to use it as a noun, often in capitalised form – 'the Diaspora' or 'in the Diaspora' – as if it were an ethno-national group or a country itself. Using the term as an adjective has the advantage of suggesting a more fluid alignment, allowing investigation of how diasporic identities, connections and claims are made and unmade in particular contexts, by communities of interest that are not stable over time or space (Van Hear 1998). Exploring diaspora from this angle thus highlights ideology and 'framing processes' (Collyer 2008; Sökefeld 2006). It permits an examination of why some people resist identifying themselves as diasporans, the circumstances that encourage or discourage diasporic positioning, and can highlight the tensions and cleavages within diasporic communities. Particularly when produced in the context of conflict, diasporic communities are characteristically fractious and riven, partly along imported political and social divides, partly through frustrations and differences opened up in countries of settlement (Griffiths 2000). As Pasura has argued, Zimbabwe's new diaspora is 'fractured and fragmented', such that generalisations about a singular diaspora can be profoundly misleading (Pasura 2008).

The emergence of diasporic identities and claims from 2000 is intimately connected to changes in the Zimbabwean homeland and cannot be understood in separation from Zimbabwe's trajectory of economic and political crisis. Although the structural adjustment years of the 1990s caused a 'brain drain' out of Zimbabwe that built upon previous trajectories of flight on the part of Ndebele speakers (following the 1980s massacres) and white settlers (before and after independence), the political violence that followed the emergence of the MDC in late 1999 signalled the onset of a new era marked by intense repression, extraordinarily rapid economic contraction and displacement on an unprecedented scale. National politics became polarised, as the MDC immediately posed a very serious challenge to Zanu(PF). Emerging out of the movement for constitutional reform led by the unions, churches and civics, the MDC crosscut regional and ethnic divisions, and won over urban constituencies and Matabeleland in the Parliamentary elections of 2000 (Rich-Dorman 2002; Raftopoulos 2001). Zanu(PF)'s counter strategy was to launch the 'Third Chimurenga' [liberation struggle], involving a return to wartime rhetoric of enemies and sellouts, and politicised land occupations led by 'war veterans', in which white farmers and farm workers were assaulted, evicted and killed. Party/ state agents unleashed a broader campaign of violence targeting MDC activists, teachers, unionists, journalists and civic leaders, while the public services were purged of those deemed disloyal. What had become a vibrant public sphere was drastically eclipsed by repressive security legislation and bans on the independent media, while the judiciary and police were forced into partisan roles, such that the presidential elections of 2002 that returned Mugabe to power, were widely regarded as stolen (Raftopoulos 2004; Hammar and Raftopoulos 2003; on state legitimating rhetoric, Ranger 2004).

Further periods of elevated violence followed the 2005 parliamentary elections, through the state's politicised programme of mass urban demolitions known as Operation Murambatsvina [Remove the Filth], through which 700,000 people lost their homes and/or their informal urban livelihoods (Potts 2006, Solidarity Peace Trust [SPT] 2005). Hunger and food shortages were further intensified through Operation Taguta [We're Satisfied], as the military commandeered food and unrealistic price controls rendered much formal trading unprofitable (SPT 2006). After the MDC's narrow victory in the March 2008 elections, state violence to punish MDC voters and influence the presidential run-off reached new levels through

Operation Mavhoterapapi? [How did you vote?] (SPT 2008 and 2008a). The violence forced the MDC to pull out and Mugabe declared himself winner, but SADC heads of state refused to see this as legitimate, leading to a political deadlock over power-sharing in which inflation levels continued their exponential rise, to the point that official rates from mid 2008 were measured in hundreds of millions of per cent. The compromise, facilitated through protracted SADC mediation, was the Global Peace Agreement (GPA) signed by Zanu(PF) and the two MDCs in September 2008, but only implemented from February 2009. Thereafter, prices stabilised, but donors delayed full re-engagement in the light of uncertainties over the workability of the new inclusive government, given Zanu(PF)'s continued control of key security ministries, and ongoing political violence from Zanu(PF)/state agents. Over this decade of intense political repression and economic contraction, life expectancy plummeted to one of the lowest on the continent, as basic services ceased to function, HIV/AIDS and later cholera took their toll, and remittances became crucial in the struggle to survive (Bracking and Sachikonye 2007).

This was the context in which Zimbabweans beyond national borders began to see themselves as, and started to organise as diasporans, exiles and in other ways. Exiled journalists and broadcasters set up Zimbabwean radio and internet news sites abroad to service diasporans and provide alternatives to the state-dominated media (discussed below). At the same time, there was a rapid extension of opposition politics beyond Zimbabwe's borders, as activists initiated a network of MDC branches in South Africa, Britain and elsewhere to campaign and raise money for the party at home and assist victims of political violence. Non-partisan groups such as the South Africa-based Zimbabwe Exiles Forum (founded by exiled lawyers in 2003) or the USA-based Association of Zimbabweans Based Abroad also lobbied against the abuses of Zanu(PF) rule. Ahead of the 2005 elections, the UK-based Diaspora Vote Action Group presented a legal challenge to the Zimbabwe Supreme Court to extend diaspora voting beyond the embassy and armed forces. Indeed, activism was such that Raftopoulos and Alexander argued that 'in its totality, Diaspora political activism has opened up a new front in the fight for democratisation in Zimbabwe' (Raftopoulos and Alexander 2006).

In campaigning for the restoration of democracy and the rule of law in Zimbabwe, these various diasporic groups found a receptive international environment, gaining support from western governments, as well as human rights groups such as Amnesty International, trade union movements, churches and others. In an extraordinary display of solidarity with Zimbabweans in 2008, South African dock workers refused to unload a Chinese shipment of arms intended for the Zimbabwean government, and a broader international campaign supported by the International Network on Small Arms, unions, churches and civil society activists led to the ship's inability to dock in alternative ports in Mozambique, Namibia and Angola (Larmer 2008). The broad international support for this particular campaign, facilitated by the rapid flow of information over email, internet and mobile phones, illuminated how a decade of activism and the consolidation of transnational networks of support helped to shift international opinion against Zanu(PF) (Larmer 2008). Indeed, the potential threat posed by diasporic activism was underlined by Zanu(PF)'s defensive counter-mobilisation beyond its borders – through efforts to jam diaspora media transmissions (using Chinese technology), and by covert destabilisation and infiltration of opposition groups (Raftopoulos and Alexander 2007; McGregor 2009). Although in 2004, Zanu(PF) belatedly woke up to the financial potential of its citizens abroad and launched 'Homelink' to try to channel remittances via the Zimbabwe Reserve Bank, the scheme raised only a fraction of the funds envisaged. The Mugabe government refused to extend diaspora voting rights, despite the legal challenge mentioned above, but rather cast 'the Diaspora', particularly those who went to the West, as traitorous and in league with imperialist forces.

Diasporic claims-making not only aimed to transform the situation at home, but also to extend the civic sphere within countries of settlement, challenging exclusionary state policies both within the southern African region and in the West, particularly with regard to asylum. The period from 2000 thus also saw a proliferation of Zimbabwean asylum-seeker support and campaign groups. Although the conflation of homeland politics with the politics of asylum was sometimes cast as a diversion (Magaisa 2006), campaigning on the issue of asylum was an important means of highlighting the abuses of Zanu(PF) rule, particularly given factionalism within the MDC that undermined the party's capacity to speak with one voice, culminating in a formal split in 2005 (on the MDC's internal problems, see Le Bas 2007; Raftopoulos 2006). It provided grounds for joint action with an array of local, national and international groups promoting migrants' rights. In South Africa, the predicament of Zimbabwean refugees was taken up by diaspora organisations such as the Zimbabwe Political Victims' Association and Concerned Zimbabweans Abroad, Zimbabwean and South African NGOs such as the Solidarity Peace Trust and Lawyers for Human Rights, as well as international bodies such as Refugees International and Human Rights Watch. Churches emerged as key actors providing humanitarian assistance and shelter, and sometimes also as critics of state policies (Sisulu et al. 2007: 560). In Britain, the Zimbabwe Association, one of a large number of support groups in cities around the country, worked with the Refugee Legal Centre to mount legal challenge deportations to Zimbabwe, joined up with churches, the TUC and Refugee Council in campaigns for asylum-seekers rights, organizing high profile events such as the church service described at the outset.

Aside from investing in such campaigns, Zimbabweans also organised themselves to recreate Zimbabwean social and religious institutions in foreign environments (Sisulu et al. 2007; Pasura this volume; Muzondidya this volume). Within countries of settlement, the development of diasporic social life means that, over time, it has become much easier for Zimbabweans abroad to meet one another, and social calendars can be punctuated by regular gatherings with compatriots to relax, drink, barbeque meat (*gochi gochi*), listen to Zimbabwean music, discuss Zimbabwean news, watch Zimbabwean soccer, or pray together in Zimbabwean church fellowships. Such socialisation also facilitates, and is enmeshed with important networks of mutual support, which can provide practical and emotional assistance in dealing with the authorities, seeking work, incidents of domestic violence, illness, bereavement and the repatriation of bodies.

At its most straightforward, the term 'diaspora' has been invoked in this extension of the Zimbabwean social and political field beyond national borders simply to mean Zimbabweans outside the country's borders. The geographical expansion of social and political life clearly does not render the border irrelevant – quite the opposite. Zimbabweans, like other transnational groups use the term diasporan to 'position themselves and each other according to who is inside and who is outside'(Turner 2008: 748). Diaspora political campaigns have often used the term in this broad way to invoke the widest possible constituency of Zimbabweans outside Zimbabwe. While many of the most prominent diasporic activists are recent political exiles who have sought asylum, Zimbabweans abroad include people in a broad range of circumstances, whose reasons for leaving were varied, and who left at different times. The term diaspora has the advantage of rendering irrelevant the state binaries that divide 'economic migrants' from 'political refugees', and are used by host states to either confer or strip the different categories of their rights. Brought together by a shared connection to a distant homeland, diasporic campaigns can incorporate labour migrants, professionals and others who left primarily to meet socio-economic goals alongside political exiles (though, as conditions deteriorated from 2000, there is a sense in which everyone experienced their move as forced). These campaigns can also incorporate older generations of migrants from the 1970s and 80s.

But the term also has other connotations, beyond simply a positioning 'abroad'. Like the term 'exile', the idea of diaspora is ancient and predates the modern state and international bureaucracies that produced the categories of refugee and asylum-seeker. Both terms have an aestheticisable quality, and are prone to romanticisation. As Said notes, the exile 'once banished lives an anomalous and miserable life, with the stigma of being an outsider', yet unlike the label 'refugee', the term '"exile" carries with it, I think, a touch of solitude and spirituality' (Said 1984). But there are also differences between the two terms. First, the idea of diaspora is broader than that of exile, as the latter forefronts the act of banishment whereas the notion of diaspora can invoke a degree of choice. Second, while the idea of diaspora is intrinsically collective, the notion of exile can be individualistic – though Zimbabweans who have mobilised as 'exiles' rather than as 'diasporans' have been able to breach this individualism and use it as a shared identity and as the basis for broader solidarity campaigns, in so doing invoking powerful historical precedents from the time of the liberation struggle. While being in exile often suggests little about the duration of time abroad or the relationship with the hostland (other than through solidarity campaigns), the term diaspora implies a degree of embeddedness in the country of residence (even if clearly also estrangement), such that diasporic demands for recognition and rights are typically made on a dual front, in relation to the host society as well as the homeland (Østergaard-Nielsen 2003). As the formation of a diaspora implies a protracted separation from home, it can also convey ambivalence about the reality of return. Indeed, some Zimbabweans have explicitly rejected the label 'diasporan' in favour of 'exile' on these grounds. Moreover, as it is used by Zimbabweans, the term diaspora clearly has elite connotations.

The elite overtones of the word mean that although all Zimbabweans living outside Zimbabwe could potentially see themselves as part of a diaspora, the term has often been taken up and applied much more selectively. The Zimbabwean migrant labourers in South Africa, the circulating traders who move between cities in the region and maintain regular contact with home are not usually labelled diasporans. When young male migrants return home to Zimbabwe from the South African townships at Christmas and other times, they are called '*majonijoni*', or '*injiva*', terms which, despite their association with money, convey none of the elite overtones of the diasporan. Indeed '*injiva*' implies criminality and violence: Maphosa argues that '*injiva*' invokes the cultural style of urban youth gangs, the popular image being 'of an individual who among other things does not hesitate to use *umese* (knife) or *isibhamu* (gun) to resolve disputes, settle grudges or demand sex' (Maphosa 2006).

There is further evidence of the elite connotations of 'diasporan' in the tensions between those 'in the Diaspora' (particularly but not only those who are in the West) and those who stayed behind - what Magaisa (2006) describes as a 'love/hate' relationship. These tensions build on the fantasy of the colonial motherland and other relatively wealthy diasporic destinations as sites of easy riches. Such perceptions can be reinforced despite the acute exclusion many in the diaspora have faced, through the difficulties of conveying realities of insecurity and hardship to those at home, and the shame of failing to live up to expectations. Those left behind may combine gratitude and resentment towards those who have

sought greener pastures, who may have prospered while those at home
have suffered, whose investments have inflated property prices, whose
money-making sheds doubt on the commitment to return and whose view
of Zimbabwean politics can be detached from the complexities of lived
reality. As Raftopoulos and Alexander describe, those still at home 'have
criticised Diaspora activists for being out of touch with the political reality
on the ground ... or for being cowards who have run away from the frontline
of the struggle against authoritarianism' (Raftopoulos and Alexander 2006:
52). Stephen T. Maimbodei, writing in *The Herald* (Zimbabwe's main state-
run daily), captures other aspects of the resentment of those left behind in
claiming 'the Diaspora syndrome' has replaced the 'been to' syndrome of
a previous generation who had studied or trained in the west. Both new
and old labels are selective, Maimbodei notes, 'my father, who worked as
a migrant labourer in Malawi and South Africa, was never called a "been
to"'.[1]

> Diaspora, which has replaced the 'been-to' syndrome, is now so rife ...
> Today's 'been-to' or Diasporan is bringing immense economic benefits
> to their families. In Zimbabwe's harsh economic environment, you hear
> many claiming that if it were not for the family members and relatives in
> the Diaspora, they would be suffering more than they are doing right now.
> Diasporans are now the new buyers and owners of property, and they are
> doing it at unprecedented levels. For a nation which is going through such an
> economic crunch to have roads littered with the latest vehicles from all over
> the world, most of them fuel-guzzling 4 x 4s, is a wonder.

The status attached to the term diasporan also emerges clearly through
contrast to meanings of 'migrant', 'refugee' and 'asylum seeker' in countries
of settlement. Indeed, the appeal of being a diasporan seems partly to
be a reaction against these other labels, which are at best alienating and
dehumanising. At worst they are terms of abuse and imply criminality: a
Zimbabwean mother (herself a recent migrant) provided a reminder of this
as we were chatting on a SE London street corner when her six year old son
pointed to a stranger and exclaimed loudly, 'Look, Mummy, it's a migrant!'
She reprimanded him with horror, 'Don't ever call someone using that
term again, it's not polite'.[2] The Independent Asylum Commission in the
UK has recently argued that the term 'asylum' has been so contaminated
with overtones of criminality that it has chosen to reactivate the older
term 'sanctuary' instead.[3] As the introduction explores further below, in
South Africa, the violence of the xenophobic attacks of May 2008 similarly
underlined the negative stereotyping around the terms of migrant, asylum-
seeker, stranger or *mukwerekwere* [babbler – speaker of incomprehensible
languages]. To be a 'diasporan', in contrast, is honourable, implies a certain
level of consumption and education, and a familiarity with technologies

such as the internet and mobile phones. It implies responsibilities and obligations, both towards family and dependents, but also in the political sphere through civic engagements to extend the boundaries of political community both *in situ* and at home. The status of the diasporan has also been validated through the churches, where leaders make biblical comparisons with the Jews in exile in Babylon and Egypt, cast a renewed Zimbabwe as the promised land, while also elaborating the moral goals of 'reverse mission' against a decadent West (Maxwell 2006).

This emergence of the idea of 'the Diaspora' and 'the Diasporan' as a means of talking about Zimbabweans abroad does not, however, mean that diasporans have spoken with a singular voice, found it easy to unite, or that imaginations of the nation have had a shared liberal content. As indicated above, much diasporic activism has explicitly aimed to contest Zanu(PF)'s narrow and commandist version of nationalism, based on ideals of rights, the rule of law, democracy and inclusiveness. Yet diasporic politics does not always take us into Brah's (1996, or others') cosmopolitan and progressive version of 'diasporic space' that transcends essentialised categories of belonging. Rather, essentialised expressions of identity have also flourished in diasporic contexts, and political divides at home have been imported. The suspicion and instability of diaspora politics between 2000 and 2008 not only reflected the main political division between Zanu(PF) and MDC and the internal factionalism of the MDC but also ethnic and racial divides (on the MDC split see Rafotopuolos 2006; Le Bas 2007; on diaspora politics see Sisulu et al. 2007; McGregor 2009). Strands of ethnic nationalism that are brought into check back home through the pragmatics of voting have flourished in diasporic contexts, such as Mthwakazi, which advocates an agenda of separatism for Matabeleland (see Peel this volume). 'Rhodesian' organisations have also mobilised outside Zimbabwe and on-line (see King 2004), while racial cleavages have been underlined by white Zimbabweans' easier access to citizenship rights abroad, differentiating their experience from the black majority who are insecure. Summarizing the diasporic divisions within the South African context, Sisulu et al. bemoan the lack of unity: 'this amorphous diaspora, with its class and ethnic divisions, has failed to act in a concerted way' (2007: 562). Raftopoulos and Alexander cast diaspora mobilisation as undermined by the MDC's internal factionalism, by conflicts between 'internals and exiles', by racial, class, ethnic, linguistic and regional divisions, by a tendency to duplicate activities and compete for political space rather than cooperate, by excessive dependence on the internet, and by the 'emergence of briefcase Diaspora organisations for whom fighting for democratic change in Zimbabwe has become a lucrative personal industry' (2006: 53). The mutual distrust that has been such a marked feature of Zimbabwean diaspora associational life was greatly exacerbated by insecurity and the fears of the police and security agents of host as well as homeland states (on the South African context, see Sisulu et al. 2007; on Britain, see McGregor this volume and 2009; Pasura 2008 and this volume)

Talking about Zimbabwean diasporic identities as they have been shaped at this particular historical juncture in specific places thus creates an avenue into broader theoretical debates. It prioritises empirical study in a literature that has often been notable in part for its detachment from ethnographies of lived experience in particular localities, or the shaping role of states or global political economy (though see recent ethnographies of African diasporic communities, Stoller 2002; d'Alisera 2004; McGown 1999; Clarke 2004; Mazzucato 2008 and essays in Koser 2003). The ambiguous status attached to the notion of a 'diasporan' by Zimbabweans still at home places questions of nation and class at the forefront of discussion, in a literature in which class in particular is often overlooked (Grillo 2007). The reproduction within diasporic settings of racial and ethnic divides raises important questions about postcolonial identities. Talking about diasporic identities being made and unmade in particular contexts moves beyond the categories used by states to classify foreigners, which are also reflected in the conventional divisions of migration studies between the economic and political, forced and involuntary, and in typologies of diaspora (Cohen 1997). It also questions assumptions about assimilation over time.

This brief discussion of how the terms 'diaspora' and 'diasporan' have been taken up by Zimbabweans has so far concentrated largely on how their use has reflected change within Zimbabwe from 2000. The next section turns to the South African and British contexts more specifically, to look further at how the structure of opportunity and constraint within these two places has influenced Zimbabwean diasporic identities and claims, before turning to the role of diasporic media.

Zimbabwean Diasporic Claims and the South African Context

Zimbabwean diasporic claims in the South African context have been shaped by a contradictory mixture of opportunities and exclusions. From 1994, post-apartheid South Africa rapidly became a magnet for migrants and refugees from other parts of the continent, who were attracted by the country's wealth, the possibilities of work and study, and expectations of asylum as these were fostered through the ANC's rhetoric of rights and an inclusionary Africanism (Crush 2000; Landau 2005 and 2006; Muzondidya this volume). Zimbabweans had a distinct advantage over many other African migrants due to the quality of Zimbabwean education and respect for Zimbabwean qualifications on the part of South African employers, such that those with education were well placed to take advantage of the opportunities created by post-apartheid indigenisation and neo-liberal economic restructuring. There were openings at the top of the socio-economic hierarchy for the business and professional classes, and in the middle for skilled artisans, nurses and others. As Sisulu et al note, Zimbabwean professionals and business people concentrated in South Africa's major cities, particularly Johannesburg, have 'enjoyed considerable success in the corporate world, especially in financial services' (2007: 555), and Zimbabweans are also prominent in the health sector, engineering, IT, security, media and journalism (Bloch 2005; Chikanda 2005). Neo-liberal economic reforms in industry and agriculture have also influenced markets in unskilled labour, and South African employers have been in a position to benefit from and exploit migrants without their papers (SPT 2007). South African corporations expanded into Zimbabwe, buying up assets, while in the border regions, supermarkets and other service providers saw a huge surge in business from Zimbabweans buying basic commodities in South Africa, and contributing to flourishing cross border industries (SPT 2007).

These opportunities for some Zimbabweans and the economic benefits accruing to sectors of South African society from the economic crisis in Zimbabwe and large-scale migration, have co-existed with mounting popular xenophobia, and a decade of state investment in restrictionist measures of immigration and asylum control. A new temporary protection arrangement was finally (and unexpectedly) announced only in early 2009 (Crush and Williams 2003; Nyamnjoh 2006; SPT 2004; HRW 2007 and 2008; Handmaker and Parsely 2001; Maharaj 2004; on the protection measures, see LHR 2009). Many poor South Africans have seen little economic benefit from the post-apartheid transition and are also newcomers to the urban spaces they have come to share, or compete over, with other African migrants. As Landau argues (2005: 1115–6), the 'nativist' discourses and restrictionist realities of South Africa's treatment of migrants 'resonate with global trends in which quests to assert sovereignty through immigration controls are resulting in actions that undermine the legitimacy and founding principles of the liberal states that undertake them'. Investing in border controls, detention and deportations for the period between 2000 and 2008 did not, however, stem cross-border movement any more than in other contexts, as it did not address the conflicts, economic decline and transnational calculations that underpinned movement (on the Mexico/ US border, Massey 2005; on Europe, de Haas 2007; see also Castles 2004). Rather, the effects were to enhance the risks and insecurities faced by Zimbabweans (and other migrants) and to create lucrative informal economies of border crossing and forged documents, in which the police and other state agents developed profitable businesses out of their role as law enforcers (Landau 2005). The professionalisation of cross border services has been embodied in the figures of the *amalayisha* [transport operators dealing in people, goods and money] and *magumaguma* [people traffickers who assist with crossing, but also prey on, rob and rape border jumpers] (see Rutherford this volume).

Unlike many other postcolonial cross border movements of this scale within the African continent, the Zimbabweans who fled repression at home were not treated *en masse* as refugees, isolated in large camps serviced by the international community. South Africa upheld a model of individual determination of refugee status, access to which was particularly restricted for Zimbabweans (HRW 2007 and 2008, Kriger this volume). This specific exclusion of Zimbabweans reflected the supportive political relationship between the Mugabe and Mbeki (then Motlanthe) governments, as there are longstanding precedents allowing for group determination and for international intervention to assist victims of war and humanitarian disasters who do not fit a narrow refugee definition, reflected both in the OAU Convention (incorporated into South African law) and the flexibility of UNHCR's mandate to assist a broader category of 'people of concern' (Crisp 2000). A government decision to roll out temporary protection for Zimbabweans was only announced in April 2009, in the context of the fragile GPA agreement between Zanu(PF) and the two MDCs, and after Jacob Zuma had taken over as South African President. The need for such protection measures reflected the inextricable entwining of state violence and economic plunge that provoked the exodus from Zimbabwe, and produced patterns of flight that have tapped into routes of self advancement followed by generations of migrant labourers, students and professionals.

In this volume, Norma Kriger extends this discussion of the politics of legal protection for Zimbabweans in South Africa since 2000, as it has been provided for through South Africa's progressive legal architecture – the constitution, immigration, refugee and employment law – and as it has been undermined through daily violations. Kriger elaborates how South Africa's official policy of support for the Mugabe government fostered and legitimated an environment of hostility toward Zimbabweans. The chapter provides an illuminating discussion of the initial limitations of rights-based advocacy, and the belated critique of the categories of the law itself in relation to Zimbabweans' circumstances of displacement. Kriger reviews the very limited legal options open to Zimbabweans prior to the new temporary protection measures, and some of the ways they tried to manipulate access to them. International organisations such as IOM and UNHCR were themselves complicit in upholding this limited structure of opportunity and the resultant suffering among Zimbabweans. IOM, in particular, as 'lead agency', cooperated in a programme of deportations with inadequate protection.

The failures of the state and international regimes operating in South Africa to provide adequate protection for those displaced forced Zimbabweans to elaborate other claims that depend on shared history and reciprocity between the two countries, often cast in terms of 'brotherhood' in the struggle against white minority rule, and to rely on their own informal networks or turn to Zimbabwean community-based organisations. Zimbabweans have also exploited the considerable scope for 'merging in' unnoticed, by emphasising common ethnic identities and languages between the two countries – Venda in the border areas, or Sotho, Shangaan or Ndebele elsewhere – or investing in relationships with previous generations of migrants who have been naturalised.

In this volume, Muzondidya elaborates on these strategies, the nature of the shared histories they invoke, and their limits. He investigates how Zimbabweans who initially saw South Africa simply as a place of temporary residence and work have gradually begun to make it home, and examines the ways in which they are engaged in an ongoing process of negotiating new spaces for themselves and their children in South African cities. The chapter argues that experiences in South African cities have been diverse, but that one response to a sense of exclusion produced by mounting popular xenophobia has been the development of new definitions of Zimbabweanness, in which the content of diasporic patriotism involves inverting South African contempt for *makwerekwere*. This patriotism deems Zimbabweans to be superior, as Zimbabweanness is associated with the values of respect for education, the law, family and authority, while South African society is condemned as violent, criminal and amoral. In diasporic venues, the banal symbols of the nation have been newly validated, with national flags and anthem-singing occupying a more prominent place than in social gatherings at home. Yet Muzondidya is careful also to delve beyond such symbols and rhetorics of diasporic unity, to explore the class, racial and ethnic cleavages and tensions within diaspora communities.

Away from the cities in the farms of the border region of Limpopo Province, the agrarian economy and histories of crossborder contact provide a rather different context for seeking to merge in or simply find temporary work and safety. Blair Rutherford's chapter examines the neoliberal policies that have reshaped the agrarian economy over the last decade, exploring the overlapping historical formations of citizenship, the cultural politics of vulnerability, and the economies of survival informing Zimbabwean farmworkers' circumstances and strategies. Rutherford highlights the importance of distinguishing between different cohorts of migrants, and also elaborates the interweaving of political and economic motivations for flight for those arriving since 2000, many of whom had direct experience of state violence though they did not try to access the asylum regime. Unlike previous generations of Zimbabweans who sought work on the farms, recent arrivals often have more education and come from more distant parts of Zimbabwe that lack historic engagements with the South African borderlands. Though some undoubtedly responded to diasporic political campaigns, such as efforts in the border region around election times to encourage Zimbabweans abroad to go home to vote or to join the mass marches against the Lindela detention centre, their capacity to move to and fro, and their predominantly non-elite class base means that most tend not to be labeled as, or to conceive of themselves as 'diasporans', in so far as that term invokes the idea of the relatively well-to-do, educated urban classes.

These chapters on Zimbabweans in the South African context thus help to illuminate both the advantages and limitations of the concept of diaspora as a means of understanding displacement and the cultural politics of survival beyond national borders within the region. The term is useful because it is being used by some Zimbabweans themselves, it is not denigrating and circumvents the state binaries of refugee/economic migrant. But the elite, educated connotations of the term mean that the idea of the diasporan is a poor fit with the circumstances and identities of the majority of those displaced within the region, or those who have exploited the scope for manoeuvre and 'blending in' within a society that is less fully penetrated by the law than Western contexts and has multiple historical cross border connections. Indeed some commentators criticise the 'careless' use of the term 'diaspora' within the African context on the grounds that it works against longstanding traditions of mobility, hospitality and incorporation and is likely to reinforce exclusion (Bakewell 2008). Yet in many African contexts, protracted exclusion is now a reality and exilic identities and mythical nationalisms have also flourished among displaced non-elites, particularly those who have been spatially isolated and contained in refugee camps, where they have become a destabilizing force (Malkki 1995; Loescher and Milner 2005). Although many Zimbabweans have been able to merge into South African society, the scale of movement, the exclusionary state response and popular xenophobia combined to undermine strategies of integration. Experiences of detention, of being herded into trucks for deportation, or assaulted as criminals, and the clustering of destitute Zimbabweans in city churches, informal shacks and cholera camps clearly have the potential to foster militant exilic and diasporic identities, underlining the urgency of a humanitarian solution *in situ* and the importance of a workable political agreement at home.

Nonetheless, this incomplete fit between the term 'diaspora' and the identities assumed by displaced communities within the region is important, and leads into the next section that reflects further on why the term appears to have a wider application in Western destinations such as Britain, and what the implications might be.

Diasporic Claims and the British Context

Despite the sympathy for anti-Mugabe diasporic campaigning on the part of the British government and exceptional media attention to events in Zimbabwe, Zimbabweans' experiences in Britain have also been shaped by the mix of opportunities and exclusions created by broader state migration policies. These have produced openings at the top for professionals (particularly in health and social care), as well as in the security arms of the state, as the army and police have looked to new African migrants to swell the number of recruits from ethnic minorities. Entrepreneurs have been able to secure loans from local authorities aiming to stimulate ethnic minority businesses. At the same time, economic growth and neoliberal restructuring created opportunities at the bottom for unskilled and irregular migrants in a range of poorly remunerated jobs, and demographic changes have also contributed to demand for workers in the care industry (on neoliberal restructuring, see Anderson and Rogaly 2005). The goal of legislative change over this last decade, guided by broader rhetorics of 'securitisation' and a xenophobic tabloid press, has been to reduce unskilled migration from outside the EU, curtail access to asylum and discourage irregular migration by stripping those arriving outside legal channels of their rights (Bloch and Schuster 2004; Flynn 2005; Huysmans 2006). These changes have undermined Zimbabweans' (and others') historical arguments for inclusion based on old colonial ties and the Commonwealth – the marginalisation of which is widely interpreted as a betrayal motivated by racism. While opportunities for integrating are increasingly sharply limited by legal channels of entry, there are also racialised constraints on 'blending in', other than through assuming the identities of other migrant groups. As in South Africa, Zimbabweans in Britain are scattered geographically – professionals, business people and students can be found in most major cities, while asylum seekers have also been subject to policies of dispersal that have taken them into hostile places of high unemployment where local authority housing is available but local residents feel most directly threatened by immigration. The importance of carework for Zimbabweans in Britain has also produced specific clusters of settlement in destinations that would otherwise be unlikely places for first generation migrants (Mbiba 2005; McGregor 2007).

The loss of status and racism many have experienced, and the hostile media response to migrants and asylum-seekers have undoubtedly been important as a context for the widespread adoption of the term diaspora among Zimbabweans in Britain (on Zimbabwean asylum seekers' experiences, see Ranger 2005). The contradictions of the status attached to movement to the colonial motherland and the realities of dirty demeaning work are captured by the jokes that cast movement to Britain as joining the 'BBC' (British Bottom Cleaners) (McGregor 2007 and in this volume). But diasporic positioning is also about other aspects of the opportunity structure, and the transnational calculations that allow even unskilled, informal workers to send significant remittances home. Diasporic mutual aid groups have often been formalised with the help of funds from the local state, charitable foundations and private donors, building on the multitude of historical ties and current solidarities alluded to at the outset. Interest among policy-makers in 'diaspora engagement', though driven by the desire to quell unskilled immigration from outside Europe has also provided incentives to organise as such (Mercer et al. 2008). Although Zimbabweans' diasporic positioning is clearly more than simply an opportunistic response to such budget lines, they clearly are influential, as evidenced perhaps by a seminar in late 2008 entitled 'Strategic Options for Zimbabwe Economic Recovery Plan in World Recession: A Case for the Diaspora', convened by the Zimbabwe Diaspora Development Interface, involving speakers from the Zimbabwe Institute of Engineers UK, the Zimbabwe Gentlemen's Club, and prominent Zimbabwean businessman Nkosana Moyo (former Minister for Trade and Industry).[4]

The essays in this volume further these debates over the take up of diasporic identities in the British context in various ways. My own article focuses directly on the differentiating effects of state policies and the law, and discusses how the close historical ties between Britain and Zimbabwe have shaped both the specific sense of betrayal over legal exclusion and the capacity for diasporic organisations to mount challenges to it. The chapter focuses primarily on those in irregular legal categories, and explores how being seen as 'low' has affected ideas about class identity. As some of those trapped in informal menial work have managed to use their earnings to maintain their class position at home and in intergenerational terms, the chapter argues that those in irregular circumstances should not be considered an 'abject class' of migrants, but rather the idea of abjection should be discussed in relation to the development of legal spaces of exclusion. Diasporic associations appear important in this light as they provide occasions for meeting where status is not judged through demeaning employment in Britain. Though they reinforce identification with the Zimbabwean homeland, diasporic associations such as community-based asylum seeker support groups also work to achieve integration in Britain and have developed a multitude of linkages to a range of British-based civic and political groups. Such linkages reflect not only the current politics of asylum in Britain, but also the legacies of a unique historic relationship.

Diasporic associational spaces are investigated further by Dominic Pasura, who explores engagement with homeland politics. He develops a classification for interpreting the mode and degrees of participation among different communities of Zimbabweans in the UK, critiquing frameworks in the existing literature (Shain and Barth 2003; Sheffer 2003). Pasura's discussion of how the idea of Zimbabwean diasporic identity is expressed, performed and made a lived reality in particular British settings, draws on the findings of a multi-sited ethnography of Zimbabwean communities in different parts of Britain, which involved socializing among Zimbabweans in a pub and '*gochi gochi*'[barbeque] in the Midlands and attending the vigil maintained by Zimbabweans outside the Zimbabwe embassy in London. Pasura distinguishes between 'visible', 'epistemic', 'dormant' and 'silent' members of Zimbabwean diasporic communities in Britain. He illuminates the motivations both for engaging and disengaging, and shows why some – particularly asylum seekers and white Zimbabweans – have performed their Zimbabweanness in public while others have tried to blend in to British society by adopting identities as Jamaicans, black British or South Africans.

 Martha Chinouya also investigates engagements with home, but focuses on family networks and the particular circumstances of HIV positive women asylum-seekers. As their legal status was insecure and the stigma attached to the disease is also acute in Britain, these women delayed seeking treatment such that they suffered acute ill health and were hospitalised, interrupting their capacity to remit to family at home. Chinouya engages with and extends the litreature on transnational families in important ways (Bryceson and Vuorela 2002; Baldassar et al. 2008): she argues that debates over transnational families have tended to assume good health on the part of lead migrants, and that there has often been an over-emphasis on financial transfers that ignores the emotional context. Considering those who are severely ill, however, highlights flows in the opposite direction, of emotional support, prayers and traditional herbal remedies from those left behind, even though most women do not fully disclose the reasons for their ill health, and tend to use euphemisms such as 'cough', 'bad blood', or 'the modern disease'. Yet the chapter also underscores the tensions within transnational families created by the combination of distance, poor health, prolonged separation and the north/south divide in access to treatment, as these are revealed in the dynamics of disclosure of HIV positive status within families, and the tendency not to tell children at home they too might be affected, given the lack of prospects for treatment.

The final chapter in this section focuses on a central concern for Zimbabweans in Britain, interlinked with their identity as diasporans – that of burial at home. This further underlines how the politico-economic crisis in Zimbabwe since 2000 has been experienced in ways that are enmeshed with the HIV/AIDS epidemic. Beacon Mbiba focuses on strategies for dealing with death and burial among Zimbabweans in Britain, and in Zimbabwe's capital city, Harare. He argues that the locus of burial can be revealing about notions of identity and belonging, and how these shift over time, in relation both to the in situ circumstances of diaspora communities and changes at home, including histories of urbanisation, changing rural/urban connections, HIV/AIDS, state planning traditions and their incapacitation, as well as other dimensions of politico-economic crisis. Mbiba highlights the effects of a crisis of space in Harare's urban cemeteries, which has disrupted a longstanding trend within Zimbabwe towards urban burial. His exploration of the changing practicalities and meanings attached to urban and rural burial in recent years highlights the growing segregation of low and high status urban burial grounds reinforced by diaspora remittances, and shows how the multi-faceted crisis has forced Zimbabweans both at home and abroad to think about the locus of burial in new ways.

Together, these chapters on the Zimbabwean diasporic communities created in the British context illustrate many similarities with South Africa diasporic groups, notwithstanding the narrower class base in the UK, the smaller numbers and greater distance from the humanitarian crisis. Zimbabwean diaspora social organisations in Britain are notably similar to those in South Africa. They draw on a shared cultural repertoire of ideas about education, family values and what constitutes a dignified death, as these have been shaped historically by the Christianisation of elite urban culture at home; they replicate the same enthusiasm for soccer, food and music from home, share the same political concerns for homeland political transformation and maintaining dignity and class standing abroad. Diasporic spaces in both contexts demonstrate the tension (also characteristic of academic theorizing) between diaspora as cosmopolitan ethos and exclusive national positioning. But the commonalities of diasporic positioning across continents, particularly as expressed by the relatively well-off and well-educated, does not only reflect common historical repertoires combined with a sense of exclusion and displacement, but has also been boosted enormously by new communications technologies that have allowed for a proliferation of web-based services for diasporans. The ready access to news, the crossfertilisation of ideas and terms (including that of 'diaspora' itself), the joined up political campaigns, the possibility of immediate exchange of ideas between the scattered locations would have been much more difficult in the absence of the proliferation of Zimbabwe diaspora internet sites, discussion forums, radio broadcasts and other kinds of texts. As such the role played by these media technologies, the texts they create and circulate and the communities of users and producers, require further discussion.

Mediating Diaspora – the Internet and Creative Writing

The 'watershed' in the 'phenomenal rise of alternative media' in the Zimbabwean context was 2003 – a year marked by the mass exodus of journalists following a reorganisation of broadcasting and the enforced closure of the *Daily News* (Zimbabwe's only independent daily newspaper) and three other private newspapers (Moyo 2007: 83). Thereafter there was an extraordinary mushrooming of Zimbabwean diaspora news and discussion sites, most of them 'promising to unearth the truth and expose the corruption and human rights abuses by the Mugabe regime', by telling 'the real Zimbabwean story' (*Zimonline.co.za*), providing 'uncensored news' (*Zimdaily.com*), and reporting 'without fear or favour' (*Zimbabwejournalists. com)* (Moyo 2007: 84). These sites provide multiple visual and narrative reminders of diasporic positioning to their users, through their advertising and links to Zimbabwe shopping, money transfer, funeral insurance companies, the latest diaspora campaigns, and asylum and immigration advice. They appear to have very widespread use among Zimbabweans abroad – Bloch's survey of Zimbabweans in Britain and South Africa revealed the internet as the most important form of social networking (2005, 2008). Zimbabwe diaspora websites thus create the possibilities of a community of directly linked-up diasporans that is larger than those who attend physical gatherings (Pasura this volume; Moyo 2007).

A growing body of work has begun to explore the role of such websites in the making of diasporic communities, drawing on broader media studies debates (Karim 2004; Moyo 2007). How alternative are these sites? How empowering to the users, how radical and transforming is their potential? What is the role of 'internet intellectuals' who 'interpret national crises, rearticulate values and construct community'(Bernal 2006). In relation to Zimbabwe diaspora websites, Moyo provides some initial answers to these questions: he emphasises the 'alternative' content of most diaspora sites when compared to the state-controlled Zimbabwean media, but also the diversity in terms of production, professionalisation and capitalisation, with sites ranging from 'shoe-string' outfits to large commercial operations involving as much as 400,000 hits a day (2007: 101). Despite an extraordinary expansion in the number of internet users within Zimbabwe over the course of the Zimbabwe crisis from 50,000 in 2000 to one million in 2007 (Moyo 2007: 101), those who are connected are still overwhelmingly outside Zimbabwe, in cities and better off than most. Moreover, some sites publish information of dubious credibility, funders are often untransparent, editors can have vested and partisan interests, which have helped to widen diasporic divides and foster distorted views of politics (Moyo 2007: 102; Raftopoulos and Alexander 2006).

Such criticism, reflected in a broader literature, has helped dispel the certainties of the initial exaggerated assumptions about the radical potential of the internet, as well as producing new interest in how new and old media interact. 'Internet intellectuals' may also be influential offline, as academics, writers, politicians, community leaders or television celebrities, while their fame may equally be promoted via radio, television, newspapers – or, even more old-fashioned, books. While new technologies can be used to break down old barriers and categories, such liberating or subversive potential is only realised through users whose political views will allow for it (Alexander and McGregor 1999). Moreover, the facilitating role of technology needs to be considered in the light of the content of the information being exchanged and the power of narrative, language and 'rhetorical pointing' in providing unconscious reminders of community (as Billig has elaborated in relation to newspapers, see Carter 2007 and Peel this volume, in relation to diaspora websites).

In the final section of this volume, a cluster of chapters contribute to these debates over media and narrative in shaping diasporic identity. Winston Mano and Wendy Willems question the 'alternative' character of communities that meet on the web, by exploring online diaspora discussions of 'Zimbabweanness'. They do so by examining reactions to the antics of Makosi Musambasi, a Zimbabwean nurse who became an overnight star in the UK television series, Big Brother, as these were expressed on *NewZimbabwe.com*. As a nurse, Makosi was to some extent an archetype of Zimbabwean diasporic experiences in the United Kingdom. To many Zimbabweans, Makosi's participation in the show demonstrated that the most recent Zimbabwean diaspora had managed to occupy a place in British society. However, she also challenged and provoked heated debate about what internet participants understood as 'Zimbabwean' morality and womanhood. The users of the discussion forums often vented views that were the opposite of tolerant and liberal, repeating exclusive definitions that cast 'Zimbabwean' in opposition to the immorality of a decadent 'West'.

Such echoing within diaspora spaces of aspects Zanu(PF)'s version of patriotism, sometimes incorporated within oppositional narratives, is a recurrent theme of various chapters in this book. As one of the features of Mugabe's patriotism has been a notion of rural authenticity that would include only 'sons of the soil' while excluding whites and others deemed foreign, it is fitting to explore displaced white Zimbabweans' narratives of nation and ideas about belonging. One (albeit partial) source for doing so is the outpouring of creative writing on the part of displaced white Zimbabweans in the form of novels and autobiographies both before and after 2000. Primorac's chapter in this volume explores this body of writing, some of which has received international acclaim, not least for its willingness to combine narratives revolving around family, cultural identity and social change with a critique of the Mugabe regime. Speaking from positions of displacement, autobiographical texts by authors such as Peter Godwin, Alexandra Fuller and Cathy Buckle reveal complex subjectivities, and articulate alternative versions of recent Zimbabwean history from those propagated by Zanu(PF). Primorac's literary exploration of these texts focuses in particular on Fuller and Godwin's respective memoirs *Scribbling the Cat* (2004) and *When a Crocodile Eats the Sun* (2007), both published by mainstream publishing houses, and widely reviewed and debated in the British as well as the Zimbabwean diasporic media. The chapter situates these texts within a genealogy of white-authored Zimbabwean writing since independence. Primorac argues that there are continuities running through strands of this work that can be traced back to a colonial-era generic blueprint and argues that by reproducing elements of this blueprint, Fuller and Godwin are contributing to the revival of an important aspect of Rhodesian discourse. Since Mugabe's notion of Zimbabwean patriotism has been predicated on claims that the forces of Empire are still alive, Fuller and Godwin's work arguably contributes indirectly and unwittingly to the survival of the very ideology they are seeking to counter.

Debates over ethnicised and racialised understandings of identity in the diaspora are pursued further by Clayton Peel, who explores the role of diaspora websites that target specific ethnic/racial constituencies – *Goffal.com,* which serves the mixed race 'Coloured' community, and *Inkundla.net,* which services Ndebele speakers. Peel is interested in whether movement into the diaspora has provided the context for challenge or reproduction of ethnic and racial categories imported from home, in the role of diaspora internet sites in fostering alternative transnational public spheres and shaping engagements in Zimbabwe. By providing space for ethnic and racial minorities and non-state players to interact with each other, Peel argues that these diaspora websites allow participants to critique Zimbabwean state policies and formulate alternatives. At the same time, these websites provide opportunities for reproducing and reinforcing sub-national identities that had been marginalised in the Zimbabwean context, despite challenges created by the difference in racial hierarchies in Britain (where 'Coloureds' are not socially recognised) and Zimbabwe. By highlighting the space within the diaspora for meeting not primarily as Zimbabweans, but as Zimbabwean-Ndebele or 'Coloureds', Peel highlights the capacity for diasporic expressions of attachment to the nation to foster both convergence and divergence with home, to harden or dismantle prior ethnic and racial divisions.

These chapters analysing the textual content of diaspora websites and diaspora literary forms all highlight the potential for displacement and new environments to challenge and undermine identities brought from home. As such they provide a link to the final contribution to this volume. The emotional content of diasporic identities (implicit in all the chapters of this book), and the sense of alienation and loss that can infuse them is, perhaps, better captured through creative writing than academic analysis. So it is fitting that the final contribution to this collection takes the form of a short story by London-based Zimbabwean writer, Brian Chikwava and a conversation on life in the diaspora with Primorac.

Chikwava won the Caine Prize for African Writing in 2004 for his witty short story *Seventh Street Alchemy* (2004), and his novel *Harare North* (2009) explores the life of a young black Zimbabwean in the UK. The title of the story published in this volume – *One Dandelion Seed-head* – suggests dispersion, and, in contrast to the diaspora internet users discussed in other chapters, the narrator's 'Zimbabweanness' is hardly visible to the reader. This unnamed narrator emanates from an elite Zimbabwean family, but is now part of the transient youth sub-culture and globalised social world of inner-city London. The narrator's voice is interrupted by a stammer, echoing Zimbabwe's most famous 'transnational' writer Dambudzo Marechera (Wylie 1999), who did so much to deflate the pieties of the first generation African nationalist leadership. Chikwava acknowledges Marechera as an inspiration while also distancing himself from the anxiety and drama associated with Marechera's life in London, and his writing lacks the nihilistic and violent tone of Marechera's work. Chikwava seems ambivalent about whether Zimbabwe is still 'home' and criticises some aspects of diaspora identity politics, particularly the militant ethnic strands. Yet he considers himself to be a Zimbabwean writer and invokes a 'rooted' kind of cosmopolitanism, close perhaps to that described by Kwame Appiah (1998). Indeed, the glimpse Chikwava's story provides of the social spaces of Britain's multicultural cities appears to mock the metaphorical extension of the idea of diaspora to include everyone equally, as the narrator and other immigrants have 'put tons of effort to repress cultural baggage so that they blend into the local order of things', while their English friends are diasporic only insofar as it is cool to 'reclaim a lost exoticism' through tales of non-English ancestors. Chikwava's story thus provides an imaginative commentary on the key themes of the volume – the contestations over space and identity, history and memory involved in the emergence of a 'new diaspora', and the shaping of this imagined community by process of displacement and the cultural politics of survival.

Concluding Comments and Future Directions

Inevitably, there are gaps in the existing body of research on Zimbabwe's new diaspora reflected in this volume, which deserve some reflection as a means of conclusion. There is clearly further scope for interdisciplinary and comparative research building on the start made here, which could elaborate the implications of the similarities, divergences and connections between the South African, UK and other diasporic shaping contexts, and could draw further insight from the different approaches and interests of historians, geographers, anthropologists, political scientists, literary and media analysts.

Perhaps the most striking gap in the research conducted on the new Zimbabwe diaspora to date is the role of the churches. Although it is clear from surveys that churches are by far the most important society in terms of the numbers of members involved (Bloch 2005, 2008), and some essays in this collection have given a glimpse of the importance of faith, there have not been detailed studies of the Zimbabwean church fellowships set up by mainline and other churches to serve the needs of diaspora communities (though see Pasura's forthcoming work on Roman Catholic communities), nor are there studies of transnational church politics and the crisis since 2000.

Second, this collection has explicitly focused on the new Zimbabwean diasporic communities formed since 2000, though it aimed to emphasise the importance of historical connections. There is, however, clearly a need for further research on continuities, changes and linkages with past migrations, exploring change over time in the contexts for integration or exclusion, connections between different generations of Zimbabwean migrants, providing more detailed elaboration of inter-generational change, reflected in politics and associational life, gendered identities and family dynamics. Such research would need to be sensitive not only to race, class, gender and ethnicity in a transnational context, but would also need to complicate the categories 'first' and 'second' generation migrant, by looking at different mechanisms for 'straddling', and strategies of managing children that deliberately try to prevent loss of connection with home.

Third, the reader of this volume will be struck by the emphasis on exclusion, distress and hardship among those displaced from Zimbabwe in both South African and British contexts, and a lack of detailed attention to those who have prospered. In this light, there is a need for further studies of the perspectives of the business elites and professionals, diaspora politicians and community leaders, their strategies of accumulation, transnational investments and development ideas. While there have been a number of surveys underlining the importance of remittances, both from the perspective of the receivers and the remitters (Bloch 2005; Bracking and Sachikonye 2007; see also the forthcoming work of Bailey, Cliffe and Mavhunga), we lack detailed studies of the various forms of diasporic and transnational entrepreneurship that have emerged in the context of the crisis, including the innovative range of web-based shopping and service schemes.

Finally, this volume is about the 'making' of new Zimbabwe diasporic ommunities through a period of protracted political and economic crisis at home, and shaped by contradictory processes of inclusion and exclusion in countries of settlement. The scale of the movement beyond Zimbabwe's borders, the tensions and insecurities that have characterised the implementation of the GPA and the certainty that economic reconstruction cannot happen over night, all mean that debates over the character and role of the new Zimbabwe diaspora are likely to persist beyond the short term. The importance of remittances to those at home, the diminished capacity of state education, health and other public services mean that families are likely to continue to try to exploit the opportunities for straddling countries and continents for the foreseeable future. Yet the prospect of political transition at some juncture and calls from the MDC for largescale donor re-engagement have already begun to provoke debates over 'sustainable return' and the role of the diaspora in reconstruction and development, transitional justice and reconciliation. Such debates have also begun to highlight the possibility of a future process not of the making of a new diaspora, but of its unmaking.

Notes

1. See the discussion of the Herald article, in the posting by CM, 11 November 2007, 'Digging beneath the surface of Zimbabwe's 'Diaspora syndrome' 11 November 2007, *Zimbabwe Review,* http://zimreview.wordpress.com/2007/11/11/ [accessed August 2008].
2. Pers, comm., SE London, July 2008.
3. Independent Asylum Commission. http://www.independentasylumcom mission.org.uk/
4. Zimbabwe Diaspora Development Interface website http://www.zimdias porainter face.org/

References

Alexander J. and J. McGregor. 1999. 'Representing Violence in Matabeleland, Zimbabwe: Press and Internet Debates'. In T. Allen and J. Seaton (eds) *The Media of Conflict: War Reporting and Representations of Ethnic Violence.* London: Zed Press.

Anderson, B. 1992. 'The New World Disorder', *New Left Review,* 193: 3–13.

Anderson, B. and B. Rogaly, 2005. 'Forced Labour and Migration to the UK'. Oxford: COMPAS in collaboration with the TUC.

Appiah, K.A. 1998. 'Cosmopolitan Patriots', in P. Cheah and B. Robbins (eds) *Cosmopolitics: Thinking and Feeling Beyond the Nation.* Minneapolis: University of Minnesota Press, pp. 91–114.

Axel, K.B. 2004. 'The Context of Diaspora', *Cultural Anthropology*, 29, 1: 26–60.

Bakewell, O. 2008. 'In Search of the Diaspora Within Africa', *African Diasporas*, forthcoming.

Baldassar, L., C. Baldock, and R. Wilding. 2006. *Families Caring Across Borders: Aging, Migration and Transnational Caregiving.* London: Macmillan.

Bernal, V. 2006. 'Diaspora, Cyberspace and Political Imagination: The Eritrean Diaspora Online', *Global Networks*, 6, 2: 161–79.

Billig, M. 1995. *Banal Nationalism.* London: Sage.

Bloch, A. and L. Schuster. 2004. 'At the Extremes of Exclusion: Deportation Detention and Dispersal', *Ethnic and Racial Studies* 28, 3: 491–512.

Bloch, A. 2005. *The Development Potential of Zimbabweans in the Diapora: A Survey of Zimbabweans Living in the UK and South Africa.* Geneva: IOM.

Bloch, A. 2008. 'Zimbabweans in Britain: Transnational Activities and Capabilities', *Journal of Ethnic and Migration Studies*, 34, 2: 287–305.

Bracking, S. and L. Sachikonye. 2007. 'Remittances, Poverty Reduction and the Informalisation of Household Wellbeing in Zimbabwe'. Conference paper, Stellenbosch, 27–28 March 2007.

Brah, A. 1996. *Cartographies of Diaspora: Contesting Identities.* London: Routledge.

Bryceson D. and U. Vuorela (eds). 2002. *The Transnational Family: New European Frontiers and the Global Network.* Oxford: Berg.

Carter, S. 2007. 'Mobilising Generosity, Framing Geopolitics: Narrating Crisis in the Homeland Through Diasporic Media', *Geoforum*, 38: 1102–12.

Castles, S. 2004. 'Why Migration Policies Fail', *Ethnic and Racial Studies,* 27, 2.

Chetsanga, C.J. and T.B Muchenge. 2003. 'An Analysis of the Cause and Effect of the Brain Drain in Zimbabwe'. SAPRN. Retrieved 20 June 2008 from http://www.sarpn.org.za/documents.

Chikanda, A. 2005. 'Medical Leave: The Exodus of Heath Professionals from Zimbabwe'. Migration Policy Series, 23. Cape Town.

Chikwava, B. 2004. 'Seventh Street Alchemy'. In I. Staunton (ed.) *Writing Still. New Stories from Zimbabwe.* Harare: Weaver Press, pp. 17–30.

____. 2009. *Harare North.* London: Jonathan Cape.

Clarke, K.M. 2004. *Mapping Yoruba Networks: Power and Agency in the Making of Transnational Communities.* Duke University Press.

Clifford, J. 1997. *Routes: Travel and Translation in the Twentieth Century.* Harvard University Press

Cohen, R. 1997. *Global Diasporas: An Introduction.* London: Routledge.

Collyer, M. 2008. 'The Reinvention of Political Community in a Transnational Setting: Framing the Kabyle Citizens' Movement', *Ethnic and Racial Studies*, 31, 4: 687–707.

Crisp, J. 2000. 'Africa's Refugees: Patterns, Problems and Policy Challenges,' New Issues in Refugee Research. Geneva: UNHCR.

Crush, J. 2000. 'The Dark Side of Democracy: Migration, Xenophobia and Human Rights in South Africa', *International Migration*, 38: 103–31.

Crush, J. and D. Tevera (eds). Forthcoming. *Zimbabwe's Exodus. Crisis, Migration and Survival.*

Crush, J. and V. Williams. 2003. 'Criminal Tendencies: Immigrants and Illegality in South Africa,' *Migration Policy Brief,* 10. Cape Town: SAMP.

D'Alisera, J. 2004. *Imagined Geographies: Sierra Leonean Muslims in America.* Philadelphia: University of Pensylvania Press.

De Haas, 2007. 'The Myth of Invasion. Irregular Migration from West Africa to the Maghreb and Western Europe'. Oxford: International Migration Institute (IMI) research report.

Dumont, A. 2008. 'Representing Voiceless Migrants: Moroccan Political Transnationalism and Moroccan Migrants' Organisations,' *Ethnic and Racial Studies* 31, 4: 792–811.

Flynn, D. 2005. 'New Borders, New Management: the Dilemmas of Modern Immigration Policies', *Ethnic and Racial Studies* 28, 3: 463–90.

Griffiths, D.J. 2000. 'Fragmentation and Consolidation: The Contrasting Cases of Somali and Kurdish Refugees in London', *Journal of Refugee Studies* 13: 281–302.

Grillo, R. 2007. 'Betwixt and Between: Trajectories and Projects of Transmigration', *Journal of Ethnic and Migration Studies* 33, 2: 199–217.

Hammar, A. and B. Raftopoulos. 2003. 'Zimbabwe's Unfinished Business: Rethinking Land, State and Nation'. In Hammar, A., B. Raftopoulos and S. Jensen (eds) *Zimbabwe's Unfinished Business: Rethinking Land, State and Nation in the Context of Crisis.* Harare: Weaver Press.

Hammar, A., Landau, L. and J. McGregor (eds). Forthcoming 2010. 'Zimbabwe Post 2000. Political Economies of Displacement'. *Special Issue, Journal of Southern African Studies.*

Handmaker, J. and J. Parsely. 2001. 'Migration, Refugees and Racism in South Africa', *Refuge*, 20, 1: 40–51.

HRW (Human Rights Watch). 2007. *'Keep Your Head Down': Unprotected Migrants in South Africa.* New York.

——. 2008. *Neighbours in Need: Zimbabweans Seeking Refuge in South Africa.* New York.

Huysmans, J. 2006. *The Politics of Insecurity: Fear, Migration and Asylum in the EU* London: Routledge.

Karim K. 2004. *The Media of Diaspora.* London: Routledge.

Kleist, N. 2008. 'Mobilising 'the Diaspora': Somali Transnational Political Engagement', *Journal of Ethnic and Migration Studies*, 34, 2: 307–323.

Koopmans, R and P. Statham, 2001. 'How National Citizenship Shapes Transnationalism: A Comparative Study of Migrant Claims-Making in Germany, Great Britain and the Netherlands', *Revue Eurohernne des Migrationes Internationales,* 17, 2: 63–100.

Koser, K. (ed.) 2003. *New African Diasporas.* London: Routledge.

Landau, L. 2005. 'Urbanisation, Nativism and the Rule of Law in South Africa's 'Forbidden Cities', *Third World Quarterly,* 26, 7: 1115–34.

——. 2006. 'Transplants and Transients: Idioms of Belonging and Dislocation in Inner-city Johannesburg', *African Studies Review*, 49, 2: 125–45.

Larmer, M. 2008. 'The Zimbabwe Arms Shipment Campaign', *Briefings, Review of African Political Economy,* 117: 486–93.

Le Bas, A. 2006. 'Poliarisation as Craft: Party Formation and State Violence in Zimbabwe', *Comparative Politics,* 38, 4: 419–38.

Levitt, P. and B.N. Jaworsky. 2007. 'Transnational Migration Studies: Past Developments and Future Trends', *Annual Review of Sociology* 33: 129–56.

LHR (Lawyers for Human Rights (South Africa) and Forced Migration Studies Programme (FMSP). 2009. *Immigration Policy Responses to Zimbabweans in South Africa: Implementing Special Temporary Permits.* Background Paper prepared for a Roundtable on 9 April 2009, Pretoria.

Loescher, G. and J. Milner. 2005. 'Protracted Refugee Situations in Africa', *Survival,* 47, 2.

Magaisa, A. 2006. 'Donors, Diaspora and Zimbabwe Democracy', 25 July 2006, retrieved 28 2008 July from http://www.newzimbabwe.com/pages/magaisa28.14451.html.

Maharaj, B. 2004. 'Immigration to Post-Apartheid South Africa', *Global Migration Perspectives,* 1. Geneva: Global Commission on International Migration.

Malkki, L. 1995. 'From "Refugee Studies" to the National Order of Things', *Annual Review of Anthropology,* 24: 495–523.

Maphosa, F. 2006. 'Undocumented Labour Migration and Transnationalism Between Zimbabwe and South Africa', Seminar Paper, retrieved 10 November 2008 from http://www.uj.ac.za/Portals/102/docs/seminar%2520papers/.

Massey, D. 2005. 'Five Myths About Immigration: Common Misconceptions Underlying US/Mexico Border Enforcement policy'. Retrieved 21 July 2008 from http://www.ilw.com/articles/2005,1207–massey.shtm.

Maxwell, D. 2006. *African Gifts of the Spirit: Pentecostalism and the Rise of a Zimbabwean Transnational Religious Movement.* Oxford: James Currey.

Mazzucato, V. 2008. 'The Double Engagement: Transnationalism and Integration. Ghanaian Migrants' Lives Between Ghana and the Netherlands', *Journal of Ethnic and Migration Studies* 34, 2: 199–216.

Mbiba, B. 2004. 'Zimbabwe's Global Citizens in Harare North (United Kingdom): Some Preliminary Observations'. In M. Palmberg and R. Primorac (eds), *Skinning the Skunk: Facing Zimbabwean Futures.* Uppsala: Nordiska Afrikainstitutet.

McGown, R.B. 1999. *Muslims in the Diaspora: The Somali Communities of London and Toronto.* University of Toronto Press.

McGregor, J. 2007. 'Joining the BBC [British Bottom Cleaners]: Zimbabweans and the UK Care Industry', *Journal of Ethnic and Migration Studies,* 33, 5: 801–24.

——. 2008. 'Abject Spaces, Transnational Calculations: Zimbabweans in Britain Navigating Work, Class and the Law,' *Transactions of the Institute of British Geographers,* 33, 4: 466–82.

——. 2009 'Associational Links with Home Among Zimbabweans in Britain: Reflections on Long Distance Nationalisms', *Global Networks,* forthcoming.

Mercer, C., B. Page and M. Evans, 2008. *Development and the African Diaspora: Belonging and the Politics of Home.* London: Zed Press.

Moyo, Dumisani. 2007. 'Alternative Media, Diasporas and the Mediation of the Zimbabwe Crisis', *African Journalism Studies* 28, 1 and 2: 81–105.

Nyamnjoh, F. 2006. *Insiders and Outsiders. Citizenship and Xenophobia in Contemporary South Africa.* London: Zed Books.

Østergaard-Nielsen. 2003. 'The Politics of Migrants' Transnational Political Practices', *International Migration Review,* 37, 3: 760–86.

Pasura, D. 2006. 'Mapping Exercise: Zimbabwe', London: IOM. http://www.iomlondon.org

———. 2008. 'A Fractured Diaspora: Strategies and Identities Among Zimbabweans in Britain', PhD Thesis. University of Warwick.

Phimister, I and Raftopoulos, 2004. 'Mugabe, Mbeki and the Politics of Anti-imperialism in Zimbabwe,' *Review of African Political Economy*, 101: 385–400.

Potts, D. 2006. '"Restoring Order"? Operation Murambatsvina and the Urban Crisis in Zimbabwe', *Journal of Southern African Studies*, 32, 2: 273–291.

Raftopoulos, B. 2001. 'The Labour Movement and the Emergence of Opposition Politics in Zimbabwe'. In B. Raftopouolos and L. Sachikonye (eds) *Striking Back: The Labour Movement and the Postcolonial State in Zimbabwe 1980–2000*. Harare: Waver Press, 1–24.

———. 2004. 'Race, Nation and History in Zimbabwean Politics'. In B. Raftopoulos and T. Savage (eds) *Zimbabwe: Injustice and Political Reconciliation*. Institute for Justice and Reconciliation, Cape Town.

———. 2006. 'Reflections on Opposition Politics in Zimbabwe: The Politics of the Movement for Democratic Change'. In B. Raftopoulos and K.Alexander (eds) Reflections on Democratic Politics in Zimbabwe. Cape Town: Institute for Justice and Reconciliation, pp. 6–37.

———. 2008. 'Reshaping Politics Through Displacement'. Presentation to the Conference 'Political Economies of Displacement in Post-2000 Zimbabwe'. Johannesburg: Wits, 9–11 June.

Raftopoulos, B. and T. Alexander (eds). 2006. Reflections on Democratic Politics in Zimbabwe. Cape Town: Institute for Justice and Reconciliation.

Ranger, T. 2004a. 'Nationalist Historiography, Ptriotic History and the History of the Nation: The Struggle Over the Past in Zimbabwe', Journal of Southern African Studies, 30, 2: 215–34.

———. 2002 'The Narratives and Counter Narratives of Zimbabwean Asylum: Female Voices', Third World Quarterly, 26, 3: 405–21.

Rich-Dorman. 2002. 'Rocking the Boat? Church NGOs and Democratisation in Zimbabwe', African Affairs, 101: 43–65.

Said, E. 1984. 'Reflections on Exile,' Granta, 13: 159–72.

Sheffer, G. 2003. Diaspora Politics: At Home Abroad. Cambridge University Press.

Sisulu, E., B. Moyo and N. Tshuma 2007. 'The Zimbabwean Community in South Africa.' In S. Buhlungu, J. Daniel, R. Southall, J. Lutchman (eds) South Africa: State of the Nation 2000. South Africa, HSRC Press.

Sokefeld, M. 2006. 'Mobilizing in Transnational Space: A Social Movement Approach to the Study of Diaspora', Global Networks, 6, 3.

Solidarity Peace Trust (SPT). 2004. No War in Zimbabwe: An Account of an Exodus of a Nations People. Port Shepstone.

———. 2005. Discarding the Filth: Operation Murambatsvina, Port Shepstone.

———. 2006. Operation Taguta/Sisuthi. Command Agriculture in Zimbabwe. Port Shepstone.

———. 2007. A Difficult Dialogue: Zimbabwe South Africa Economic Relations since 2000. Port Shepstone.

———. 2008. Punishing Dissent, Silencing Citizens: The Zimbabwe Elections 2008. Port Shepstone.

_____. 2008a. Desperately Seeking Sanity: What Prospects for a New Beginning in Zimbabwe? Port Shepstone.

Stoller, P. 2002. Money has no Smell: The Africanization of New York City. University of Chicago Press.

Turner, S. 2008. 'The Waxing and Waning of the Political Field in Burundi and its Diaspora', Ethnic and Racial Studies, 31, 4: 742–65.

Van Hear, 1998. New Diasporas: The Mass Exodus, Dispersal and Regrouping of Migrant Communities. London: Routledge.

Vertovec, S. and R. Cohen. 1999. 'Introduction' In S. Vertovec and R. Cohen (eds.) Migration, Diasporas and Transnationalism. Aldershot: Edward Elgar.

Waldinger, R. 2006. '"Transnationalisme" des Immigrants et Presence du Passé', Revue Europeenne des Migrations Internationales, 22, 2: 31–41.

Werbner, P. 2000. 'The Materiality of Diapsora: Between Aesthetics and "Real Politics"' Diaspora, 9, 1.

Wylie, D. 1999. 'Taking Resentment for Wisdom: A Posthumous Conversation Between Marechera, N. H. Brettell and George Grosz'. In A. Chennells and F. Veit-Wild (eds), Emerging Perspectives on Dambudzo Marechera. Trenton NJ: Africa World Press, pp. 315–31.

Zimbabwean Diasporic Communities in South Africa

1

Makwerekwere: Migration, Citizenship and Identity among Zimbabweans in South Africa

James Muzondidya

For many Zimbabweans who left their country for South Africa following 2000, their new places of residence and work are now becoming home. They are engaged in an ongoing process of negotiating new spaces for themselves and their children. In so doing, they are debating shared and contrasting experiences with Zimbabwean compatriots, and are developing new ideas about the future of Zimbabwe. This chapter investigates how experiences in South Africa have helped to reshape notions of citizenship, belonging and nationhood, as these have developed through a process of definition and counter-definition between Zimbabweans and South Africans, and as they have been shaped by race, ethnicity and class. I hope to show that this contestation over labelling and stereotypes of the other is producing a new cultural content of 'Zimbabweanness' within Zimbabwe diaspora communities in South Africa.

Experiences of racism and xenophobia have been potent influences on this process of reshaping national identities, and on other dimensions of difference. As Stuart Hall (1996), Willemsen (1994) and Fukui and Markakis (1994) have all poignantly observed, identities are constructed at the point of intersection between external discourses and practices and the internal psychic processes that produce subjectivities about self and others. Said argues that identities are defined less by what one is and more by what one is not, through a process of othering (1978). There is a rich literature on the South African context, that discusses not only the mounting xenophobia

African migrants face from the South African media, public and state officials (Crush 2001; Nyamnjoh 2006; Abdullah 2000; Human Rights Watch 2006; Solidarity Peace Trust 2004), but also the defensive counter-strategies migrants themselves have developed (Landau 2004, 2005). Migrants have deployed a range of historical and pan-Africanist arguments elaborating common ethnicity and race, shared African struggles against apartheid, and indebtedness to past generations of labour migrants. They have also inverted xenophobic and 'nativist' discourses that cast foreigners as criminals, by labelling South Africans and South African society as criminal and amoral, in contrast to idealised memories of the societies migrants themselves emanate from (Landau 2004, 2005).

In this chapter, I explore the diverse ways Zimbabweans living in South Africa's cities have responded to the difficulties of the South African context. The longstanding relationship between the two countries, and multiple ties created through precolonial mobility, decades of labour migrancy and naturalisation within South Africa, a shared border, white settlers' movements and interlinked African nationalist politics mean that there is a particularly rich body of shared historical memory and connections that can be invoked in claims to belonging in South Africa. Yet the current climate within South Africa has undermined past receptivity to these arguments, particularly for black Zimbabweans, which in turn is fostering a defensive reaction and reinforcing diasporic identifications. My argument is based on thirteen formal interviews[1] and informal discussions with Zimbabweans and South Africans in the cities of Cape Town, Pretoria, Johannesburg and Musina, with whom I have interacted over the course of the decade that I have been studying and working in South Africa.

The starting point for this discussion is a brief exploration of the history and diversity of Zimbabwean migrants in South Africa, which has provided such a rich resource of connections and arguments to claim belonging.

Differentiating Zimbabwean Migrants' Experiences

The community of Zimbabweans living abroad in South Africa is both sizeable and diverse. Estimated to number between 1 and 1.5 million (Goliber 2004; Polzer 2007: 5, IRIN, 3 April 2008), Zimbabweans are South Africa's largest foreign nationality. They comprise documented and undocumented labour migrants, informal traders, skilled professionals and business people, students and refugees. Some have been resident for decades, have settled permanently and are naturalised as South African citizens, while others conceive of their stay as temporary and arrived recently, particularly in the period following 2000.

Their place in the country has been shaped by complex histories of migration and contact. These include the precolonial northward displacements of the *Mfecane*, through which Mzilikazi's Khumalo clan moved from Zululand across the Limpopo in the late 1830s and established the Ndebele state in what is now South West Zimbabwe (Rasmussen 1978; Cobbing 1976; Etherington 2001), the movements of white settlers within the region over the course of the twentieth century, and the drawing of African migrant labour southwards to work on the South African mines, which was implicated in early transnational worker, religious and Africanist politics (Ranger 1970; Hodder Williams 1983; Mlambo 2002). Most of the Zimbabwean migrants who serviced the country's mines, farms, factories, provided domestic labour in private homes, or moved in search of tertiary education in the colonial period were temporary migrants (Crush, Jeeves and Yudelman 1991; Van Onselen 1976). Yet some stayed on and started families in South Africa as they married into local communities. If they settled permanently, they came to be referred to back home as *amagewu* (Ndebele) or *zvichoni* (Shona) – those who were never heard of again and lost contact with relatives.[2]

After independence, the numbers moving from Zimbabwe to South Africa continued to grow. Not only did whites continue to depart (Selby 2006: 117–18; Simon 1988: 1), but there were also outflows from Matebeleland and parts of Midlands during and after the state-orchestrated *Gukurahundi* killings of 1983 to 1987 (Hanlon 1986: 181–3; Alexander, McGregor and Ranger 2000: 192, 195–7). Labour migrants continued to seek work, particularly from the drought prone, southern districts of Masvingo, Midlands and Matebeleland South whose residents were historically better connected to the South African farms, mines and towns than to the main Zimbabwean labour markets (Maphosa 2008; Amanor-Wilks and Moyo 1996). Many of these early post-independence migrants slipped into the country unnoticed and blended in: their cultural and linguistic affinity with the white, Nguni or Venda communities in South Africa enabled them to settle and integrate. Some of these Zimbabweans eventually acquired South African citizenship, both lawfully and unlawfully (Sisulu, Moyo and Tshuma 2007: 554; Solidarity Peace Trust 2004), and came to assume South African identities. But others continued to feel they belonged in Zimbabwe, where they maintained their families by remittances. Some formed self-help organisations to develop their communities in Zimbabwe and to repair public facilities like schools and clinics damaged during Gukurahundi (Muzondidya and Chiroro 2008). These (stereotypically young, male) migrants who came back to Zimbabwe during holidays were known as *injiva*, a term that invokes not only the idea of money, but also the style of South African urban youth culture, associated with criminality as much as cash (Solidarity Peace Trust 2004; Maphosa 2004: 16).

Although the decade of the 1990s saw an increase in the numbers of skilled and semi-skilled Zimbabweans leaving Zimbabwe as the effects of adjustment bit (Amanor-Wilks and Moyo 199; Tevera and Crush 2003), the scale of migration from 2000 has been unprecedented, given the political uncertainty and economic 'meltdown' at home (Human Rights Watch 2006). While the stereotypical Zimbabwean migrant of the pre-2000 movements was the *injiva* – the young single male from the southern parts of the country, in the last decade migrants have comprised the young and old; men, women and children; married and unmarried; northerners and southerners. The movement of women and children became notable particularly after the 2005 elections when the economy rapidly deteriorated and the disastrous 'Operation Murambatsvina' destroyed the livelihoods of many urban-based households (United Nations 2005). In some cases, entire families have relocated because of the increasing economic hardships in Zimbabwe and the growing shortages of basic services and commodities, or persecution from ZANU PF and government security agencies.

Unlike the earlier migrants, many of these post-2000 migrants, especially the unskilled and semi-skilled, have struggled to settle down in the highly competitive and increasingly hostile environment of South Africa. With limited financial resources and irregular employment, many of Zimbabwe's recent migrants live in makeshift, plastic houses in informal settlements alongside poorer South Africans in living conditions that are overcrowded and unsafe. Others are found in the inner city areas where the rent is low but crime rates high (Solidarity Peace Trust 2004). Aside from the many working on the border farms (see Rutherford this volume), Zimbabweans have found niches in unskilled labour markets in security and bricklaying. Women have more limited employment opportunities than their male compatriots, and the few who find secure employment usually work as domestic servants in the homes of South Africans or assistants in retail shops owned by Asian migrants, where wages are low and sexual abuse is also rampant.[3] To make ends meet, some female migrants end up turning to prostitution or taking up low-paying jobs, such as being employed as street sales/advertising agents by small private companies and other self-employed migrants.[4] Many of these sales agents are paid on commission, while those who are paid a fixed wage earn an average of R150 per week.[5] Semi-skilled workers and professionals are better off, but often only marginally so. Many find no suitable jobs within their professions and end up doing menial work in the security and service industries. Others have been exploited, even if they find professional openings, such as Zimbabwean teachers in private colleges, who are paid very low wages (Sisulu, Moyo and Tshuma 2007).[6]

The few recent migrants who have found it relatively easy to settle in South Africa are those at the upper end of the labour market, such as accountants, engineers and academics, whose services are desperately needed because of the critical skills shortage in South Africa (SA Government Information, 3 March 2006, Sisulu, Moyo and Tshuma 2007). Business entrepreneurs also fare well, and many such Zimbabweans like Strive Masiyiwa, the founder and Chief Executive Officer of Econet; Trevor Ncube (publisher of both the Zimbabwe Independent and South Africa's most popular weekly, Mail and Guardian) or Nigel Chanakira (the founder of Kingdom Bank), have successfully relocated and established themselves in South Africa. Some of the Zimbabwean farmers who left Zimbabwe after 2000 have also been successfully absorbed into that country's farming industry.[7] Living a more comfortable life than the rest, such Zimbabweans who have secured formal employment or established businesses in South Africa have bought homes and invested in South Africa, and some have been granted South African permanent residency or citizenship. Many have sought to integrate and to raise their children in South Africa: while they commonly still look to Zimbabwe as home, these Zimbabweans generally anticipate being in South Africa for the long term.[8]

Despite these differences, professional and skilled Zimbabweans share with unskilled compatriots a host of problems associated with being outsiders. They have all had to deal with xenophobia and racism, as well as problems in dealing with South African immigration bureaucracies, as officials have often failed to approve, or delayed the processing of applications for business, work, citizenship and permanent residence permits.[9] The following section explores how Zimbabweans' experiences of racism and xenophobia have contributed to on-going debates about identity, alongside other factors, such as the challenges of living away from home and the attraction of living in a more prosperous country.

Xenophobia and Racism in the New South Africa

Zimbabweans have often been particular targets in the rising xenophobia in South Africa, alongside Nigerians, Mozambicans and others, and are accused of overwhelming South Africa by their large numbers. They have been alleged to peddle drugs and engage in criminal activity, while their national leaders are seen as economic and political competitors to South African aspirations of leadership of the continent (Centre for Development Enterprise 2008; Southern Africa Migration Project 2008). The largest South African daily, the tabloid, the *Daily Sun*, and biggest Sunday newspaper, the *Sunday Times*, have both published inflammatory articles scapegoating Zimbabweans. In one such inflammatory article in 2006, the *Daily Sun* claimed 70 per cent of housebreaking in Gauteng was committed by foreigners, 'mostly Zimbabweans',[10] while the *Sunday Times* alleged that Zimbabweans were responsible for some very high profile crimes committed in South Africa since 2000, such as the 2002 and 2005 Johannesburg International Airport cash heists in which a combined R185 million was stolen and a number of bank robberies across the country allegedly committed by the infamous 'Hammer Gang'.[11]

Zimbabweans and migrants from other African countries are also accused of queue jumping, fraudulently taking state welfare, and occupying government houses built for South African low-income earners (Pillay and Barolsky 2008). For instance, *The Star* of 6 February 2006, ran two headline stories on Zimbabweans – 'Foreigners are stealing our birthright' and 'How else are we supposed to survive' – which alleged that Zimbabweans were acquiring RDP houses and receiving social grants meant for unemployed South Africans.[12] The same newspaper further claimed that the government hospital in the South Africa-Zimbabwe border town of Musina was experiencing 'a new phenomenon of heavily pregnant Zimbabweans arriving in South Africa, just in time to give birth [and] then register their children at the Home Affairs department, even when the fathers were not South Africans ... for social grants'.[13]

The image of a Zimbabwean, as constructed in contemporary South African media and public discourse, is that of a murderous criminal also responsible for a host of other vices such as prostitution, drug abuse, spreading HIV-AIDS, impregnating young girls and leaving them to raise the children alone.[14] Zimbabweans tend to be cast universally as illegal, such that 'criminality and illegality' have become main defining characteristics of a Zimbabwean. Very little distinction, if any, is made between the recent and old migrants who have been in the country for generations and have naturalised.[15] Because Zimbabweans appear to have become the largest group of foreign nationals in South Africa, the word 'Zimbabwean' has also become a generic term for foreigner.

These xenophobic discourses have tried to assert South African superiority over African migrants, drawing on western notions of modernity as well as apartheid supremacist ideologies, which conjured up an image of a chaotic and uncivilised post-independent Africa. They have borrowed from colonial and racist discourses about African bodies to depict African migrants, Zimbabweans included, as inferior human beings, as despicable and filthy subjects with smelly bodies.[16] This ideology of superiority is constructed within the context of a widely shared prejudice of exceptionalism among both black and white South Africans, partly based on the fact that South Africa is more industrialised and advanced in relation to other countries of the continent (Mamdani 1996: 27; Neocosmos 2008). This notion of exceptionalism, fostered through isolation from the rest of the continent during apartheid, cuts across class and educational divisions among South Africans and upholds the idea that while South Africa is geographically in Africa, it is separated from the rest of the African continent culturally, politically and economically (Mamdani 1996b: 3–4, 1998: 1). The reference point for South Africa is thus the developed world of Europe and America rather than underdeveloped Africa. For many South Africans, Africa continues to be the 'dark continent', and there is very little knowledge of, or interest in, the countries that exist beyond the Limpopo (Willliams 2008).

Formulated within this framework, South African public discourse about Zimbabweans and other African migrants casts them as primitive and uncivilised beings migrating from the 'African jungles north of the Limpopo'.[17] The rural background of most Zimbabwean migrants and their cultural conservativism is viewed as a sign of backwardness. In the black townships, migrants are stereotyped as sorcerers who use witchcraft to succeed in business, gain employment ahead of South Africans and snatch other people's wives, husbands, girlfriends or boyfriends.[18]

Although some recent studies have suggested that strong regional 'Southern African' identities have protected migrants from within the region from more negative attitudes towards foreigners from further afield (CDE 2008; SAMP 2008), the experiences of Zimbabweans do not accord with this view. Unlike migrants from Botswana, Namibia, Swaziland and Lesotho who are favourably received by South Africans, Zimbabweans are viewed as culturally different and closer to other Africans from sub-Saharan Africa. Focusing on the gulf between the dominant Nguni languages and cultures of South Africa and that of the predominantly Shona-speaking Zimbabwean migrants, they are projected as babblers who speak incomprehensibly – *makwerekwere*. Even Nguni-speaking Ndebele and Shangaan migrants from Zimbabwe are often not distinguished from the rest of Zimbabweans, and are included in the category *makwerekwere* or *kalanga* (foreigners).[19]

Zimbabweans have been among the targets in the recent xenophobic violence directed against African migrants in townships and informal settlements.[20] Levels of intolerance towards African foreigners reached an all time high in May 2008 when South Africans violently attacked and killed African migrants in Johannesburg, Pretoria, Cape Town and Durban, leaving sixty dead of which twelve were Zimbabwean, and 80,000 displaced.[21] Businesses belonging to African migrants were looted and their shacks destroyed by residents who accused them of taking up their jobs and committing crime.[22] Although the South African government has initiated anti-xenophobia campaigns, individual ANC leaders have spoken out against the attacks and former president of South Africa, Mbeki, has tried to emphasise South Africa's bonds with the rest of the Africa (Williams 2008), many other prominent politicians have been hostile to migrants, such as former minister of Home Affairs-Mangosuthu Buthelezi. At the same time, state officials, ranging from immigration officials at the

Department of Home Affairs to soldiers and police officers routinely ill-treat Zimbabweans and other African migrants (Landau 2005; SPT 2004).[23]

Zimbabweans in South Africa, like other African migrants, also have to deal with being black in a country where categories of race and ethnicity are still used to mark boundaries of social location and status. Race remains important for most South African whites who are struggling to accept blacks as equals in a post-apartheid South Africa (Habib and Bentley 2008; Burger and Jaftaa 2006). As Ibrahim Abdullah, a Sierra Leonean academic who lived in South Africa in the 1990s elaborates, 'while refugees and working class immigrants are constantly hounded by law enforcement agents and angry citizens because of their visible prosperity as hawkers, petty traders, craft entrepreneurs and drug dealers, middle class professional African immigrants face racial discrimination from their white counterparts in the white controlled or dominated cities and institutions' (Abdullah 2000). Both skilled and unskilled Zimbabweans I have encountered in my almost one decade of living in South Africa complain bitterly about racial discrimination in both their working and living spaces.

The Politics of Repositioning

Xenophobia and racism against Zimbabweans and other African migrants is more than just a general antipathy towards foreigners generated by discourses of fear and danger. It is part of the identity dialectic and contemporary nation-building process in contemporary South Africa involving social hierarchies or binaries between 'South Africans' and others viewed as not belonging, in which non-South Africans are placed in diametric opposition to South Africans in terms of class, culture, ethnicity and modernity. As Hall (1996) notes, there is a dynamic of ongoing power-play in this identity politics, and the historical, cultural, linguistic and colour characteristics that can be used as symbolic marks of exclusion or inclusion are used by the competing groups to give themselves an alternative or counter-position to gain access to resources and power, to gain space and to create collective identities.

Within this identity dialectic in contemporary South Africa, Zimbabweans and other African migrants have tried to create space for themselves by developing their own counter-hegemonic discourses. Mobilising history and memory and calling on norms of reciprocity, they have tried to argue for rights in South Africa by emphasising the role played by their countries in ending apartheid (Landau and Haupt 2007: 14). In this process, which Landau and Haupt (2007: 9–15) describe as 'tactical cosmopolitanism', Zimbabweans have specifically argued for a regional citizenship based on the mutual interdependence of southern African countries, highlighting

Zimbabwe's role as frontline state in the struggle against apartheid, and the debt owed to them by South Africans for hosting ANC exiles. They have also argued that South Africa's economic development would not have been possible without the exploitation of cheap labour from the countries of the regional hinterland.[24] Through this line of argument, Southern African citizens in South Africa not only deserve to be treated fairly as 'regional citizens' but also have a right to benefit from the development their parents and grandparents helped to bring about.

Other historical claims to rights draw on pan-Africanist arguments emphasising cultural and political bonds between South Africans and other Africans (Landau and Haupt 2007:13–2007). African migrants have challenged the notion of South African exceptionalism, by appealing to notions of geography, race and indigeneity and arguing that the real 'aliens' are Europeans, Asians and Americans. Landau and Haupt have described this invocation of pan-Africanism by African migrants as 'rhetoric and tactic' meant to legitimise access to South African space (Landau and Haupt 2007: 13). But, in some cases, it is more than simply strategic: for many migrants, especially the educated, whose viewpoints are shaped by African nationalism, there is a political conviction that 'South African exceptionalism' is a misinformed philosophy and that South Africa's destiny is bonded to the rest of the continent.

Other historical arguments for inclusion have drawn on memories of the *Mfecane*, and other precolonial migrations, particularly on the part of Venda, Ndebele and Shangaan speaking migrants from Zimbabwe. For instance, Douglas, a Shangaan-speaking Zimbabwean from the south-eastern district of Chipinge, who has lived in South Africa since the late 1980s makes claims to South Africanness on the basis of his surname – Sithole – which he traces back to South African origins. Similarly, the Matabeleland-born Mduduzi, claims South African roots from his *isibongo* [totem/clan name] Mlambo, which is also found among the Nguni groups of South Africa.[25] But, as Ndlovu-Gatsheni argues, contemporary Ndebele *izibongo* and clan names have complex histories that are belied by such straightforward claims to common ancestry. For instance, the *izibongo* or clan names Ndlovu, Moyo and Mlambo do not lead to single apical ancestors, but rather to a multitude of distinct clans and divergent family histories and ethnicities. The Ndlovus, for example, include the Ndlovu (Gatsheni) who are Nguni, the Ndlovu (Gabula) who are Kalanga, the Ndlovu (Mthombeni) who are Gaza-Nguni as well as a number of other Ndlovus of diverse ethnicity. There are numerous people of Rozvi-Shona origin who adopted Nguni surnames for purposes of acceptability within the Ndebele state (Ndlovu-Gatsheni 2004; Ndlovu Gatsheni forthcoming). Of course, history and facts are not the key issue for Zimbabweans engaged in the politics of identity and claim-making in South Africa. As they attempt to insert and reposition themselves in their new spaces, they are reimagining, reinventing and reconstructing their family histories with the strategic goal of emphasising their historical connection to South Africa, unravelling their Zimbabwean histories and national identities to trace common pre-colonial ties.

The process of repositioning and reconstitution of identities on the part of African migrants in South Africa is not all about history. It also involves learning local languages, cultures and sub-cultures. Almost all the Zimbabwean migrants interviewed during this research could speak at least one of South Africa's official eleven languages, the commonly spoken ones being Zulu, Sotho, Venda and Tsonga/Shangaan. Zimbabweans from the southern districts, who spoke Nguni languages at home find it relatively easier to assimilate than their Shona-speaking counterparts, who have an advantage only in the Venda-speaking communities of northern Limpopo province. Some Zimbabweans have adopted South African sounding names and try to cut contacts with Zimbabwean friends and relatives. Those who successfully integrate into South African society, can end up assuming ambivalent multiple identities (Maphosa 2008), may feel emotionally that they are 'in-between', as they experience leaving home but at the same time do not feel they have arrived (Krzyzanowski and Wodak 2007: 115).

Despite these possibilities, it is the constraints on Zimbabweans' capacity to blend in and assume South African identities that is notable in the recent context, even if they speak local Nguni languages or have family ties to South Africa. Zimbabweans are easily distinguishable by their accent and gestures: Bheki, who has lived in Johannesburg for over a decade, shares a common view that Zimbabweans stand out in the streets South African cities because of their body language, their gait, conversation and style of dress.[26] Within the townships, the younger generation of South African blacks have developed *tsotsi taal* sub-cultures, which also differ between one South African township to another (Molamu 2002). Originating as a gangster sub-culture, mixing Afrikaans, English and Zulu words, at the beginning of the twentieth century, *tsotsi taal* singles out insiders from outsiders, even among South Africans themselves. Furthermore, the popular discourses outlined above work against acceptance of Zimbabweans' attempts to claim 'South Africanness' on the basis of common histories, languages and cultures. The May-June 2008 xenophobic attacks were indicative of the difficulties of integration, as their targets included not only recent migrants, but also naturalised South Africans of Zimbabwean and Mozambican origin with long histories of residence in South Africa.[27]

This difficulty in integration has been racialised, as white Zimbabweans have not faced the same problems as their black compatriots. Those with family connections, have been absorbed particularly easily, and there are multiple linkages, given the numbers who moved to white-ruled South Africa in the late 1970s and early 1980s, and the then need for skills, such that doctors, accountants, engineers and teachers, were easily absorbed into South Africa's private sector, or set up their own businesses (Sinclair 1979: 41). Former members of the Rhodesian security services with military backgrounds, were absorbed into the apartheid government's military and intelligence services (Godwin and Hancock 1993: 314–19; Stiff 2002). There were, of course, differences in identity, language, memory, and belonging that shaped the positioning and integration of white, English-speaking, immigrants, especially in predominantly Afrikaans speaking areas. Some authors emphasise the difficulties this created, such as Godwin 1993: 316, for an Australian comparison, (see Venables 2003), yet, for many, notions of shared racial and cultural identity, and in some cases family links, with white South Africans nonetheless facilitated this process.

White Zimbabweans who have moved to South Africa after 2000 have been able to acquire citizenship relatively easily, or have secured permanent residence and working permits because of their family and business connections. They have not experienced the same economic hardships and problems as their African counterparts in settling in South Africa because of their skin colour. They are economically privileged in comparison to their black compatriots under the country's prevailing system of 'economic apartheid' which continues to guarantee unequal access to jobs and services for whites over blacks (Bond 2000 and 2002). It is rare to find white Zimbabweans singled out for criticism or hear of xenophobic-inspired violence against them.[28] Race, as Ibrahim Abdullah has correctly argued, is thus 'not only implicated in the whole process of emigration, from the officials in the Home Affairs Department to the people in the street, it is also the racial discourse about the Other Africa and its people, propagated to signify relations between African immigrants and white/black South Africans'(Abdullah 2000). In this hostile context, of exclusion and 'otherness', black Zimbabweans have also tried to find each other and have reimagined the meaning of 'Zimbabweanness'.

Emerging Diaspora Nationalisms

Zimbabweans' counter-discourses combine anti-host country sentiments with efforts to assert their superiority over South Africans, and are important in the development of diaspora nationalisms. Through these counter-hegemonic discourses, Zimbabweans try both to correct negative perceptions about themselves and their country and develop a positive image of Zimbabwe and everything Zimbabwean. Zimbabweans interviewed for this study speak of Zimbabwe and Zimbabweans in general, in very endearing and exaggerated terms. Zimbabwe, to these Zimbabweans abroad, is superior to South Africa and the other neighbouring countries in everything, from food to moral deportment.

Combining their own experiences of South African society, especially the negative aspects which include crime and violence, with ideas and assumptions in local media and intellectual discourses about these issues (Bornman Van Eeden and Wentzel 1998; Emmett and Butchart 2000), Zimbabweans try to define themselves in antithesis to South Africans. For instance, responding to South African public denunciation of Zimbabweans as criminals who take jobs ahead of South Africans, they have projected Zimbabwe as a nation of 'diligent, hard and intelligent workers', incomparable to the 'lazy, dishonest and uneducated' South Africans who are 'good only at drinking, fighting and criminality'.[29] They have sought to depict South Africans collectively as idle, alcoholic and morally decadent, while projecting themselves as saintly and law-abiding. To these diasporans, Zimbabwe remains a place of virtue notwithstanding current political and economic problems: it is cast as devoid of South African social ills such as the high incidence of rape and other violent crimes. Zimbabwean men project themselves as 'perfect gentlemen'– loving and caring, unlike their South counterparts who are caricatured as 'violent savages' who 'cannot care for their women and children'.[30] Being Zimbabwean also means being 'educated' and 'well-mannered'.

As Zimbabweans in South Africa seek to deal with the huge assault on their national pride brought about by displacement and xenophobia, they have thus utilised the same ideas and assumptions underlying xenophobic discourse, turned them upside down to cast South Africans in negative terms while portraying a positive image of themselves and their country. This type of Zimbabwean diaspora nationalism can express itself in feelings of cultural superiority or ethnocentrism. The content of this nationalism, which seeks to reify and essentialise the difference between Zimbabweans and South Africans, also tends to redefine Zimbabwean nationhood in mythical terms. The result is that a growing number of Zimbabweans in South Africa are increasingly beginning to see their national character largely in these mythic terms defined as polar opposites of the South African.

The combination of discrimination and the emotional void created by being away from home has led many Zimbabweans abroad to display very high levels of patriotism. Even those Zimbabweans who are pessimistic about the future of their country and do not support the incumbent government are also quick to defend Zimbabwe and its government when outsiders make generalisations about their country.[31] Such patriotic sentiments are not only the preserve of recent migrants, but are also frequently expressed also by the many Zimbabweans who have acquired permanent residence or citizenship in South Africa (48 per cent of Zimbabweans from

Bulilimamangwe and Beitbridge had South African passports and other identity documents and many have established families and homes in South Africa [Maphosa 2004; 2008 and Chetsanga 2003]). Many of these Zimbabweans who have some security in South Africa sought to naturalise their status simply as a pragmatic and temporary survival strategy and not a matter of commitment to South Africa. Almost all my interviewees expressed a desire to retain their Zimbabwean identity and to return to Zimbabwe when the economic and political conditions changed.[32] The importance of burial at home in Zimbabwe is indicative of the strength of this sentiment (Maphosa 2008: 5; Dzingirai 2007; Mbiba this volume).

The feeling of patriotism is almost palpable, in particular among professionals who strongly resent discrimination at their places of work and residence.[33] Embracing an ardent patriotism, these Zimbabweans have placed great emphasis on national days, such as Independence Day, national institutions and national symbols, such as the national flag. In fact, these Zimbabweans abroad embrace the Zimbabwe national flag and national colours more enthusiastically than Zimbabweans in their own country. Whenever the national football, cricket and tennis teams are playing, most immigrant Zimbabweans are dressed in their national colours, ardently supporting their national teams.[34] Diasporic communities in South Africa also display their patriotism in their taste for music. Harare based music salesman, Tererai claims that the Zimbabwean diaspora in South Africa and the UK has become their largest market for local music,[35] while the *The Star* claimed that Zimbabwean residents in Musina can easily be identified through 'the music of Zimbabwean band System Tazvila Chazezes and Challengers [sic] blaring from their homes'.[36]

Zimbabweans in South Africa depend crucially on networking with each other, and on formal and informal occasions to socialise among themselves. Working class migrants rely heavily on kinship and extended family ties for both accommodation and employment, and new arrivals are helped by compatriots who have been in South Africa for a longer period.[37] These social networks are maintained through social visits during weekends or important family events like birthdays, weddings and regular phone calls to discuss developments at home (Muzondidya 2008). Many continue to live with friends or relatives after they have found jobs, sharing room rentals and groceries in order to cut down on accommodation and food costs.[38] The many burial societies formed by Zimbabweans in South Africa further cement these ties – such as the Johannesburg-based, Masasane Burial Society (formed by migrants who moved to South Africa during the 1980s),[39] the Zvishavane Burial Society, and the Pretoria-based Maranda and Mberengwa Burial Societies. In these societies, members meet once a month or more, pay monthly subscriptions of between R30 and R50 redeemable when there is bereavement in the family.[40] Society contributions have sometimes been used to facilitate development at home, such as in Tsholotsho, where burial society money has been invested into the building of a library and a laboratory for a secondary school.[41]

While burial societies have mostly brought working class migrants together, professionals have formed alumni associations. Former students and teachers of Marist Brothers Secondary School of Dete, for example, have organised themselves into Marist Old Students Association (MOSA) South Africa (www.mosadete.info.ms/). Johannesburg professionals created the Batanai-Bambanani Zimbabwean Association, which is devoted to mutual support in business and fund-raising for good causes, and has over 200 members, mostly professionals occupying senior positions in South African businesses and institutions (Sisulu, Moyo and Tshuma 2007). In Cape Town, parents in professional families formed the Zimbabwe Social Forum in 2006, which aimed to provide a platform 'through which Zimbabweans can network and meet each other and our children can interact and be able to speak to each other in either Shona or Ndebele'.[42] Similarly, students have set up the Association of Zimbabwean Students in South African Universities (AZISSU) to provide help in times of need (Sisulu, Moyo and Tshuma 2007). Zimbabweans also come together in weekend parties and braais to eat Zimbabwean food and listen to music from home, or watch amateur football tournaments – 'boozers soccer' – and exchange gossip and discuss Zimbabwean politics.[43]

Zimbabweans living in those parts of South Africa with large 'home communities' have established shebeens and pubs serving drinking and music needs of Zimbabwean patrons as well as restaurants. Zimbabweans in Johannesburg, for instance, drink and dine at such places as 'KwaMaGumede', a restaurant and pub owned by a Zimbabwean businessman and which serves Zimbabwean dishes. These venues provide reminders of Zimbabweanness, but also promote integration – as Bigman, an owner of a shebeen in a Pretoria informal settlement argued 'Many actually say that *kwaBigman ndiko kumusha, saka todzokerei kuZimbabwe*' [why should we return to Zimbabwe when Bigman provides us with all the entertainment we miss about Zimbabwe].[44] Zimbabwean church fellowships also operate in many of South Africa's townships and informal settlements, providing crucial networks and support for women.[45]

While these diasporic spaces have thus provided spaces where Zimbabweans come together, there are nonetheless tensions and cleavages. Despite the unitary patriotism invoked in some contexts, the diaspora has also reproduced and exacerbated ethnic, class, racial and other divides imported from home. These tensions are important for understanding the ambiguous and contradictory nature of diaspora nationalism.

Ambiguities and Contradictions

While Zimbabweans in South Africa have often displayed high levels of diaspora nationalism, not everyone has participated or articulated such views. For those who are illegal, fear and insecurity have encouraged them to remain underground and not to make public displays of their Zimbabwean nationality. Others opt to conceal or reject their national origin, instead seeking to pass as South African and gain entitlement to the privileges this brings. The strategies people have used include avoiding associating with fellow Zimbabweans or using Zimbabwean languages in public.[46] In some extreme cases, rejecting Zimbabwean identity involves cutting off contact with friends and relatives from Zimbabwe. For such Zimbabweans, the scorn, suspicion and ridicule they have faced has dealt a severe blow to their national pride: they feel their stigmatisation in the region is just another negative consequence of their country's collapse, which has contributed to their antipathy towards both their government and country.

Some white Zimbabweans, for example, have found it difficult to continue identifying with Zimbabwe after moving to South Africa. Many whites lost their Zimbabwean citizenship status through the Citizenship of Zimbabwe Amendment Act (2001), which required Zimbabweans of foreign descent to provide documentary proof to the Registrar General that they had legally renounced their foreign citizenship or entitlement to foreign citizenship (Government of Zimbabwe 2003; Human Rights Forum 2002). They have also been vilified by the Zimbabwean state and constructed as foreigners since the beginning of the chaotic but populist fast track land reform programme in 2000 (Raftopoulos 2003: 230). Belonging in the Zimbabwean nation has been defined in racial terms, such that only 'native Africans' or '*vana vevhu/abantwana bomhlabathi*' (sons of the soil) can be the original and true inhabitants of Zimbabwe, and claim rights to the country's land and other resources (Muzondidya 2007: 333–40). Constructed as aliens on the basis of their race and stripped of their legal citizenship by the amendment, white Zimbabweans living outside Zimbabwe have increasingly become naturalised citizens of South Africa, Britain and other countries.

Some black Zimbabweans have also turned their backs on Zimbabwe, frustrated by the economic and political crisis and unfair treatment, such that they have adopted citizenship in those countries where they now live. Political activists and black businessmen who fled from Zimbabwe under threat of arrest after falling out of favour with ZANU PF, for example, have now become naturalised citizens of South Africa.[47] While some have sought temporary refuge others are bitter over their experiences in Zimbabwe and have decided to sever connections with home and settle permanently in their new countries of residence.

Among those Zimbabweans in South Africa who have continued to identify with Zimbabwe, the racial divide between white and black Zimbabweans experienced at home, has been reproduced in the diaspora (Makunike 2005). This divide is particularly felt between the 'Rhodies' who could not accommodate themselves to majority rule, and black Zimbabweans, whom they blame collectively for their dislocation. Black Zimbabwean interviewees felt such white Zimbabweans generally try to disassociate themselves from Zimbabwe and black Zimbabweans. According to Wozha, a Zimbabwean professional who has been in South Africa since the 1990s, 'Rhodies always try to conceal their Zimbabwean identities and the closest they ever get to acknowledging their connection to Zimbabwe or Zimbabwean identity is for them to say "I once lived or went to school in Zimbabwe"'.[48]

Ethnic and regional divisions from home have also been deepened in some diasporic contexts. Much of the socialisation among black Zimbabweans discussed above occurs within limited circles of people who know each other from home or organise in linguistic, ethnic and regional groupings. In one of the informal settlements in Pretoria, Zandspruit, Karanga-speaking migrants from Masvingo normally socialise alone, as do the Shangaan-speakers from Chiredzi and Chipinge, and Venda-speakers from Beitbridge. The various groups rent accommodation in different quarters of the informal settlement, rarely mix when drinking at shebeens and often engage in ethnic fights.[49] There is also mutual antagonism between Ndebele migrants who fled Zimbabwe during the *Gukurahundi* violence and killings of the 1980s who are often collectively branded ZIPRA dissidents, and Shona migrants who are often collectively identified with ZANU PF by the other group.[50] In the Johannesburg branch of the MDC, the tension and hostility within the diaspora erupted into violence in 2005, resulting in two rival groups - MDC South Africa and MDC Zimbabwe Action Support Group, both of which competed to be recognised as the legitimate representative of the party in South Africa.[51]

Divisions among Zimbabweans abroad have given rise to tribally exclusive organisations. For instance, diaspora political activists from Matebeleland who are bitter about the marginalisation of their region from national development and the perceived ethnic hegemony of the majority Shona ethnic group have formed separatist organisations, such as *Mthwakazi Action Group on Genocide and Ethnic Cleansing in Matebeleland and Midlands* and *Mthwakazi People's Congress (MPC)*. These organisations have not only provincialised Ndebele identity and tried to construct it as an antithesis to Shona identity, but have also agitated for Ndebele self-determination through the creation of an autonomous Ndebele state (Mthwakazi 2006). Tribally based political parties within Zimbabwe such as the Patriotic Union of Matabeleland (PUMA), the Federal Democratic Union (FDU),

ZAPU-Federal Party (ZAPU-FP), have all found more support among the young Ndebele generations in the disapora, where displaced Ndebele communities are linking up via the internet, through web-based forums such as inkundla.net, to promote a distinct Ndebele political identity (Muzondidya and Gatsheni-Ndlovu 2007).

Conclusion

In this chapter, I hoped to convey some of the diverse and contradictory experiences of Zimbabweans in South Africa, and to show how their differential circumstances were shaping the formation of the new Zimbabwean diaspora communities. Although some recent Zimbabwean migrants in South Africa are integrating and beginning to see their longterm future in their country of settlement, this process has often been combined with a renewed attachment to home, encouraging the development of diasporic sentiments and spaces for meeting as Zimbabweans. Xenophobia, racism and discrimination within South Africa have reinforced this sense of distinctive Zimbabweanness, even on the part of those who have lived in South Africa for some time.

The new diasporic spaces in which Zimbabweans seek to find emotional support, socialise and re-define the meanings and nature of ties with home at a distance are shaped by contradictory trends. On the one hand, Zimbabwean diasporic spaces are infused by a resurgent patriotism that inverts the denigrating stereotypes of the South African media and re-invests Zimbabweanness with a shared moral superiority, giving elevated importance in diasporic venues to symbols of the Zimbabwean nation, such as the flag, national colours, national anthem and Independence Day. At the same time, regional, ethnic and racial divides from home have been imported and widened, as the frustrations and insecurities of displacement have undermined mutual trust. While they renegotiate their relationships and problems with their fellow compatriots and find new ways of understanding their identity as Zimbabweans abroad, Zimbabweans in the diaspora have also delved into history to find pragmatic arguments to justify their presence in South Africa and create bonds with South Africans, have struggled to learn South African languages and to acquire the documents that can legitimate their stay.

Notes

1. I would like to express my gratitude to Johannes Muzondidya for conducting all the interviews held with Zimbabweans living in Pretoria's informal settlements in August 2008.

2. Discussion with Mbuya Murinda, Zaka December 2007
3. Discussion with Rose, Pretoria, May 2007, Interview with Mutsai, Pretoria 17 August 2007.
4. *Mail and Guardian Online* 20 April 2006, *The Zimbabwean* 23 December 2005
5. Discussion with Rose, Pretoria May 2007.
6. See also *The Zimbabwean* 2 March 2006.
7. *The Zimbabwean* 18 January 2005, IRIN 2 June 2006
8. Interview with Bheki, Pretoria 27 February 2006, Zipho Cape Town 7 April 2006.
9. SW Radio Africa 21 March 2006.
10. *Daily Sun* 5 April 2006.
11. *Sunday Times* 2 July 2006. See also Mail and Guardian online 29 June 2006, which blames Zimbabweans for robberies in Gauteng, Mpumalanga and Limpopo.
12. *The Star* (SA) 6 February 2006.
13. *The Star* 6 February 2006.
14. *Business Day* 19 November 2007, IRIN 21 September 2007, Discussion with Thabo Pretoria May 2007.
15. Interview Tariro Cape Town 10 April 2006.
16. Remarks from a public conversation, Cape Town August 1995.
17. Informal Conversation with Lerato Cape Town August 1995.
18. Discussion with Geoff Pretoria September 2008, Interview with Philip Pretoria 18 August 2007.
19. Busani, a Ndebele-speaking Zimbabwean who is married to a local South African woman, emphasised this point. Discussion with Busani Pretoria November 2007.
20. *Business Day* 25 October 2000, *New Zimbabwe Online* 1 April 2006, *Sunday Times* 18 May 2008.
21. *The Herald* 4 June 2008, *Mail and Guardian* 23–29 May 2008.
22. *Sowetan* 2 April 2008, *Mail and Guardian* 31 March 2008, *Pretoria News* 18 April 2008.
23. IRIN 25 November 2004, *The Herald* 16 February 2007.
24. *The Herald* 3 February 2004.
25. Discussion with Douglas November 2007, Mduduzi Pretoria 2008.
26. Bheki 27 February 2006.
27. South African Home Affairs Parliamentary Committee, 29 May 2008.
28. *JhbLive* 2006.
29. Informal Conversation with Zimbabweans, Beitbridge Border Post 27 September 2008. These are also common expressions from my personal interaction and discussions with Zimbabweans living in South Africa.
30. Informal Conversation with Zimbabwean professionals Cape Town 2006.
31. These are also personal impressions I have made from my interaction and discussions with Zimbabweans living in South Africa.
32. See for example, interviews with Zipho Cape Town 7 April 2006, Professor Johannesburg 26 February 2006, Bheki Pretoria 27 February 2006, David, Chris, Nyarai and Simon Pretoria 2007.

33. Interview with Bheki 27 February 2006, Discussion with Wellington, October 2006
34. Personal Observations South Africa 1995–2001, 2004–2008.
35. Tererai September 2005.
36. The Star 6 February 2006.
37. Working class migrants interviewed in Pretoria indicated that they got their jobs through friends or relatives who have been in South Africa for a much longer period than them. Interviews with Senior, Pretoria 25 August 2007, Manuel Sango Pretoria 25 August 2007, Professor Johannesburg 26 February 2006.
38. Discussion with David, Chris, Nyarai and Simon February & March 2007, Interviews with Philip Mbengo Pretoria 18 August 2007.
39. IWR Africa Report No. 92, 30 January 2007.
40. Interview with Bigman Pretoria 19 August 2007.
41. IWRAfrica Report No. 92, 30 January 2007.
42. Inaugural meeting of the Zimbabwe Social Forum May 2006.
43. Personal Observations Cape Town 2004–2006, Pretoria 2006–2008.
44. Interview with Bigman Pretoria 19 August 2007.
45. Interview with Mutsai, Ruth and Belinda Pretoria, 17 and 18 August 2007.
46. Discussion with Netsai Cape Town 2006.
47. Many prominent individuals were forced into exile in the ZANU PF succession battle in 2004 following threats of arrest for alleged illegal business dealings. See *Financial Gazette* 15 June 2006
48. Discussion with Wozha, Pretoria October 2007.
49. Interviews, Ruth, Philip and Manuel Pretoria 17 and 18 August 2007
50. *Newzimbabwe.com* 15 June 2005, Inter Press Service 24 November 2005
51. *Newzimbabwe.com* 15 June 2005.

Bibliography

Abdullah, I. 2000. '"I'm Not an Alien": African Immigrants in Post-Apartheid South Africa'. Paper Presented at the African and Afro-American Studies 30th Anniversary Conference, University of North Carolina, http://www.unc.edu/ depts/afriafam/ AnniversaryConference/abdullah.htm.

Amanor-Wilks, I. and S. Moyo. 1996. 'Labour Migration to South Africa During the 1990s', Harare: ILO/SAMAT.

Anderson, B. 1983. *Imagined Communities: Reflections on the Origin and Spread of Nationalism.* London:Verso.

Beach, D.N. 1994. *The Shona and Their Neighbours.* Oxford: Blackwell.

Bond, P. 2000. *Elite Transition: From Apartheid to Neo-Liberalism in South Africa,* London: Pluto Press.

Bornman, E., R.van Eeden, M. Wentzel (eds). 1998. *Violence in South Africa: A Variety of Perspectives.* Pretoria: HSRC Press.

Britain Zimbabwe Society. 2006. 'Brief Report of Open Forum: Zimbabwe Skills & Reconstruction', 16 September, http://www.britain-zimbabwe.org.uk/OFN. htm

Burger, R. and R. Jaftaa. 2006. 'Returns to Race: Labour Market Discrimination in Post-Apartheid South Africa', Department of Economics, Stellenbosch University, Working Papers.

Cobbing, J. 1976. 'The Ndebele Under the Khumalos, 1820–1896', PhD Thesis. University of Lancaster.

Crush, J. and D. Yudelman. 1991. *South Africa's Labour Empire: A History of Black Migrancy to the Gold Mines.* Cape Town: David Philip.

Dzingirai, V. 2007. 'The Role of Kinship in Displacement', Lives for Transformation and Development Workshop, Nordiska Afrika Institute and Centre for Rural Development. Wild Geese Lodge: Harare, 28–29 June.

Emmett, T. and A. Butchart (eds). 2000. *Behind the Mask: Getting to Grips With Crime and Violence in South Africa.* Pretoria: HSRC Press.

Etherington, N. 2001. *The Great Treks: The Transformation of South Africa, 1815–1854.* London: Longman.

Godwin, P. and I. Hanlon. 1993. *Rhodesians Never Die: The Impact of War and Political Change on White Rhodesia, c. 1970–1980.* Oxford: Oxford University Press.

Habib, A. and C. Bentley (eds). 2008. *Racial Redress and Citizenship in South Africa.* Pretoria: HSRC Press.

Hall, S. 1996. 'Politics of identity.' In S. Hall (ed) *Culture, Identity and Politics.* Aldershot: Avebury.

Harries, P. 1994. *Work, Culture, and Identity: Migrant Labourers in Mozambique and South Africa, c.1860–1910.* Johannesburg: Witwatersrand University.

Hodder-Williams, R. 1983. *White Farmers in Rhodesia, 1890–1965: A History of the Marandellas District,* London.

Human Rights Watch. 2006. *Unprotected Migrants Zimbabweans in South Africa's Limpopo Province,* Volume 18, Number 6(A), August 2006, http://hrw.org/reports/2006/southafrica0806/5.htm

Krzyzanowski, M. and R. Wodak. 2007. 'Multiple Identities, Migration and Belonging: Voices of Migrants'. In Michael Krzyzanowski and Ruth Wodak (eds) *Identity Troubles.* Palgrave MacMillan: Basingstoke.

Landau, L. and I.M. Haupt. 2007. 'Tactical Cosmopolitanism and Idioms of Belonging: Insertion and Self Exclusion in Johannesburg'. Migration Studies Working Paper Series No. 32. Forced Migration Studies Programme, University of the Witwatersrand.

Mamdani, M. 1996. *Citizen and Subject: Contemporary Africa and the Legacy of Late Colonialism.* Princeton: Princeton University Press.

——. 1996b. 'Centre for African Studies: Some Preliminary Thoughts', *Social Dynamics,* 22, 2: 1–14.

——. 1998. 'Is African Studies to be Turned into a New home for Bantu Education at UCT?' *Seminar on the Africa Core of the Foundation Course for the Faculty of Social Sciences and Humanities. University of Cape Town, Wednesday, 22 April.*

Mandava, T. 2001. 'Call for Regional Policy on labour Migration'. *Afrol.com,* 11 March 2001. http://www.queensu.ca/samp/sampresources/samppublications/pressarticles/ 2001/labour.htm

Maphosa, F. 2004. 'The Impact of Remittances from Zimbabweans Working in South Africa on Rural Livelihoods in the Southern Districts of Zimbabwe'. Research report submitted to the Council for the Development of Social

Science Research in Africa (CODESRIA), July 2004. http://www.Livelihoods. org/hot_topics/migration/remittancesindex.html

———. 2008. 'Transnational Experiences of Undocumented Migrants from Zimbabwe's South Western Borderlands'. University of Pretoria, Department of Archaeology and Anthropology Seminar, 22 July.

Markakis, J. and K. Fukui, 1994. 'Introduction.' In J. Markakis and S. Fukui (eds) *Ethnicity and Conflict in the Horn of Africa*, eds London: James Currey.

Mathe, R. 2005. *Making Ends Meet at the Margins: Grappling with Economic Crisis and Belonging in Beitbridge, Zimbabwe*. Dakar: CODESRIA.

Mlambo, A.S. 2002. *White Immigration into Rhodesia: From Occupation to Federation*. Harare: University of Zimbabwe Publications.

Molamu, L. 2002. *Tsotsitaal: A Dictionary of the Language of Sophiatown*. Pretoria: UNISA.

Muzondidya, J. 2008. 'Majoni-joni: Survival Strategies Among Zimbabwean Immigrants in South Africa'. Paper Presented at the International Conference on Political Economies of Displacement in post-2000 Zimbabwe, Wits University, Johannesburg, 9–11 June.

Muzondidya, J. and B. Chiroro. 2008. 'Diaspora Philanthropy and Development: Help and Giving among Zimbabweans in South Africa'. Paper presented at International Society for Third Sector Research Conference, University of Barcelona, Spain, July 9–12.

Muzondidya J. and S.J. Ndlovu-Gatsheni. 2007. 'Echoing Silences: Ethnicity in Post-colonial Zimbabwe, 1980–2007'. *African Journal of Conflict Resolution*, 27, 2: 275–297.

Ndlovu-Gatsheni, S.J. 2004. 'The Dynamics of Democracy and Human Rights Among the Ndebele of Zimbabwe', PhD Thesis. University of Zimbabwe.

Neocosmos, M. 2006. *From 'Foreign Natives' to 'Native Foreigners': Explaining Xenophobia in Post-Apartheid South Africa* Dakar: CODESRIA.

———. 2008. 'The Pogroms in South Africa: The Politics of Fear and the Fear of Politics'. 5 June 2008. http://libcom.org/library/the-pogroms-south-africa-the-politics-fear-fear-politics-05062008

Nyamnjoh, F. 2006. *Insiders and Outsiders: Citizenship and Xenophobia in Contemporary Southern Africa*. Dakar: CODESRIA.

Pillay, S. and V. Barolsky. 2008. 'Citizenship, Violence and Xenophobia in South Africa: Perceptions from South African Communities'. Pretoria, Human Sciences Research Council Report, June.

Raftopoulos, B. 2003. 'The State in Crisis: Authoritarianism, Selective Citizenship and Distortions of Democracy in Zimbabwe'. In A. Hammar, B. Raftopoulos and S. Jensen (eds) *Zimbabwe's Unfinished Business: Rethinking Land, State and Nation in the Context of Crisis*. Harare: Weaver Press.

Ranger, T.O. 1970. *The African Voice in Southern Rhodesia, 1898–1930*. London: Heinemann.

———. 1989. 'Missionaries, Migrants and the Manyika: The Invention of Ethnicity in Zimbabwe'. In L. Vail and L. White (eds.) *The Creation of Tribalism in Southern Africa*. London: James Currey.

————. 2004. 'Nationalist Historiography, Patriotic History and History of the Nation: The Struggle Over the Past in Zimbabwe'. *Journal of Southern African Studies* 30, 2: 215–34.

Rasmussen, K. 1978. *Migrant Kingdom: Mzilikazi's Ndebele in South Africa.* London: Rex Collings.

Rutherford, B. 2006. 'Zimbabwean Farmworkers in Limpopo Province, South Africa'. Presentation at the BZS Research Day, Oxford University, 17 June.

Said, E. 1978. *Orientalism.* New York: Vintage Books.

Selby, A. 2006. 'Commercial Farmers and the State: Interest Group Politics and Land Reform in Zimbabwe', D. Phil Thesis. Oxford University.

Simon, A. 1988. 'Rhodesian Migrants in South Africa: Government, Media and a Lesson for South Africa', *African Affairs* 87, 346: 53–68.

Sisulu, E., B. Moyo and N. Tshuma. 2007. 'The Zimbabwean Community in South Africa.' In R. Southall et al. (eds) *State of the Nation; South Africa, 2006–2007.* Pretoria: HSRC Press.

South African Government Information. 2006. 'Address Delivered by the Deputy President, Phumzile Mlambo-Ngcuka, at the Launch of the Joint Initiative for Priority Skills Acquisition (JIPSA)'. Presidential Guest House, 27 March 2006, http://www.info.gov.za/speeches/2006/06032810451001.htm.

South African Home Affairs Parliamentary Committee. 2008. 'Xenophobia Attacks: Ministerial Briefing'. 29 May 2008. http://www.pmg.org.za/report/20080529–xenophobia-attacks-ministerial-briefing.

Statistics South Africa. 2006. *Mid Year Population Estimates.* 1 August 2006. http://www.statssa.gov.za/.

Stiff, P. 2002. *Cry Zimbabwe: Independence-Twenty Years On.* South Africa: Galago Publishing.

Tendi, B.M. 2008. 'Patriotic History and Public Intellectuals Critical of Power', *Journal of Southern African Studies* 34, 2: 379–96.

Unendoro, B. 2006. 'Zimbabwe: Mbeki Policy Failing'. Institute for War and Peace Reporting, AR No.53, 7 February 2006, http://www.zimbabwesituation.com/feb10_2006.html.

Van Onselen, C. 1976. *Chibaro: African Mine Labour in Southern Rhodesia 1900–1933.* London: Pluto Press.

Venables, E.S. 2003. 'The Women from Rhodesia: An Auto-Ethnographic Study of Immigrant Experience and [Re]Aggregation in Western Australia', Ph.D. Thesis. Murdoch University, Perth.

Williams, V. 2008. 'Xenophobia a Deep Rooted Phenomena', 21 May 2008. http://www.amandlapublishers.co.za/content/view/676/73/

Wilmsen, E.N. 1994. 'Introduction: Ethnicity, Identity and Nationalism in Southern Africa', *Journal of Southern African Studies*, 20, 3.

2

Zimbabwean Farmworkers in Limpopo Province, South Africa[1]

Blair Rutherford

As a way to introduce the working conditions, uncertainties and anxieties that mark the social experience of the group of displaced Zimbabweans who work on South African farms in the border-zone with Zimbabwe, I start with a quotation from a Zimbabwean man who began working on a South African border farm a few months before I met him in June 2005:

> Work is tough. You must be strong to work on farms. The only reason we do these shit jobs is because we are foreigners so we work here. We work harder than the South Africans as we need money ... . [But] staying in Zimbabwe is horrible – eeee, that country is shit; there are no jobs or future there! How can we look after our children and our children's children if I can't find a job there? It is better to be here [in South Africa] and to keep moving rather than just sitting and doing nothing (Zimbabwean farm worker in Tshipise, 29 July 2005).

Zimbabweans working on the farms in northern Limpopo province, South Africa, are intimately entangled in overlapping discursive practices of sovereignty and historical formations of citizenship, cultural politics of vulnerabilities, and economies of survival. In the occasional moments that they have merited passing public attention since the late 1990s, the analytical lenses and responses by policymakers and activists have been grounded largely in categories and structures of feeling associated with the long history and institutional arrangements surrounding migrant labour, or more recent ones marked by xenophobic sentiments and/or principles of human rights. The latter has been ascendant particularly since 2000 when the extent of the ZANU (PF) government's desire to maintain power at all costs became viscerally evident to the vast majority of Zimbabweans through the politicised violence and the dramatic economic decline that have devastatingly reverberated throughout that country from that ambition. With the greater attention given to the important issues of refugee processes for Zimbabweans and xenophobic attacks against Zimbabweans and other foreigners (e.g., SPT 2004, HRW 2007, FMSP and MLAO 2007), Zimbabweans who are working in jobs long marked for foreign workers can be overlooked, and thus the political and economic issues arising out of their precarious terrain of economic survival become obscured.

This is clearly seen in Solidarity Peace Trust's critical and thorough report concerning the generally grim situation Zimbabweans face in South Africa, *No War in Zimbabwe: An account of the exodus of a nation's people* (SPT 2004). While mounting a vital argument that Zimbabweans should be more easily granted asylum in South Africa given the politically-induced crisis in their homeland that is causing so many to flee, the report predominantly focuses on Zimbabweans living in South African urban areas. It only has a short section on the South African border-zone with Zimbabwe, noting in passing that there are a large number of Zimbabweans working on the farms there while observing that only those who have been recently displaced by the ZANU (PF) regime (citing Refugees International 2004) qualify for asylum as they do 'not fit the previous seasonal workers' mould' (2004: 61). The implication here is that the vast majority of these Zimbabweans working on the farms fall under the category of (im)migrant labour and thus fall outside the purview of their advocacy.

South African government officials and politicians and civil society activists have often had similar concerns. There are two dominant tendencies in their perspectives and efforts of intervention, pivoting around the concern of national sovereignty: either trying to find laws and policies to regulate these Zimbabweans as seasonal migrant workers or calling for their removal as they are largely undocumented migrants who are said to readily take jobs away from South Africans, thereby enabling farmers, particularly white farmers, to continue to mistreat all their workers, including South Africans. Important as these interventions and discourses operating through forms of national sovereignty and boundaries of citizenship are in shaping the lives and possibilities for these Zimbabwean farm workers in South Africa, I am going to suggest that they inhibit other ways of understanding and responding to them; ways of understanding and responding that are grounded more in the economies of survival they are pursuing.

This essay privileges the social experience of Zimbabwean farm workers in northern South Africa, examining their strategies, networks and tribulations in relation to wider political and economic contexts and hegemonic representations. In so doing, I draw on the three-pronged heuristic strategy of the anthropology of social suffering (Kleinman, Das and Lock 1997) that looks at cultural representations, social experience and political and professional processes. In this literature, 'cultural representations' refers to the public discussions, images and narratives concerning 'suffering', which I relate here to displacement to South Africa. These cultural representations, in turn, inform the routinized social experience – the social practices, structures of feeling and being-in-the-world. While wider political processes inform responses to suffering, particularly given the increased social power of mass media-ted narratives and images, these anthropologists argue that by attending to social experience one seeks to counter what can be an imbalance in representations, which can fixate on a specific, narrow understanding of suffering. In the authors' words: `What we represent and how we represent it prefigure what we will, or will not, do to intervene. What is not pictured is not real. Much of the routinised misery is invisible; much that is made visible is not ordinary or routine` (Kleinman, Das and Lock 1997: xiii). Analogously, the social experience of Zimbabwean farm workers in northern South Africa tends to be 'out-of-focus` of much of the discussion of Zimbabweans in South Africa.

Following this heuristic framework, I will put greater emphasis on the social experience of these Zimbabwean farm workers in regards to their livelihood strategies in South Africa. Elsewhere I have attended to some of the issues concerning cultural representations and political and professional processes (Rutherford and Addison 2007, Rutherford 2008). This chapter seeks to provide greater insight into the lives of these Zimbabweans working on farms in northern South Africa by sketching out some of their social relations and working conditions, the transnational pathways they have taken and have forged between Zimbabwe and South Africa, and, in the conclusion, drawing a few implications arising out of their survival strategies in terms of possible solidarity work. Through analyzing some of the South African contexts in which these Zimbabweans' lives are entangled and the transnational pathways that brought many to the farms and with which some utilize in their livelihoods, the aim is to deepen the understandings of the livelihoods and the particular enmeshing cultural politics of these Zimbabwean farm workers in northern South Africa.

This chapter is based on two short periods of ethnographic fieldwork in July 2004 and July and August 2005 and a brief follow-up research in June 2008 in Limpopo province, South Africa. I carried out fieldwork and interviews on five farms near Musina, the South African town just south of Zimbabwean border town of Beitbridge, and conducted a survey of 143 Zimbabwean farm workers, seventy-nine males and sixty-four females, in the last half of 2005. Although the wider contexts have changed in 2008 and 2009 (which I will touch upon in an Afterword), the social experience of these Zimbabwean farm workers in South Africa has not changed greatly since 2004–2005, the time in which most of this research for this chapter was conducted.

'Weipe is full of Zimbabweans!' Zimbabwean Farm Workers in Northern Limpopo

Every commercial farming area found in the semi-arid region south of the Limpopo River and north of the Soutpansberg mountains, a 130 kilometer long strip of volcanic and sedimentary rock ranging in altitude up to 1,700 meters, is said to be 'full of Zimbabweans' these days. These include Weipe, a commercial farming area hugging the south bank of the Limpopo River West of the official border-crossing and Tshipise, a commercial farming area between Musina and Thohoyandou in Venda. Zimbabwean farm workers are also found in other parts of Limpopo province (formerly Northern province and before 1994 part of Transvaal) as well as elsewhere in South Africa. However, they are especially concentrated in this seventy kilometer belt between the Soutpansberg range and the Limpopo River which marks the international boundary between South Africa and Zimbabwe. The presence of Zimbabweans working on these farms is not new, but their numbers, their geographic origins and their social characteristics have changed in the last six years.

It is difficult to determine the exact number of Zimbabweans who have been working on these farms during various periods, just as it is for figuring out the total number of Zimbabweans living in South Africa today. On the 200 or so South African commercial farms found north of the Soutpansberg range, different estimates from studies such as a 1998 survey by David Lincoln and Claude Maririke (2000: 52), one conducted by the provincial Department of Labour in early 2000 (NPDoL 2000: 2), work done by the International Organization for Migration (IOM 2003: 18, IOM 2004: 17) and my recent discussions with white farmers in this border area, all suggest that seventy to eighty per cent of the farm workers here are Zimbabwean, with at least 15,000 to 20,000 of them working and living on these citrus, horticultural and game farms (Rutherford and Addison 2007, HRW 2006, 2007).

Nearly all observers with whom I spoke – farmers, farm workers, government and NGO officials – claimed that there has been a dramatic increase in the number of Zimbabweans 'jumping the border,' including those seeking work on the border farms since 2000. This is also evidenced by the increasing number of Zimbabweans caught and deported from the border area: whereas the Department of Home Affairs deported 5,363 Zimbabweans apprehended throughout South Africa in 1990 (Crush 1998:

4), in 2002 the South African National Defense Force (SANDF) that patrols the border with Zimbabwe caught nearly 45,000 Zimbabwean 'infiltrators' only in the borderline area itself (excluding those caught at the border-post), while in 2007, an estimated 200,000 Zimbabweans were deported (HRW 2008: 8). In forty days of June and July 2008, 17,000 Zimbabweans were deported, despite the growing documented violence in Zimbabwe surrounding the presidential run-off election (UNHCR 2008). Farmers in this area also told me in 2005 that given the number of Zimbabweans seeking work from them they no longer relied on labour contractors to recruit workers as they had done in the past and as was common when Lincoln and Maririke (2000: 46) did their research in 1998.

In addition to the increasing number of Zimbabweans working on these border farms since 2000, many of the observers also suggested that in the 1990s and, especially, earlier, the majority of these migrants were predominantly Venda from the Beitbridge area of Zimbabwe. Since 2000, Zimbabweans have come from throughout Zimbabwe to work on northern South Africa commercial farms. I have met Zimbabwean farm workers in northern Limpopo province who came from Hwange, Nyanga, Banket, Chimanimani, Mberengwa, Bulawayo, Zvishavane, Gokwe, and, especially, Harare, to name but a few of their diverse Zimbabwean homes. My survey of farm workers reinforces these observations. In the survey, less than eighteen per cent identified themselves as 'Venda,' while fifty-eight per cent identified themselves as 'Shona' or 'Karanga.' The increasing numbers and changing social origins and characteristics of these farm workers in northern Limpopo province signal the growing crisis in Zimbabwe itself.

Leaving Zimbabwe: On Displacement

Before 2000, Zimbabweans who came to the farms did so almost exclusively because of dwindling economic opportunities in Zimbabwe largely as a consequence of the adoption of a structural adjustment policy (see Zinyama 2000). As others have noted, this transnational movement was facilitated by the 'opening-up' in post-Apartheid South Africa that attracted increased immigrants from southern and other parts of Africa, even though Apartheid immigration policies and attitudes continued to hold sway in the 1990s (see Crush 1998, Harris 2001). The politically induced crisis in Zimbabwe after 2000 has added a very different dimension to the migration. All the Zimbabwean farm workers I met who came after 2000 saw the need to find work in South Africa arising out of the drastic reduction of economic possibilities back in Zimbabwe as a consequence of the ZANU (PF) regime. Let me give a few examples of the predicaments some told to me.

A number of workers had educational and trade qualifications that had given them reasonable jobs in Zimbabwe that they had lost due to the disruptions since 2000. The average, median and mode educational level achieved of the surveyed workers was Grade Seven. Twenty-four per cent had achieved their O levels and one worker their A levels. Over fifty per cent of the workers who had arrived since 2000 had some secondary school education. Nearly seventy per cent had at least seven years of schooling, significantly higher than Lincoln and Maririke's (2000: 50) 1998 sample in which only forty-four per cent had that educational achievement.

One young Zimbabwean man who had his O levels had been working at a tourist lodge in Hwange that closed down in 2001 due to thefts and harassment by war veterans camped nearby. He eventually moved to Beitbridge but was not making much money. Then he met some Zimbabweans playing on a soccer team from a farm on the South African side of the Limpopo who told him how to jump the border and find work there. He has been working on the farm since 2002 as a lower management worker, periodically returning to Zimbabwe.

The notorious state-organized youth groups, the 'Green Bombers' (see, e.g., Solidarity Peace Trust 2003) figured in narratives of displacement of others. One man said he worked in a printing company in Bulawayo until 2003 when the employers caved in to political pressure to hire more 'Green Bombers,' the colloquial term for graduates from the Border Gezi youth training camps as they commonly have worn green uniforms when on duty intimidating or attacking people for the state or individual ZANU (PF) leaders, and all employees suspected of voting for MDC lost their jobs. Some young men lamented that they could not find work because they refused to enroll in the 'Border Gezi' youth camps, whereas others tried to get into these programs to get a job in the police or army but were told that all the spots were full. Both groups felt that without certificates of completion at these camps their job opportunities in Zimbabwe were limited so they 'jumped' the border to look for work.

I also met a number of young men and women – who claimed to be in their late teens, but some looked younger – who came to earn money to try to pay school fees to continue with their education. For example, one worker I knew who had been working on a farm since 2003 had two young relatives, two boys aged sixteen, spending a few nights with him, before they headed further south looking for work on another farm where they had a relative working. Others were working at their *musha* (a rural home and land) and found it difficult to produce enough because of drought and/or lack of inputs. One man I met had farmed on his Masvingo *musha* for fifteen years and never had a wage-labour job before crossing the border in July 2005 to find work on a commercial farm as he failed to harvest anything from his fields. The survey showed that seventy-seven per cent of the Zimbabwean workers had access to a *musha*. Over sixty-five per cent of those with access to land said nothing was harvested from the land the previous growing season in 2004–2005, due likely to drought and/or lack of access to agricultural inputs.

One woman said she worked as a store-keeper in rural Masvingo from 1999–2000 but left the job as her earnings were too low to help look after her daughter and her mother. She moved back to her mother's *musha* but they were unable to grow enough food to survive on, as they could not afford any inputs and the rains were paltry. She now alternates between working at her mother's *musha* in Masvingo during the rainy season and coming to a borderland farm with her brothers to work in a orange packing shed from May until August to earn money to pay for some agricultural inputs and 'basic necessities.' As she solemnly put it, 'It is difficult to be away from my family, but there is nothing to eat and there are no jobs in Zimbabwe. One needs to force oneself to cross the border to survive … .'

This sense of pushing oneself to come to South Africa to survive on one's own and, typically, for one's dependents was a strong sentiment. These sentiments were often explicitly gendered. For men, many stressed that they had to come to South Africa as they were 'the man of the household' and thus they were responsible to look after their family. Accordingly, they crossed the Limpopo like a 'man.' As one put it, 'we are the fathers, we must be brave and cross the river to find money …' Others configured themselves as continuing a tradition forged by their male relatives and ancestors who previously had made the trek to work in South Africa. In contrast, women farm workers often stressed to me their duties as a mother to find work, particularly for those who were single mothers. As one woman declared, 'No one is looking after my children or my mother who is looking after them. I need to do what I can, even if it is difficult.' And there definitely were difficulties these displaced Zimbabweans faced, starting with crossing the Limpopo River itself.

Along the border the Limpopo River is comprised largely of stretches of dry sand with scattered pools and pockets of water behind weirs save for the short rainy season typically commencing in December – a time in which border-jumpers face the potential threat of crocodiles, who, a number of Zimbabwean farm workers suggested to me, 'have acquired a taste for Zimbabwean flesh' since 2000. Drowning was also a large concern. In June 2008, one Zimbabwean farm worker witnessed a group of Zimbabweans holding hands as they crossed the Limpopo in December 2007 being washed away and told me accounts of others about finding drowned bodies on the banks.

On the Zimbabwean side one risked encounters with young men deemed *maguma-guma*, those who seek money and goods 'the easy way' who could rob, beat, rape or kill you (see, also, SPT 2004:56–58). I have met a number of Zimbabweans seeking work on the farms who had cuts and bruises after being beaten up by *maguma-guma* or lost their money, clothes, shoes and any other belongings they had brought with them. Those who have worked on the farms for some time typically had strategies to try to avoid encounters with these gangs, albeit they were not always guaranteed to be successful.

On the South African side, border-jumpers face 137 kilometers of fences running along most of the border, including a high security 'NOREX fence.' The latter has had its electric current switched off since the 1990s but it has sensors indicating to South African National Defence Force (SANDF) soldiers camped along the fence when it has been contacted. SANDF soldiers also have patrolled along the 225 kilometer border, though in 2008 they have been replaced by South African Police Services officers, who currently patrol South Africa's borders with its other neighbours. Finally, border-jumpers also risk encountering wild animals.

By 2008, unlike in 2004 and 2005, the *maguma-guma* also were operating on the South African side of the border. I met one Zimbabwean near Musina in June 2008 who had crossed into South Africa for the first time the week before – he had worked for a farm merchandise store as a sales clerk in Harare the previous five years until his number of hours dropped so much given a precipitous decline in sales that it made no more economic sense to continue with the job. As he explained, 'I was paying more on public transport to work than I was earning.' He said he and others had learned of *maguma-guma* operating along the rail line heading south from the border and other routes which Zimbabweans took. Like their counterparts patrolling the Zimbabwean side of the border, these men rob, rape and even murder Zimbabweans entering into South Africa. He said these *maguma-guma* included Zimbabweans who had been living in South Africa for some time as well as South Africans – 'anyone who wants to prey on us has easy targets,' he grimly observed.

Once over the border, many head further south, trying to join relatives in Guateng province or elsewhere or to look for better remunerative jobs outside the agricultural sector. Some head to farms because of previous contacts there, relatives or friends working on farms, or hearing about the existence of jobs back in Zimbabwe on particular farms. Others seek work on the farms as they have no money, are starving, had their clothes and other belongings stolen by *maguma-guma*, and so forth. Some may move from farm to farm seeking work or stealing to survive. Others find work on these farms for a short or long duration. Seasonal workers, which most Zimbabweans are, work on these farms during picking season from April/May to August/September. Some then return to Zimbabwe with the likely intention of returning next picking season while others move onto other South African farms or seek employment elsewhere in South Africa. In addition to facing this wide range of risks which other Zimbabweans face when 'jumping' the border, these Zimbabwean farm workers also have to face life on the farms themselves.

Working and Living Conditions on Border Commercial Farms

The social experience of these Zimbabwean workers on South African farms are shaped both by individual farm owner's predilections and the historical and current positioning of commercial farms within the political economy and the institutional arrangements and politics of the South African state itself. As post-Apartheid farmers were encouraged to take advantage of greater export opportunities while adjusting to a significant reduction in government support, there was a drastic drop in the number of farmers and farm workers as processes of concentration occurred in the sector (Greenberg 2003, Hall 2004). Many farmers in the border area that were still around and had capital went into or expanded their citrus and vegetable production for export, increasing their demand for workers, particularly for seasonal harvesting and packing (Rutherford and Lincoln 2007).

Most of these border-land farms were settled by Afrikaners in the first half of the twentieth century (Lahiff 2000). Although never completely autonomous and under various forms of state sanction and law, racialised paternalistic rule informed labour relations then and continues to be influential today on these northern Limpopo farms still largely owned by Afrikaners. As others have noted (e.g. Ewert and Du Toit 2005), post-Apartheid farmers now face new legislation and ethical market regulations covering aspects of their relations with workers that had been outside the purview of state legislation and translocal regulation in the past. But Zimbabwean workers told me about the range of wages they received, mostly under the statutory minimum wage, the common disregard for protection against pesticides, the illegal deductions on their monthly pay-cheques, the bribes of the rare Labour or Union official to appear and the staged performances for the annual EUREPGAP (Euro-Retailer Produce Working Group Good Agricultural Practices) ethical inspections for exporters to Europe as farmers selectively comply with the regulations and dodge irregular enforcement mechanisms.

Most workers I talked to saw their situation as grim. Many complained about their working conditions – low wages, long hours, nontransparent calculations of piece-rates and monthly salary deductions, pesticide exposure, etc. – and about their living conditions – crowded rooms for seasonal workers or poor housing overall, unsafe drinking water, unclean or non-existent toilets and so forth. Nonetheless, there was a great variation in living conditions from farm to farm and on farms between different groups of farm workers, with typically senior workers, if not permanent workers more broadly, living in much better housing than seasonal workers.

Racism and sexual harassment were also common complaints. Workers had tales about how Afrikaner farmers treated Africans as a 'different species.' They also talked about occasional sexual abuse of women workers by foremen and management workers who used their gate-keeping positions over hiring and allocation of work tasks to demand sexual favours from women workers (see also Lincoln and Maririke 2000). Conditions did vary as some farmers gave minimum wages to many of their permanent workers, provided protective clothing and brick houses with electricity and ablution blocks, more or less following legislation and regulations governing commercial farms in South Africa and 'ethical trade' (EUREPGAP) rules for exporters to the Europe Union. Nonetheless, the general impression many workers gave was that regulations were typically not followed, a point also reinforced in the survey.

My survey was biased towards permanent workers, which comprised just over fifty per cent of the sample, whereas far more Zimbabweans are seasonal workers. It does show though that some Zimbabweans are quite ensconced in these farms. On average, they had been working for fifty-one months, but the median and the mode were twenty-four months. The average pay was R571 per month, below the then minimum wage of R785. The mode was R300 per month. Minimum wage at the time was R785.79 per month. Piecework regimes were a common way to organize citrus harvesting, even though labour regulations prohibited them. Concerns raised in the survey related mainly to working, living and health conditions and issues of dignity, of being treated as inferior by farmers – complaints that are common for many farm workers with or without South African citizenships (see, e.g., Crush 2000; Ewert and Du Toit 2005). Whereas the Zimbabwean farm workers I met recognized that they faced similar working and living conditions as South Africans, the difference in 2004 and 2005 was that Zimbabweans felt employers took advantage of their desperation and the fact that their legality was unclear. Many noted how vulnerable they were to harassment and limited in potential recourse when they face a problem in South Africa; as put by one, 'If you have a problem you may get arrested if you go to the government to complain'.

The legal status of these Zimbabwean workers has been contested and highly ambivalent. Until the late 1990s, state officials had made exceptions for the farmers between the Soutpansberg mountains and the Zimbabwean border by enabling them to 'legally' hire Zimbabwean workers without going through normal worker permit state administrative channels until the late 1990s (Lincoln and Maririke 2000; Eveleth 1999; see Crush 2000 for an overview of the debate). At that time, this special dispensation was increasingly challenged by media exposés, NGOs, and others (see, e.g.,

Ratshitanga 1998, City Press February 22, 1998, Eveleth 1999, SAPA 2001, SAHRC 2003, Sowetan 1999, NPDoL 2000, HRW 2006, 2007). Some of these critics generally demanded that 'national sovereignty' be enforced, particularly against what they viewed as an egregious continuation of the authority of white (Afrikaner) farmers in post-Apartheid South Africa, with the aim of deporting those Zimbabwean workers who were not there legally (see Rutherford 2008).

Today, the so-called 'special employment zone' north of the Soutpansberg is officially no more and any farmer in South Africa can make a request to recruit Zimbabwean workers applying to Home Affairs for a corporate permit. Despite this attempt at legalising Zimbabwean farm workers as state-sanctioned migrant workers, in 2005 there were still relatively few farmers who took this route due, I was told, to bureaucratic delays. A Home Affairs official told me in August 2005 that eighty-nine corporate permits were approved in Limpopo covering about 11,000 Zimbabwean farm workers, though many more borderland farmers have gone this route since then. Moreover, I found in 2005 that a number of provincial government officials and authorities still were concerned about ensuring the ease of these farmers to get Zimbabwean farm workers, making exceptions if the workers were not exactly legal. This was most obvious with 'farm identification cards' that typically documented the worker's dates of employment at the farm, with his/her photo and Zimbabwean national registration number, and sometimes a fingerprint – echoes of passes used in Apartheid and colonial periods. Indeed, for most of the surveyed workers (over sixty percent), they had some form of permit – twenty per cent issued by the farmer and forty per cent having a corporate permit. These cards typically sufficed to avoid deportation if the Zimbabwean worker encountered SANDF soldiers or Home Affairs officials outside the farm or in a raid of the farm, whereby only Zimbabweans living there and lacking proof of employment are typically deported, I was told. Such accommodations were not made for Limpopo farmers outside this northern border zone, attesting to the lingering effects of the previous exemptions made for this region (Rutherford 2008).

In 2008, many of the farmers with a number of farm workers used corporate permits (see also HRW 2007), though employers still complained about what they saw as unnecessarily long bureaucratic delays in receiving the permits and a range of difficulties they faced when dealing with Zimbabwean and, especially, South African border authorities. Moreover, there were still a number of informal arrangements between South African border authorities and farmers to permit the use of farmer identification cards to act as a proxy for corporate permits as some farmers did not want to give the individual corporate permit identification to each farm worker in case they 'ran away,' as some farmers put it. Nonetheless, given the high numbers of Zimbabweans crossing the border and the high numbers of recent migrants sheltering on these farms looking for work, farmers, workers and civic activists said South African police and Home Affairs officials were carrying out a number of raids in June 2008, occasionally arresting and deporting Zimbabwean farm workers who had corporate permits along with those who had no documentation permitting them to be in South Africa.[2]

On the farms themselves, Zimbabweans occasionally openly or covertly resisted these power relations, even taking job action to try to improve their conditions (Rutherford and Addison 2007). Yet they often acquiesced, as they did not want to jeopardize the source of foreign currency that is crucial for their own and often multiple dependents' survival or livelihood. As a relatively sanguine worker explained his situation on the farm and his relative impoverishment, despite working as a lower management worker on a Tshipise farm for over ten years: 'My place is modest but it works. I must just keep my eye on 'the project' ... [which is to] look after my family back in Zimbabwe. And it is safe here [compared to Zimbabwe] ....' As many have pointed out (e.g. Potts 2000; Crush and McDonald 2000), migration has long been part of livelihood strategies for many people in southern Africa – for some this is crucial to survival strategies, while for a few, migration is a way to try to get ahead, or what these Zimbabweans called 'projects'.

Transnational Connections and 'Projects'

Most Zimbabwean workers I met anxiously tried to keep in touch with family members and dependents back in Zimbabwe (West and Selian 2005), finding ways to send money, food items, and occasionally other consumer products back to them.

When workers recounted what they brought back to Zimbabwe on their return trips – be it at the end of the month when they received their salary, the end of the picking season, when they hear of family emergencies, or whenever they could cobble enough money to head back to Zimbabwe to see a spouse, children, parents or other family members – it was often a list of items that were once basic to many Zimbabwean homes. Maize meal, cooking oil, sugar, and soap were the most commonly mentioned, given such 'necessities' were scarce in Zimbabwe or too exorbitant in price. For example, in June 2008, one Zimbabwean farm worker I know arranged to have his sister who worked on the same farm as he did to go to Bulawayo on the weekend, transporting cooking oil, salt and maize meal to his wife who was staying at her parent's place waiting to give birth to their first child. 'It is far for my sister to travel,' he admitted, 'but my wife sent a message to me that she and her family have no basics at home.' A few who had money saved up would bring radios, CD players, televisions, clothes, and bicycles, among other items. They would also bring South African Rand to convert into Zimbabwean dollars at the blackmarket rate to give to dependents, buy food and clothes, pay school fees and so forth.

The survey showed respondents try to regularly go back to Zimbabwe. Over eighty-five per cent had returned to Zimbabwe in the year before, on average nine months previously. All but three of the surveyed workers who returned to Zimbabwe brought food, while less than fifty per cent also brought money back, on average just under R490. The surveyed workers had on average just under four dependents back in Zimbabwe. Two-thirds of the respondents also regularly sent money or food back to dependents, mainly by sending it with others, while a few sent items by mail.

A few also carried out what they call 'projects,' investments into activities that they hoped would result in more income for them. These projects were more commonly carried out by permanent workers, who have some longevity on the farms to have potentially built some ties to farmers to acquire resources from them and some certainty over their future on the farm. From my research, not many were able to carry out such 'projects' – instead the money they earn went to basic survival for them and their dependents. Only thirteen per cent of the survey respondents said they had 'projects' in Zimbabwe, mostly gardening ventures or 'business' activities.

From my research, it seems that permanent Zimbabwean farm workers in management or lower-management positions were the ones involved in some form of projects (Rutherford 2008). For example, a Zimbabwean farm clerk on a South African farm bordering the Limpopo River told me in 2005 that he received an old irrigation pump and other irrigation supplies from the farmer which he then arranged to have people help him carry them over the river bed and to have transport meet them on the Zimbabwean side to take them to his rural home about 130 kilometers away. His wife and relatives used the equipment to grow tomatoes to sell in Bulawayo.

In short, the transnational livelihood strategies of these Zimbabwean farm workers in northern Limpopo province were largely strategies of survival for the majority and strategies of potential economic gain for a few. These farm worker strategies, of course, have been predicated on employment on the South African border farms, whose owners clearly profit from their labour. Such predicaments deeply marked the social experience of these displaced Zimbabweans.

Conclusion

Crossing the national border pressed heavily on the men and women I met as they recognised the explicit linkages between the reconfiguration of their identification as Zimbabweans when working on South African farms, leading to a different set of vulnerabilities and narrow possibilities due to how they are disadvantageously placed by the dominant formations of citizenship and assertions of sovereignty. Ways to normalise their legal status and calls to end human rights abuses on farms are all important as are political and economic changes back in Zimbabwe. Indeed, many Zimbabwean farm workers expressed to me their desire to return 'home' if they could earn a living; that is the catch. In all likelihood, after the struggle eventually succeeds to bring in a government that has wider national and international legitimacy it will take more struggles before many can sustain themselves, if not achieve a reasonable livelihood, from carrying out activities solely within Zimbabwe. This is clear in the early days of the national unity government in Zimbabwe that took power in February 2009. There have been some improvement in economic indicators and the provision of social services, but there is still very high unemployment, human rights problems and a variety of other forms of insecurities in Zimbabwe. And the growing unemployment problem in South Africa and elsewhere in the region shows the magnitude of this dilemma in a neoliberal climate.

This leads me back to economies of survival – the hazardous routes taken by Zimbabweans, those with educational qualifications, those seeking resources to attain such qualifications, and those without such schooling or ambition, to South African farms where they are typically underpaid and vulnerable to a range of abusive conditions; harsh conditions that as Andries Du Toit (2003) and others (Crush 2000) show, are also common in the Cape and elsewhere in South Africa where the sentiments of belonging are predicated not necessarily on national citizenship but also on distinctions within South African formations of citizenship concerning class, gender and ethnicity. Henry Bernstein (2004, 2007) makes the point in his caution against conventional appeals to agrarian and land reform that such struggles of survival on farms need to be placed within an 'agrarian question of labour' as they are often driven, in part, by fragmenting and multi-sited pursuits of individual and household livelihoods through varied forms of wage labour, informal sector activity, and farming. These activities of survival and possibly accumulation for displaced Zimbabweans are poorly captured by the phrase 'seasonal workers' mould.' While recognizing the dense intersection of discursive practices of sovereignty, citizenship, and production informing the vulnerabilities of Zimbabweans working on the farms in northern South Africa, I suggest it is vital to work against and through such discourses in a way that does not neglect how they play out in the economies of survival and the struggles of those of any nationality who must take 'shit jobs' on either side of the Zimbabwean/South African border. A focus on their social experience in relation to the wider cultural representations and political and professional processes provides a way of doing so.

Afterword

Since the middle of 2008, there have been significant changes in the legal situation of Zimbabweans in South Africa with implications for Zimbabwean farm workers in northern Limpopo province. In July 2008, Department of Home Affairs opened up a refugee reception centre in Musina, enabling non-South Africans fleeing their homelands to acquire an asylum-seeker permit which enables them to work legally in South Africa and to receive a hearing to make an asylum claim. Previously, the closest refugee reception centre was in Pretoria, over 500 kilometres from the South African border with Zimbabwe. As a consequence, more and more Zimbabweans went to Musina seeking this permit, along with many others from other countries (including those who had been already living in other parts of South Africa). There have been a variety of humanitarian and administrative issues with this Musina office (see, e.g., MSF 2009). Indeed, national and international mass-mediated attention combined with pressure from South African and international organisations led to a surprise announcement by the Minister of Home Affairs just before the South African elections in March 2009 that there will be special visa status for Zimbabweans and a halt to the deportations for Zimbabweans. Although the special status for Zimbabweans is currently being revisited by the new cabinet and its status is unclear, the suspension of deportations has meant that Zimbabwean farm workers have not been subject to many, if any, raids in the border-zone. During a brief research trip in June 2009, I did not see any border patrols along the fence and none of the farms I visited had a raid in the last six to ten months. The permanent Zimbabwean farm workers expressed how they felt 'freedom' for the first time in South Africa. Farmers and workers were also saying there were fewer Zimbabweans looking for work in April and May 2009 as Zimbabweans were more able to travel to other parts of South Africa with their asylum-seeker permits and the cessation of deportations. The farmers with whom I talked were still largely using the corporate permit to legalize their Zimbabwean farm workers and also were not worried about any possible labour shortage. It is too early to tell how this will affect the social experience of Zimbabwean farm workers in the short term, or how long these changes in the immigration status of Zimbabweans in South Africa will last and with what effects on social experience and wider cultural representations.

Notes

1. An earlier version of this paper was given at the Britain Zimbabwe Society Research Day, Oxford, 17 June 2006, where it received helpful comments and suggestions. I also gratefully thank the Social Sciences and Humanities Research Council of Canada for their financial support of this research. Parts of this chapter are published in Rutherford and Lincoln 2007.
2. In June 2008 when visiting the detention camp just south of Musina where Zimbabweans caught from the area await deportation, I learned about a South African man who was detained by the soldiers and was waiting to be sent to Zimbabwe. He was a worker hired to work on the border fences and had no identification on him as he feared being robbed by the *maguma-guma* and the soldiers picked him up, disregarding his explanations in chiVenda that he was a South African.

References

Bernstein, H. 2004. '"Changing Before Our Very Eyes": Agrarian Questions and the Politics of Land in Capitalism Today', *Journal of Agrarian Change*, 4, 1–2: 190–225.

———. 2007. 'Agrarian Questions of Capital and Labour: Some Theory about Land Reform (and a periodisation).' In L. Ntsebeza and R. Hall (eds) *The Land Question in South Africa*. Cape Town, 27–59. *City Press*, 22 February 1998.

Crush, J. 1998. 'Introduction: Immigration, Human Rights & the Constitution'. In J. Crush (ed.) *Beyond Control: Immigration & Human Rights in a Democratic South Africa*. Kingston, ON, 1–17.

———. 2000. 'Introduction: Making Hay with Foreign Farmworkers.' In J. Crush (ed.) *Borderline Farming: Foreign Migrants in South African Commercial Agriculture*. Kingston, ON, 1–13.

Crush J. and Clarence Tshitereke. 2001. 'Contesting Migrancy: The Foreign Labour Debate in Post-1994 South Africa', *Africa Today*, 48, 3: 49–70.

Crush J. and David McDonald. 2000. 'Transnationalism, African Immigration, and New Migrant Spaces in South Africa: An Introduction', *Canadian Journal of African Studies*, 34,1: 1–19.

Du Toit, A. 2003. 'Hunger in the Valley of Fruitfulness: Globalization, "Social Exclusion" and Chronic Poverty in Ceres, South Africa'. Paper presented at conference *Staying Poor: Chronic Poverty and Development Policy*, University of Manchester 7–9 April.

Eveleth, A. 1999. 'Government to Meet on Phantom Farm Labour "Agreement"', *Mail & Guardian* (SA), 19 February.

Ewert J. and Andries Du Toit. 2005. 'A Deepening Divide in the Countryside: Restructuring and Rural Livelihoods in the South African Wine Industry', *Journal of Southern African Studies*, 31, 2: 315–32.

FMSP and MLAO (Forced Migration Studies Programme and Musina Legal Advice Office). 2007. *Special Report: Fact or Fiction? Examining Zimbabwean Cross-Border Migration into South Africa,* Johannesburg.

Greenberg, S. 2003. 'Land Reform and Transition in South Africa', *Transformation,* 52: 42–67.

Hall, R. 2004. 'A Political Economy of Land Reform in South Africa,' *Review of African Political Economy,* 31, 100: 223–37.

Harris, B. 2001. 'A Foreign Experience: Violence, Crime and Xenophobia during South Africa's Transition', *Violence and Transition Series,* Vol. 5, Braamfontein, South Africa: Centre for the Study of Violence and Reconciliation.

HRW (Human Rights Watch). 2006. *Unprotected Migrants: Zimbabweans in South Africa's Limpopo Province,* New York City.

——. 2007. *'Keep Your Head Down': Unprotected Migrants in South Africa.* New York.

——. 2008. *Neighbours in Need: Zimbabweans Seeking Refuge in South Africa.* New York.

IOM (International Organization for Migration). 2003. *Mobility and HIV/AIDS in Southern Africa: A Field Study in South Africa, Zimbabwe and Mozambique,* Pretoria.

——. 2004. 'Developing Regional Guidelines on HIV and AIDS for the Commercial Agriculture Sector in the SADC Region', *Workshop, Centurion, South Africa,* Pretoria: Partnership on HIV/AIDS and Mobile Populations in Southern Africa (PHAMSA), 2–3 December.

Kleinman, A., V. Das and M. Lock. 1997. 'Introduction'. In A. Kleinman, V. Das and M. Lock (eds) *Social Suffering.* Berkeley: ix-xxvii.

Lahiff, E. 2000. *An Apartheid Oasis? Agriculture and Rural Livelihoods in Venda,* London.

Lincoln, D. and C. Maririke. 2000. 'Southward Migrants in the Far North: Zimbabwean Farmworkers in Northern Province'. In J. Crush (ed.) *Borderline Farming: Foreign Migrants in South African Commercial Agriculture.* Kingston, ON: 40–62.

MSF (Médecins Sans Frontières). 2009. *No Refuge, Access Denied: Medical and Humanitarian Needs of Zimbabweans in South Africa.* Cape Town, South Africa.

NPDoL (Northern Province Department of Labour). 2000. *Report on Foreign Labour North of the Zoupansberg, Northern Province,* Polokwane, South Africa.

Potts, D. 2000. 'Worker-Peasants and Farmer-Housewives in Africa: the Debate About 'Committed' Farmers, Access to Land and Agricultural Production', *Journal of Southern African Studies.* Special issue on African Environments, 26, 4: 807–32.

Ratshitanga, M. 1998. 'Unions to Tackle Border Farmers', *Mail & Guardian* 9 January.

RI (Refugees International). 2004. *Zimbabweans in South Africa: Denied Access to Political Asylum.* Washington.

Rutherford, B. 2008. 'An Unsettled Belonging: Zimbabwean Farm Workers in Limpopo Province, South Africa', *Journal of Contemporary African Studies* 26(4): 401–15.

Rutherford B. and Lincoln Addison. 2007. 'Zimbabwean Farm Workers in Northern South Africa', *Review of African Political Economy,* 34, 114: 619–35.

SAHRC (South African Human Rights Commission). 2003. *Final Report on the Inquiry into Human Rights Violations in Farming Communities,* Johannesburg.

SAPA (South African Press Association). 2001. 'Illegal Zimbabwean Workers Must be Treated Humanely: says Mbeki', 13 November.

SPT (Solidarity Peace Trust). 2003. *National Youth Service Training -'Shaping Youths in a Truly Zimbabwean Manner': An Overview of Youth Militia Training and Activities in Zimbabwe,October 2000 – August 2003.* Port Shepstone, South Africa.

———. 2004. *No War in Zimbabwe: An Account of an Exodus of a Nations People.* Port Shepstone, South Africa.

UNHCR (United Nations High Commission for Refugees). 2008. 'Zimbabweans Struggle For Asylum In South Africa'. Press release, 13 July.

West A. and Audrey Selian. 2005. 'Experiencing Technical Difficulties: The Urgent Need to Rewire and Reboot the ICT-Development Machine', *Article 19.*

Zinyama, L. 2000. 'Who, What, When and Why: Cross-Border Movement from Zimbabwe to South Africa'. In David McDonald (ed.) *On Borders: Perspectives on International Migration in Southern Africa.* Cape Town, pp. 71–85.

3

The Politics of Legal Status for Zimbabweans in South Africa

Norma Kriger

Legal status for foreign migrants in principle guarantees rights and protection from ill-treatment by government, employers and citizens. Although Zimbabwean migrants are a mixed group, including refugees and economic migrants, the vast majority fled the deteriorating humanitarian crisis that began in 2000. In South Africa, most Zimbabweans are looking to find work to help their families at home to survive, but because they are deemed to be in the country illegally, they are vulnerable to arrest, detention and deportation by government officials and open to exploitation by employers.

This chapter examines the politics of legal status for Zimbabweans in South Africa from the vantage point of a variety of actors – the South African government, Zimbabwean migrants and organisations that advocate for and protect migrants' rights. It begins by assessing the legal statuses available to all foreign migrants in South Africa before showing how the circumstances of most Zimbabweans do not fit the legal options and discussing how Zimbabweans seek to avoid or cope with their status as 'illegal foreigners'. The chapter then examines the perspective of the South African government whose migration policy has been critically shaped by its supportive foreign policy toward Zimbabwe and xenophobia. Finally, it explores how multilateral, local and international rights and pro-migrant groups converged by 2008 to recommend that the South African government should grant Zimbabweans temporary legal status as a group. In April 2009, the South African government announced new migration policies for Zimbabweans: a moratorium on deportations, a 90-day free visa, and a one year special permit for undocumented Zimbabweans already in the country. Only the first two of these policies were brought into action immediately. This chapter discusses the prior legal situation for Zimbabweans. Implementing these policy changes will have to contend with the same challenges of powerful xenophobic forces inside and outside government and the pursuit of foreign policy objectives vis-à-vis Zimbabwe that have shaped migration policy and practice over the last decade.

Current Legal Status Options

The South African migration system falls under the jurisdiction of the Ministry of Home Affairs and is governed by the Refugees Act (No.130 of 1998), which came into force in 2000, and the Immigration Act (No. 3 of 2002), which was implemented on 7 April 2003 and was amended by the Immigration Amendment Act (No.19 of 2004). The Refugees Act creates legal statuses for asylum seekers and recognised refugees, as well as permitting asylum-seekers to enter and stay in the country until their applications for refugee status are determined. Temporary residence permits, some of which allow the holder to work are provided for through the Immigration Act, while all migrants who do not have legal status are liable to deportation as 'illegal foreigners'. Although the number of 'illegal foreigners' is not known, it is clear that they constitute the largest legal category and the numbers of asylum seekers, refugees, and work permit holders are small in comparison.

Asylum Seekers and Refugees

Under the Refugees Act, it is possible to qualify for refugee status on one of two grounds. First, by demonstrating that one has a well-founded fear of persecution on the grounds of one's race, tribe, religion, nationality, political opinion or membership of a social group (s.3(a) RA), which is an almost verbatim adoption of the refugee definition from the 1951 UN Convention.[1] Second, by showing that one was compelled to leave one's country because of 'external aggression, occupation, foreign domination or events seriously disturbing or disrupting public order in either a part or the whole of his or her country of origin or nationality ...' (s.3(b) RA), which is a verbatim adoption of the refugee definition from the 1969 OAU Convention.[2] The inclusion of the additional grounds in the OAU Convention for obtaining refugee status means that the Refugees Act provides a broader definition of refugees than is conventional, and also allows dependants of refugees to qualify as refugees (s.3(c)).[3]

Each asylum application for refugee status is decided by the Department of Home Affairs (DHA) personnel on its individual merits. This case-by-case approach to refugee status determination is unusual in the rest of Africa (World Refugee Survey 2004).Upon entry to the country, asylum seekers must go directly to lodge their claims for asylum at one of the five Refugee Reception Offices (RROs), where Refugee Reception Officers are supposed to fill out an application form based on asylum seekers answers to the questions on the form and immediately issue them with an asylum seeker permit (s.22 RA). An asylum seeker permit gives asylum seekers the right to be in the country until their claim has been adjudicated, and, since April 2004, the right to work and study (NCRA 2006: 6–7, Landau et al. 2004: 16).

Within a specified time period, the asylum seeker must return to the RRO for an interview with a Refugee Status Determination Officer (RSDO), who decides whether or not to grant refugee status. If the RSDO rejects the application as 'manifestly unfounded, abusive or fraudulent',[4] the decision is automatically reviewed by a Standing Committee on Refugee Affairs (s.25 (1) RA). If the RSDO rejects the application for some other reason, the asylum seeker may lodge an appeal to the Refugee Appeal Board (s.26 (1) RA), after which, if the RSDO decision is upheld, the asylum seeker may seek judicial review by a High Court. Regulations associated with the Refugees Act require that asylum applications must be adjudicated or finalised by the DHA within six months from the date of lodging a claim (NCRA 2006:6). If the application for asylum is approved, the DHA must issue the asylum seeker with a refugee permit (or section 24 permit) or formal refugee identity document (s.27 (d) and s.30 RA, NCRA 2006: 34).[5]

These documents permit the refugee to be in the country legally, and to exercise other rights, such as the right to work, study, and access social services and social assistance. The Refugees Act explicitly provides protection and general rights to refugees (but not asylum seekers), including the right to seek employment, the right to the same basic health care and basic primary education which the inhabitants of South African receive, and the right to full legal protection, including the rights set out in the Bill of Rights of the constitution (section 27). After five years of refugee status, one may apply for permanent residence if the SCRA determines that the person will remain a refugee indefinitely (s.27(c)).[6]

SA is currently a top destination country for individual asylum seekers, along with the US, Sweden, France, UK, Canada and Greece (UNHCR 2008). At the end of 2007, it hosted about 144,700 refugees and asylum seekers, including 48,400 Zimbabweans, 24,800 Congolese, 12,900 Somalis, 7,500 Ethiopians, 7,200 Malawians and 5,900 Angolans. Most were in the 89,000 asylum application backlog; only 36,700 held refugee status (WRS 2008). Both the refugee and asylum seeker population in South Africa is comprised of about eighty per cent adult men – an unusually large percentage where adult women globally represent close to half the adult refugee population (CoRMSA 2007: 13; WRS 2004).

Most asylum seekers do not succeed in becoming recognised refugees. Of 5,879 asylum applications decided in 2007, about one-third (1,705) were granted refugee status (CoRMSA 2008: 17); of roughly 5,000 new asylum applications decided in 2006, only about sixteen per cent (796) were given refugee status (CoRMSA 2007: 13).[7] The acceptance rate of asylum applications between 1994 and 2000 was nearly thirty per cent (WRS 2002), falling to just over fifteen per cent between 2000 and 2006 (CoRMSA 2007: 13). While the number of refugees has grown almost two and a half times since 1999 – from 14,530 refugees to 36,700 (WRS 2000; WRS 2008), South Africa is host to a small number of refugees relative to its population.[8] Between 2000 and 2005, about eighty per cent of recognised refugees came from the DRC, Somalia, and Angola, with Burundi and Congo Brazzaville also supplying sizeable numbers of refugees (WRS 2000–2003).

Temporary Residence

Under the Immigration Act of 2004, all foreigners who are not permanent residents require a temporary residence permit and a passport to enter the country (s.9 (4)). There are thirteen different types of temporary residence permits (s.11–23), all of which require applicants to hold a passport. Most temporary residence permits, such as a visitor's permit (s.11) and a study permit (s.13), prohibit the holders from conducting work. To obtain a visitor's permit, one needs a visa (s.10A). During the financial year 2007/8, DHA issued 63,460 visitors' permits.[9]

Four temporary residence permits allow foreign nationals to work. The quota work permit is only available to foreign nationals who fall within specific skilled professions identified from time to time by the Minister of Home Affairs, who also fixes a quota. Skilled foreign nationals can also qualify for a general work permit, and must produce an employment contract when they enter the country. Employers may apply for a corporate permit which entitles them to hire a predetermined number of foreign workers (s.21) – typically unskilled or semi-skilled workers in the mines and on commercial farms. To obtain a work permit or to hire foreigners under a corporate permit, employers must demonstrate that South African citizens and permanent residents are not available and that the terms and conditions of work meet specified labour standards.

Only a small proportion of foreign migrants in the country have the right to work. For example, in financial year 2007/8, the DHA issued 32,344 general work permits and 1,133 quota permits. These figures of foreign migrants with the right to work are small in comparison to the nearly 313,000 'illegal foreigners' who were deported in 2007/8.[10]

'Illegal Foreigners'

The Immigration Act defines a 'foreigner' as an individual who is not a citizen (s.1 (xvii)) and an 'illegal foreigner' as a foreigner who is in South Africa in contravention of the Immigration Act (s.1 (xviii)). 'Illegal foreigners' are subject to deportation (s.32 (2)). The number of deportations increased each year since 2003, to over 300,000 in 2007 (CoRMSA 2008: 17), reflecting both a more stringent deportation policy and an increase in 'illegal foreigners'. South Africa increased border controls by enhancing police and army patrols, and an old army warehouse is being used as a detention facility in Musina unconstitutionally since a court order in May 2009, to alleviate the daily pressure of accommodating and feeding deportees at Musina police station (FMSP 2007: 5–6). The 2008 DHA annual report identifies the Chief Directorate's strategic goal as reducing the size and annual growth of illegal migration (DHA 2008: 24).

Zimbabweans in South Africa

While the sheer numerical preponderance of Zimbabwean migrants in South Africa and aspects of their social, demographic and economic profile are noteworthy, the distinctive characteristic of Zimbabweans in South Africa is that most have arrived since 2000 and seek work to assist their families to survive the deteriorating humanitarian crisis in Zimbabwe (AI 2008). The legal status options available to them – refugees fleeing persecution or economic migrants seeking to better their lives – leave most as 'illegal foreigners'. Many do try to obtain asylum, but South Africa's restrictive and discriminatory asylum determination process often denies even legitimate asylum seekers refugee status. Some Zimbabweans seek asylum status fraudulently merely to obtain the right to be in the country legally and to work; still others who might qualify for refugee status apparently prefer the risks of illegality to giving up their freedom to cross the border to visit family. Like other migrants, Zimbabweans bribe officials to avoid arrest, detention and deportation. The number of Zimbabweans, their profile, the misfit between their circumstances and the legal options available to them, and their different strategies to remain in the country are all discussed below.

Profile of Zimbabweans

There are more Zimbabweans in South African than there were Mozambican refugees during its civil war in the 1980s and 1990s (FMSP 2007:5), though the numbers are subject to ongoing contention. Rights and pro-migrant groups argue for lower numbers than often appear in the South African media and most estimate that there are 1.5 million Zimbabweans in South Africa today (FMSP and Musina Legal Advice Office 2007, HRW 2008: 23, FMSP 2008: 5). UNHCR puts the figure higher, estimating between 1.5 million and 3 million (UNHCR 2008). If the UN population estimate of 12.5 million people in Zimbabwe in 2008 is accepted, then fifteen per cent of the population of Zimbabwe might be in South Africa. But it is not at all certain that there are 12.5 million people in Zimbabwe. Recently, a Wall St Journal op-ed reported that informed sources in Harare suggested that the resident population might be only 6.5 million, half the population of four years ago (Wall Street Journal 2008) while *The Economist* referred to a resident population of only 8–9 million (The Economist 2008). Supporting the case for a major downward revision of the population inside Zimbabwe is the unsuccessful effort of an organisation conducting a survey in four districts in South Matabeleland to find anyone to interview in the 18–25 year old range (Eppel 2008; Eppel and Raftopoulos 2008: 20).[11] Should there be far fewer than 12.5 million people in Zimbabwe today, obviously the proportion of Zimbabweans and their absolute numbers in South Africa will be correspondingly higher.

Until recently, about ninety per cent of Zimbabweans in South Africa were single young men between twenty and forty years old. Over the past few years, increasing numbers of women and unaccompanied children arrived in the Limpopo border area, but few Zimbabwean families with children (CoRMSA 2008: 66). But, in July 2008, UNHCR reported an increasing number of families arriving as a result of election-related political violence in Zimbabwe (UNHCR 2008a; FMSP 2007: 8). Although Zimbabweans have settled all over the country (in cities, medium and small towns, industrial and mining areas, in the Limpopo border area and rural villages), the majority live in the major urban areas where they seek work or engage in trade (FMSP 2007: 6; CoRMSA 2008: 66). The Zimbabwean population in South Africa is well-educated compared to South Africans, with nearly one-third of Zimbabwean migrants having completed at least one tertiary degree (CoRMSA 2008: 67). According to the Zimbabwe Reserve Bank in 2007, fifty per cent of Zimbabwean households are being sustained by remittances from Zimbabweans working in South Africa and elsewhere, which are estimated to inject nearly US$500 million into the national economy each year (CIGI 2008: 16–17) .

Zimbabweans and Legal Status Categories: A Poor Fit

The vast majority of Zimbabweans enter South Africa as 'illegal foreigners', either crossing the border illegally or bribing immigration officials; many use the services of agents servicing the border, known as *Malaitsha*[12]

(HRW 2008: 107; Mawadza 2008: 4). To enter South Africa legally, one must present a passport to a border official, yet for almost a year the Zimbabwean government issued no passports because of lack of paper and is now issuing passports only to clear the backlog and not to new applicants. Most Zimbabweans cannot afford the cost of a passport (HRW 2007, 2008; Mawadza 2008: 7). Moreover, the government of Zimbabwe can take up to a year to issue a passport (IRIN 2008). Without a passport, one cannot apply for a work permit or a visitor's permit.[13] While eight SADC neighbouring countries have bilateral agreements with the SA government for their citizens to enter the country on visa-free visitor's permits for thirty days, Zimbabweans must still produce a financial security deposit of SA R2,060 for a visa, approximately US$250, which most are unable to do (HRW 2008: 107). Zimbabwean civil servants, however, are exempt from the visa requirement (HRW 2008: 109). Interestingly, students and others intending to migrate sometimes buy pay slips from civil servants, which cost at least sixty-six times less than the financial deposit required to obtain a visa (Mawadza 2008: 4).

Zimbabweans migrants overtook Mozambicans as the largest national group of deportees around 2005 (Trimikliniotis 2008: 1327; HRW 2007: 18).[14] In the first six months of 2007, the IOM's reception center in Beitbridge, which provides humanitarian assistance to Zimbabwean deportees registered 102, 413 deportees, and by no means do all deportees choose to register with the IOM (HRW 2008: 101).[15]

A small but rapidly growing proportion of Zimbabweans seek asylum. There were 10,181 asylum seekers between 2000 and 2004, rising to 17, 667 in the year of 2007, and over 10,000 in the first four months of 2008 (IRIN 2008; CoRMSA 2007: 13; CoRMSA 2008: 17). In each year between 2005 and 2007, over one-third of all asylum applicants were from Zimbabwe (CoRMSA 2007: 13; CoRMSA 2008: 17; HRW 2008: 31). Since 2006, Zimbabweans have been the largest single group of asylum seekers. The next largest national group of asylum seekers was from the DRC, which accounted for less than 6,000 claimants in 2006 and 2007 (CoRMSA 2007: 13; CoRMSA 2008: 18). Electoral violence following the March 2008 elections produced a significant surge in the numbers of Zimbabwean asylum seekers, such that around 4,000 Zimbabweans stood in line to apply for asylum at the Johannesburg Refugee Reception Office on the two days a week set aside for accepting Zimbabweans asylum seeker applications (UNHCR 2008). At the RRO office in Musina, which opened in July 2008, as many as 800 Zimbabweans reportedly lined up daily to apply for asylum permits (IRIN 2008).

Yet only a small number of Zimbabweans have won refugee status. Of the 66,578 Zimbabwean asylum applicants between 2000 and April 2008, 710 were granted refugee status, some 4,000 were rejected, and over 62,000 cases are still pending (IRIN 2008; CoRMSA 2007: 13; CoRMSA 2008: 17). Although the 700,000 people in cities across Zimbabwe who were directly targeted under Operation Murambatsvina[16] were not recognised as refugees, some rights organisations argued that they had strong claims under international refugee law (LHR 2006: 12; HRW 2008: 61–74).

Zimbabwean Strategies with Respect to Legal Status

While many Zimbabwean asylum seekers face DHA discrimination in lodging their claims and having their asylum seeker and refugee documents recognised by the police, there is widespread acknowledgement by rights groups, pro-migrant groups and the UNHCR that many Zimbabweans also use the asylum system to stay in the country legally and secure the right to work. The long backlog in assessing asylum claims means that asylum seekers can remain in the country for extended periods while their applications await status determination (HRW, 2008; IRIN 2008). To avoid the long wait, Zimbabweans offer bribes to officials, just as migrants from other countries are known to do (NCRA 2006; CoRMSA 2007 and 2008).

In sharp contrast, many legitimate Zimbabwean refugees apparently do not apply for refugee status because they consider it more important to be able to travel home periodically to deliver food and money to their families than to have legal status of asylum seeker or refugee (RI 2007). Under the Refugees Act, refugees must give up status if they voluntarily return home (s.5 (1)(a)), and an asylum seeker permit lapses if the holder departs from SA without the consent of the Minister (s.22 (5)(a)) and if the application is rejected or found to be manifestly unfounded, abusive or fraudulent (s.22(6)(b)).[17] According to the World Refugee Survey, there were about 18,900 de facto refugees in South Africa – legitimate refugees who did not apply for refugee status – about 11,800 of whom were Zimbabweans (WRS 2008).[18]

Like other foreign migrants, Zimbabweans also seek to obtain South African documents to avoid arrest, detention and deportation. Zimbabweans can do so because DHA officials are involved in issuing and selling both real and fictitious documents. The Ministry of Home Affairs' budget request in 2006 acknowledged the existence of 'significant corruption and fraud in acquiring South African citizenship, including through fraudulent marriages' (Home Affairs 2006: 44; Business Day 2005). In September 2005, the chairperson of the Home Affairs Portfolio Committee said in parliament that South Africa was under siege from illegal immigrants who had acquired false documents (PMG 2005). Crime syndicates have operated inside the DHA for years, selling forged and genuine South African documents, apparently mainly to 'economic migrants' (Business Day 2004; AP 2004; Mawadza 2008: 6). It is evidently public knowledge that migrants themselves are also involved in forging asylum papers and ID documents at known premises. For example, African migrants produce forged documents until late at night in about forty-three hair salons on a single street in Sunnyside, a suburb of Pretoria (Mawadza 2008: 6).

In the wake of the xenophobic violence in May 2008, South African citizens interviewed by Suren Pillay blamed foreign nationals and government agencies for foreigners' fraudulent access to identity documents (Pillay 2008: 17–18). Pillay recommended that government address the 'apparently endemic corruption within both the department of home affairs, local municipalities and within some relevant divisions of the SA Police Service, including the issuing of false or corruptly acquired identity documents ...' (Pillay 2008: 26).

Like other 'illegal foreigners', Zimbabweans who are unable to obtain legal status seek to work illegally, and domestic, agricultural and construction sectors employ large numbers of undocumented migrants, paying them less than minimum wage. Even professional and skilled Zimbabweans resort to such jobs to survive. Others are self-employed, as street traders or in the informal urban settlements where many live. Better educated Zimbabweans are also finding work in private schools, where police and immigration officials are less likely to detect them (Mawadza 2008: 5). Zimbabweans, like other foreign migrants, have learned from government officials seeking bribes from them that they can offer to bribe police and other government officials if they are found working illegally or arrested for being in the country without documents, and may also bribe immigration officials to release them rather than deport them (HRW 2007).

The Impact of Foreign Policy and Xenophobia

Official discrimination against Zimbabweans has stemmed from both South Africa's foreign policy support for the ZANU PF regime – and for ZANU PF as a party since the formation of a government of national unity in February 2009 – and widespread xenophobia towards all foreigners. The interplay of foreign policy support for the Zimbabwe regime and xenophobia and the imploding situation in Zimbabwe have combined to make the situation of Zimbabwean migrants both distinctive and precarious.

Xenophobia

In 2006 the South African Migration Project undertook a national survey of the attitudes of South Africans toward foreign nationals in the country and compared the results with surveys it had conducted in the 1990s. The findings are sobering. Compared to citizens of other countries worldwide,

South Africans were the least open to outsiders and wanted the greatest restrictions on immigration. South Africans favouring a total ban on immigration increased from twenty-five per cent in 1999 to thirty-five per cent in 2006, and in 2006 nearly fifty per cent supported or strongly supported the deportation of foreign nationals, including those living legally in South Africa. The same report showed South Africans to be divided on refugee protection with forty-seven per cent supporting protection, thirty per cent opposing it, and nearly twenty per cent having no opinion. Fifty per cent favoured making it mandatory that all refugees lived in border camps, and only thirty per cent agreed with allowing refugees to work (SAMP 2008: 1–3). These figures indicate a wide gap between South Africans' attitudes to foreigners and both South African law and policy and the advocacy positions of rights and pro-migrant groups.

SAMP's study noted that South Africans continued to view foreign nationals as a threat to the country, 'Indeed, along certain indicators, attitudes have hardened since 1999' (SAMP 2008: 3). The proportion of South African who believed that foreign nationals 'use up resources' grew from fifty-nine to sixty-seven per cent between 1999 and 2006 and the percentage associating migrants with crime also increased from forty-five to sixty-seven per cent over the same period, while the proportion of those who viewed migrants as bringing disease rose from twenty-four to fifty per cent (SAMP 2008: 3).

While the majority of South Africans had an unfavorable impression of migrants wherever they came from, with respect to African migrants, they had the most favorable attitudes to migrants from Botswana, Lesotho and Swaziland. Only fourteen per cent of South Africans had favorable attitudes to Mozambicans and twelve per cent to Zimbabweans, while the most unpopular of all African migrants were Somalis, Angolans and Nigerians (SAMP 2008: 4). Interestingly, the percentage of South Africans with no contact at all with foreigners has declined sharply in less than a decade from eighty per cent in 1997 to sixty per cent in 1999 and to thirty-two per cent in 2006. In 1999 and 2006 around a third of respondents said it was likely or very likely that they would take action against foreign nationals living in their communities. Most said they would merely report foreigners to the police, community associations, and employers. But sixteen per cent said they would join with others to force foreign nationals to leave the area and nine per cent would use violence to do so (SAMP 2008: 4–6). The authors of the SAMP study noted: 'This surely indicates that the violence of May 2008 could well have been even more widespread or may become so in the near future. At the very least, it suggests that a sizeable minority approves of the actions of others' (SAMP 2008: 6).

The SAMP authors concluded that 'the vast majority of South Africans form their attitudes in a vacuum, relying mainly on hearsay and media and other representations' (SAMP 2008: 4). On the issue of whether or not contact between foreigners and citizens hardened or softened xenophobic attitudes, the SAMP report states: 'Contact ... cannot be isolated from the circumstances of interaction' (2008: 32). Reports about the xenophobic violence in May 2008 contain interesting allusions to the nature of contact between foreigners and citizens in the housing market. Housing policy excludes foreigners from access to subsidised housing. Based on limited research conducted during the xenophobic violence, Pillay reported that foreign nationals often rented formally built homes and backyard shacks from citizens, and that in at least one location where researchers visited, the impression was that citizens 'overcharged' foreign nationals for rent and electricity. In other areas, it emerged that citizens had sold or rented out low-cost government-built homes that they had been allocated to foreigners, while they went back to live in shacks and placed their names again on waiting lists for housing. Consequently, foreigners were seen to have access to low-cost housing ahead of many citizens (Pillay 2008: 22–23). Another short-term investigation into the xenophobic violence of May 2008 reported similar findings about tensions around foreigners' ability to purchase low-cost housing built by the government because they have the income while citizens have been on waiting lists for five to ten years (Steinberg 2008: 7). Before the May violence, a researcher reported that Zimbabwean migrants had been accused of getting low-cost government-built homes – Reconstruction and Development Programme (RDP) housing – ahead of legitimate South Africans (Mawadza 2008: 4).

Following the outbreak of xenophobic violence in South Africa in May 2008, Amnesty International said an inquiry should examine the role of possible contributory factors, including 'the longstanding pattern of discriminatory practices and attitudes shown towards asylum-seekers, refugees and migrants by officials, including from the Department of Home Affairs (DHA), the police services and also the magistracy.' AI continued: 'Legal and advocacy organisations ... have repeatedly raised with the government their concerns that these practices and attitudes result in effective denial of access to asylum determination procedures, place individuals at risk of arbitrary arrest, unlawful deportation, or forcible return to their countries of origin where they may be subjected to further human rights violations' (AI 2008). Amnesty International referred to the 'implicit official denial that Zimbabweans in South Africa may be in need of international protection' perhaps having contributed to the hostility toward this group, who have been targeted in the current violence (AI 2008).

South Africa's Foreign Policy Toward Zimbabwe

As President, Thabo Mbeki was a pivotal player in SA's foreign policy toward Zimbabwe; after his resignation as President, effective from 25 September 2008, he continued to serve as SADC's appointed facilitator between

ZANU PF and the opposition MDC, until President Zuma took over in November 2009. In fact, Mbeki had been attempting to mediate a political solution in Zimbabwe since at least 2002 when President Mugabe's re-election as president was not recognised by the MDC or Western observers. The South African government, and Mbeki in particular, have given strong support to ZANU PF and most of the time to Mugabe since 2000.[19] South Africa's policy toward Zimbabwe appears to have been shaped by concern not to alienate the Zimbabwe state by overt and aggressive pressure and to prevent other institutions and states from doing the same (Southern Africa Litigation Centre 2006). The government's oft-repeated stance has been that Zimbabweans can solve their own problems 'through a combination of reconciliation and a regeneration of the existing political elite ...' (Alden and Schoeman 2003: 14); outsiders should not dictate. South Africa was willing to help Zimbabwe find solutions but it would respect state sovereignty (Todd 2007: 444; Alden and Schoeman 2003: 2).

South Africa's support for Zimbabwe has taken different forms. First, government officials, including ex-President Mbeki, ex-Foreign Affairs Minister Dlamini-Zuma (the current Home Affairs Minister) and former ANC Secretary-General Kgalema Motlanthe, all endorsed key elements of Mugabe's version of the problem in Zimbabwe in public statements, including the following: Zimbabwe's problems began when Mugabe decided in 2000 to redress the historical injustice of deeply skewed racial land inequalities. Britain, rather than the Zimbabwe government, has a responsibility to compensate white farmers for the confiscated land because white settlers stole the land during the colonial era. The West, and in particular, the former colonial power, Britain, angered by the Zimbabwe government's violation of property rights, especially of white farmers, unfairly introduced punitive sanctions, which have had a devastating impact on the economy (Phimister and Raftopoulos 2004; Freeman 2005). South African officials also regurgitated Mugabe's fiction that the crisis is between Zimbabwe and Britain, as when ex-ANC Secretary General Motlanthe said the ANC supported the appointment of former Tanzanian president, Benjamin Mkapa, as a mediator in the crisis with Britain (Todd 2007: 442).

Second, most independent observers would agree with the MDC that Mbeki has been partisan to ZANU PF in the negotiations that occurred on and off since 2002, asking the MDC to make compromises while avoiding pressuring Mugabe's government to make changes it did not embrace. Third, South Africa strengthened its defense and intelligence ties with Zimbabwe in an agreement signed in Cape Town on 17 November 2005. The establishment of a South Africa-Zimbabwe Joint Permanent Commission on Defence and Security was to boost cooperation and tackle specific areas of mutual concern, including cross-border crime and illegal immigration (SW Radio Africa 2005, Todd 2007). Fourth, South Africa has voted against efforts to condemn Zimbabwe's human rights record or obstructed putting Zimbabwe on the agenda in multilateral institutions and has denounced efforts to exclude Mugabe from international meetings, including the EU-Africa summits (Southern Africa Litigation Centre 2006). Finally, the South African government refused to engage in any form of sanctions against the Mugabe regime. Hence the government continued to supply Zimbabwe with its electricity and oil needs, even when it did not pay its bills. It also supplied arms and ammunition to the regime. For example, when Mugabe and ZANU PF were implementing a policy of organised violence against Zimbabweans who voted for the opposition in the March 2008 election, South Africa issued a permit allowing Chinese arms and ammunition to be transported across South Africa to Zimbabwe (Home Office 2008: 8).

Why South Africa persists in its pro-ZANU PF/Mugabe policy is not obvious. Some have explained South Africa's foreign policy toward Zimbabwe as 'driven by the combined ... class interests of South Africa's emergent black and traditional (white) bourgeoisie (whether located in the public and/or private sectors),' or, put differently, 'a renewed South African sub-imperialism' (McKinley 2004: 357). Others maintain that South Africa has failed in its foreign policy objectives toward Zimbabwe because it lacks hegemonic power even in southern Africa. Notwithstanding its dominant economic and (arguably) military position, proponents of this view argued that the South African government has failed to influence events in Zimbabwe because of the popularity of Mugabe's anti-imperialism discourse within elite circles and amongst the African population in relation to Mbeki's support for neo-liberal values and South Africa's desire to court regional and continental allies (Alden and Soko 2005: 388–9; Alden and Schoeman 2003: 14). Others maintain that Mbeki and the ANC have aligned with Mugabe and his regime chiefly around 'a politics of liberation solidarity': a struggle against colonialism and imperialism (Phimister and Raftopolous 2004: 390).

Whatever the reasons for SA's support for the regime in Zimbabwe, there has been no marked change under either former President Motlanthe, who succeeded President Mbeki, or since President Jacob Zuma was elected in April 2009. Prior to becoming South Africa's President, Zuma, who is also President of the ANC, publicly asserted his opposition to using sanctions against Zimbabwe and his commitment to continuing Mbeki's approach to Zimbabwe (WSJ 2008).

Both South Africa's support for the Mugabe regime and xenophobic attitudes combined to affect Zimbabweans in a specific way. The nature of discrimination against Zimbabweans may be illustrated by the problems they experience accessing the asylum system. Initially, when Zimbabweans applied for asylum at RROs, they were told that because 'there is no war in Zimbabwe', they had no right to apply for asylum. In June 2002 the Wits Law Clinic tested the legality of this practice in a case involving five Zimbabwean exiles. The case was settled when the DHA conceded that any Zimbabwean had a right to apply for asylum (LHR 2006: 17–18). Nonetheless, in a 2006 survey of Zimbabweans in South Africa, some respondents still experienced a similar attitude from DHA officials and the police. For example, one Zimbabwean male who was granted refugee status in October 2005 was still waiting for his documentation a year later. Among other unlawful experiences with the police, Hillbrow police officers arrested him for having an asylum permit, because they claimed that 'the permit is not issued to Zimbabweans'. He had to pay a bribe to stop the police from tearing up the permit. Then in 2005, police officers stationed at Jeppe police station threatened to shoot him after an argument 'over my being a Zimbabwean and having an asylum permit'(LHR 2006: 19). A thirty-five year old Zimbabwean asylum permit holder told LHR she was harassed and detained by two Germiston police officials two weeks after she arrived in the country in November 2004, and secured her release by paying a bribe. She also complained that DHA officials at the Rossettenville RRO had told her in December 2004 and again in March 2005 to 'go back to Zimbabwe because there is no war'(LHR 2006: 21) After the opposition party and the ruling party signed a power-sharing deal in September 2008, Zimbabwean asylum seekers allege they were told by DHA officials that they could now return to their country (Zimbabwe Times 2008 and 2008a, Zimbabwe Exiles Forum 2008).

Whether they fear South African government officials or Zimbabwean Central Intelligence Organisation officials who operate on both sides of the Limpopo border or for some other reason, it is striking that Zimbabwean asylum seekers prefer to cross the border illegally rather than enter through a formal border post, as they are entitled to do by law (HRW 2008: 84, FMSP 2007: 7). According to DHA, only one Zimbabwean national claimed to be an asylum seeker at the Beitbridge border post in the first six months of 2007 compared to 938 from the DRC, 443 from Somalia and 433 from Ethiopia (DHA 2007).

The Politics of Legalising Zimbabwean Migrants

While the South African government remained steadfast in its view that Zimbabweans were overwhelmingly economic migrants illegally in the country, many organisations came to acknowledge the humanitarian crisis in Zimbabwe and to advocate that the South African government should offer temporary legal status to Zimbabwean migrants.

The strategies adopted by rights groups and pro-migrant organisations with respect to Zimbabwean migrants changed dramatically from 2006. Initially, these organisations resisted calling for special treatment for Zimbabweans. When appeals were made for the regularisation of legal status, they were general rather than for specific nationalities. For example, Lawyers for Human Rights recommended that undocumented migrants be legalised, and in particular those resident in SA for a considerable time, those forced migrants who did not meet the strict confines of the Refugees Act but who had compelling reasons to stay in the country (surely an implicit reference to Zimbabweans), and migrant workers and their families, employed and self-employed in the informal sector (LHR 2006: 30). Indeed, the generalised appeal for regularising the status of undocumented migrants through the introduction of a period of amnesty was still being made by the Human Sciences Research Council following the xenophobic violence against foreign migrants in May 2008 (Pillay 2008: 26).

The reluctance to single out the plight of Zimbabweans was at least in part because domestic NGOs recognised the political problems of advocating special circumstances for Zimbabweans to the South African government whose foreign policy was strongly partial to Robert Mugabe and ZANU PF. These organisations also were aware that many South Africans did not consider the political and economic situation in Zimbabwe to be worse than in Swaziland, for example, and had adopted the official ANC and government rhetoric that race and land issues in Zimbabwe were unresolved colonial legacies.[20]

As Zimbabweans continued to come in large numbers to South Africa, a public debate ensued as to whether Zimbabweans were economic migrants or refugees. Even in late 2007, the UN emphasised that Zimbabweans were fleeing for economic reasons and saw them as economic migrants (RI 2007). While the UN recognised that some were refugees (DHA AR 2008: 9), it opposed treating all Zimbabweans as refugees (FMSP 2008: 10). The UN and the DHA were in agreement in that both saw the vast majority of Zimbabweans as economic migrants (Lefko-Everett 2007). A wide range of civil society groups, however, called for all Zimbabweans to be recognised as refugees as they had been forced to leave because of 'events seriously disturbing public order' – part of the OAU Convention's broader definition of refugees which was incorporated in the Refugees Act (RI 2007; NCRA 2006).[21] In July 2007, the chief opposition party, the Democratic Alliance, suggested that all Zimbabweans were 'economic refugees' and called for the Minister of Home Affairs to use her powers under the Refugees Act (s.35) to create refugee camps for Zimbabweans (VOA 2007; FMSP 2007: 8–9). But the Minister rejected the construction of camps on the grounds that Zimbabweans were not 'refugees', and the DHA backed this position by noting that neither the UNHCR nor UNICEF had indicated an influx of refugees (DHA media release 2007). The UN itself has supported the Minister's opposition to building refugee camps (BBC 2007).

In November 2007, the US-based Refugees International recommended that the UN should provide humanitarian assistance to Zimbabweans in the region and that host countries, in particular Botswana and South Africa, should work towards creating new legal frameworks that acknowledge the nature of Zimbabwean migration – neither all refugees nor voluntary economic migrants – and provide adequate protection and assistance to those in need, including documented status. Until such time, RI called for a halt to Zimbabweans' arrest, detention, and deportation in SA and Botswana (RI 2007).

Actually, there is no need for legal reform in South Africa. Under the Immigration Act, the minister for home affairs may use her discretion where special circumstances exist to set terms and conditions under which to grant 'a category of foreigners the rights of permanent residence ...' (s.31(2)((b)). In its 2008 annual report, CoRMSA advocated that the government stop deportations of Zimbabweans and use existing provisions under the immigration law to confer legal status on them as a group (CoRMSA 2008). In June 2008 Human Rights Watch (HRW) made an extended case for regularising the status of Zimbabweans because they were victims of forced displacement since 2000.[22] HRW called on the minister to use s.31 of the Immigration Act to end deportations of Zimbabweans, allow them to enter SA legally and without having to pay for a visa, grant them the right to work for a limited period of time, and proposed the minister may limit rights to work, and not include rights to housing assistance, to food and social security (HRW 2008: 121). These proposals were endorsed by the government when it announced a new migration regime for Zimbabweans in April 2009. HRW also advocated providing group-based refugee status to eligible Zimbabweans, including those who had been direct targets of Operation Murambatsvina in May 2005. Whether to employ group-based or individual status determinations has been a subject of policy discussions (LHR and FMSP 2009) .

Under the Refugees Act, the Minister of Home Affairs may declare 'any group or category of persons' to be refugees, and may impose conditions provided that they are in conformity with the constitution and international law. After consultation with the UNHCR representative and the Premier of the province into which the mass influx of asylum seekers has taken place, the Minister may 'designate areas, centres or places for the temporary reception and accommodation of asylum seekers or refugees or any specific category or group of asylum seekers or refugees who entered the Republic on a large scale, pending the regularisation of their status in the Republic'.

(s.35, RA). The Minister may also make regulations relating to a large-scale influx of asylum seekers into the country (s.38(1), RA).

The UN High Commissioner for Refugees underwent a change of heart on Zimbabwean migrants in South Africa after ZANU PF's orchestrated violence against the MDC during the presidential run-off campaign following the March 2008 election. He appealed to SA to halt all deportations of Zimbabweans until the crisis in Zimbabwe had been resolved, to ensure that asylum seekers were able to lodge their claims, and to exceptionally grant Zimbabweans a temporary legal status allowing them to stay in the country (UNHCR 2008a; Foreign Affairs, 2008). There was thus a new consensus among the key local and international actors on foreign migrants that SA government should halt all deportations of Zimbabweans and give them temporary legal status.

Following the establishment of this consensus, South Africa had its first experience with granting group-based legal status under the Immigration Act (s.31(2)(b)).[23] After the xenophobic violence in May 2008 and the SA government's establishment of temporary camps for displaced foreigners, the government, responding to calls from the UNHCR and others, decided in July 2008 to issue a six month temporary permit to residents of the displaced camps. The camps held, at their peak, about 40,000 displaced individuals (JRS 2008). The objective of the temporary permit was to ensure the immediate protection, including against deportation, for the displaced and to allow them a period of time in which to make decisions about their options and/or replace or extend documents lost in the violence. Amnesty International documented numerous human right violations and other unlawful practices against the displaced, including: a fast-track asylum process that resulted in a ninety-eight per cent rejection rate in Guateng province and even higher in the Western Cape – far higher than the ordinary case-by-case approach to asylum determination – and entailed most of the unlawful practices that critics have complained about in the ordinary asylum process and new breaches of the law; government termination of the validity of the permits and the halt on deportation well before the expiration of the six month period; and mandatory registration by camp residents that required completing a form that would mean that those who were asylum seekers and refugees effectively agreed to give up rights they already held (AI 2008b and 2008c).

South Africa's first experience with issuing group-based legal status under the immigration law is a cautionary tale of how implementing a legalisation process generated fresh rights violations against the very population that it was intended to protect. The number of Zimbabweans who would need to be processed is at least one million – a bureaucratic task of a different magnitude from the 40,000 displaced foreign migrants who went into the temporary camps.

South African government officials and politicians will be mindful of the high levels of xenophobia among citizens before they introduce 'enlightened' migration policies, such as regularising Zimbabweans' legal status. In the aftermath of the xenophobic violence in May 2008 that resulted in sixty-two deaths, 670 wounded, and tens of thousands of displaced foreigners, Amnesty International observed: 'There is currently great sensitivity on the part of the government not to appear to be "privileging" "foreigners" in terms of access to essential services in the context of high levels of poverty and unemployment in South Africa' (AI 2008b: 4). More generally, one may anticipate that the South African government will make every attempt to avoid giving the impression that they are 'privileging foreigners', and in particular, those fleeing a regime the South African government supports. Should the government actually grant Zimbabwean migrants temporary legal status, as it has declared it intends to, coping with likely xenophobic responses will be a major challenge.

Conclusion

This chapter discussed the politics of legal status for Zimbabwean migrants in South Africa from the vantage point of numerous stakeholders – the government of South Africa, the opposition party, the migrants, the UNHCR, and domestic and international civil society organisations involved in human rights and migrant issues. What makes the Zimbabweans' predicament so pressing is that most have been forced to leave their home country because of its ever-growing humanitarian crisis but they do not fit the conventional legal definition of refugees. Consequently, most are 'illegal foreigners' in South Africa – the most vulnerable migrant group. If the South African government moves ahead with its stated intention of granting Zimbabweans temporary legal status, this new migration policy will have to contend with challenges from foreign policy interests with respect to Zimbabwe and concerns about stoking xenophobic attitudes among its citizens.

Notes

1. South Africa acceded to the 1951 UN Convention in January 1996.
2. South Africa acceded to the 1969 OAU Convention in December 1995.

3. In terms of the Refugees Act, a dependant 'includes the spouse, any unmarried dependent child or any destitute, aged or infirm member of the family of such asylum seeker or refugee' (s.1(ix)).

4. A 'manifestly unfounded application' is one made for asylum on grounds other than those on which an asylum application may be made under the Refugees Act (s.1(xii), RA); a 'fraudulent application for asylum' is one 'based without reasonable cause on facts, information, documents or representations which the applicant knows to be false and which facts, information, documents or representations are intended to materially affect the outcome of the application (s.1(xi), RA).

5. NCRA (2006: 26–37) discusses some of the problems that recognised refugees experienced with their s.24 permits that led the DHA to introduce formal refugee identity documents in 2001. When these latter documents had their own problems, the DHA decided in 2005 to test its smart cards – a computerised system planned for all South Africans – on refugees renewing their documents.

6. The Refugees Amendment Bill seeks to streamline administrative practices, primarily through the removal of the Standing Committee for Refugee Affairs as well as the Refugee Reception Officers and the Refugee Appeals Board and to create a Refugee Appeals Authority (CoRMSA 2008: 24).

7. CormSA (2007: 13) states that those granted refugee status in 2006 do not include asylum seekers who might appeal their RSDO rejections.

8. Many other African countries host much larger refugee populations: Tanzania (432,500), Kenya (319,400), Sudan (310,500), Chad (294,100), Uganda (235,800), Ethiopia (210,700), DRC (177,500). Of these countries, only the DRC and Ethiopia have populations greater than South Africa's 48 million people; the others have smaller populations (3–40 million) except for Chad (10.7 million) (WRS 2008).

9. DHA Annual Report for year ended 31 March 2008.

10. DHA Annual Report for year ended 31 March 2008, pp.24, 62.

11. Eppel and Raftopoulos (2008: 20) report that women respondents predominated in the survey as a result of Matabeleland's rural population having joined the diaspora. Conceivably, the absence of 18–25 year olds in South Matabeleland may reflect not only an external migration but also internal migration.

12. *Malaitsha* derives from an Ndebele verb, *laitsha*, that refers to carrying something. *Malaitsha* used to carry, for a fee, only groceries for Zimbabweans in South Africa back to their families; increasingly they are transporting people too. The *malaitsha* bribe immigration officials at the border posts to allow them into South Africa (Mawadza 2008: 4,8).

13. Farmers with corporate permits have hired Zimbabwean farm workers who have been issued with inexpensive ETDs by the government of Zimbabwe.

14. South Africa no longer publishes figures of deportations by nationality.

15. In four months in 2006, less than fifty per cent of deportees registered with the IOM (HRW 2007: 32)

16. The government of Zimbabwe launched Operation Murambatsvina (Operation Remove the Filth) in May 2005 allegedly to enforce by-laws that prohibit all

forms of illegal activities in areas such as vending, illegal structures and illegal cultivation. However, most people recognized the military-style operation as a government-sponsored vendetta against urban people who had voted for the MDC in the March 2005 parliamentary election.

17. HRW (2008: 78–79) shows that the 1951 convention permits refugees to return to their home country for brief periods without having their refugee status revoked and only requires revocation if the refugee voluntarily reestablishes in the country where persecution was feared, as this is interpreted to mean making the country the primary residence.

18. WRS does not discuss how it arrived at the number of de facto refugees.

19. Under President Mbeki, SA policy was to encourage the rise to power of a younger political elite in ZANU PF as a way of removing Mugabe.

20. The author was present at a Human Rights Watch seminar held in Johannesburg and attended by many local rights groups and migrants' advocacy groups in August 2006. Domestic organisations discussed the difficulties of advocacy for Zimbabwean migrants.

21. According to HRW (2008: 108 fn.327) no African government or court has ever explicitly used the 'events seriously disturbing public order' phrase to declare a group of persons to be refugees. However, FMPS (2008:22) claims 'Conferring group refugee status according to the 1969 OAU Convention is a common response to large-scale migration around Africa'. One civil society group advocating for all Zimbabweans to be recognised as refugees under the 1969 OAU Convention is Jesuit Refugee Services (FMSP 2008: 20).

22. HRW (2007) had called for the documentation of Zimbabweans but had not developed the rationale that Zimbabwean migration was a product of a growing humanitarian crisis in Zimbabwe.

23. Between 1995 and 1999 the South African cabinet offered three immigration amnesties in terms of which eligible foreigners received permanent residence. These amnesties were not issued under the Immigration Act, which was only passed in 2002 (Human Rights Watch 2007: 27).

References

Alden, C. and M. Soko. 2005. 'South Africa's Economic Relations with Africa: Hegemony that Wasn't: South Africa's Foreign Policy Towards Zimbabwe', *Strategic Review for Southern Africa*, 25, 1: 1–28.

Amnesty International. 2008. *Zimbabwe: Time for Accountability*. AI: London, Index: AFR46/028/2008.

——. 2008a. *South Africa Must Protect Those At Risk Of 'Xenophobic Attack'*, 23 May 2008.

——. 2008b. *South Africa: Talk for Us Please – Limited Options Facing Individuals Displaced by Xenophobic Violence*. AI: London, Index: AFR 53/012/2008.

——. 2008c. *South Africa: Displaced At Risk As Camps Close*, 7 October 2008.

Associated Press. 2004. 'Terrorists Obtain S.Africa Passports', 28 July 2004. Retrieved 20 October 2008 from http://www.chinadaily.com.cn/english/doc/2004–7/28/content_352358.htm

Bate, R. 2008. 'Zimbabwe is on the Ropes', *The Wall Street Journal*, 14 November 2008.

BBC News. 2008. 'Anger at S. Africa Camp Closures', 1 October 2008.

BBC News, Peter Greste. 2007. '"No camps" for Zimbabwean Migrants', 24 August 2007. Retrieved 20 October 2008 from http://news.bbc.co.uk/go/pr/fr/-/2/hi/africa/6962609.stm

Besada, H. and N. Moyo. 2008. *Zimbabwe in Crisis: Mugabe's Policies and Failures Centre for International Governance (CIGI).* Working Paper 38, October 2008.

Business Day. 2004. 'Home Affairs to Ask for Forgery Proof Passports. Pressure from US, EU over Document Theft', 20 February 2004. Retrieved 28 October from http://www/businessday.co.za/PrintFriendly.aspx?TarkID=953008

———. 2005. 'Home Affairs in New Pledge to Root Out Graft, 11 July 2005. Retrieved 28 October 2008 from http://www.queensu.ca/samp/migrationnews/

Constitution of the Republic of South Africa (No. 108). 1996.

CoRMSA (Consortium for Refugees and Migrants in South Africa). 2007. *Protecting Refugee and Asylum Seekers in South Africa*, Johannesburg,19 June 2007.

———. 2008. *Protecting Refugees, Asylum Seekers and Immigrants in South Africa*, Johannesburg, 18 June 2008 and June 2009.

Department of Home Affairs. 2006. Vote 4, Budget, 2006.

———. 2007. Media release. Issued by the Chief Directorate: Communication Services, Jacky Mashapu. Statement on Zimbabwean Nationals Entering SA. 1 August 2007. Retrieved 28 October from http://www.dha.gov.za/media_releases.asp?id=419

———. 2008. *Annual Report for the Year Ended 31 March 2008.*

Eppel, S. 2008. *Transitional Justice Options in Zimbabwe for 2009.*

Eppel, S. and B. Raftopoulos. 2008. *Political Crisis, Mediation and the Prospects for Transitional Justice in Zimbabwe.* Series: Developing a Transformation Agenda, Idasa, November 2008.

Forced Migration Studies Programme (FMSP). 2007. *Responding to Zimbabwean Migration in South Africa – Evaluating Options.* Background document prepared for a meeting on 27 November 2007 at the Chalsty Centre, University of the Witwatersrand, Revised Version – 28 November 2007. Hosted by Lawyers for Human Rights, the Wits Law Clinic, and the Wits Forced Migration Studies Programme.

Forced Migration Studies Programme (FMSP) and Musina Legal Advice Office. 2007. Special Report: *Fact or Fiction? Examining Zimbabwean Cross-Border Migration into South Africa*, 4 September 2007.

Freeman, L. 2005. 'Contradictory Constructions of the Crisis in Zimbabwe' *Historia*, 1, 2: 287–310.

Garcia, S. and P. Duplat. 2007. 'Zimbabwe Exodus', *Refugees International Bulletin*, 7 November 2007.

Guterres, A. 2008. 'Millions Uprooted', *Foreign Affairs*, 87, 5: 90–9.

Home Office, UK Border Agency. 2008. *Country of Origin Information Key Documents: South Africa*, 6 May 2008.

Human Rights Watch. 2007. *'Keep Your Head Down': Unprotected Migrants in South Africa*, 19, 3(A), Feb. 2007.

———. 2008. *Unprotected Migrants: Zimbabweans in South Africa's Limpopo Province*, 18, 6(A), July 2008.

———. 2008a. *Neighbours in Need: Zimbabweans Seeking Refuge in South Africa*, June 2008.

Immigration Act (No. 13). 2002.

Immigration Amendment Act (No. 19). 2004.

IRIN. 2008. 'Zimbabwe: 'Double-ups' not Packing for Home', 19 Sept 2008.

Jesuit Refugee Services. 2008. *Dispatches No. 243*, 29 August 2008.

Landau, L., K. Ramjathan-Keogh and G. Singh. 'Xenophobia in South Africa and Problems Related To It', Background Paper prepared for: Open Hearings on 'Xenophobia and Problems Related to It', hosted by the South African Human Rights Commission with the Portfolio Committee of the Departments of Foreign Affairs and Home Affairs. Johannesburg: South Africa, 2 November 2004.

Lawyers for Human Rights (South Africa). 2006. *The Documented Experiences of Refugees, Deportees and Asylum Seekers in South Africa: A Zimbabwean Case Study.* A Written Submission prepared by Civil Society Organisations Working on the Refugee and Asylum Seekers' Human Rights Issues in South Africa. For Presentation to the Minister of Home Affairs. Johannesburg: South Africa, April 2006.

Lawyers for Human Rights (South Africa) and Forced Migration Studies Programme (FMSP). 2009. *Immigration Policy Responses to Zimbabweans in South Africa: Implementing Special Temporary Permits.* Background Paper prepared for a Roundtable on 9 April 2009, Pretoria.

Lefko-Everett, K. 2007. *Principle and Pragmatism in Dealing with Migrants*, 10 September 2007. Retrieved 28 October 2008 from http://www.idasa.org.za/output_details.asp?RID=1222&OTID=26&PID=11

McKinlay D. 2004. 'South African Foreign Policy towards Zimbabwe under Mbeki', Review of African Political Economy, 100: 357–364.

Mawadza, A. 2008. *The Nexus Between Migration and Human Security: Zimbabwean Migrants in South Africa*, Institute for Security Studies, Paper 162, May 2008.

NCRA (National Consortium for Refugee Affairs) in collaboration with University of Witwatersrand, Forced Migration Studies Programme. 2006. *Refugee Protection in South Africa 2006.*

Nyamnjoh, F. B. 2006. *Insiders and Outsiders: Citizenship and Xenophobia in Contemporary Southern Africa.* Dakar: Codesria in association with Zed Books.

Parliamentary Monitoring Group, Home Affairs Portfolio Committee. 2005. Retrieved 28 October from http://www.pmg.org.za/viewminute.php?id=6282

Phimister, I. and B. Raftopoulos. 2004. 'Mugabe, Mbeki & the Politics of Anti-Imperialism', *Review of African Political Economy*, 31, 101: 385–400.

Refugees Act (No. 130). 1998.

Save the Children. 2007. *Child Migration in Southern Africa.* Weaver Press and Save the Children UK and Save the Children Norway in Mozambique.

Schoofs, M. and N. Brulliard. 2008. 'South Africa's Zuma Rules Out Sanctions on Zimbabwe', *Wall St. Journal*, 25 October 2008. Retrieved 28 October from http://online.wsj.com/article/SB122488514654968023.html?mod=googlenews_wsj

South African Human Rights Commission (SAHRC). 2004. *Report of the Open Hearings on Xenophobia and Problems Related to it*. Hosted by the SAHRC and the Parliamentary Portfolio Committee in Foreign Affairs, November 2004. Retrieved 28 October from http://www.sahrc.org.za/sahrc_cms/downloads/Xenophobia%20Report.pdf

South African Migration Project (SAMP). 2008. *The Perfect Storm: The Realities of Xenophobia in Contemporary South Africa*. Migration Policy Series No. 50.

Southern Africa Litigation Centre. 2006. *South Africa's Foreign Policy on Zimbabwe's Human Rights Violations*, Johannesburg.

Steinberg, J. 2008. *South Africa's Xenophobic Eruption*, ISS Paper 169.

SW Radio Africa. 2008. 'UN Urges South Africa to Halt Deportation of Zimbabweans', 14 July 2008.

____. 2008a. 'South Africa, Zimbabwe Strengthen Defence, Intelligence Ties', 17 November 2005, http://www.swradioafrica.com/news171105/saties171105.htm.

The Economist. 2008. 'Reaching Rock Bottom', 6 December 2008.

Todd, Judith. 2007. *Through the Darkness: A Life in Zimbabwe*, South Africa: Zebra Press.

Trimikliniotis, N., S. Gordon and B. Zondo. 2008. 'Globalisation and Migrant Labour in a 'Rainbow Nation': a Fortress South Africa?', *Third World Quarterly*, 29, 7: 1323–1339.

UNHCR. 2008. July Update, Zimbabwe Update.

____. 2008a. 'South Africa: Changing Patterns of Displacement from Zimbabwe', 11 July 2008. http://www.alertnet.org/thenews/newsdesk/UNHCR/9b5f1376 0bad72187f0a5f31debda2fe.htm

____. 2008b. 'South Africa Cuts Nearly 500 km off Zimbabweans' Asylum Journey', 7 August 2008. http://www.unhcr.org/cgi-bin/texis/vtx/news/opendoc.htm?tbl=NEWS&id=489ae61d4.

United States Committee for Refugees and Immigrants. 2000. *World Refugee Survey 2000 – South Africa*.

____. 2001. *World Refugee Survey 2001 – South Africa*.

____. 2002. *World Refugee Survey 2002 – South Africa*.

____. 2003. *World Refugee Survey 2003 – South Africa*.

____. 2004. *World Refugee Survey 2004 – South Africa*.

____. 2005. *World Refugee Survey 2005 – South Africa*.

____. 2006. *World Refugee Survey 2006 – South Africa*.

____. 2007. *World Refugee Survey 2007 – South Africa*.

____. 2008. *World Refugee Survey 2008 – South Africa*. Online. UNHCR Refworld. Retrieved 28 October 2008 http://www.unhcr.org/refworld/docid/485f50d2c.html

Voice of Africa. 2007. 'S. Africa Opposition Presses Case for Refugee Camps for Zimbabwe', 24 July 2007. Retrieved 28 October from http://www.voanews.com/english/archive/2007-07/2007-07-24-voa71.cfm

Zimbabwe Exiles Forum. 2008. 'SA Withdraws Asylum for Zim Exiles', 29 September 2008.

Zimbabwe Times. 2008. 'MDC Meets SA Authorities Over Asylum', 11 October 2008.

———. 2008a. 'South Africa Stops Issuing Asylum Permits', 8 October 2008.

The Cultural Politics
of Survival in Britain

4

Zimbabwean Transnational Diaspora Politics in Britain

Dominic Pasura

This chapter is about Zimbabwean transnational diaspora politics, and seeks to understand both the character and motivation of different forms of political engagement on the part of Zimbabweans living in Britain. To do so, it develops a classification for interpreting the mode and degrees of participation in diaspora politics, which critiques and extends those in the existing literature (Shain and Barth 2003; Sheffer 2003), and illuminates how the idea of Zimbabwean diasporic identity is expressed, performed and made a lived reality in particular British settings. It is based on multi-sited ethnographic field research in different parts of Britain, and involved participation in different sorts of diaspora social and political gatherings. Many authors have pointed to 'the complicated relationship between dispersed ethnic groups, the states in which they live (host states), and the actions of governments that might make some historical or cultural claim to represent them (kin states)' (King and Melvin 1999: 108: Sheffer 2003), yet this complex triadic relationship requires further empirical investigation not least because diasporas can play a role not only in democratising their countries of origin (Østergaard-Nielsen 2003a; Sheffer 1986), but also in fomenting conflict (Fair 2005; Shain and Barth 2003). As Rogers (cited by Østergaard-Nielsen 2003b: 764) observes, there has been less attention to migrants' transnational politics in Europe than on the other side of the Atlantic: European-based research has tended to focus on migrant political participation in so far as it relates to improving their situation in the country of settlement rather than as a phenomenon in its own right.

This chapter contributes to debates over transnational diaspora politics by seeking to answer the following set of questions: To what extent, and in what ways, do Zimbabweans in Britain participate in transnational diaspora politics? How do different legal and geographical circumstances in Britain influence Zimbabweans' attitudes towards, and participation in transnational diaspora politics? What is the nature of transnational diaspora politics?

Before beginning to answer these questions, it is important first to clarify some terms. Although the intensity and regularity of transborder activity is essential to the definition of transnationalism, Guarnizo (cited by Levitt 2001: 198) usefully distinguishes between 'core' transnationalism (activities that are a regular, patterned, sustained and an integral part of an individual's life), and 'expanded' transnationalism (more occasional practices). Although there are many definitions of diaspora, the way the concept has been formulated by classical theorists is narrower than transnationalism, as Levitt explains:

> Transnational communities are building blocks of potential diasporas that may or may not take shape. Diasporas form out of the transnational communities spanning sending and receiving countries and out of the real or imagined connections between migrants from a particular homeland who are scattered throughout the world (Levitt 2001: 202–3).

Not all diasporas are transnational, only those diasporas whose 'core' or 'expanded' activities transcend borders can be considered as such. It thus makes sense to speak of Zimbabweans abroad who maintain links and connections with the homeland as a transnational diaspora,[1] and to explore what Hagel and Peretz (2005: 472) refer to as 'transnational diaspora politics'.

The chapter draws on my year long multi-sited ethnography of Zimbabweans in Britain, conducted in 2005–6, which included thirty-three interviews[2] in Coventry, Birmingham, London and Wigan. My research sites included one of the most prominent of Zimbabwean diaspora political activities in Britain – the Vigil in front of Zimbabwe House on the Strand in central London. I also patronised two informal social venues – the Zimbabwean pub in Coventry and *gochi-gochi* (barbeque) in Birmingham. I also wanted to study Zimbabweans who did not live in one of Britain's large multicultural cities, and thus made regular visits to Zimbabwean refugees and asylum-seekers in Wigan, a small town in northwest Britain.[3] The assumption of multi-sited ethnography is that the different contexts will alter people's responses, and I hope to reveal below how these different places all provide different insights into transnational diaspora politics and the factors that influence engagement and disengagement.

Transnational Diaspora Politics: A Four-Fold Classification of Members

In order to understand Zimbabwean migrants' participation in transnational diaspora politics in Britain, I have devised a malleable four-fold classification of members, which I use as a heuristic tool. The classification builds both on empirical investigation and a critique of earlier formulations by other scholars (Shain and Barth 2003; Sheffer 2003).

Sheffer (2003: 100) classifies diaspora members as 'core members', 'members by choice', 'marginal members' and 'dormant members' as an attempt to bridge the 'conceptual difficulties in identifying various categories of people in migrant ethnic groups who have experienced varying degrees of acculturation, integration and assimilation in their host countries.' Yet this categorisation is problematic as it is based on 'ancestry', which Brubaker (2005: 11) describes as 'a poor proxy for membership in a diaspora' and also tends towards a static and bounded notion of ethnic identity. Because the Zimbabwe diaspora is diverse in racial and ethnic terms, defining 'core' members in this way would also encourage the charge of racism. The fact of being born within a particular ethnic group should not be used as a primary tool for classifying the manner in which members participate in transnational diaspora politics.

A rather different classification is developed by Shain and Barth (2003), who distinguish members, as 'core', 'passive' or 'silent'. 'Core' members here are defined not in ethnic terms or through birth, but through their activities and role, as:

> the organising elites, intensively active in diasporic affairs and in a position to appeal for mobilisation of the larger diaspora. Passive members are likely to be available for mobilisation when the active leadership calls upon them. Silent members are a larger pool of people who are generally uninvolved in diasporic affairs (in the discursive and political life of its institutions), but who may mobilise in times of crisis (Shain and Barth 2003: 452).

However, Shain and Barth's (2003) categories are largely descriptive and they lack the analytic edge to tell us why particular diaspora members are in the core, passive or silent category. The 'core members' are clearly indispensable for the diaspora's survival, but we understand little about what might motivate them, and it is not clear why passive members are always available for mobilisation. Who are these people? In which social class do they belong? What inhibits them from being part of the core group?

My modification of these typologies distinguishes between 'visible', 'epistemic', 'dormant' and 'silent' members of the Zimbabwe diaspora. The extent to which Zimbabweans in Britain engage in political and/ diasporic activities defines the group to which they belong. Members do not 'naturally' belong to any one category. Due to the fragmented and mobile nature of the diaspora, the categories are subject to change, and internal conflicts and external pressures make the semblance of diaspora unity a temporary feature. The divisions between the categories are 'virtual boundaries' (Sheffer 2003: 12) and should not be regarded as rigid, as it is possible for diaspora members to belong simultaneously to two different categories. Moreover, as Waldinger and Fitzgerald (2004: 1177) remind us, 'migrants do not make their communities alone: states and state politics shape the options for migrant and ethnic trans-state social action'. In formulating the classification, I have considered how institutions in the hostland and homelands might influence the category to which members belong.

Visible members of the diaspora, as the word suggests, are those intensively active in political and diasporic life. Visible members initiate and participate in diasporic activities that seek to improve their lives in the hostland and homeland. They would include participants at the Zimbabwe Vigil, activists in the Zimbabwe Association (one of many asylum seeker support groups), members of one of the Movement for Democratic Change (MDC) branch committees in the UK, or members of the Diaspora Vote Action Group (who in 2004 made an unsuccessful appeal to the Zimbabwe Supreme Court to allow Zimbabweans abroad the right to vote in homeland elections). I hope to show some of the complex motivations for this sort of visible engagement through the account of the Vigil, developed below.

The second category comprises the epistemic members, derived from the Greek word *episteme* which means 'to know'. Epistemic members of the Zimbabweans diaspora might also be referred to as 'cyberspace activists', or 'desktop activists'. Predominantly these are intellectuals engaging in cyberspace debates about the political and economic future of Zimbabwe. What distinguish epistemic members from visible members of the diaspora are their cultural capital and their means of engaging in diaspora politics. Epistemic members have amassed cultural capital in the country of origin or in the country of destination in the form of advanced educational qualifications and social status, but eschew grassroots political involvement: they rarely take part in demonstrations and protests but make use of online discussion groups, internet radio debates and conferences to influence public opinion on issues relating to the hostland and homeland. Epistemic members of the Zimbabwean diaspora have built cross-border networks linking Britain, South Africa, the US and the homeland engaging in robust debates on how to guide the country out of its political and economic crises. They participate in web-based discussions in a number of Zimbabwean news sites, such as newzimbabwe.com, zimonline.co.za, zimdaily.com, changezimbabwe.com or the London-based Zimbabwean internet radio stations such as Afrosounds, Zimnetradio, Nehandaradio, Zonetradio and SW Radio Africa. The frequency and intensity of these debates has led to the development of an 'epistemic community' that actively discusses the politics of the homeland, and that is considerably larger than the 'visible' diaspora who associate in person, though membership in these two categories clearly overlaps.

The actions of epistemic members of the diaspora have caused great anxiety within the homeland government. One example can be provided by the campaign 'Fair Deal',[4] launched through the Zimdaily website, which aimed to identify children of ZANU PF ministers and prominent party activists studying at western universities for deportation back to Zimbabwe. As result of this (and related) campaigns, Australia deported eight Zimbabwean students whose parents had links with ZANU PF (Guma 2007). The influence of this epistemic community has also provoked efforts on the part of the homeland government to control cyberspace by jamming SW Radio Africa with Chinese technology (NewZimbabwe 2006) and passing the Interception of Communications Act [Chapter 11:20] of 2006, authorising the interception of all phone, internet and mail communications. Comparing visible members and epistemic members, it can be observed that both members regularly participate in diaspora politics and attempt to control the public space of diaspora politics, in so far as they try to shape authentic and legitimate narratives about homeland politics. Whereas visible members meet in physical space, epistemic members act in cyber space.

The third category of diasporic Zimbabweans is comprised of dormant members. As the word suggests, these members are inactive. Their inaction is caused by several factors: undocumented status and fear of the Zimbabwean Central Intelligence Organisation (CIO) or the British Home Office, lack of time caused by the need to do extra shifts to increase earnings, or a general disillusionment about the prolonged political and economic crisis in the country of origin. Dormant members may occasionally participate in diaspora politics, and can be seen to correlate to Shain and Barth's (2003) passive members. However, the word passive denotes an unresponsive attitude to a common cause. As for the dormant members of the Zimbabwean diaspora, they may remain committed and wired into political and economic events in the country of origin but internal and external factors restrict them from full participation. The uncertain future of undocumented migrants creates a fundamental insecurity in everyday life and can drive them to political marginalisation.

The last category is that of silent members. Shain and Barth (2003: 452) called silent members 'a larger pool of people who are generally uninvolved in diasporic affairs (in the discursive and political life of its institutions), but who may mobilise in times of crisis.' Yet for the Zimbabwean diaspora in Britain, they are not a large pool of people but rather a minority of people who are not involved in diaspora politics because of their desire to disown and distance themselves from their Zimbabwean background and conjure an alternative belonging. Some white Zimbabweans, for example, who emigrated after, as well as prior to independence have maintained an identity as Rhodesians. They have an uneasy relationship with the majority of the Zimbabwean diaspora as they disassociate themselves from anything Zimbabwean. They link with one another through websites including http://www.rhodesia.com; http://www.rhodesia.org. Some black Zimbabweans, on the other hand, prefer to be identified as South Africans or Jamaicans, for fear of deportation, humiliation at the representation of Zimbabwe in the media and other reasons. Indeed, one of the most contentious themes to emerge from this study is the number of black Zimbabweans who disown their Zimbabwean identity and forge new ones. Silent members are unlikely to participate in diasporic activities or develop a commitment to diaspora politics as they regard themselves as non-Zimbabweans. For the majority of black silent members, this is a strategic suppression, contingent on external factors both in the hostland and the homeland. Silent members can also include those who have fully integrated into the country of settlement. By suppressing or forging an alternative national identity, silent members exist on the periphery of the diaspora. Consequently, silent members may slip into non-members through assimilation, integration and creolisation. Although silent members' activities may be described as diasporic they are not transnational if they lack connection to the original homeland. While visible members and epistemic members are passionate in identifying themselves as Zimbabweans and maintaining strong ties to the homeland, silent members suppress their Zimbabwean identity and define themselves in some other way.

Having developed this schematic representation of Zimbabwean diasporic members, the next section describes and analyses detailed ethnographic data from the Zimbabwe Vigil, *gochi-gochi* in Birmingham, a pub in Coventry and Wigan in order to illustrate how the classification can help us understand the nature of transnational diaspora politics.

Contexts for Engagement and Disengagement: Ethnographic Vignettes

The Zimbabwe Vigil demonstrates outside the Zimbabwe Embassy in central London. It occupies a prime position and is perhaps the most regular and visible of gatherings that extend homeland opposition politics into the diaspora. Morgan Tsvangirai and several opposition Members of Parliament from the country of origin have visited this place to offer their moral support, as have a number of British MPs, among them Kate Hoey Labour MP, Lembit Opik Liberal Democrat MP, Michael Ancram Conservative MP, and Lord Triesman. Indeed, unlike many exile groups, who find it difficult to access the political establishment in Britain (on Turkish Cypriots lack of access, see Østergaard-Nielsen 2003a: 683) Zimbabweans in Britain have an unusual degree of access and support from British political actors, as well as the support of refugee organisations (RefugeeCouncil 2005). The UK government and the EU have placed Zimbabwe on their political agenda by imposing targeted sanctions on the government of Zimbabwe. In response to the accusations of human rights abuses, the Zimbabwean government counters with claims of neo-colonialism (Phimister and Raftopoulos 2004). While the British government's receptiveness to oppositional strands of diaspora activism has encouraged the development of diaspora opposition politics, such lobbying and access has also had the effect of deepening the rift between the diaspora in Britain and the Zimbabwean government.

According to the Vigil coordinators, the idea of protesting weekly at the Zimbabwean embassy was first mooted by Roy Bennett, MDC MP and Tony Reeler (a prominent member of the NGO community), who remembered the successful pickets outside South Africa House during the apartheid era, and the Central London Branch of the MDC then went on to set up the Zimbabwe Vigil in October 2002. By allowing demonstrations outside the Zimbabwe Embassy and the House of Commons, the British government provides a symbolic gesture of approval, a kind of implicit validation of the Vigil's activities and intentions.

The following account is based on my participation and observations at the Vigil on a number of occasions. Although the Vigil is open to all Zimbabweans, it draws its participants primarily from asylum seekers, refugees, MDC members and white Zimbabweans. White Zimbabweans, more than ten of whom were present during each of my visits, are central to the organisation and logistical operation of the Vigil, bringing tents, table, fliers and other material. The number of participants ranged between forty and eighty would typically be lower on a rainy day. Predominantly white Zimbabwean women coordinate the Vigil activities, though black women also play a part, and both Shona and Ndebele speakers participate.

Although the Vigil is linked to the MDC (specifically to the pro-Tsvangirai faction of the MDC from late 2005), it aims to draw on a broader oppositional constituency.[5] Huge banners of close to ten metres in diameter enhance the visibility of the Vigil to passersby, with Zimbabwean flags tied to the makeshift tent. When I attended the Vigil, the banners pronounced: 'Mbeki blood is on your hands'; 'Wake up world before Zimbabwe becomes another Sudan'; 'No to Mugabe no to starvation'; 'Arrest Mugabe for torture'; 'End murder, rape, and torture.' There was a big poster with the words: 'Wanted' in bold with Mugabe's photo underneath and a list of 178 people allegedly killed by Mugabe during the political violence that gripped the country after the 2000 parliamentary elections. A dartboard with Robert Mugabe's face on it had the words: 'Take a shot at Mugabe'. In front of the makeshift tent was a placard with Zimbabwean notes and the bearer cheques introduced to deal with the effects of hyperinflation, with an explanation of what the Zimbabwean dollar is worth compared to the British pound.

At the Vigil, members are asked to sign the attendance register placed on an improvised table and passers-by were solicited to sign a petition to the former UN secretary general, Koffi Annan, for human rights abuses committed by Robert Mugabe. Pamphlets on the table chronicled the political and economic state of Zimbabwe; copies of *The Zimbabwean* paper were for sale, and there was also a bowl for donations. Vigil coordinators were selling MDC t-shirts for £15, and an open palm (MDC symbol) with the words 'Join the MDC Today' for £2 and green ribbons inscribed 'Make Mugabe history' were being sold for £1. An important part of the experience of the Vigil involved singing – mainly liberation war songs recycled to suit the collective anti-Mugabe conviction. The singing, mainly in Shona or Ndebele, was accompanied by drumming and dancing and could be particularly eye-catching in that, for most of the time, white Zimbabweans were beating the drums. Members of the Vigil cheered *'Murehwa'* to encourage harder beating of the drums (Murehwa is the name of a place in Zimbabwe, but has also come to stand for a whiteman who identifies with black Zimbabweans). The Vigil advances particular agendas, invoking universalised themes of human rights abuses, starvation, rule of law and democracy to appeal to the sympathy of the British public and entice the international community to intervene in the homeland.

There are multiple forces operating within and outside the Vigil that influence members' participation beyond support or criticism of its particular political objectives. To participate, undocumented members in particular, had to overcome their fears both of the Zimbabwean intelligence services, the CIO, and that of the Home Office. Indeed, the former appeared to be paramount for those I spoke to, even though most did not have legal status. In all of my visits, Vigil coordinators would ask members to pose for pictures, and took turns to grab *The Zimbabwean* newspaper to see if their photos make them recognizable.

Within the Vigil itself, there are those who direct and who have information, those who are listened to and the rest who come for advice. As Itzigsohn (2000: 1146) correctly observes, 'transnational politics reflects the social mobility of certain groups of immigrants abroad, creating new elites.' The Vigil coordinators have an instrumental role, but the political elites as they appeared at this site were the MDC leaders, particularly in relation to asylum seekers, for whom they acted in some ways as gatekeeper. They supply letters to authenticate the validity of Vigil members who are seeking or intending to seek political asylum. Whether through choice or necessity, many women come to the Vigil to have their immigration problems sorted out. This explains the importance of the weekly register as asylum seekers come to the Vigil 'to be seen and counted', as one Vigil participant put it to me.

In the eyes of some critics, the role the Vigil is playing in the asylum process is problematic, but this is not the only criticism I heard. Some were also uneasy about the prominence of white Zimbabweans in coordinating and organising Vigil activities, given their conspicuous absence from grassroots and national political activities in the homeland (particularly prior to the formation of the MDC, in which they did play a part). The beating of drums makes them African, perhaps to distinguish themselves from other white people in Britain. I met former white farmers, who had lost their farms and hoped a change of government would be in their interests; they had dual nationality. In contrast, the black Zimbabweans I met at the Vigil were undocumented migrants, and one such, Kennedy, articulated the problematic divide he felt: 'if you go to the Vigil, you will discover that the majority of every white person there has had himself a farm taken over by the government or a relative has been affected. That's why they come to the Vigil, it's personal, for them it's personal not national.' This view illuminates the racial tensions within the diaspora and antagonism towards even those white Zimbabweans who are genuine political activists. Kennedy's broader perspective echoed and fed into a particular way of looking at the Zimbabwean crisis that borrowed heavily from Mugabe's rhetoric of Britain versus Zimbabwe, whites versus blacks.

The dividing line between the Vigil activists and the MDC branch is rather thin if not difficult to disentangle, given that the Vigil coordinators sometimes wore MDC t-shirts and sell MDC regalia. For many Vigil participants, the assumption seemed to be that freedom comes through and with the MDC. The MDC has always appealed for financial assistance from those living in the diaspora. Unlike my other research sites such as the *gochi-gochi*, the pub and diaspora churches, where members have divergent political views and opinions, the Vigil members expressed an homogeneous response to crises in the homeland and perceived the opposition party, the MDC, as the only legitimate and democratic force capable of changing the political and economic fortunes of Zimbabwe.

Yet the view of Vigil members is not representative of the attitude of Zimbabweans in the diaspora towards homeland politics. The discussions at the *gochi-gochi* in Birmingham and the pub in Coventry reveal a broader spectrum of opinion, different types of engagement and motivations for participating or disengaging with transnational diaspora politics. Here I briefly elaborate the insights these social gatherings can provide, starting with the *gochi-gochi*. The *gochi gochi* venue appears well known among Zimbabweans in Birmingham and beyond, and both Ndebele and Shona travel to frequent it, but there is also an underground quality to it. The Jamaican pub that hosts it has a dual purpose, serving both to introduce and conceal *gochi-gochi*. It introduces Zimbabweans to the black community in Birmingham and the wider public as well as shielding them from the risk of immigration raids by the Home Office. *Gochi-gochi* is located in the backyard of a Jamaican pub in an African and Asian neighbourhood of Birmingham. The Zimbabwean owner, Ndunduzo, came to the UK in 1997, is in his late thirties, married with two children. He was a mechanical engineer in Zimbabwe, but now runs the *gochi-gochi* as his source of income and refers to himself as 'marketing adviser' for Zimbabwean musicians such as Oliver Mutukudzi and Aleck Macheso. Ndunduzo first started the idea of a *gochi-gochi* in a disused shop, operating it more like a *shebeen*.

There are no signs outside the Jamaican pub describing the Zimbabwean *gochi-gochi*, yet it is central to the pub's survival. Ndunduzo does not sell beer to his customers; he simply plays Zimbabwean music *miseve* (sungura) and cooks *sadza* (hard porridge) and roast *bruvosi* (meat sausage) for his customers, charging £7 per plate (like other nostalgic Zimbabweans, he travels considerable distance to buy his meat from a British Indian butcher in Milton Keynes who specialises in African products). During winter, the turnout is low but Ndunduzo would not go home with less than £120. Ndunduzo does not have a license as his activities are construed as part of the Jamaican pub, and he does not pay rental to the Jamaican owner as his mainly Zimbabwean customers buy beer in the pub. On one of my visits, the table was littered with flyers about Zimbabwean and South Africa artists coming to perform in the UK. The physical environment is not prosperous – old chairs, a scruffy floor and broken windows – but the *gochi-gochi* can evoke 'home' through music, food, beer, dance, language and memories. It is not a political site as such, but it is a place where communities are formed and motivations for various forms of involvement are debated.

Many Zimbabweans frequent *gochi-gochi*, both Shona and Ndebele, men and women, and people of different political persuasions. It has become a popular venue for birthday parties and baby showers. Ndunduzo explained *gochi gochi's* appeal, 'everyone has that longing for the homeland. People would imagine themselves roasting meat kwaMereki, kwaMushandirapamwe, kuMabvuku – this place acts as a memory for those places back home.' The *gochi-gochi* does not peddle a particular strand of politics, and in relation to the memory of the male Zimbabwean spaces it invokes, it is also more open to women. I met 'visible' diaspora opposition political activists there as well as members of the 'epistemic' opposition community, such as Farai, one of those banned from returning to Zimbabwe for his role in setting up Radio SW Africa. But I also met ZANU PF supporters and Ndunduzo himself tried to cater to all as Zimbabweans, including by organising a celebration of Zimbabwe's Independence Day, which met with diverse reactions from some patrons: 'Normally we hold Independence Day celebrations; however some tend to personalise it saying we are from MDC and we aren't free. I say no to this because we were free in 1980 and that is why we are celebrating our freedom from colonialists'.

As a social arena where politics is openly discussed, the *gochi-gochi* could provide further insight into transnational diaspora politics: people debated their justifications for their own stance of activism or disillusion, making and remaking political opinions and strategies through conversation with others. One of the patrons, Prosper, spoke to me about his support for ZANU PF, justified less in terms of agreement with its actions, than through the observation that the ruling party was where power lay as well as disillusion with the factionalism of the opposition. Prosper, who came to Britain in 1998 to work in the telecommunications industry, explained to me:

> I am pro-Zanu (PF) because I believe that if anybody wants to make change in Zimbabwe it has to be within Zanu (PF). To be honest with you, people are saying Mugabe made good thing by making the unity accord with PF-Zapu. That's not true, the hero is Nkomo. He came and joined Zanu (PF), and made changes within. In Zimbabwe, if you want to change things you change things in Zanu (PF) and not in any political party, forget it. Right now, what is the opposition doing? They are fighting within, some for Tsvangirai and others for Ncube.

Politics is also the favourite subject in the Zimbabwean pub in Coventry, and you likewise hear people arguing about MDC and ZANU PF; the state of the economy in Zimbabwe; the land issue; the exchange rate; immigration raids. I made twenty separate visits to the Zimbabwean pub in Coventry, which also attracts Zimbabwean men (I rarely saw women there) from a broad swathe of the West Midlands, though it has a typical English name, suggesting no connection to Zimbabwe. The pub is owned by a Swaziland-born British woman who sells Zimbabwean beer (Zambezi, Castle Lager, Bohlingers and Lion). The Zimbabwean patrons of the pub were Ndebele and Shona, documented and undocumented, and held all types of political opinion, from those who praised Mugabe for 'correctly articulating the problem of land issue', to those who accused him of destroying the country and the likes of Steven, who explained, 'both Zanu (PF) and MDC are hopeless. What we want in Zimbabwe is none of them; we want professional people who have a heart for the people.' What the patrons shared was their age (most were young men from their early twenties to early forties) and their style – to fit in, one would have to wear baggy jeans, dreadlocks and earrings; American black artists seem to have inspired these black Zimbabweans in their lifestyle – what music they listen to and how they dress, perhaps not so much what they drink. You rarely find white or Asian people in the pub although the pub is located in an Asian-dominated locality.

The pub is also a place for gossip; that someone has bought a house back home; that someone has changed his phone card; internet chat rooms; the stressful life of work in Britain. In the background, the disc jockey plays African music, mainly from Zimbabwe and South Africa. To the right side of the counter is an American pool table, a game Zimbabweans are not used to, which was obvious in the way they struggled to play the game. *Gochi-gochi* and the pub provide an opportunity for members to celebrate 'the glorious old days in the homeland' and inescapably conversations also engaged political questions on the cause of their predicament in Britain. To apply the classification I have espoused in the beginning of this chapter, *gochi-gochi* and the pub can be said to embody members from all the different diaspora categories – the visible, epistemic, dormant and even the silent diaspora. Whereas Zimbabweans I met in Birmingham were proud of their Zimbabwean-ness, in Coventry they were more inclined to express shame and to try to hide their identity: it was in Coventry that I found Zimbabweans most inclined to try to pose as South African or Jamaicans. It is unclear why this was so, but those without papers were particularly insecure during the time of my visits to the pub, due to high profile Home Office raids on the Walker Crisp factory where many worked, which may have contributed to the prominence of such claims.

These social haunts for Zimbabweans in Britain's large multicultural cities provide contexts for relatively open engagement in diasporic social and political activities that are very different from the patterns of socialisation in Wigan, where the Zimbabwean community is comprised of refugees and asylum-seekers who are isolated and stand out markedly from the local community. Along with other African refugees, they are a focus for the wrath of the local people as they are viewed as strangers who have come to 'dilute' a largely white, working-class community and stretch out its resources. Disturbing stories of racist attacks and abuse that the Zimbabwean community and other refugee communities have had to endure in this part of the country has forced them to form a closely bonded community. In the homeland and in some diasporic sites, ethnicity tends to divide Zimbabweans but in Wigan, Zimbabweans come together across these cleavages. The unique characteristic of Zimbabweans in Wigan is group solidarity despite internal differences on the basis of ethnicity, gender and class.

Nothing in the respondents' homes would give away that they come from Zimbabwe. There were no symbols of their place of origin hanging on the walls. Upon close inquiry, I realised that artefacts like Zimbabwean t-shirts, national flags, or anything that points to being Zimbabwean were hidden. However, they listened to music from the homeland, borrowed each other's homeland soap operas, drama and video cassettes (Mukadota family and Gringo – Zimbabwean TV dramas of the early1980s and 1990s respectively – were particularly popular). Music videos of Zimbabwean gospel artists were also among some of the treasured symbols. In fact, a market for these homeland products has been created with some Zimbabweans making extra copies of these products and selling them for £5.

While the dominant white community constructs them as outsiders and aliens, the Zimbabweans in Wigan have found a sense of belonging and welcome in the local Methodist church. Against this feeling of rejection and being unwanted, the Zimbabwean community perceive race as a defining characteristic of their exclusion and lack of social and political participation in public diasporic activities.

None of those I met in Wigan expressed an interest in the subject of Zimbabwean politics. Asked if they participate in diaspora politics Hlangani exclaimed, 'No, no!' although he had heard about the Vigil in London and MDC meetings in Manchester. Similarly, Tonderai laughs and says 'we don't even think about it'. Kudakwashe said she has 'no time for it.' The life of the Zimbabweans in Wigan can be summarised as a triangular routine, that is, home, work and the local Methodist church, because of the fear of racial violence on the streets. Although most I spoke to were refugees with documented status, they wanted to remain dormant because of harsh external conditions. By contrast, undocumented migrants in Birmingham, Coventry or London are less isolated and many have a sense of belonging to the broader local community. In relation to other research sites, Wigan has peculiar conditions of isolation and racism that has made participation in diasporic politics dangerous.

The Nature of Transnational Diaspora Politics

The vignettes of the various ethnographic sites have, I hope, thrown some light both on the diverse forms of engagement, and different motives for participating or withdrawing in transnational diaspora politics. But the decisions people make and their reflections on their relationship with the homeland and with Britain also need to be cast within the broader, uneven relationship that exists between the diaspora and the homeland, and the state policies promoted by the Zimbabwean government. Below I highlight the important role of the homeland government in shaping diaspora politics before highlighting the main roles and motivations for transnational diaspora politics expressed by my respondents: mobilising funds for the MDC, creating alternative democratic space and achieving legal status in Britain.

From the year 2000, the Zimbabwean government's attitude towards its diaspora was clearly discernible: it was treated as anti-ZANU PF and unpatriotic. Mugabe, driven by a narrow nationalist ideology, led an onslaught attacking the West for their neo-imperial ambition, excluding those with dual citizenship and targeting those deemed disloyal. Yet it has also tried to raise money through the diaspora, through Homelink and the Diaspora Housing Scheme, launched in 2004 by Governor of the Reserve Bank, Gideon Gono who travelled to the UK, the US and Australia encouraging the diaspora to send money through these government schemes.[6] These initiatives can be seen as an effort to redefine its relationship with its diaspora and led to high expectations in the diaspora that Zimbabweans abroad may be allowed to vote in the 2005 parliamentary and presidential elections. Indeed, when the government rejected any moves to allow its diaspora to vote, the Diaspora Vote Action Group petitioned the Supreme Court to force the government to allow them the right to vote (Maphosa 2005).

These governmental positions – the diaspora as a source of capital but as comprised of unpatriotic citizens contaminated by western democracies – have had important effects on attitudes within the diaspora, particularly the latter claim. Grace, for example, who operated a Safari Guide in Zimbabwe which was taken over by the government during the Fast Track land reform and came to Britain with her husband in 2000 regards participation in diaspora politics as problematic because 'the government at large presents those of us who do speak out as traitors sympathetic to the West and enemies of the state'. Equally, Hlangani explains his fear of participating in diaspora politics 'because there are a lot more government agents here in [the] UK'. Both these attitudes and the insight from the vignettes above highlight the need to rethink what has become a truism in diaspora and transnational studies that diaspora communities transcend nation states. As this study illustrates, the fear of government intelligence operatives infiltrating diaspora organisations and determining the behaviour of diaspora members, a constant theme among all of the research participants' narratives, shows how the nation state remains a significant actor in transnational diaspora politics.

Diaspora politics in Britain is not divorced from homeland politics, but rather about augmenting political parties in the homeland, the more prominent political grouping being appendages of opposition political parties or civic organisations in the country of origin. One particularly important role of the diaspora is to mobilise funds for the party in the homeland (despite the fact that the Political Parties Finance Act of 2001 made it a criminal offence for a political party in Zimbabwe to rely on donor funds from abroad). For Blessing, the only viable diaspora political participation is 'the MDC method in which people here are the ones who are sponsoring it back home'. Kennedy agrees that diaspora politics should be about mobilizing 'funds for the party (MDC) instead of trying to splinter political groups that is what Mugabe wants ... ZANU PF wants that, it thrives on divide and rule'. Tapfumanei acknowledges that political meetings in the diaspora are only part of the struggle but 'the real political theatre is in Zimbabwe'. By contrast, Prosper and Tigere, complained that the entire MDC leadership in the UK are just 'opportunists' using donor funds for their personal use. According to Prosper, 'the MDC chairman in the UK has three nightclubs and … has nursing agencies and whatnot. From donor funds'.

Others envisaged a different role for the diaspora in homeland politics, which was not just about raising money but about creating alternative democratic space. Given the harsh laws that undermine the capacity of the opposition or civics to function openly,[7] the role of those in the diaspora was to highlight the problems and issues Zimbabwe is facing to the international community. As Sihle put it 'the lack of a democratic space to manoeuvre as a political party' means diaspora politics is more important than often it appears. According to John, diaspora politics has the potential of working well because 'there are no barriers to stop you from expressing your opinion and to make a difference on the international front which is very important'. Putting Zimbabwe in the global context of preventing world conflicts, Farai explains what the diaspora has achieved so far:

> The international community's most powerful blocks like the UN, IMF, and EU have come to condemn the Zimbabwean government without a gun being fired in the country. You know in Africa many problems have come to the eyes of the western world after people have died, after a genocide. Look at what happened in Rwanda, what happened in Uganda, what happened in Darfur … But in Zimbabwe before things have reached that point, Zimbabweans were able to articulate the troubles and suppressions that they were experiencing. I give credit to people in diaspora for doing that.

This may be tantamount to what Smith (2003: 726) termed the 'transnational or diasporic public sphere', a political space within which members of the 'diaspora operate, inside and outside the state'. The extent of the coverage of the Zimbabwean crisis in the international media demonstrates how both visible and epistemic members of the Zimbabwean diaspora use their positions outside the nation state to influence what is happening within.

From my ethnographic observations and interview material, I would argue that the lack of legal status is an important catalyst, albeit not the only one, for the development of transnational diaspora politics among Zimbabweans in Britain. Kennedy explains, 'we have certain individuals who were known ZANU PF members but when they come here they want to claim asylum but at the same time we have genuine MDC members who are genuine political activists.' Another example comes from Tigere, who makes an estimation of the number of Zimbabwean undocumented migrants in country: 'three quarters of people in England don't have papers and these people have claimed political asylum, no matter [whether] they are ZANU PF or MDC'. Lizzy occasionally participates at the Vigil because she has observed that political gatherings in the UK are being 'used by opportunists to generate money for themselves or to gain papers to reside here permanently'. Thus, for the majority of black Zimbabweans, there is a close relationship between a person's immigration status and their participation in political activism. The majority of asylum seekers and refugees participate in transnational diaspora politics in contrast to labour migrants, who tend to be much less involved. As I have elaborated elsewhere (Pasura 2008), colonial history can further augment and motivate for protests over rights: in 2005, more than 400 Zimbabweans protested against forced deportation back home outside the Home Office in London. Arthur Molife, chairperson of the campaign said, 'we suffered under colonialism, and we have the right to be here. We are not going back until we do so voluntarily. We are not dogs, we are not criminals. We want to go back to a free Zimbabwe' (Kimber 2005).

Conclusion

In this chapter, I hope to have shown that transnational diaspora politics has taken various forms, but some of the most important ways it has been envisaged and expressed are in terms of extending homeland politics, particularly by giving financial support to the MDC, as creating an alternative democratic space from the shrinking and repressive conditions in the homeland, and as an avenue for rights to permanent settlement in Britain.

The four-fold classification of the Zimbabwean diaspora as visible members, epistemic members, dormant members and silent members highlighted the different modes of engagement or disengagement, and some of the motivations for doing so. It has also begun to throw light on the characteristics and circumstances of the different types of social actor. I hope to have shown that visible members and epistemic members of the diaspora are the main actors in transnational diaspora politics, and correspond to 'core transnationalism' and intense engagement in political activities in Britain. But participating in political activism in the diaspora should be expanded from those visible in public space to include those engaged in cyberspace political activism. Even dormant members should be included as participants in diaspora politics, as their role suggests 'expanded transnationalism', that is, occasional participation in political activism. Silent members may slip into non-members because either they have fully assimilated and integrated in the host country or because they conjure an alternative identification which does not emphasise connection to the original homeland. Although silent members' activities may be described as diasporic, if they still meet up with other Zimbabweans in social venues, follow Zimbabwean affairs and express nostalgia for their homeland, as we have seen, they may not be transnational if they lack further connection to the original homeland.

Guarnizo, Portes and Haller (2003: 1239) studied political transnationalism among the Salvadoran, Dominican and Colombian in the United States and note that 'it is not the least educated, more marginal, or more recent arrivals who are most prone to retain ties with their home country politics' but the educated and those who have acquired US citizenship. My findings suggest a more complex picture about the degree of involvement in diaspora politics. The majority of visible members who participated regularly in transnational diaspora politics were asylum seekers, marginal in relation to their immigration status. However, the prominence of those with dual nationality (white Zimbabweans) and those granted refugee status means that immigration status on its own was not the sole motivation for engaging in transnational diaspora politics.

Moreover, the role of epistemic members further complicates the picture: using human and social capital acquired both in the homeland and hostland, 'cyber diaspora politics' (Ong 2003: 82) provides a new innovative way of engaging in transnational diaspora politics, perhaps least appreciated in earlier studies of migrants' political transnationalism. The advances in modern technology and communication facilities such as internet, email, faxes, discussion groups and online forums provides an opportunity for diasporas to confront oppressive homeland governments that rely on physical violence and oppressive laws to limit democratic spaces in their countries.

Yet for many Zimbabweans in Britain, the motivation for engaging in transnational diaspora politics was pragmatic and instrumental to other ends. For instance, on gaining refugee status and rights to settlement visible members have displayed the tendency to become dormant. The majority of dormant members in the diaspora are more worried about sending remittances and 'sorting out' their immigration status in other ways than engaging in visible political mobilisation and fear of the CIO and the Home Office act as external pressure dissuading participation. Yet it would be reductive to suggest that the construction of a distinct political identity of opposition at the Vigil is simply an epiphenomenon of the hostland's tight control on immigration, rather it is driven primarily by the organisers' aims of democratising their homeland as well as broader support for this goal. The other sites I explored in this chapter – the *goch-gochi* and the pub – were primarily social, organised around cultural symbols of food, music, beer, language and memory, but in providing quasi public venues for Zimbabweans to meet and relax they were also fostering an arena for open political discussion that in itself was significant. Wigan's peculiar conditions of isolation and racism, in contrast, have worked against participation in transnational diaspora politics, as residents fear any such visible engagement. These different ethnographic sites, and the different circumstances they reveal highlight the varied ways in which the diaspora in Britain is both being made and unmade, and show this diaspora is both shaping as well as being shaped by the political relationship between diaspora and homeland.

Notes

1. For a full discussion about the key features of this transnational diaspora in Britain see Pasura 2008.
2. All names in this study have been changed to protect respondents.
3. Other 'sites' studied for my thesis, but not drawn upon in this article, included religious gatherings, specifically the Forward in Faith Ministries International (or Zimbabwe Assemblies of God, ZAOGA), a globalised Zimbabwean Pentecostal church led by Dr Ezekiel Guti and the Catholic church in Birmingham, where weekly Sunday masses are celebrated in Shona.
4. The following is the campaign message behind Fair Deal: 'Millions of Zimbabweans are going without basic commodities, while Zanu-PF officials kids enjoy western lifestyle. Help us send Mugabe's crooks [sic] kids to their evil fathers.'
5. On the 12 October 2005, the MDC National Executive disagreed on whether or not to participate in senate elections and this resulted in the formation of two antagonistic groups. On the one hand, there was an anti-senate MDC led by Morgan Tsvangirai. On the other hand, there was a pro-senate MDC led by Professor Welshman Ncube. Later, Arthur Mutambara became its leader. Although this division is also manifested in Britain, it is largely the anti-senate MDC led by Morgan Tsvangirai that participates at the Vigil.
6. Homelink was the term coined by the government, representing an amalgamation of official money transfer agencies.
7. The Public Order and Security Act of 2002 require political parties to apply to the police, loyal to Mugabe, for permission to hold meetings.

References

Brubaker, R. 2005. 'The "Diaspora" Diaspora', *Ethnic and Racial Studies* 1, 28: 1–19.

Fair, C.C. 2005. 'Diaspora Involvement in Insurgencies: Insights from the Khalistan and Tamil Eelam Movements', *Nationalism and Ethnic Politics* 1, 11: 125–56.

Guarnizo, L. E., A. Portes and W. Haller. 2003. 'Assimilation and Transnationalism: Determinants of Transnational Political Action among Contemporary Migrants', *American Journal of Sociology* 6, 108: 1211–48.

Guma, L. 2007. 'Australia Deports 8 Students Whose Parents Have Links with Zanu PF' *Swradioafrica.com*. Retrieved 12 September 2007 from http://www.swradioafrica.com/news040907/oz040907.htm

Hagel, P. and P. Peretz. 2005. 'States and Transnational Actors: Who's Influencing Whom? A Case Study in Jewish Diaspora Politics during the Cold War', *European Journal Of International Relations* 4, 11: 467–93.

Itzigsohn, J. 2000. 'Immigration and the Boundaries of Citizenship: The Institutions of Immigrants' Political Transnationalism', *International Migration Review* 4, 34: 1126–54.

Kimber, C. 2005. 'Don't Send Us Back to Mugabe', *Socialist Worker*, 5 February.

King, C. and N. J. Melvin. 1999. 'Diaspora Politics – Ethnic Linkages, Foreign Policy, and Security in Eurasia', *International Security* 3, 24:108–38.

Levitt, P. 2001. 'Transnational Migration: Taking Stock and Future Directions', *Global Networks* 3,1: 195–216.

Maphosa, T. 2005. 'Supreme Court Denies 3.5 Million Zimbabweans Abroad from Voting' *Voice of America*. Retrieved 13 September 2005 from http://www.voanews.com/english/archive/2005-03/2005-03-18-voa18.cfm?CFID=92660981&CFTOKEN=35693264

NewZimbabwe. 2006. 'D-Day for Zimbabwe's SW Radio Africa', *NewZimbabwe.com*. Retrieved 17 October 2006 from http://www.newzimbabwe.com/pages/fm11.12705.html

Ong, A. 2003. 'Cyberpublics and Diaspora Politics among Transnational Chinese', *Interventions* 1, 5: 82–100.

Østergaard-Nielsen, E. 2003a. 'The Democratic Deficit of Diaspora Politics: Turkish Cypriots in Britain and the Cyprus Issue', *Journal of Ethnic and Migration Studies* 4, 29: 683–700.

——. 2003b. 'The Politics of Migrants' Transnational Political Practices', *International Migration Review* 3, 37: 760–86.

Pasura, D. 2008. 'A Fractured Diaspora: Strategies and Identities among Zimbabweans in Britain'. PhD Thesis. University of Warwick

Phimister, I. and B. Raftopoulos. 2004. 'Mugabe, Mbeki & the Politics of Anti-Imperialism', *Review of African Political Economy* 101, 31: 385–400.

Refugee Council. 2005. 'The Right to Work: The Future for Zimbabwean Asylum Seekers in the UK'. Retrieved 27 December 2005 from http://www.refugeecouncil.org.uk/news/2005/Dec05/media_briefing.pdf

Shain, Y. and A. Barth. 2003. 'Diasporas and International Relations Theory', *International Organization* 3, 57: 449–79.

Sheffer, G. 1986. 'A New Field of Study: Modern Diasporas in International Politics'. In G.

——. (ed.). 1986.*Modern Diasporas in International Politics*. London: Croom Helm, pp. 1–15.

——. 2003. *Diaspora Politics: At Home Abroad*. New York: Cambridge University Press.

Smith, R.C. 2003. 'Diasporic Memberships in Historical Perspective: Comparative Insights from the Mexican, Italian and Polish Cases', *International Migration Review* 3, 37: 724–59.

Waldinger, R. and D. Fitzgerald. 2004. 'Transnationalism in Question', *American Journal of Sociology* 5, 109: 1177–95.

5

Diaspora and Dignity: Navigating and Contesting Civic Exclusion in Britain[1]

JoAnn McGregor

The central contradiction between the elite connotations of the term 'diaspora' as it has entered Zimbabwean popular discourse and the realities of life in Britain, is the acute loss of status most Zimbabweans have experienced. Such loss of status has been particularly acute for asylum seekers, failed asylum seekers and those forced into the informal economy to survive. This chapter explores the routes into, circumstances and perspectives of those Zimbabweans who have ended up in irregular legal categories where they lack basic rights, investigating how people coped with insecurity and the assault on their class identities. It contributes to broader debates over responses to restrictionism by discussing how the close historical relationship between Britain and Zimbabwe has shaped individual expectations and reactions to exclusion, as well as enhancing the capacity of Zimbabwean diasporic organizations to challenge it.

I draw on interviews conducted in 2004–5 with more than eighty Zimbabweans in different work and legal situations and on my own engagement with a Zimbabwean asylum-seeker support group (The Zimbabwe Association [ZA]).[2] The chapter elaborates joint action with British-based migrant and asylum-seeker advocacy groups, and involvement in broader social movements aiming to restore dignity to the process of seeking asylum, enhance migrants' rights and contest the narrowing of the civic sphere. The emergence of such movements has been a recent feature of Western countries, following the 'deportation turn' in state policies

(Gibney 2007). It has characteristically involved interesting national and local level civic coalitions among migrants themselves, community-based and other advocacy groups, faith organisations, schools, trades unions, local authorities, individual MPs and others (Nyers 2003; Laubenthal 2007; Rodier 2007).

Lobbying for rights in Britain has been an important aspect of Zimbabwean diaspora politics. There is a significant overlap between Zimbabwean activism on the issue of asylum and the extension of Zimbabwean opposition politics in Britain – a conflation of host and homeland politics that is characteristic of diaspora political engagement (Østergaard-Nielsen 2003). While asylum seekers who are insecure provide key constituencies and have played important roles in pushing the boundaries of the civic sphere in Britain, diasporic associations engaged in such challenges also incorporate activists from a broader social base. Such campaigns typically also have individuals in leadership roles with security and longer histories in Britain – including professionals and others who have made successful asylum claims, exiles from the 1970s or 1980s and white Zimbabweans who have mostly qualified for citizenship in Britain.

By discussing this aspect of diaspora politics and the experiences of exclusion it seeks to challenge, I hope to shed light not only on how people's response to 'being seen as low' and the role diasporic associations can play in maintaining dignity and social status, but also on the role of diasporic associations in promoting civic engagement in Britain. The chapter extends the argument that there need be no contradiction between diasporic positioning and integration in countries of settlement (Werbner 2002; Mercer et al. 2008). Demonstrating social embeddedness is central to anti-deportation campaigns, and for individuals who are insecure, being known and playing public roles within diasporic organisations that have developed broader social and political links in Britain can make the difference between remaining and being removed. Community-based organisations supporting asylum seekers can thus play the dual role of reinforcing diasporic identities and at the same time enhancing inclusion in British society.

A Contracting Civic Sphere: Routes into Irregularity

The structure of opportunity within Britain for Zimbabweans (and other non EU migrants) has changed radically since the late 1990s. While legal routes have opened up and allow a path to full citizenship for those entering via channels for skilled migrants (reinforced in the recent shift to a points-based system), other 'strata' of entry are now reserved for EU citizens (such as unskilled work), access to the asylum system has been radically restricted, and those who find themselves in irregular categories are barred from all prospects of inclusion, stripped of the privileges of citizenship and are liable to detention and enforced removal (Kofman 2002; Morris 2003; May et al. 2007; Bloch and Schuster 2005; Flynn 2005; MRN 2007).

Zimbabweans had been encouraged to come to Britain partly because of the opportunities for work and study, and the ease of entry. Over the structural adjustment decade of the 1990s, the horizons of the Zimbabwean middle classes had begun to shift beyond national borders and beyond the region, especially to Britain as former colonial motherland. Increasing numbers were taking advantage of openings, particularly in feminised occupations such as nursing and social care, and young women formed a significant component of migrants (McGregor 2008a). British-based recruitment agencies were targeting Zimbabwe a source of nurses, social workers and teachers – a process in which colonial legacies were deemed an asset. As a multitude of Zimbabwean transnational social networks to Britain were elaborated, so migration was encouraged by fantasies of a luxurious life: 'I imagined I would live like the Queen, and would return rich after a few months', one young woman (a secretary from Harare) recalled thinking when she left for Britain in 1998 to save for a house and her children's education.[3] Flights could be purchased relatively cheaply in Zimbabwe dollars up to 2002 and there was a degree of flexibility for those arriving speculatively that allowed them to regularise their stay and work (for example, by enrolling for nursing bursaries, or taking out student visas to legitimate employment). By the time state violence became acute in Zimbabwe in 2000, economic migration networks from Zimbabwe were thus in the process of expansion.[4]

Removing such flexibility and enhancing state control over migration from outside the EU has been a major goal of policy-making since the late 1990s (Flynn 2005; MRN 2007). This tightening up has coincided with the period of drastic deterioration in Zimbabwe and the arrival of people seeking not only to work, study and make money, but also to escape violent persecution. The number of Zimbabweans (and others) in irregular circumstances has grown as the structure of opportunity in Britain has become more rigid, and the 'deterence' of stripping irregular migrants of their rights has not functioned as intended, as it has not taken into account transnational calculations related to dramatically deteriorating conditions in Zimbabwe.

The routes Zimbabweans have taken into irregularity in Britain are varied. The new visa requirement Britain imposed in 2002 was particularly important, as, aside from inflating costs, claiming asylum was not a legitimate reason for applying for a visa, such that people began to arrive in Britain on false Malawian and South African passports (Ranger 2005). Many people have not been able to access Zimbabwean passports, either for political reasons, or because the Government of Zimbabwe has lacked ink and paper for printing new passports, and there have been major delays of up to a year even for those reapplying for old passports. Those arriving on false South African and Malawian passports have been in a particularly precarious situation, given the difficult of proving Zimbabwean nationality (even for well-known political activists as discussed below), making them vulnerable to deportation as non-Zimbabweans. Yet most Zimbabweans have not arrived in Britain irregularly: rather they entered through regular routes and became irregular afterwards, by overstaying students' and visitors' visas, or by breaching restrictions on work (visitors are not allowed to work, while students are permitted to work only twenty hours a week). The renewal of student visas has become much more difficult over time, with the aim of excluding 'students' who had registered with bogus colleges simply to legitimate work.

But the asylum system itself has also become a major route into irregularity. It has become much more difficult to make claims, or to appeal negative decisions: access to the system has been constrained by a host of measures, such as the need to make claims within a very short period after arrival in Britain, by reduced availability of legal aid and a dramatic fall in the number of firms taking on asylum cases and reduced rights of appeal. Amnesty International (AI) has condemned the high refusal rate on first applications, arguing that the high success rate of cases brought to appeal is evidence of the extent of flawed decision-making (AI 2004: 25). The Independent Asylum Commission (IAC) report on interim findings commended the government for recent improvements, while also condemning a 'culture of disbelief' among those adjudicating initial claims and describing the treatment of asylum-seekers as 'well below the standards to be expected of a humane and civilised society' (IAC 2008: 3–4). It went on to criticise levels of and access to welfare support within the system, the stigmatising nature of vouchers, and the policy of dispersing asylum-seekers, which has taken people away from support networks, placing them in deprived white neighbourhoods characterised by high unemployment, where they have faced racist abuse (IAC 2008: 25–6). The IAC casts the 'enforced destitution' of refused asylum-seekers as 'indefensible' (IAC 2008: 3). Moves to fast track the process of making a claim through the New Asylum Model (from 2007), have raised further concerns about the likelihood of unsafe decisions, due to the difficulty of accessing supporting documents within that period and the short time frame for appeals amongst other issues (IAC 2008: 25).

Zimbabwean asylum-seekers' experiences from 2000 are testimony to the erosion of the system and enforced criminalisation of people who have been forced to work illegally in order to survive (ZA 2007). A large proportion of the total 26,165 Zimbabwean asylum claims made between 2000 and the first quarter of 2009 were made in the period 2000–2 (10,260 claims). There were particularly large numbers in 2002 (7,695 claims), when Zimbabwe topped the chart of asylum seeking nations in Britain (Home Office Quarterly Asylum Statistics 2000–8).[5] But the visa requirement imposed in November of that year drastically reduced the numbers, such that claims in 2003 were less than half those in 2002.[6] Moreover, claims after that date were increasingly made not at airports by individuals coming directly from Zimbabwe, but within Britain, by individuals already in the country.[7] After 2002, it appears that deteriorating conditions in Zimbabwe could translate much less readily into movement to Britain, and the deepening humanitarian crisis and mass displacements thereafter were largely contained within the region and neighbouring countries (ZA 2007). There were only slightly elevated claims following Operation Murambatsvina in 2005, while the surge in claims following the acute violence of 2008 has been overwhelmingly from individuals already living in Britain rather than new arrivals from Zimbabwe.

During the period 2000–2, when just under half of all Zimbabwean asylum claims in Britain were made, the system was 'overloaded to bursting point and competent legal representatives were in short supply' particularly for the large numbers who ended up in detention centres because they lacked contacts in Britain who could provide surety for bail (ZA 2007). Unscrupulous private firms exploited ignorance about legal aid to charge as much as £800 per case while failing to provide basic representation (ZA 2007). The Home Office 'country guidance report' used at the time to guide the adjudication of claims was inaccurate and misleading, and was subsequently discredited, but it contributed to a large number of unsafe decisions in the period it was used (Ranger 2005). Asylum-seeker support groups are still 'struggling to help people whose cases were dismissed during that period', and the delays have caused 'much suffering' (ZA 2007). The Home Office aims to hear such outstanding 'legacy cases' from this period by 2011, but for some, this will mean having spent up to eleven years living in Britain in fear of deportation and without basic rights. Many have been circulating between detention centres and prisons, having been arrested for offences such as working illegally or using false documents before being transferred to immigration removal centres at the end of their sentences: a significant number have spent more than 300 days in detention (ZA 2007). The Haslar detention centre Visitors Group recently raised concern about Zimbabweans being held, including one individual who had already served a nine month prison sentence and served a further two and a half years in detention centres (Haslar Visitors Group 2008). Another such case – 'LP' – is described by Zimbabwe Association as a 'documented torture victim' who was interviewed while still traumatised and with little understanding of the legal ramifications of his comments': had he received appropriate legal advice at this initial stage the case might have been quickly resolved in 2003, but instead, he has 'had to face numerous court hearings, has been detained, faced with removal more than once as his case hinges on disputed nationality, and his case is still ongoing' (ZA 2007). The ZA submission to the IAC provides further examples of de facto refugees being refused recognition, such as 'RM' who gave the correct answer to a test on knowledge of MDC politicians, by accurately naming the shadow minister of education, yet the interviewer recorded the answer as incorrect on the grounds that it should have been Aeneas Chigwedere, who was then Minister of Education. The case is still on-going five years later (ZA 2007).

Aside from those trapped within the asylum system, there are significant numbers of failed asylum seekers still living in Britain, as refusal rates have been high throughout the period since 2000: in late 2007 refusal rates on first claims ran at seventy-four per cent.[8] Many claims that are accepted are not accorded full recognition as refugees, but are rather granted various types of temporary leave to remain (on the 'fractioning' of statuses all of which confer fewer rights than full refugee status, see Zetter 2007). As deportations to Zimbabwe have been suspended for the greater part of the period between 2002–9 (due to legal challenges discussed below), so the pool of irregular migrants from Zimbabwe includes large numbers of failed asylum seekers, among whom are likely to be significant numbers of de facto refugees.

This erosion of asylum has been combined with attempts to restrict access to unskilled jobs for those outside the EU. The largescale migration from the new EU Accession states to Britain from 2004 (amounting to as many as 500,000 people in the first six months) enhanced competition for unskilled work. Zimbabweans described how employers suddenly began asking to see papers and agencies with a history of recruiting Zimbabweans shifted to the use of Eastern European workers[9] (on competition between EU/non-EU migrants, see also McIlwaine et al. 2006). The effects of this competition seem likely to have reinforced the importance of Zimbabwean employers, and further squeezed Zimbabweans without papers into niches where they had already established a reputation, such as in care, where language initially seems to have proved a disadvantage to Poles, Lithuanians and others (McGregor 2007). The gender dimension to polarised opportunities in Britain has probably also become more acute in this process: many of the female nurses and carers I interviewed complained of what they perceived as the acute 'shortage of quality Zimbabwean men' in Britain,[10] sometimes naturalising the 'uselessness' of their male compatriots unable to find work or gain stability.

As a result of these changes in state migration policy, increasing numbers of Zimbabweans have found themselves in irregular circumstances – they are legally resident in Britain (given the suspension of deportations) but lack rights to work or to welfare, and have thus continued to swell the ranks of Britain's informal workforce. As Williams and Winderbank have shown, illegal work is 'normal' in many sectors of the economy, particularly in subcontracted service markets (Williams and Windebank 1998; Anderson and Rogaly 2005). This is not just attributable to the 'supply' of irregular migrants looking for work, but also to the 'demand' created employers' interests and encouragement through state policies (Samers 2005; Jordan and Duvell 2002). Over the period 2000–7 there was little effort invested in targeting employers of illegal immigrants (only thirty-seven employers were fined), while the new civil penalty regime introduced in early 2008 has been criticised as 'a poor instrument for tackling exploitation of migrants workers' (MRN 2008: 2). The principle effects have been 'to weaken the position of migrants in the labour force and to strengthen the hand of employers who would wish to take advantage of this position': it has been implemented in a discriminatory manner, by targeting ethnic minority businesses (particularly Chinese- and Turkish-run), and has had a particularly negative impact on the capacity for undocumented migrants with permission to remain to secure work, enhancing the risk of destitution (MRN 2008: 2).

Zimbabweans (and others) forced to survive by working irregularly live on the margins of state protection: they occupy legal 'states of exception', where normal rights are suspended (McGregor 2008, Zylinska, 2005). People designated illegal migrants have an acute awareness of dehumanisation, of their potential exploitation and exposure to bodily risk. As I have argued elsewhere, the notion of abjection can throw light on the ways the experience their circumstances – abjection being defined as a forceful and dehumanising act of exclusion, in which those expelled are rendered disgraced and shamed, and accorded purely negative value (McGregor 2008; Nyers 2003). Yet, in discussing the ways in which Zimbabweans in this situation have coped with this exclusion, sought to maintain their dignity and mounted public challenges, it is important to capture the agency and diverse circumstances of those with irregular legal status, and to avoid imputing the abject with the qualities of victimhood implied by their position. Nyers writes against such slippage by using the conjuncture 'abject cosmopolitanism' – through which he explores irregular migrants' political agency as expressed by participation in anti-deportation and pro-regularisation campaigns (Nyers 2003 and 2006).

Navigating Legal and Social Exclusion

The popular Zimbabwean discourses surrounding movement to Britain are an appropriate place to start this discussion of experiences, as they cast the process of moving to the UK in contradictory terms, both as a mark of status in itself but also as subjection to dirty, demeaning, feminised work. This is captured in jokes that associate Zimbabweans in the UK with cleaning and carework, caricaturing them as 'BBC' (British Bottom Cleaners), 'bum technicians' or 'madot.com' (dot implying dirt; and dot. com invoking the dependence of the diaspora on internet connections) (Mbiba 2004; McGregor 2007). These jokes, which function partly as a putdown by those still at home, deploy the language of loss of status, even of abjection. The jokes were elaborated in interviews with accounts of the shame and humiliation associated with being 'seen as low', the disgust of handling dirt and for men, of emasculation. Women described weeping when they got to work before being able to compose themselves, or of how relatives had tried to hide the realities of their work, such that arriving in Britain and being faced with menial work was a huge shock (McGregor 2007).[11]

People often described this as one dimension of their experience even if they also felt satisfaction in helping others, made friendships with colleagues, or had positively opted for carework, given its flexibility and the possibilities of relatively high earnings. A live-in careworker with one of the better agencies can earn £20,000 per annum or more, which translates into a fortune back in Zimbabwe: one careworker talked at length about her disgust at length whilst also emphasizing how she 'didn't think of the dirt at month end' and described her MSc studies in International Development and the construction plans for her new ten bedroom house in Zimbabwe with animation.[12] Indeed, as Zimbabwean inflation rose exponentially, so the transnational discrepancy became more and more pronounced. The phenomenon of the 'BBC' was widely discussed in the press in Zimbabwe, and Mugabe used it to sneer at those 'who will be thrown out and return crippled in wheelchairs, clutching their pounds'.[13] Yet the idea of the BBC also conveys much about postcoloniality: about the way people looked up to the former colonial motherland only to be faced with the crude bodily realities of servile work, with overtones of colonial master/servant relations. It also illuminates the dishonesty and difficulties in communication between those in the diaspora and those at home (ma.dot.com, in particular), by the disjuncture between the status attached to regular use of modern communications' technologies and dealing with dirt.

The notion of broken postcolonial responsibilities is particularly important in explaining reactions to exclusionary treatment in Britain, enmeshed with an emphasis on race and experiences of racism. Some people argued that the history of colonisation in itself conferred a moral right to be in Britain (Pasura 2008). Moreover the policy of privileging EU migrants over Commonwealth migrants in unskilled work was widely discussed as a betrayal, and as evidence of racism (cf McIlwaine et al. 2006:

19–20). 'We are your children' is a phrase I heard repeatedly in describing postcolonial relationships and responsibilities dishonoured, 'we were taught your history, taught to look up to you, to want to be like you'.[14] 'What makes me feel angry and very bitter here, we're in the UK because of our history, because of the commonwealth, we were shaped by that history, but now preferential treatment is going to Europeans over Africans, it's racism'.[15] 'Now Zimbabwe has been expelled from the commonwealth' another argued 'we have no claim, we are strangers'.[16]

For some, informality in itself constituted an assault on status. There were diverse reactions, but for many of those coming from Zimbabwe's professions, who had little prior engagement with the informal economy, the experience of taking on false names and papers, or posing as someone else, was very stressful. Many were ill-prepared for negotiating the world of bogus agencies and colleges or unscrupulous lawyers and employers – their experiences were of being ripped off and exploited in their first months in Britain (by other Zimbabweans, by a range of British employers, as well as other longer established African and other migrants).

The pervasive fear of deportation is, of course, centrally important to those without papers, particularly for those who have experienced violence at the hands of the Zimbabwean state. One woman for example, who had come to Britain for economic reasons nonetheless recalled how fear had engulfed her: 'I was very scared those first few months, I didn't want to show my face, all the time I was worrying about being arrested, what would I say, what would happen. My heart would be thumping when I saw a policeman in the street, what can you say when you know you're illegal? I really wanted to be legal, I hate that illegal life, you're always worried, always afraid. People were telling me other Zimbabweans will inform on you, so I didn't want to meet or talk to others ... then one I knew was deported, so those rumours were true, I heard that £500 is what the informers are paid for that information'.[17] A man and his wife (former teachers, working irregularly in care) pointed out how fearful it was to be aware of living beyond state protection: 'you don't have your basic rights without the papers, people treat you like trash, trample on you, you're not a human being, push you around – who will protect or stop them from killing you?'.[18] Given that lack of papers acted as an insurmountable 'brick wall' blocking advancement in Britain, some found ways to accommodate the prospect of deportation into their strategy for remittances, making sure not to accumulate property and finance in the UK that might be lost: 'I had a friend who is worried about the deportations' one carer described, 'she's waiting for the call from immigration. So what she did, she packed all her property, and shipped it back home with a removal company. Now she has a small suitcase on top of the cupboard, it's ready packed. So when immigration come to the door, she will grab the suitcase and she is prepared, all her property is already transferred back home. When they come, she'll go and just get a free ticket home'.[19]

For some of those who fled violence in Zimbabwe, such insecurity has proved too much, and has cost people their lives. The six Zimbabweans who feature among the recent suicides of asylum-seekers and detainees documented by the Institute of Race Relations are indicative: they include Kwanele Siziba, aged 27, who fell 150 feet to her death, when bailiffs whom she believed were immigration officers threatened to kick in the door; Forsina Makoni, an elderly seventy-nine year old woman who set herself alight after her asylum claim was rejected; Edmore Ngwenya, a twenty-six year old failed asylum seeker facing deportation, who died after jumping into a canal. A further two suicides were the result of lack of access to medical treatment; Lizwane Ndlovu, a failed asylum seeker, who died from TB in hospital two weeks after being released from detention following a hunger strike, and Star Engwenya, a destitute and mentally unstable asylum seeker, who had failed to access treatment after suffering a stroke (Institute of Race Relations 2006: 6, 13, 22, 23). This is but a small number of the suicides and other deaths that have actually occurred, which have had ramifications way beyond those immediately involved, as community organisations and faith groups have stepped in to help – to offer emotional support to those bereaved, to deal with authorities in place of relatives/ friends lacking papers themselves and to help raise funds to repatriate bodies (at a cost of around £3000 per body, Mbiba 2006 and this volume; see also ZimCare 2007). The head of a network of Brethren in Christ house churches in the Midlands described being asked to intervene personally in five suicide cases.[20] It is unlikely that this is exceptional.

But the experience of living and working irregularly in Britain has not turned those occupying them into a universally victimised 'abject class' (McGregor 2008). Migration to Britain has worked for some of those without papers, despite the insecurity and other costs: in transnational and transgenerational terms, it has often been a successful strategy. For some, it has allowed for the reproduction of elite or middle class status, or for social mobility, enabling the accumulation of high status assets, new qualifications and good education for children – as well as preventing the starvation of those at home. One illustration can be provided by a mother from a politically well connected family with property in the former white suburbs who left Zimbabwe in 2001 to fund the higher education of her sons and worked informally under a false name as a live-in carer following a failed asylum claim made on arrival. By the middle of 2007, her eldest son was in the final stages of his accountancy qualifications in the UK, and she had successfully completed an Open University BSc in Business Studies. When her son secures his first professional job, she plans to retire to Zimbabwe to rest, as her son will be in a position to take over maintaining the family's elite status. She envisages him assuming the greater part of the burden of remitting funds to support those back in Zimbabwe and securing his siblings' education. This is far from an isolated example.[21]

Given the difficulty of mobilising to counteract exploitation for those without documents, there have been informal efforts to marginalise unscrupulous employers. When one new Zimbabwean employment agency was set up in 2004 (providing temporary labour in care, cleaning, catering and security), the managing director (a former opposition activist with refugee status) described his motivation as being to assist those in a situation of bonded labour in the only way he felt possible – by providing work for compatriots himself. By offering better terms of employment, the agency was able to take over the workforce of another Zimbabwean agency with a notorious reputation for underpaying and bonding irregular workers, whose boss was infamous for boasting about the property and girlfriends he had accumulated in the UK.[22] After three years, the agency had been so successful that the directors were planning to extend business operations in South Africa.

While some employers of irregular migrants have undoubtedly 'taken advantage', others are thus providing support and minimal security in a context where the state does not. Some of those working without papers referred to the agencies that employed them not only as a 'foot in the door', but also as a 'protection of some sort', and 'safety net'. One such – a former banker turned failed asylum-seeker working as a carer – described how it was better to get work with other agencies (rather than with a Zimbabwean agency that underpaid), but felt that the Zimbabwean agency was useful as a last resort 'if you face a problem [with your employer] you can go back, at least you have your own people there, they feel for you, they're not strict with papers, they identify with you'.[23]

While many people regarded doing informal work as an acute challenge to the status they had enjoyed at home, there was also enormous resistance to being defined by unskilled work in Britain. Some described doing manual work not as diminishing their own class standing but rather as an encounter with the British class system. As a former university lecturer, briefly an 'overstayer' who found himself lifting boxes in a supermarket warehouse in the UK, explained to me: 'I never thought that I would be doing manual work, but it has been a good experience in some ways, it has opened my mind: now I understand the infamous British class system. I have been teaching Marx all these years, but now I understand what he was talking about!'[24] A careworker felt 'humbled, but we needed that lesson – back home we had that pride, look at how we treated Mozambican and Zambian labourers, we only looked up to South Africans'.[25] Many spoke of themselves as sojourners, joked about doing gap years, or described themselves as observers and critics of British society, such as a pastor (working as a security guard), who felt two things had saved him from going under in Britain – his wife and the training the church had given him in anthropology.[26] As many of those in informal work were also studying, or had aspirations to do so, they defined their stay in Britain by their studies rather than in terms of the work that supported it. As long as doing servile work could be cast in terms of personal and professional uplift, or as a temporary break, even a learning experience, so it could be upheld positively as a means to self advancement, greater knowledge, further qualifications. Metaphors of stepping stones, ladders and the like were frequently used.[27]

Contesting the Boundaries of the Civic Sphere in Britain

Zimbabweans have also mounted public challenges to the civic exclusion they have faced in Britain. These campaigns have contested deportations, sought to uphold asylum-seekers' rights and demanded permission to work and study for those who, by virtue of a moratorium on deportations, are allowed to reside in Britain. In so doing they have joined up with a range of broader British based campaigns: the Trades Union Congress campaign for asylum seekers' 'Right to Work', the London-based campaign 'Strangers into Citizens', or 'Still Human Still Here', a campaign against destitution among asylum-seekers, which is supported by Amnesty International, the Medical Foundation for the Care of Victims of Torture, church and students groups, Refugee Legal Centres, the Immigration Law Practitioners Association and others. Zimbabweans have been well placed to organise by virtue of their unusual embeddedness in Britain, the extent and manner in which the British media has covered the Zimbabwe situation (Willems 2005) and the unusual networks of support to both conservative and liberal establishments, described in the introduction to this volume. In mid 2005, for example, pressure on the British Government to restore the moratorium on removals to Zimbabwe was supported by what the *The Times* described as 'an unusual combination of dissident Labour MPs, the Conservative Party, the Liberal Democrats and media outlets normally anchored at different ends of the ideological spectrum', the Archbishop of Canterbury, Dr Rowan Williams and former Labour leader Lord Kinnock.[28] The possibilities of mobilisation have also benefited enormously from the organisational experience and motivation of a highly educated group, many of whom have histories of civic and political activism.

As Zimbabweans began to arrive in Britain in very large numbers from 2000, so asylum-seeker support and campaign groups mushroomed in the UK's major cities, at the same time as other diasporic associations were being formed – such as Zimbabwean church fellowships, MDC committees and the vigil outside the Zimbabwe Embassy in London was established (McGregor 2009, Pasura this volume). Diasporic mutual aid associations filled a range of crucial social, emotional and practical needs. From the outset there has been a notable degree of overlap between these mutual aid and political organisations despite their explicitly different primary functions; individual activists have also commonly played leadership roles in more than one sort of organisation. The conflation of the politics of asylum with homeland politics has been a major source of controversy, widely cast in negative terms by Zimbabwean political commentators, as contributing to the internal problems of the MDC in the diaspora. Alex Magaisa (2006), for example, summarises the contradictions of diaspora politics in Britain in the following terms:

> In most cases, unscrupulous individuals have jumped on board for personal gain only to disappear into thin air once their interests had been satisfied. In desperation some individuals have also taken advantage of the situation, joining political organisations in the diaspora, not to play any significant role but to gain the necessary labels of political involvement for purposes of seeking asylum in their host countries. Political divisions at home are replicated in the diaspora causing confusion and most well-meaning individuals lose interest and retreat to the margins. But others are genuine in their desire to fight for political change and are often let down by those that take unfair advantage. They organise rallies and meetings and show immense solidarity.

A former member of the MDC UK executive (who has subsequently withdrawn from politics) argued similarly 'The asylum issue destabilised MDC politics here – people get involved just so that they can be 'known' so they'll be jostling for positions, just to say I'm a branch or district chair. Just for the position, not because they're going to be lobbying effectively ...'[29]

Other asylum-related issues that have proved controversial include disputes within the MDC over authority to write letters supporting asylum claims, as well as allegations against prominent diaspora MDC politicians of 'taking advantage' in various ways, such as by selling support letters, and the exposure of scams involving Zimbabwean refugee support groups assisting ZANU PF elites to gain entry through the asylum system. The 'Zimbabwe Community in the UK', founded by Albert and Grace Matapo in Birmingham, for example, was alleged to have assisted the asylum claims of four close relatives of Cabinet Ministers subject to travel sanctions, to have charged £1000 for false documents and coaching on how to manipulate the asylum system through 'lying to the white man'.[30]

Yet this negative characterisation of the effects of the imbrication of the politics of asylum with homeland politics requires some modification. The discrepancy between the more than 26,000 asylum seekers in Britain (noted above) and the numbers of MDC members in the UK (around 3,000 were claimed in 2006, rising to 4,000 by 2008), while sometimes upheld as a sign of abuse of the asylum system and the fabrication of MDC histories, could equally be interpreted as suggestive of the ways the insecurity associated with making an asylum claim has undermined public diaspora political engagement. Secondly, the cause of asylum seekers has been a potent means of drawing public and media attention to the abuses of ZANU PF rule and has been used effectively in lobbying and campaigning. As violence in Zimbabwe has been perpetrated overwhelmingly by ZANU PF and the state, focussing on asylum-seekers' persecution had the useful effect of rendering irrelevant the acute internal problems faced by the opposition, which split into two competing factions from late 2005, lacked a stable leadership in Britain, and whose fractious meetings had a reputation for provoking disengagement (McGregor 2009).

Zimbabwean asylum seeker support groups have achieved some notable successes – in campaigning and assisting in legal challenges to deportations to Zimbabwe, as well as providing invaluable help to those trying to navigate the pitfalls of a rapidly changing asylum system. The Zimbabwe Association (ZA) was one of the first such groups to be formed, in 2001 and is now a registered charity. Its volunteers (mostly themselves asylum-seekers or former asylum-seekers) have visited detention centres, supplied phone cards and other support to detainees, provided surety for bail and built a network of contacts with reputable lawyers, organisations such as Bail for Immigration Detainees (BID), and those providing counselling and other services for asylum-seekers. The ZA has developed a network of press, legal, political and church contacts for lobbying. In January 2002, as a result of extensive lobbying on the part of ZA and others (including BZS President Prof. Terence Ranger) deportations were suspended. When the Home office resumed removals in late 2004, the ZA supplied evidence of torture and other forms of abuse suffered by removed Zimbabweans on return to Harare, which was used by the Refugee Legal Centre (RLC) in a successful legal challenge in October 2005 (and in further litigation in subsequent years).[31] Outside London, other groups have been active: in Leeds for example, support for detained Zimbabwean hunger strikers protesting their removal in summer 2005 came from the Zimbabwe Community in Leeds (the head of which also held an executive position in the MDC-UK (Tsvangirai)) who mobilised a local coalition including the Refugee Council (Yorkshire and Humberside), Leeds No Borders, DeletetheBorder.Org and the local MP.[32] The scope of such support coalitions can be extensive: the campaign against the deportation of one Zimbabwean community activist in January 2009, for example, involved not only his lawyers and six different Zimbabwean diaspora groups, but also Westminster Abbey, London Citizens, the Refugee Council, Amnesty International, GreenNet, several journalists and newspapers, BID, a considerable number of individual MPs and Lords from the three main British political parties, the Archbishop of York, the Community of Holy Fire and a Facebook Group.[33]

These community-based groups are interesting not only for their links with a range of British-based civic and political groups, but also for the nature of the networks they have built among Zimbabweans, which have often crossed the ethnic, racial, class and other divisions commonly widened in diasporic contexts. The ZA, for example, brings together recent asylum seekers, refugees with status, white Zimbabweans who had left before the crisis, British 'friends of Zimbabwe' with longstanding histories of engagement dating back before independence. The Zimbabwe Community Campaign to Defend Asylum Seekers (also London-based) is headed by Authur Molife, who describes himself as an 'exile' from the 1970s who 'never accepted independence'. Like a considerable number of others from Matabeleland, he did not return to Zimbabwe in 1980, a decision reinforced when the Zimbabwean security forces caused the death of a close relative in 1982 during the *gukurahundi* conflict. Molife has not taken up full British citizenship, in order not to be declared a non-Zimbabwean: despite accumulating several Masters-level qualifications and a period in professional work for a London borough, he complains of racist exclusion and describes himself as a 'stranger in Britain – I'm just here until things change …'[34]

Yet the politicised environment in which diaspora organisations operate (created by a combination of imported political divides and insecure legal status for many in Britain) has had a profound impact on civics and mutual support organisations and their capacity to mobilise. Civic activists describe the necessity to 'be vigilant' at all times in relation to the activities of the Zimbabwean Central Intelligence Organisation (CIO), emphasise the need to 'vet' volunteers to filter out potential ZANU PF agents, feel 'edgy' about some individuals, and consider themselves less open than they would like to be.[35] Take the following explanations of the difficulties of organising within the diaspora, voiced at the Zimbabwe Open Forum in London in 2005. Sunanda Ray, founder of Zimbabwe Health Training Support, spoke of what she saw as an unwillingness to engage or assist beyond family, partly due to politicised suspicion: 'Zimbabweans here are very focused on looking after themselves and their own families whether here or in Zimbabwe. It is very difficult to organise people to look after others … here we [Zimbabweans] are still sceptical of attempts to work together. People have little to spare and if ever there is a meeting, everyone asks, "Who's paying?" or "Who's supplying the food and drink or transport?" and "Who's an informer?"'[36] Itai Garande of the internet forum TalkZimbabwe.com described ZANU PF agents disrupting a community group: 'In 1999 we tried to set up an organisation in Luton to support Zimbabweans. Bright Matonga was part of that organisation and so was Themba Mliswa; but now we see one of them is Deputy Minister of Information. So there are disruptive elements. It is not easy to organise and we need to be vigilant about who defeats our purpose.'[37] Yvonee Marime, coordinator of the Zimbabwe Womens Network UK put more emphasis on the insecurities of irregularity, created by the abuses of restrictive asylum and migration policies in Britain: 'We have many problems here. The Zimbawean diaspora is rich in skills but we are a divided community – criminalised, detained, unable to work, and suspicious. We are very angry with the British government who force good people to be criminal'.[38]

Exclusion, Dignity and Diaspora Formation

Returning to the effects of British state policy and legal exclusion on diasporic identities and the shaping of the new Zimbabwe diaspora in associational terms, it is clear that there are contradictory trends. On the one hand, any emergent differences created by legal status are cross cut by multiple diasporic networks and a common idea of Zimbabwe as home. The diaspora associations that can bring people together across the divides of legal status, are not only the campaigning and mutual support organisations described above but also churches, burial associations, football clubs, barbeques, weddings, funerals and the like. The mutual support provided by diaspora associational life is important partly because it can provide not only material and practical help, but also connections and a sense of belonging where status is judged within a different frame of reference and not in terms of work in Britain and legal relations to the British state, providing spaces where 'you can feel at home a little bit',[39] and where 'people know where you come from and don't look on you as low'.[40] One church fellowship leader explained: 'we try to provide a space where the stress can come down and where there is some support. Otherwise, without something to turn to people can end up hanging themselves. We pray for each other. Know where you're coming from, that's what I advise. Take whatever you can get and don't argue [as you don't have rights], treat it as a stepping stone to something else'.[41] Nothwithstanding or perhaps because of the background of divisive politics at home, exclusion and division in countries of settlement, there is a striking commitment among diaspora associations to recovering an inclusive interpretation of national community, to upholding and articulating the importance of national unity and pride, which has undergone a huge blow in the course of the conflict, economic catastrophe and movement to often low status work in the UK. Many of the mutual support groups in the British context see 'fostering unity' or 'restoring pride' as a primary concern. Take for example the website of the Zimbabwe Women's Network in the UK, formed in 2003, which declares 'We are organising ourselves to foster unity among Zimbabweans, in particular women: to promote our culture and traditions and to contribute to the welfare of all Zimbabweans in the UK and at home … Pride of identity is important'.[42]

Diaspora organisations are thus important in allowing the public expression of status in contexts where people judge this through transnational calculations and Zimbabwean rather than British social hierarchies. Yet legal status also matters crucially and can be divisive. Some Zimbabweans who are increasingly well embedded in the British context through mortgages and children in British schools, can echo the right wing British tabloid press, by repeating the state's categorical differences, complaining that Zimbabwean asylum seekers are mostly economic migrants rather than political refugees, criticizing their compatriots who try to bend the rules and blaming them for giving all Zimbabweans a bad name. Some deliberately try to avoid Zimbabwean events where they might meet asylum seekers and others without status.[43] 'People will try to bend all the rules. I don't blame the British government,' a group of nurses explained to me, 'they shouldn't be here, and then those who are doing that are making things worse for those of us who are here legitimately'.[44]

The combination of fear and the practicalities of life on the margins of the law for those without papers can also reinforce divisions created by legal status. Many of those without papers deliberately keep a very limited network of friends – out of fear of the Home Office, Zimbabwean politics, informers, or shame. One man who came forward to the Zimbabwe Association for assistance in 2008 after working irregularly in care for six years, said he had been following the advice of his 'agent' who instructed him to lay low and avoid all contact with Zimbabweans.[45] A man with refugee status (a former business man and shopkeeper in Zimbabwe) explained why he had not formed a burial society with his friends, most of whom were in irregular situations, in the following way: 'it's very difficult to organise something like that, most people want it, I wanted it, but to organise a group is very hard. Those societies, you need to meet at weekends, to see each other regularly. But we can't do that, because of the work pattern, and because you find your friends are scattered, they move around, they can be dispersed as asylum seekers, or they'll move to try to find a better opportunity, or their agency will move them, or they'll be worried about deportations, it's very hard. You find that you just can't get together regularly one time a week, which is what you need in those groups'.[46] Another refugee with status (formerly a trainee accountant, but working in a warehouse in the UK to support siblings at university in Zimbabwe) described how friends with irregular status withdrew contact – 'disappeared' - when fear of deportations resumed: 'out of fear, everyone is keeping himself to himself'.[47] Many others described themselves as 'too tired' to go to Zimbabwean churches or other community events.[48] The interviews with those with irregular status were striking for the evidence of ultra-mobility within Britain, for the frequency of double shifts, descriptions of exhaustion and depression, and lack of social engagement beyond work and close family or friends. Yet those who have withdrawn in this way in fear or shame, and are not 'known' to activists have also found it more difficult to mobilise support should they be detained and threatened with deportation.

Conclusion

This chapter aimed to think through the impact of restrictionist trends in British state migration and asylum policy on the shaping of the new Zimbabwean diaspora in the UK, and to discuss the ways Zimbabweans have coped with, circumvented and challenged the indignities of irregular status, and the criminalisation of asylum-seekers. It aimed to highlight the ways in which the unique historic relationship between Britain and Zimbabwe had shaped both the specific expectations of Britain as former colonial motherland, and the heightened sense of betrayal when Zimbabweans were treated as any other stranger. Yet it also tried to show how the same special relationship provided networks and openings for mounting challenges to legal exclusion, which were welcomed by British actors contesting restrictionism and treated as a political opportunity, given the high profile granted by the British media to events in Zimbabwe, and the Foreign Office's consistent condemnation of Mugabe's ZANU PF regime. The result has been a contradictory set of opportunities and exclusions – deportations to Zimbabwe of failed asylum seekers have been suspended for most of the period between 2000 and 2009, but those allowed to remain in Britain as a result of this suspension have not been granted basic rights, such as to work.

The diaspora associations that have sprung up to provide support and assistance to asylum seekers have had to operate in a politicised climate of intra-communal distrust with a constituency that is vulnerable and insecure. The diasporic identity they reinforce is important as a means of preserving dignity, counteracting the acute loss of status many have experienced in Britain. Yet Zimbabwean community-based asylum seeker support groups are notable not for their isolation from the British social and civic sphere, but rather for their engagement and multiple linkages with non-Zimbabwean British-based groups and social movements – a reflection not only of the contemporary politics of asylum in Britain, but of the legacies of a unique historical relationship.

Notes

1. This research was funded by the ESRC, grant number R000220630. Grateful thanks to the Zimbabwe Association, and those who helped facilitate the interviews: Brighton Chireka, Angelous Dube, David Mandiyanyike, Mqondobanzi Nduna Magonya and others who did not wish to be named.
2. Those interviewed were working as carers (32), nurses and teachers (37), in other unskilled work (14), or were themselves employers (managing directors of labour agencies) (5). The majority of the careworkers and unskilled workers were working irregularly, either because they were in the asylum system or had made unsuccessful claims, had overstayed visas or were students working more than twenty hours. I became a member of the Zimbabwe Association in 2001 and trustee in 2007.
3. Interview 57, nurse who trained in the UK after several years working as a carer.
4. The 2001 British census recorded just under 50,000 Zimbabweans in Britain, approximately half of whom were white. It seems likely this figure is below actual numbers. From 2005, the Home Office and IOM began working with estimates of around 200,000 Zimbabweans in Britain (Pasura 2006).
5. Home Office quarterly statistics, available up to the first quarter of 2009 at the time of writing. http://www. rds.homeoffice.gov.uk/rds/.
6. 3280 in 2003, 2045 in 2004, 1070 in 2005, 1625 in 2006, 1770 in 2007, 2630 in 2008, and 2925 in the first quarter of 2009. Home Office quarterly statistics.
7. Home Office statistics show this shift: most applications were made 'at port of entry' rather than in country up to 2003, but thereafter, the balance switched, and applications from those already in Britain have increased while applications at airports have fallen.. The cases brought to the attention of the ZA also appear to bear this out.
8. Home Office quarterly asylum statistics. http://www.homeoffice.gov.uk/rds.
9. Interviews 35–41 (unskilled warehouse workers), 12, 9 (careworkers).
10. E.g., Interviews 57 and 58
11. Interview 27
12. Interview 17. See also Interviews 20 and 54.
13. Interview 80, discussing President Mugabe's interventions in 2004
14. E.g., interviews 49 and 50
15. Teacher, retrained as nurse, Interview 67
16. Interview 73. For accounts of racism in professional and unskilled workplaces, see McGregor 2007 and 2008a.
17. Interview 56.
18. Interviews 10 and 11
19. Interview 32
20. Interview 44
21. Other cases from the interviews include two teachers working as carers likewise supporting their children's secondary/higher education, a former mechanic turned asylum-seeker/manual worker supporting a sibling's studies at the University of Zimbabwe, and a number of others funding their own studies or building themselves houses in Zimbabwe. Interviews 76, 42, 43, 10, 11.

22. Pers comm., October 2004
23. Interview 21
24. Pers comm., November 2004
25. Interivew 89
26. Interview 44
27. See for example, Interviews 10 and 11
28. 'An Exceptional Case', *The Times* 29 June 2005, 'Confusion Over Halt to Zimbabwe Deportations' *The Times* 6 July 2005.
29. Interview 25 April 2005.
30. See Foster Dongozi 'Mau Mau Faces Deportation', *Zimbabwe Standard* 27 June 2004. Retrieved 10 August 2008 from http://www.zimbabwesituation.com/. See also 'Alleged Asylum Fraud Linked to Mugabe', *Daily Telegraph* 20 June 2004.
31. For a fuller narrative of the successive Asylum and Immigration Tribunal decisions that have suspended or resumed deportations see ILPA, http://www.ilpa.orga.uk. Deportations resumed through a further AIT decision in October 2006 and in other more recent decisions, yet the categories of people considered unsafe to be removed have been expanded in each hearing.
32. See press reports: http://www.indymedia.org.uk/en/2006/09/350740.html?c=on
33. The list is derived from the circular email offering thanks after his release.
34. Interview, 18 March 2005.
35. Pers. comm., activists in asylum-seeker support groups, various junctures 2004–8.
36. Sunanda Ray, intervention at Zimbabwe Open Forum June 2005, minutes on http://www.britain-zimbabwe-org.uk/
37. Itai Garande, intervention at Zimbabwe Open Forum
38. Yvonne Marime, intervention at Zimbabwe Open Forum
39. Interview 31.
40. Interview 9, careworker and dependent of asylum-seeker, a secretary in Zimbabwe, married to a university lecturer.
41. Interview 44.
42. http://www.zimwomenuk/org/.
43. Interview, two teachers in professional jobs, Interviews 49 and 50
44. Group interview, with three nurses and one student/waiter, interviewees 61–3.
45. Pers. comm., Zimbabwe Association staff, April 2008.
46. Interview, refugee and warehouse worker, 42.
47. Interview, warehouse worker, 46.
48. Interview 12, carer and single mother of two.

References

Amnesty International (AI). 2004. *Get It Right. How Home Office Decision Making Fails Refugees.* London.
Anderson, B. and B. Rogaly. 2005. *Forced Labour and Migration to the UK.* Oxford: COMPAS in collaboration with the TUC.

Bloch, A. and L. Schuster. 2005. 'At the Extremes of Exclusion: Deportation, Detention and Dispersal', *Ethnic and Racial Studies*, 28, 3: 491–512.

Flynn, D. 2005. 'New Borders, New Management: the Dilemmas of Modern Immigration Policies, *Ethnic and Racial Studies*, 28, 3: 463–90.

Gibney, M. 2008. 'Asylum and the Expansion of Deportation in the United Kingdom', *Government and Opposition*, 43, 2: 146–67.

Haslar Visitor's Group. 2008. 'Zimbabweans in Indefinite Detention', August 2008. Retrieved 20 August 2008 from http://www.haslarvisitors.org.uk/hvgnews.htm

IAC (Independent Asylum Commission). 2008. *Fit for Purpose Yet: Interim Findings*. London.

Institute of Race Relations. 2006. *Driven to Desperate Measures*. London: IRR.

Jordan, B. and F. Duvell. 2002. *Irregular Migration: the Dilemmas of Transnational Mobility*. London: Edward Elgar.

Kofman, E. 2002. 'Contemporary European Migration: Civic Stratification and Citizenship', Political Geography, 21, 8: 1035–54.

Laubenthal, B. 2007. 'The Emergence of Pro-Regularisation Movement in Europe', *International Migration*, 45, 3: 101–34.

Magaisa, A. 2006. 'Donors, Diaspora and Zimbabwe Democracy', 25 July 2006. Retrieved 20 August 2008 from http://www.kubatana.net/html/archive/

May, J., J. Wills, K. Datta, Y.Evans, J. Herbert and C. McIlwaine. 2007. 'Keeping London Working: Global Cities, the British State and London's New Migrant Division of Labour', *Transactions of the Institute of British Geographers* NS 32: 151–67.

Mbiba, B. 2004. 'Zimbabwe's Global Citizens in Harare North (United Kingdom): Some Preliminary Observations', in M. Palmberg and R. Primorac (eds) *Skinning the Skunk: Facing Zimbabwean Futures*. Uppsala: Nordiska Afrikainstitutet.

McGregor, J. 2007. '"Joining the BBC" (British Bottom Cleaners): Zimbabwean Migrants and the UK Care Industry', *Journal of Ethnic and Migration Studies*, 33, 5: 801–24.

____. 2008. 'Abject Spaces, Transnational Calculations: Zimbabweans in Britain Navigating Work, Class and the Law', *Transactions of the Institute of British Geographers*, 33, 4: 466–82.

____. 2008a. 'Children and "African values": Zimbabwean Professionals in the UK Reconfiguring Family', Environment and Planning A, 40, 3: 596–614.

____. 2009. 'Associational Links with Home Among Zimbabweans in the UK: Reflections on Long Distance Nationalisms', *Global Networks* forthcoming.

McIlwaine, C. 2007. 'Living in Latin London: How Latin American Migrants Survive in the City'. Retrieved 1 August 2008 from http://www.carila.org.uk

McIlwaine, C., K. Datta, Y. Evans, J. Herbert, J. May and J. Wills. 2006. 'Gender and Ethnic Identities Among Low-paid Migrant Workers in London', Dept of Geography Queen Mary. Retrieved 20 August from http://www.geog.qmul.ac.uk/globalcities/reports/docs/workingpaper4.pdf

Mercer, C., B. Page and M. Evans. 2008. *Development and the African Diaspora: Place and the Politics of Home*. London: Zed Press.

Morris, L. 2003. *Managing Migration: Civic Stratification and Migrants' Rights* London: Routledge.

MRN (Migrant Rights Network). 2007. 'Enforcement Policy: at the Heart of Managed Migration?' Briefing paper, Migrant Rights Network. Retrieved 20 August from http://www.migrantsrights.org.uk/files/enforcement.doc
——. 2008. 'Papers Please. The Impact of a Government Campaign on the Employment Rights of Vulnerable Migrants'. London, September 2008. Retrieved 1 December from http://www.migrantsrights.org.uk/files/paper/paperpleasesummary.pdf
Nyers, P. 2003. 'Abject Cosmopolitanism: The Politics of Protection in the Anti-Deportation Movement', *Third World Quarterly*, 24, 6: 1069–93.
Nyers, P. 2006. *Rethinking Refugees: Beyond States of Emergency*. Routledge: London.
Østergaard-Nielsen. 2003. 'The Politics of Migrants' Transnational Political Practices' *International Migration Review*, 37, 3: 760–86.
Pasura, D. 2006. 'Mapping Exercise: Zimbabwe', London: IOM. http://www.iomlondon.org
——. 2008. 'A Fractured Diaspora: Strategies and Identities Among Zimbabweans in Britain', PhD Thesis. University of Warwick.
Ranger, T. 2005. 'Narratives and Counternarratives of Zimbabwean Asylum', *Third World Quarterly*, 26, 3: 405–21.
Rodier, C. 2007. 'The Migroeurop Network and Europe's Foreigner Camps', in M. Feher (ed.), *Nongovernment Politics*. New York: Zone Books, pp. 446–7.
Samers, M. 2005. 'The "Underground" Economy Immigration and Economic Development in the European Union: an Agnostic-Skeptic Perspective', *International Journal of Economic Development*, 6, 2: 199–272.
Werbner, P. 2002. *Imagined Diasporas Among Manchester Muslims. The Public Performance of Transnational Pakistani Identity Politics*. Oxford: James Currey.
Willems, W. 2005. 'Remnants of Empire? British Media Reporting on Zimbabwe' Special issue, 'The Media and Zimbabwe' Westminster Papers in Communication and Culture, November 2005. Retrieved 20 October 2008 from http://www.wmin.ac.uk/mad/pdf/zim_art6.pdf
Williams, C. and J. Windebank. 1998. *Informal Employment in the Advanced Economies: Implications for Work and Welfare* London: Routledge.
Wills, J. 2006. 'Subcontracting, Labour and Trade Union Oganisation: Lssons from Homerton Hospital and the London Living Wage Campaign', ESRC Identities Programme: Work, Identity and New Forms of Political Mobilisation. Working paper 2.
Zetter, R. 2007. 'More Labels, Fewer Refugees: Remaking the Refugee Label in an Era of Globalisation', *Journal of Refugee Studies* 20, 2: 172–92.
Zimbabwe Association, 2007. Evidence to Independent Asylum Commission. November 2007.
ZimCare, 2007. 'Funeral Arrangement Services'. Retrieved 28 October from http://www.zimcare.co.uk
Zylinska, J. 2005. 'The Biopolitics of Immigration'. Retrieved 21 April 2008 from http://www.signsofthetimes.org.uk/asylum[textonly].html

6

Burial at Home? Dealing with Death in the Diaspora and Harare

Beacon Mbiba

For Zimbabweans in newly formed diaspora communities around the globe, burial at home in Zimbabwe is a crucially important concern. This is the case not only for those living within the Southern Africa Development Community (SADC) countries, where bodies can be transported over land relatively easily and cheaply, but also for those beyond Africa living in Australia, USA, New Zealand and Europe, particularly the large numbers in the United Kingdom (Gaidzanwa 1999; Mbiba 2005). Zimbabweans outside their country save up to ensure that they will not rest for ever on foreign soil, invest in insurance schemes to that end, partake in burial associations that require weekly or monthly donations and meetings, or contribute to church groups that also help fulfill important financial, practical and emotional aspects of the process of bereavement and repatriating bodies for burial. But when Zimbabweans talk of burial at home, what do they mean? Do they chose to be buried within often overcrowded urban cemeteries in Zimbabwe, or do they want to be buried in rural homes? How has the recent crisis affected decisions? What might such decisions reveal about rural/urban connections or the tensions between local/ethnic attachments and national sentiment within Zimbabwe and in the diaspora?

This chapter aims to explore some of these issues, contributing to a growing recent literature on death and burial, and the influence of diasporisation (Mazzucato et al. 2006; Gardner 2002). The preference for burial at rural homes rather than in Zimbabwe's cities often continues to be expressed as an ideal both by many of those in the diaspora and in Zimbabwe's capital city Harare, notwithstanding a longstanding historical trend in practice toward urban burial in Zimbabwe. As this article elaborates, this trend appears to have been dramatically reversed, or at least disrupted in the short term from 2002. Such shifts are important, and have attracted debate in the broader literature, as the changing locus of burial can provide insight into notions of identity and belonging, can highlight important changes in rural and urban economies, shifting ideas of the nation or the effects of growing diaspora communities (Geschiere and Gugler 1998; Jua 2005; Page 2007). Geschiere and Gugler (1998) discuss the recent move towards a heightened emphasis on rural burial in Cameroon as indicative of the developing crisis of the postcolonial state, and the weakness of national identities, which appear fragmented by resurgent ethnic attachments provoked in part by the impact of neoliberal political reforms.

The Zimbabwean case discussed here, however, is not appropriately discussed in terms of a resurgence of ethnic claims undermining ideas of national belonging. Rather, the article seeks explanations for changing burial patterns by examining the multiple political-economic, planning and health crises, the surging cost of transport between urban and rural areas, the overcrowding and inadequate capacity for urban burial, segregation of low and high status burial grounds, choices on the part of families to send members with HIV/AIDS back to the rural areas for their final few years, electoral violence and other state actions such as the mass demolitions of Operation Murambatsvina (Remove the Filth) in 2005. By investigating decisions over, and planning for death and burial among Zimbabweans in Britain and South Africa, and examining the attitudes of planners in Zimbabwe's capital city, Harare, the article shows that the answer to the question of the relative desirability of rural or urban burial has not remained constant over time for different social groups, nor do there appear to be simple linear trends, and the multiple crises that have affected Zimbabweans in the last decade mean that Zimbabweans still living at home as well as those abroad have also been forced to think about this issue in new ways.

The argument is based on data from Zimbabwean funeral parlours in London and interviews with Zimbabweans in Britain (a small survey conducted in 2004, plus follow up phone calls in 2008), as well as web and media coverage of issues related to burial. It also draws on official data on death in the city of Harare, supplemented with field observations and discussion with city planners, in 2004.

Death in the Diaspora

Dying in the diaspora is certainly a traumatic experience for all those involved. It is also very expensive, and the costs of repatriating a body from the UK amount to around £3000[1] and about R10,000 from Johannesburg, South Africa. Although Zimbabweans who have moved to the UK and other western destinations are predominantly youthful, and are drawn from the country's middle and elite socio-economic classes, death rates are nonetheless high among Zimbabweans in Britain. This is partly due to the prevalence of HIV/AIDS in the diaspora: Health Protection Agency figures show that Zimbabwe rose quickly through the top ten countries of infection for heterosexual cases in Britain, ranking fourth in 1994 and first in 2004 (Health Protection Agency 2005, New Zimbabwe 2004). Deaths were particularly high in the early days of largescale immigration from 2000, before new migrants living with HIV/AIDS realised that they could get help by approaching British health services, and many treated health as a secondary priority in their struggle to negotiate responsibilities across continents, immigration, accommodation, employment, income and emotional challenges in a foreign land (Chinouya 2003). There was (and is) continued stigma towards those with HIV/AIDS, ignorance and a sense of denial among Zimbabweans many of whom perceive themselves as not at risk of contracting HIV/AIDS once in the diaspora (Chinouya 2003 and this volume). Some General Practitioners have also refused to attend to patients lacking papers, such that access to medical care has sometimes depended on interventions by NGOs. While, initially, these were run by other African groups (such as a Ugandan-run NGO approached by this author for assistance in relation to two bedridden Zimbabweans refused medical care in London), services specifically for Zimbabweans have expanded rapidly, both through community-based and state initiatives (Chinouya 2003 and 2004).

There is, unfortunately, no centralised system of record keeping in the UK from which one can compile figures on the numbers of dead bodies shipped back to Zimbabwe. Neither the Office of National Statistics, (ONS), nor the Birth and Death Registrars or the Coroner's office compile these figures,[2] while Air Zimbabwe and British Airways also refused to provide information.[3] Yet the records of one funeral parlour in SE London patronised by Zimbabweans – the Beckenham-based IPS Ltd – are indicative that the scale of repatriation is considerable, as they show that between 2002 and 2005 500 bodies were sent back from this one organisation alone. The bodies they repatriated were mostly in their prime reproductive years, probably reflecting HIV/AIDS related mortality: no children under the age of five were sent back, perhaps because they are not considered fully socialised, perhaps because they have benefited from access to medical care in Britain.

Although we still know little about death among Zimbabweans in the global diaspora today, we do know that for past generations of Zimbabwean migrants within the Southern African region, burial societies were perhaps the most persistently important type of migrant organisation (Van Onselen 1976; Yoshikuni 1999), and we also know that Zimbabweans displaced within Southern Africa and recent migrants in Zimbabwean towns continue to form burial societies although their viability in the Zimbabwean context is threatened by unemployment and rampant inflation.[4] The societies provided spaces for political mobilisation during the struggle for independence and in the recent crisis have been used by opposition activists in a similar manner to penetrate deep into ruling party constituencies under cover, to mobilise supporters, share strategies and distribute literature, as Edmund Shava, a Zimbabwean asylum seeker and member of Zvishavane Burial Society in Johannesburg described:

> We have discovered that we should not limit ourselves to discussing funeral issues in the burial society meetings, but work on ways to assist our relatives back home...Exiles return with the bodies of relatives for the funeral gatherings back home and these give them an opportunity to convene meetings where discussions can be held freely without being arrested by police under the draconian Public Order and Security Act.[5]

Although burial societies are one of the most enduring and effective civil society organisations in Zimbabwe, and the region, they remain outside mainstream development practice. They have not developed into instigators of development projects in rural areas as in other African contexts (such as Cameroon; Page 2007), perhaps due to the authoritarian nature of both the colonial and post-colonial states, their monopoly on development and suppression of civil society.

Research among Zimbabweans in the UK has revealed that burial remains a primary concern even if burial societies tend to be less prevalent in Britain than within the southern African region (Mbiba 2005; McGregor 2009). McGregor (2009) has highlighted some of the many constraints on forming burial societies in the UK, particularly dispersal through the asylum system, movement in search of work or study, and constraints on socialising for those without papers. Her interviews with eighty black Zimbabweans revealed that none had formed burial societies (though some had tried to do so) and only one had taken an insurance policy over the web from a Zimbabwean company, Moonlight. Instead, people have tended to rely on family and informal networks, as well as Zimbabwean church fellowships. Yet, there are some burial societies within the UK, especially within communities that have achieved a degree of stability over the years since moving to Britain, though their character differs considerably from the stereotypical beer hall-based male drinking club familiar from the southern African literature. Some professionals such as thirty-six year old Baba Chiendambuya of East London, do not have funeral policies, but Baba would like to be buried in what he considers his home, next to his father's grave in rural Gokwe in Zimbabwe's Midlands Province, and has catered for this through a support network that will fund the repatriation of the body in the event of his death. He described how his burial support group operated:

> I am a member of a fifteen member Zimbabwe Support Network that we formed a year ago. We have a constitution and a bank account and when we started, each member would contribute £20 per month into the account and without knowing we had over £2000 in the account. ... Yes you could say it's a burial society although we do not call it that. If any of the members die, then we each have to immediately contribute £100 towards funeral expenses ... repatriating the body to Zimbabwe for example. It means the family of the deceased would have £1400 to work with and we can top up from the collections if need be. Each member can also make claims for funeral expenses for up to six members of his/her family when they die in Britain or in Zimbabwe. So in a way it's a funeral policy for many relatives in Zimbabwe. When such a claim for a relative is made, members of the group contribute £50 each thus the bereaved member will have £700 pounds to use immediately.[6]

As demands on the group's funds have not consumed all the capital, they are now considering investment strategies that will yield profit. Over a one year period, they have had three claims:

> Last year one of our members had to attend a funeral for a relative in Zimbabwe. With the £700 from immediate contributions, he was able to buy an air ticket on the same day he received the news of death. On his own it would have been tough. As we speak we have a bereavement in the group. One of our members lost his mother in-law who has been living with him in Britain and we assume she will be buried in Zimbabwe ...[7]

The option of buying insurance policies has not been widely taken up within the diaspora, partly on grounds of lack of finance, partly on grounds of youth, as Magumede, a thirty year old mother of two, separated from her husband, but who has uncles and sisters in Britain explained: 'I am still young ... and really, death is something I have not thought about ... If I take a funeral policy, it's like I am anticipating or hastening my death or wishing myself death'.[8] Living in South East London since late 1990s, Magumede works long hours in the health sector, but creates time to be with her young children and to go drinking with friends from her home town Bulawayo, or to travel to 'gigs' when South African or Zimbabwean musicians come to perform in the UK, such as at the annual Zimfest, in Raynes Park, London attended by up to five thousand Zimbabweans.[9]

Many Zimbabweans in the diaspora thus do not make advance plans but rely on contacting *pachivanhu* (those surrounding/known to the deceased) only in the event of death, in the assumption that they will contribute to the costs. As Sinyonyo from South London recalled:

There was this girl who died less than a year ago following a short illness. I got to know her when I came to Britain but she was not a close friend. When she died, text messages were sent round requesting people to contribute and I contributed £50 towards costs of sending her body to Zimbabwe.[10]

In the absence of widespread formation of burial societies or adoption of funeral policies, it is not uncommon for deaths of Zimbabweans in Britain to be a time of financial crisis, as friends and relatives scramble around to raise the repatriation costs. Family members in Zimbabwe contribute to the demands for the body to be repatriated, even if they do not help meet the costs; children or spouses in the UK may have little say in the decision. Moreover, this last minute money-raising can often fail to cover the bill. As Nyakuita from Edinburgh, recalled:

... This woman fell ill for a few days and died ... There was no money to take her body to Zimbabwe as demanded by her family there. In the UK, she had her two teenage children as her closest family members but obviously they had no money. Her body was in the fridge for two months. As usual calls for contributions were made, but people would only throw in ridiculous amounts like five pounds, partly because they do not have money but also because they would rather go and have a beer. Eventually, people had to approach charities that chipped in with top up funding to cover repatriation costs ...[11]

The importance of burial at home has also been underlined by the practices of the 'nouveaux' rich and famous who die abroad and have their bodies transported to Zimbabwe – such as the former national soccer star Francis Shonhai, who died in South Africa in 2006 – and by the politicisation of some efforts to secure home burial. Notable among the later is the case of Christopher Muzvuru, a twenty-one year old Zimbabwean who joined the British Army in 2001 and was killed in active service in Basra, Iraq in 2003. His family and friends requested he be buried in Gweru, but the Zimbabwean authorities declared the body unwelcome: the pro-government media vilified him as a mercenary and sellout, whose body should be buried in the country he had chosen to die for – Britain.[12] Family members were visited in Zimbabwe by secret police officers, and feared assault from state aligned militias/vigilante groups.[13] Eventually, Zimbabwean authorities relented, allowed the body to be returned but insisted on burial in an unmarked grave in Gweru town – like a pauper. The incident had wider ramifications among the networks of those Zimbabweans working in occupations considered traitorous at home (in the police and security services in Britain, or who deserted Zimbabwean security services). In the wake of the Muzvuru case, such 'sell out' Zimbabweans spoke of deciding not to accompany home the bodies of their deceased parents, spouses, brothers, sisters and children, and also declined to travel home for funerals or weddings.[14] For those who are asylum seekers or irregular migrants, constraints on movement and finance are also severe.

There are, however, costs of not traveling home to attend funerals – not only in the trauma of loss, but also in the risk of witchcraft accusations or exacerbation of other conflicts. As Jua (2005) notes, death and burial can unleash a myriad of conflicts, not only when international movements are involved, but also over the consequences of intermarriage (between different races, ethnic groups or classes) or the distribution of property and assets (cf Bolling 1997). Guerillas who died in the bush and were buried away from home without proper funeral rights during the liberation war were regarded by rural people in the vicinity of the graves as an unsettling presence, and by relatives as a cause of misfortune and ill-health, such that agencies such as the Amani Trust later worked to identify and exhume the graves and allow for proper burial (on unsettling legacies of improper burial during the liberation war, see Reynolds 2003, Maxwell 1996, Alexander et al. 2000).

This discussion has already begun to touch on a range of issues surrounding the locus of burial that concern not only the diaspora, but also those living in Zimbabwean towns. The next section turns to explore the changing dynamics of urban burial in Harare, investigating the light it sheds on trends towards urban burial and their disruption in 2002.

Planning for Burial in Zimbabwe: Death in the City, 1980–2003

Harare, like other towns in Zimbabwe, was deemed a 'white space' in segregationist ideology and Africans living within it were predominantly extra-territorial migrants until relatively late in its history. It was only in the early 1960s that African migrants from the southern Rhodesian countryside began to take over urban spaces (Yoshikuni 1999). In Harare, Africans from the Zimbabwean countryside often considered themselves to be sojourners and often remained 'anti-urban' in outlook, such that urban burial could be stigmatised, and was associated with failure, or with foreigners labeled derogatorily as *mwidi* or totemless. The motivation for rural burial and for the formation of burial societies in Zimbabwe's towns was thus partly about avoiding the stigma of a pauper's burial (cf Geschiere and Gugler 1998: 311). Thus despite the provision of cemeteries for urban burial in colonial Zimbabwe, many urbanised Africans initially continued to ferry their dead for burial in the rural 'tribal trust lands' designated as their 'homes' by the colonial administrators. The Warren Hills cemetery (then known as Kambuzuma) is memorably embedded in urban shabeen folklore through dance and song, such as the lyrics '... *Where shall I be buried*

… Kambuzuma I don't want … I want to be buried home …'. Ranger (2004) argues that in Bulawayo after the Second World War, there was a gradual trend towards the Christianisation of burial and an increased use of urban burial facilities, despite initial reactions against urban burial on the part of traditionalists and non-elites (cf Ngahyoma 2003, in relation to Tanzania), and a similar trend also occurred in Harare.

In a postcolonial context, the trend towards the Christianisation and urbanisation of burial in Zimbabwe has taken place in the context of strict bureaucratic mediation. While in West Africa people can be buried anywhere in the city where they own land including under their houses (Ogu 1999; Bah 2000) or in residential compounds,[15] in Harare burials take place only in officially designated, planned and regulated cemeteries. Urban burial bureaucracies have provoked tensions and controversy, and have also not provided an equitable service for urban residents. As I have detailed elsewhere (Mbiba 2003: 478), official urban burial procedures have been criticised for undermining the performance of death and burial rituals, even of Christianised variants on tradition, as they outlaw access to graves outside public servants' working days between 8 and 5pm. This prevents the possibility of dawn and dusk burials, of nightlong vigils with processions, dancing and drinking, slaughtering stock and so on. For a discussion of the importance of avoiding midday and graveside vigils through grave-side fires in Karanga tradition (see Shoko 2007: 85).[16] The impracticality of much of this in urban settings can help explain why some still opt take their deceased for burial to the rural 'home'.

But the magnitude of death in recent years has introduced further changes in official management of burial in the city, as well as in popular practices in both urban and rural areas. Some preliminary insight into these changes can be gleaned from an interpretation of official Harare city death figures, and interviews with officials responsible for managing Harare's cemeteries. In Zimbabwe, all deaths are recorded and it is a criminal offence to transport or bury a dead body without an official burial order that is later used to prepare a death certificate.[17] Only government registrars at a limited number of offices in the country can issue these orders and certificates, and in Harare, there is only one office where death certificates can be obtained. In rural areas, the chief makes a record of the death and provides a letter that relatives of the deceased have to take to the relevant government registrar (usually at a local district administrative office) who then issues a burial order or a death certificate (if the burial has already taken place). The system has worked effectively until the recent past in that almost all deaths and burials are recorded even in remote rural locations (the exception being in periods of political violence, such as *gukurahundi* in Matabeleland and Midlands, where people killed by the fifth brigade of the Zimbabwe National Army or abducted by officers of the Central Intelligence Organisation CIO were unable to obtain death certificates).

The death records available for Harare (derived from death certificates from the Registrar of Births and Deaths, Harare District) are limited in various ways. They relate to Harare residents only, excluding 'non residents' such as visitors who die within Harare municipal boundaries, or Harare residents who had not registered officially as such.

Table 1: Summary Death Statistics for City of Harare 1995–2003

Year	1995	1996	1997	1998	1999	2000	2001	2002	2003
Total population		1408091	1486944	n.a.	n.a.	n.a.	n.a.	1444534	
Total Deaths Recorded at Harare District Office	11595	13106	13315	n.a.	n.a.	15662	17078	17504	17645
% Change in Total		0.1	1.6	n.a.	n.a.		9	2.5	0.8
% of Deaths at Home	30	34	33	n.a.	n.a.	35.2	39.9	38.5	42.1
% of hiv/aids Deaths	n.a.	13.4	9.9	n.a.	n.a.	12.9	12.9	9.8	11
% of death in 25 to 44 year age group	n.a.	34.8		n.a.	n.a.			42	45

n.a. Statistics not available
Source: Compiled from City of Harare, City Health DepatmentAnnual Reports.

Nonetheless, the official figures reveal various interesting patterns. Firstly, they show that non-residents' deaths outnumber residents' deaths (City Health Department, 2002: 13–14). In 2002 for example, of the total 35,000 deaths in Harare, residents deaths were approximately 15,000 compared to 20,0000 non-resident deaths. It is not clear why there is such a discrepancy, whether registers of 'residents' were not being kept up to date, or more likely because people were coming into town to hospital when they were sick. Secondly and perhaps more importantly, the number of deaths in Harare increased steadily from the late 1990s to 2003 (see Table 1), over which time, deaths occurring at home also increased, accounting for forty-two per cent of all deaths by 2003. The rise in home deaths is probably explicable by the decay of central hospitals in the city where terminally ill people would have died in the past: strikes by junior doctors and nurses, lack of medicines and decline in care has convinced relatives and patients that public hospitals are now spaces of death rather than recovery and that dying at home is more decent. Health staff have also encouraged terminally ill patients to go and die at home.[18] In addition to the lack of care at the hospitals, home deaths also reduce subsequent costs for the family and help them better prepare for burial. This is significant where the deceased is to be buried at a rural home, which may be hundreds of kilometres from Harare. As noted by Page (2007: 434), it is easier to move the ill than the dead. Thirdly, the high number of deaths in the 25–44 year age group is also notable (amounting to forty-five per cent in 2003), the majority of which are due to HIV/AIDS-related infections. The figure of HIV/AIDS deaths in the city has been relatively stable, at just below fifteen per cent (though there may be under-reporting), which is likely to be explained by poor families travelling to die at rural homes once they are aware of their HIV/AIDS status.

The total figure of around 35,000 deaths in Harare per year indicates a high demand for cemetery land. While about half of these bodies are non-Harare residents (in official terms) who are ferried to places outside Harare, the remainder are black residents who overwhelmingly refuse cremation in preference for burial (Table 2). To put the high and rapidly rising figures in perspective, Harare's annual burials at the end of the 1990s were about seventy-five per cent those of London. Yet London's population is about seven million while Harare has about one and half million. At a more local level, the London Borough of Bexley has a total population of about quarter of a million. Expecting its burial space to run out in 1995, the borough opened Hillview cemetery whose capacity was estimated at 6,500 (six thousand five hundred graves that would last approximately 30 –35 years.)[19] The demand of burial plots in Harare would use up this capacity in less than six months.

Table 2 shows that the overwhelming majority of Harare residents are buried in the city (around eighty-eight per cent in 2000). Yet this proportion has fallen in subsequent years, and in 2002 in particular, the number of bodies ferried out of the city for burial more than doubled. It is not clear why in 2002 the number of residents not buried in Harare shot up so significantly, but it may be linked to the shortage of burial land in the city, or administrative and political challenges facing the city. By this year, the Harare cemeteries had reached full capacity and, from 2000, local authorities had been scrambling to get more land for burial purposes. It is also plausible that political violence contributed to this shift, though we lack evidence on how elevated violence around the 2002 elections and in its aftermath might have contributed to the trend of people increasingly burying the deceased out of Harare.

The government has tried to respond to the shortage of space in the cemeteries in various ways. One strategy has been to encourage cremation, but as Curator of Harare Cemeteries Eladino Zimbwa lamented in 2000, this was not received favourably by black Zimbabweans:

We are running out of space in the graveyards. At the moment in our two open cemeteries (the five others are full), we have two burials per hour, every hour, between 10am and 3pm, seven days a week. ...The cremation campaign is not working, despite a lot of media coverage, because it is against our culture. Last year in Harare there were 717 cremations, only one of them for a black person. But I am hoping we will increase the figure thanks to economic necessity. Even though a cremation is as expensive as a coffin burial, the exercise is cheaper for those who want to take their dead back to the village... They can just put the urn on their lap in the bus, rather than having to arrange a minibus.[20]

There is no evidence that cremation has increased among black Zimbabweans even with the rising costs of burials, coffins and transport of deceased to rural areas: rather it continues to be cast as a 'foreign practice with no place whatsoever in our society'.[21]

Table 2: Deaths and Burials in Harare city 2000–2003

Year	Total Deaths (Residents Only)	Total Buried in Harare Cemeteries*	Not Buried in Harare	Daily Burials per Cemetery	Average Monthly Burials in Harare
2000	15 662	13 853	1809	n.a	1154
2001	17 078	15 127	1951	35	1261
2002	17 504	13 171	4333	38	1098
2003	17 645	15 228	2417	45	1269

*Figures include all pauper burials and burials on reserved sites. However, they exclude cremation (569) and burial of ashes (30) for 2003 and (655) and 83 for 2002 respectively. They exclude cremations (866) and ash burials (73) for 2001 and (840) and 65 for 2002 respectively.

Source: Compiled from City Health Department Annual Reports, 2000–2003.

The Harare City Council also took measures to deal with the rising demand for burial land by opening up new cemeteries, among them the notorious Granville site to the south of the city east of the Harare-Pretoria Highway, which was intended as a burial place for the poor, in response to the rise in HIV/AIDS related deaths and has the largest capacity of any of Harare's cemeteries. The cemetery has gained the nickname *KuMbudzi* (place for goats), partly because it is close to an informal place for goat-trading, but also because it is a place where people are 'treated like goats'. This cemetery is notorious not only because of how rapidly it filled up, but also because of poor landscaping and undignified burials. In seven years from the time it was opened in 1997, the *Mbudzi* cemetery had taken up as many as 14,000 burials.[22] Unlike in other cemeteries such as Warren Hills, people are buried as close as forty-five cms apart, several burials take place simultaneously and if these are on adjacent burial plots, the parties have to give each other turns in order to provide separate mourning for each of the deceased and to avoid each drowning out the other's singing.

The Harare City Council also allowed private cemeteries to open on the periphery of the city on private land. These operate as private businesses and empirical documentation would be needed to establish how they have faired. Within the older existing cemeteries, the local authority has undertaken to reserve graves for 'citizens of status', who can pay market rates. Anecdotal information also points to cases of grave banking where individuals buy large numbers of graves from the local authority;[23] these individuals then sell them off to desperate families at extortionate prices. Only one cemetery, Dzivarasekwa, is totally closed while the others recorded as closed have reservations and were semi-active in 2004, including Pioneer Cemetery which initially opened in 1897. Warren Hills, which should have been closed in 2000 has continued to operate, as any open space within it is now utilised: in 2008, several opposition MDC activists were buried there including Abigail Chiroto and Tonderai Ndira – both victims of political violence.[24]

The provision and use of cemeteries in Harare remains segregated not entirely along racial lines as was the case in the past (cf Christopher 1995 in relation to South Africa) but certainly according to class. Europeans

Table 3: City of Harare cemetery statistics

Name	Hectare	Capacity	Date Opened	Date Closed	Reserved graves	Burial rate*
Active Cemeteries						
Granville A	71	92 300	26/12/97	–	6 871	28
Granville B	115	149 500	07/03/95	–	0	9
Mabvuku	35	45 500	21/05/69	–	322	6
Warren Hills	(10)[25]	(13 000)	n.a		0	n.a
Totals	221 (231)[26]	287 300			7 193	–
Closed Cemeteries						
Dzivarasekwa	0,98	237	1964	1990	0	None
Greendale	2	5 875	12/01/54	23/08/96	380	3/week
Highfield	13	16 900	1950s(1971)[27]	29/02/95	228	1/month
Mbare	20	26 900	1953	1966	38	1/month
Warren Hills	65	84 500	1964	2000	587	3/week
Pioneer	20	24 753	1897	1979	540	2/week
Totals	120.98	159 165			1 773	

*Source: Various Sources, Harare City Council. * per day*

and Asians are not buried *kuMbudzi,* nor are rich Africans. While Voltaire observed that all men are born equal and die equal, in Harare, it could be argued that men are born unequal and die unequal.[28] Urban planners and administrators perpetuate the unequal way space for the dead is consumed in the city.

Getting a decent space in the urban cemeteries is thus now a matter of money and those able to get foreign currency (for example those in or with relatives in the diaspora) are in a better position to secure such spaces. Rising costs of burial have led to poor families not collecting their deceased relatives from the government owned mortuaries hoping that these can eventually be given a paupers burial. Unemployment and inflation have eroded the capacity of the poor to have a decent funeral. In 2008, when newspapers were reporting that a Chitungwiza family had to remove doors from their house to make a coffin for their dead son,[29] a standard coffin cost Z$1billion with caskets going for over Z$5 billion each while Z$300 million would be needed to hire a bus to ferry mourners to Granville Cemetery where a grave cost Z$112 million.[30] Families who cannot afford the cheapest commercially made coffins have resorted to making their own or burying their loved ones wrapped in a mat or in cloth.

While funerals and death have become a financial nightmare for many poor people, both at home and in the diaspora, there is a class that contributed to the sharp rise in flamboyant funerals that are used as a means of displaying wealth and are a marker of status (cf Geschiere and Gugler's description of West African elite funerals 1998: 311).[31] Driven by 'foreign currency laden diasporans' the practice includes buying elegant custom-designed coffins in shapes of cars, planes or anything fancy, elegant hearses, horse drawn hearses and expensive cars in the funeral processions that snake through city centres and growth points enroute to the cemetery, costly tombstones, lots of food and elegant funeral attire. Funerals and burials are also recorded on film with the recordings sent to members in the diaspora. Such flamboyant funerals have been controversial, as a member of the diaspora explained:

> It is the diaspora that rules these days. But I think they are driven by guilt. Because they are not at home and cannot be at home to see their relatives during their last days of illness, or to be there when they are buried, they compensate for that by sending a lot of money for these funerals. It makes them feel better … but the money could actually be put to better use.[32]

Those in the 'business of death' who provide services, coffins, transport, or food for mourners have often had booming businesses. In Harare in 2007, it was reported that ten registered and fully equipped funeral parlours were operating on a twenty four hour basis, competing for business with unregistered parlours, and continuing to draw subscriptions as inflation rocketed, and initial rates had been paid several times over.[33] Mr. Edmund Chako the marketing executive at Harare's long-standing Doves Morgan funeral parlour elaborated:

> We don't depend on policy holders only. Some families are paying as much as Z$6 million for us to provide them with funeral services. ...Our policies have increased by 400 per cent. The premium policy, which is the cheapest, was recently going for only $2,500 but we have since raised it to $10,000 per month. However, that has not deterred our customers who are still coming in large numbers.[34]

Since then, costs have escalated further as hyperinflation has spiraled further out of control, and there are also economies of theft around urban burial, in which people have been reported to steal flower vases from graves for resale to mourners the following day, or caskets and coffins are dug up for a similar reason. Those with the funds are reported to pour cement in the graves to prevent such exhumations. All this has increased the costs of a decent urban burial as well as perpetuating the stigma of an undignified urban burial for many.

Sending the Dead Back Home: Rural-Urban Linkages

Considering the trend towards increased urban burial as an indicator of identity, one could argue that there is now a significant proportion of Zimbabweans who consider the urban area as their home and prefer to be buried or to bury their deceased there. 'If I am buried *kumusha* (home*)* in Zaka, and not in Harare, my children will not be able to tend my grave and place flowers as and when they feel like' commented a female resident of Msasa Park.[35]

Yet, it is important to discuss the various factors that contributed towards this trend, as it could be argued that it reflects high costs of transport to rural areas and a range of other practical issues rather than amounting to an increased sense of urban belonging. These high costs forced many families to bury their deceased in urban areas even if they may have wished to ferry them to the rural/communal area home. Particularly in the structural adjustment years of the 1990s, there were sharp increases in transport costs, and poor urban households were affected disproportionately (Mbiba 1999; Bryceson and Mbara 2003). More recently the dramatic economic collapse, increased costs and non-availability of fuel has also meant that the middle classes have had to take the option of urban burial more seriously. In January 2005, the City Council raised burial charges twenty fold from Z$750 000 to Z$8.5 million for the grave of an adult, with a further hike to Z$17 million planned for mid-year. At the time, average monthly take home pay for Zimbabwean workers was Z\$3million.[36] In the same year, Operation Murambatsvina created further hardships, such that Harare residents in high density suburbs increasingly saw death as 'a luxury only the rich can afford'.[37] The Harare Residents Association charged that the city fathers were seeking to cash in on the people's misery at a time when options were non-existent:

> Very few people can afford that kind of money to buy a burial space for their departed ones. Right now the country has no fuel and it is very expensive to ferry the deceased to the rural areas where burial ground is free and many residents were resorting to these urban cemeteries. With the latest hikes, I am not sure how the residents are going to cope.[38]

In this context, company directors in the Building and Construction industry revealed in 2006 that workers opted not to take cash benefits, but asked their employers instead for support in the form of transport to take deceased family members for burial in the rural areas.[39]

It is thus not clear to what extent the trend towards increased urban burial is indicative of a decline in the ideal of rural burial. Rather people continue to invest in measures to rectify the inadequacies of urban burial, and the circulation between town and rural areas has increased rather than decreased in recent decades, both in the context of ESAP, and later, Operation Murambatsvina (Mbiba 1999; Bryceson and Mbara 2003). Relocations to the rural areas on the part of those sick with HIV/AIDs are supported by time series and micro-demographic data analysed by Kinsey (2006), and although HIV/AIDS deaths peaked in 2000–01, such relocations are still important. The departure into the diaspora of the middle/upper urban classes may also have had an impact on movement to the rural areas by enhancing urban unemployment, as domestic workers, garden boys, assistants and workers in family enterprises found themselves without work. Although urban in their everyday livelihoods, many Zimbabwean city residents remain attached to rural localities as a place where they belong, as well as relying on rural production as urban livelihoods have declined in the context of ESAP or the aftermath of Operation Murambatsvina (UN Habitat 2005; GoZ 2005).

Conclusions

This discussion has highlighted the wide range of factors necessary to explain the locus of burials, which is linked not only to urbanisation or the development of urban notions of belonging, but to changes in urban and rural economies, shifts in the linkages between town and countryside, the effects of HIV/AIDS, political violence and the creation of a new diaspora. The magnitude of death in Harare, the shortage of burial lands within the city and the bureaucratic administration of these grounds has also shaped decisions. Rural-urban linkages continue to be an engaging subject for social scientists and development planners, as the dichotomous view of rural versus urban does not capture more complex and interlinked realities. We have seen how the importance of rural/urban connections for many urbanites has been renewed in contexts of adjustment, or the crisis provoked by Operation Murambatsvina. As Harare's middle classes have now moved into the diaspora (or depend on remittances from relatives who have done so), the diaspora is now influencing, as well as being influenced by these changing rural/urban linkages. As one of the major occasions on which ideas about identity or home are revealed, planning for burial in Zimbabwe takes place in the light of assessments of the realities of conditions in urban cemeteries, among other factors. Indeed I hope to have shown the wide range of economic, political, health and other factors that can impinge on the way Zimbabweans in the diaspora and in Harare negotiate expectations and practicalities surrounding burial at home.

By highlighting the specifics of the Zimbabwean context, the chapter also aimed to highlight differences with the West African contexts discussed by Geschiere and Gugler (1998), where a rise in rural burial has been taken as indicative of an undermining of a sense of national belonging and a resurgence of ethnic identification. The changes in decision-making over burial by Zimbabweans within and beyond national borders reflect the acute crises of recent years, but not a diminution in a sense of national belonging, despite the large scale exodus and mass displacements.

Although this chapter argues that the idea of rural burial remains important for many urban and diasporic Zimbabweans, this ideal has been maintained in the context of a long-term trend in practice towards urban burial. Yet the chapter also discussed the possible reasons for the dramatic reversal of the trend towards urban burial in 2002, when Harare residents dying in the city suddenly began to be ferried to rural homes in much larger numbers. Again, the factors that might explain this shift point less to changes in whether people see themselves as belonging primarily in rural or urban locations, still less to any undermining of national identity, but relate to the far-reaching socio-economic, political, health and planning challenges of that year. Although Harare administrators responded to a critical shortage of urban cemetery space by changing rules of access and opening new burial grounds, these measures were inadequate and have also led to increasing differences between social classes. As residence in the diaspora, or access to diaspora finance has become increasingly important to the maintenance or definition of middle class/elite status back home, so the desire within the diaspora for burial at home, and diaspora perspectives on what constitutes a dignified burial are contributing in important ways to debates over dying and its management in Zimbabwe.

Notes

1. Interviews with Zimbabweans (2005, 2008); IPS funeral parlour, South London, 2005.
2. Letters of inquiry were sent and telephone calls made May – July 2005.
3. British Airways officers professed ignorance and did not reply to written requests for information, while an Air Zimbabwe senior manager conceded that such information was kept, but the sensitivity of this issue meant that information could only supplied by headquarters in Harare, who did not respond. Letters sent by author to Air Zimbabwe, 28 July and to BA, 2 August 2005.
4. See 'Inflation Undermines Burial Societies,' *The Zimbabwean* 27 May 2008. Retrieved 28 August from http://www.thezimbabwean.co.uk/.
5. See Zakeus Chibaya 'Burial Societies' Influential Role in Zimbabwe,' Institute for Peace and War Reporting, Johannesburg (AR no. 92) 30 January 2007. Retrieved 20 August from http://www.kubatana.net/html/ .
6. Interview, August 2008.
7. Interview, August 2008.
8. Interview respondent South East London, August 2008.
9. See 'Record Crowds at ZIMFEST' 30 August 2008. Retrieved 28 August from http://www.newzimbabwe.com/.
10. Sinyonyo, interview August 2008.
11. Interview with Mr Nyakuita, August 2008.
12. See 'Slain Zim Soldier a 'Sell-Out', *Cape Argus* 15 April 2003. Retrieved 21 August from http://www.capeargus.co.za/.
13. Jan Raath, 'Soldier's Family Fear for safety', *The Times* 21 April 2003. Retrieved 27 August from http://www.timesonline.co.uk/.
14. Respondents have requested not to be identified in this text.
15. Personal observations, Dome area of Accra, 2002.
16. In the late 1980s, the author witnessed several such grave side fires and vigils in Southern Zimbabwe. However, they seem to have disappeared in recent years probably because there to many deaths to cope with.
17. It is a legal requirement that all deaths be notified and registered before burial.
18. By 1996, home-based care programmes (training, supervision and support to home based care givers) had become a priority for Harare City Health Department (Report 1996: 76).
19. 'Borough is no Longer Dying for Grave Plots', *The Bexley Express* Wednesday 21 May 2003.
20. See Alex Duval Smith 'Aids Deaths Overwhelm Zimbabwe's Mortuaries', *The Independent* 10 February 2000.
21. See 'Funeral Services Business Booms', *The Herald* 17 February, 2007. Retrieved 18 February 2007 from http://www.herald.co.zw/.
22. 'Donor Mistrust Worsens Aids in Zimbabwe', *New York Times* 12 August 2004. Retrieved 20 August 2008 from http://www.zwnews.com/.
23. The City could not provide details of this private sector scheme in time for this paper.

24. See 'The Burial of Abigail Chiroto', *The Zimbabwean*, 26 June 2008, http://www.thezimbabwean.co.uk/.
25. This is the planned expansion of existing cemetery hence the bracketing of the figures.
26. This will be the total available hectare under active cemeteries.
27. Highfield was once closed and reopened in 1971 and final closed in 1995 after expansion of the old cemetery whose closure date was not recorded.
28. The gini-coefficient (the measure of in-equality) in cities of southern Africa is on average about 0.7 meaning that the level of inequality is seventy per cent.
29. *The Zimbabwean* 6 February 2008, http://www.thezimbabwean.co.uk/ .
30. *The Zimbabwean* 6 February 2008, http://www.thezimbabwean.co.uk/.
31. See 'Funeral Services Business Booms', *The Herald* 17 February, 2007. Retrieved 18 February 2007 from http://www.herald.co.zw/.
32. Interview, Respondent Mudiki, South London, 2004.
33. 'Funeral Services Business Booms'.
34. Ibid.
35. From 1998 surveys, see Mbiba (1999).
36. See 'Dying in Zimbabwe Now Only a Luxury Afforded by the Rich', *Zim Online* 12 December 2005.
37. Ibid.
38. Ibid. Mike Davies of the Harare Residents Association
39. Decent work surveys conducted jointly with Michael Ndubiwa, March – April 2006.

References

Alexander, J., J. McGregor and T. Ranger. 2000. *Violence and Memory: One Hundred Years in the 'Dark Forests' of Matabeleland.* Oxford: James Currey.
Bah, N.J. 2000. 'Burial in Ok, Cameroon: An Eyewitness Account of the Death Celebration of Fai Ndongdei (Phillip Njakoi)', *Tribus* 49: 49–64.
Bolling, M. 1997. 'Contested Places: Graves and Graveyards in Himba Culture', *Anthropos,* 9, 1–3: 5–50.
Bryceson, D.F. and T. Mbara. 2003. 'Sustainable Livelihoods, Mobility and Access Needs,' TRL Report 544.
Chinouya, M. 2003. 'Zimbabweans in England: Building Capacity for Culturally Competent Health Promotion'. In T. H. MacDonald (ed.) *The Social Significance of Health Promotion.* London and New York: Routledge, chapter 7.
____. 2004. *Zimbabweans in Luton: The Pachedu-Zenzele Health and Social Care Intervention Model, Luton.* Luton: NHS Primary Care Trust.
Christopher, A.J. 1995. 'Segregation and Cemeteries in Port Elizabeth, South Africa', *The Geographical Journal,* 161,1: 38–46.
Gaidzanwa, R. 1999. *Voting with Their Feet: Migrant Zimbabwean Nurses and Doctors in the Era of Structural Adjustment.* Uppsala: Nordiska Afrikainstitutet.
Gardner, K. 2002. 'Death of a migrant: transnational death ritual and gender among British Sylhetis', *Global Networks* 2(3): 191–205.

Geschiere, P. and J. Gugler. 1998. 'The Rural-Urban Connection: Changing Issues of Belonging and Identification', *Africa,* 68, 3: 309–319.

GoZ (2005), *Response by the Government of Zimbabwe to the Report By The UN Special Envoy on Operation Murambatsvina/Restore Order, August, 2005.* Harare, Government of Zimbabwe.

Halcrow, F. 1997. *Burial Space Needs in London,* Halcrow Fox, in conjunction with the Cemetery Research Group and the Landscape Partnership, report for London Planning Advisory Committee (LPAC).

Health Protection Agency. 2005. 'HIV/AIDS Report Slide Set'. London: Centre for Infections, Health Protection Agency Scotland, and Institute of Child Health. Retrieved 20 January 2007 from http://www.hpa.org.uk/infections/.

Jua, N. 2005. 'The Mortuary Sphere, Privilege and the Politics of Belonging in Contemporary Cameroon', *Africa* 3: 325–355.

Kinsey, B. 2006. 'Who Went Where and Why? Some Micro-Dynamics Following Jambanja and Murambatswina,' presentation to the British Zimbabwe Society Research Day, Oxford, 17 June 2006.

Maxwell, D. 1999. *Christians and Chiefs in Zimbabwe: A Social History of the Hwesa People, c. 1870–1990s.* Edinburgh: Edinburgh University Press.

Mazzucato, V., Kabki, M. and Smith, L. 2006. 'Transnational Migration and the Economy of Funerals: Changing Practices in Ghana', *Development and Change,* 37(5): (10441069).

Mbiba, B. 1999. 'Urban Property Ownership and the Maintenance of Communal Land Rights in Zimbabwe,' PhD Thesis. Department of Town and Regional Planning, University of Sheffield.

____. 2003. 'A Clash of Time, Cultures and Planning; Reflections from Zimbabwe' *Planning Theory and Practice: Interface,* 4, 4: 477– 481.

____. 2005. 'Zimbabwe's Global Citizens in Harare North (United Kingdom): Some Preliminary Observations'. In M. Palmberg and R. Primorac (eds) *Skinning a Skunk: Facing Zimbabwean Futures.* Uppsala: Nordic Africa Institute.

McGregor, J. 2009. 'Associational Links With Home Among Zimbabweans in the UK: Reflections on Long Distance Nationalisms', *Global Networks,* forthcoming.

NewZimbabwe. 2004. 'Zimbabwe Immigrants Account for Half of Aids Cases in the UK'. Newzimabwe.com 22 March 2004.

Ngahyoma, J. 2003. 'Tanzania Demo Over Graves'. BBC News. Retrieved 8 August from http://news.bbc.co.uk/.

Ogu, V.I. 1999. 'Housing as Graveyard: A Tale of Housing Culture in Nigeria', *Third World Planning Review,* 21, 3: 317–29.

Page, B. 2007. 'Slow Going: The Mortuary, Modernity and the Hometown Association in Bali-Nyonga, Cameroon', *Africa,* 77, 3: 419–41.

Potts, D. 1995. 'Shall we go Home? Increasing Urban Poverty in African Cities and Migration Processes', *The Geographical Journal,* 161, 3: 245–64.

Ranger, T. 2004. 'Dignifying Death: The Politics of Burial in Bulawayo', *Journal of Religion in Africa,* 34, 1–2: 111–44.

Reynolds, P. 1996. *Traditional Healers and childhood in Zimbabwe.* Ohio University Press.

Roys, C. 1995. 'Widows and Orphan's Property Disputes: The Impact of AIDS in Rakai District, Uganda', *Development in Practice* 5, 4: 345–51.

Shoko, T. 2007. *The Karanga Indiginous Religion in Zimbabwe: Health and Well-being.* Ashgate: Aldershot.

UN-HABITAT. 2005. *Report of the Fact Finding Mission to Zimbabwe to Assess the Scope and Impact of Operation Murambatsvina by the UN Special Envoy on Human Settlements, Mrs. Anna Kajumulo Tibaijuka.* Nairobi: UNHABITAT. http://www.unhabitat.org/

Van Onselen, C. 1976. *Chibaro: African Mine Labour in Southern Rhodesia 1900–1933.* London: Pluto Press.

Whyte, S.R. 2005. 'Going Home? Belonging and Burial in the Era of AIDS', *Africa* 75, 2: 154–72.

Yoshikuni, T. 1999. 'Notes on the Influence of Town Country Relations on African Urban History Before 1957: Experiences of Salisbury and Bulawayo.' In B. Raftopoulos and T. Yoshikuni (eds.) *Sites of Struggle:Essays in Zimbabwe's Urban History.* Harare: Weaver Press.

7

Negotiating Transnational Families: HIV Positive Zimbabwean Women's Accounts of Obligation and Support

Martha Chinouya

This chapter investigates the ways HIV positive Zimbabwean women have renegotiated their health and family relationships after moving to Britain. The growing literature on transnational families has tended to assume good health on the part of the 'lead migrants' who cross continents to seek work and support those left behind through remittances (Bryceson and Vuorela 2002; Parreñas 2005). Yet a significant proportion of Zimbabwean women in the UK who have moved abroad in the context of political and economic crisis at home have also had to deal with the consequences of HIV/AIDS in their families. Their capacity to work and remit all important funds to their relatives at home has commonly been undermined by late diagnosis and acute illness, such that even when they have managed to secure access to treatment in Britain, they have not been able to continue to make the kinds of financial transfers home that they themselves, and their relatives left behind expected. For many, who have sought asylum, insecurity over legal status and prohibitions on working have further reduced their capacity to remit. Exploring the experiences of Zimbabwean women living with HIV/AIDS in Britain thus sheds a different light on the workings of transnational families: it reveals different sorts of transfers between family members, and different sorts of tensions. The article brings together insights from two literatures that have developed separately – that on HIV/AIDS and that on transnational families, highlighting emotional as well as financial exchanges within families, and revealing the difficulties of caring at a distance (Baldassar et al. 2006).

How have such women managed their health and obligations with dependents in Britain and at home while unable to earn? Have they disclosed the nature of their ill-health to family members, if so to whom, and what were the consequences? How have those at home in Zimbabwe reacted to the knowledge of illness on the part of overseas remitters they depend on and how have they sought to help? By examining these and other questions, this chapter highlights aspects of obligation, support and tension within transnational families that have not received significant discussion in the existing literature. By exploring the narratives of women who have experienced a health crisis that has interrupted support for dependents both in the UK and back home, this chapter reveals the emotional and other support family in Zimbabwe has provided, including through sending prayers and efforts to find traditional drugs. At the same time, however, the stigmatising nature of an HIV positive diagnosis and the unequal nature of disclosure to different family members highlights the tensions and inequalities within families, as these have been shaped by north/south divides in access to treatment.

The chapter is based on interviews with forty-four HIV positive Zimbabwean women, who were part of a larger Nuffield Foundation funded study of more than sixty Zimbabweans living with HIV/AIDS in the UK.[1] The majority of these women were asylum seekers and their experiences of living with HIV were enmeshed in complex ways with their experiences of asylum. As asylum-seekers they were not permitted to work, but received financial support and accommodation from the National Asylum Seeker Services and were eligible for free treatment as their cases were still pending (see Department of Health, 2008 guidelines). All the women were on HAART (Highly Active Anteretroviral Therapies) and received their first clinical diagnoses confirming their status as HIV positive while in the UK. Approximately half were widowed and had experienced the death of the father of their children, and suspected these deaths were from AIDS (though in most cases, there had been no verbal disclosure on the part of their menfolk prior to their death). These widowed women preferred to call themselves 'single mothers', as 'widow' was construed as stigmatising and as a form of disclosure about HIV/AIDS in itself. Some were still married (either through the courts or through *lobola* [traditional bridewealth] payments), some lived with their husbands whilst others were co-habiting. All women were responsible for children and other dependents – they had left some children behind in Zimbabwe where they were mostly cared for by their own mothers, whom they also needed to support. Some also provided for orphaned relatives, and some had small children in the UK.

These Zimbabwean women, like most of those who are HIV positive in the UK, acquired their infections in Africa. Most individuals infected through heterosexual intercourse in the UK were born in Sub-Saharan Africa with Zimbabwean women and men forming a large part of this group (HPA 2006). This reflects the acute epidemic in Zimbabwe, where it is estimated that 1.7 million (out of a population of 13 million) have HIV (UNAIDS 2007). Zimbabwe has not been able to achieve universal access to anteretroviral treatments, though numbers receiving treatment have risen from 25,000 in 2005 to 60,000 in 2006 (UNAIDS 2008). Although HIV prevalence in Zimbabwe has fallen to eighteen point six per cent from thirty-three point seven per cent in 2001 (UNAIDS 2007), the reasons for this are unclear. Gregson et al. (2006) emphasise behaviour change among young people, but the effects of international and regional migration are also likely contributing factors.

Transnational Families, Remittances and Intimacy

We know from the large body of research on transnationalism that migrants' family connections and obligations to those left behind are critically important. Kane, for example, emphasises migrants' 'moral duty' and sense of 'social debt' towards those left behind, 'the prestige migrants gain from assisting development in their village of origin', which 'confirms their success ... and compensates for feelings of loss and marginality they experience in the host country' (Kane 2002: 251). The flow of resources can also be the material basis for family life, embedded in negotiating reciprocities and obligations within and across generations (Finch and Mason 1993; Ncube et al. 1997; Cattell 1997; Weisner 1997). Some authors argue such obligation can be considered a form of 'normative contract' comprising rules and guidelines (Finch and Mason 1999) and discuss 'family wealth contracts' between parents and their children, which can incorporate labour, exchange of wealth, emotional and practical support. Similar forms of obligation also exist between siblings as well as peer support groups (Chinouya 2002). Levitt describes 'a transnational moral economy of kin, which involves putting family first' (2001: 137). In the Zimbabwean case, as the crisis in Zimbabwe deepened, dependence on remittances increased dramatically for middle/class elite families in the suburbs as well as less well-to-do households in the high-density areas (Bracking and Sachikonye 2007). For Zimbabwean migrants in Britain and South Africa, remittances to relatives at home are a major concern, regardless of whether they left primarily for political or economic reasons (Bloch 2005). Moreover, unlike previous generations of migrants, women were prominent in the flows to Britain, partly due to the importance of work in social care and nursing

(McGregor 2007, 2008). Many such women migrants left their children at home, for a range of reasons, reflecting insecurity and lack of legal status for some, the difficulty of supporting children in Britain as a single parent on low wages, the desire for the children to grow up as Zimbabweans, and reactions against British norms of parenting and child rights (McGregor 2008).

It is important to see these economic flows between different parts of families as embedded in unequal social relations of power, shaped not only by gender but also generation and other axes of difference. These social inequalities are in turn shaped by state policies, such as asylum and immigration policies, and global relations of inequality and unequal development that also impinge on the options open to families (Levitt 2001; Parreñas 2005). Transnational family relationships also embody tensions, and 'transnational motherhood takes a toll because care-giving at a distance is emotionally stressful for parents and children' (Levitt 2001). This is notwithstanding the importance of new and cheaper forms of communication – telephone, SMS and email – that can act as the 'social glue' of transnational families (Vertovec 2004), allowing mothers to be much more involved in the lives of the families left behind, not only economically but also as nurturing figures (Parreñas 2005). Parreñas reminds us that 'transnational mothering is not a one-way process' (Parreñas 2005: 319), that children and other kin left behind also contribute to the relationships, shaping their form, the emotional support they can provide, as well as the worries and conflicts that are an inevitable part of 'long distance intimacy' (Parreñas 2005). There are multiple tensions produced by reliance on international remittances, as money sent to kin left behind can undermine the purchasing power of households lacking migrating kin, as a result of asset price inflation and inflationary effects of parallel currency markets (Bracking and Sachikonye 2007). There can also be tensions within families produced by the difficulties of honest communication with home, and mutual misunderstandings. It is common, for example, for money sent back to be obtained under very difficult and demeaning working circumstances, involving irregularity and deskilling, such as in the care industry, and relatives still at home in Zimbabwe may lack comprehension of the criminalisation and insecurities of asylum seekers; stress is also caused to the remitters by their inability to fully control the use of remittances (McGregor 2007).

Although these studies of transnational families are increasingly sensitive to inequalities and non-economic flows between members, and to the perspectives not only of remitters but also those left behind, they have not distinguished between healthy and unhealthy migrants, or looked at the effect of episodes of ill-health either on international remittances patterns or caring relationships. Yet it is clear from the vast literature on HIV/AIDS in Africa that incomes fall dramatically when heads of households are incapacitated by, and subsequently die of AIDS, and that such illness is intimately connected to patterns of mobility – within countries to urban areas or to kin, within the region to more prosperous neighbouring countries such as to South Africa, or back to rural homes in the final years of the disease (Cliggett 2005; Maphosa 2008). Networks of care in turn are transformed and upended as breadwinners become dependents, and grandmothers, children and other kin become carers instead of receivers of care (Van Blerk and Ansell 2007; Thomas 2006).

This chapter extends these literatures by beginning to explore the economic and emotional content of long distance exchanges between HIV positive Zimbabwean women in the UK and their dependent families at home. It highlights how ill-health can reveal the supporting role of family left behind and not just the obligations, while also remaining sensitive to the tensions involved.

As such it reveals the importance of linking up and integrating insights from fields of study that tend to be treated separately: debates over transnational families, remittances and HIV/AIDS have tended to proceed with too little cross-fertilisation.

This study also broadens understanding of emotional support and flows within families to include faith. The HIV positive Zimbabwean women in this study were all practicing Christians: most attended church in the UK (either a local church or a Zimbabwean church fellowship), had been church-goers at home, and their relatives still in Zimbabwe were also practicing Christians. For these women, their personal faith was central to the ways they discussed both their obligations to family and their health. It was also an important part of transnational communication – relatives at home texted prayers, and involved local church groups to pray for sick relatives. Such prayers were critical to the emotional support HIV positive women received from distant family in Zimbabwe. While several studies have begun to explore the role of African churches in the UK (Maxwell 2006; Ter Haar 1998), this literature is still undeveloped in its relationship to understandings of families, remittances and support networks during times of ill-health and other crises. Part of my argument here, is that there is a need for greater integration of studies of transnational religion with studies of the experiences of HIV/AIDS and the development of cross-continental family support networks.

Getting the Diagnosis and Making Sense of HIV

The women in this study had mostly arrived in Britain before the visa requirement in 2002, and made claims to asylum after they had been in the UK for some time. Before their diagnosis, most had been students, visitors or were working in unskilled jobs, particularly in care. Most had sought medical attention and been hospitalised after contracting TB. HIV positive status itself is most commonly referred to through euphemisms, and following their diagnosis, people talked of themselves as living with 'the modern illness' (*Chirwere chemazuva ano* in Shona) or simply 'the illness' (*Umkhuhlane* in Ndebele). There were related indirect means of speaking about TB, which women spoke of as 'the modern cough' (*chikosoro chemazuva ano*) in Shona, or 'the cough' (*isikwehlelo*) in Ndebele. These were also the terms in which HIV positive women disclosed their status to their relatives, and very few liked to speak directly of their status as HIV positive. Although, from a policy and clinical point of view, HIV has slowly been redefined as a chronic illness in the UK, reflecting effective clinical treatments, most of the Zimbabwean women in this study made very late clinical presentations with AIDS-defining illnesses, which had an acute impact on their capacity to work and remit. As a result of these delays, most had experienced periods of hospitalisation in the UK. As I have described elsewhere, although they suspected they were ill, most Zimbabweans with HIV delayed presenting to the health authorities, sometimes because they feared contact with the state officials if their legal status was insecure, sometimes because they could not countenance the idea of illness when so many others depended on their remittances. Some felt that after moving to the UK they had left all their problems behind in Zimbabwe (Chinouya 2002). The stigma attached to HIV/AIDS, which is acute in the UK just as it is in Zimbabwe, was also an important reason for delaying.

These attitudes are important, as the delays they caused in seeking treatment were directly responsible for the acute shift in the capacity to work and remit that was such a worry to the women in this study. A mother, who used to send money, described working until she virtually collapsed, and was then incapacitated for a long period in hospital, with severe impacts on her ability to send money home: 'I was very sick. Really sick with *chikosoro chemazuva ano* (the modern cough, TB). I could not walk. I was admitted in hospital. I was there for a very, very long time. All the money that I was earning suddenly dropped to zero and the people at home, besides worrying about my health were also worried whether they will get the pound [money]'. (Mother, age 53).

These anxieties over health and money were greatly exacerbated by the insecurities generated by their status as asylum-seekers. Some had been waiting for decisions for years, having gone through a series of appeals, and some spoke of the stress and anxiety they had experienced in relation to their claims as worse than managing their illness, not least as they feared being returned to places where treatment was not available. Seeking asylum also created structural barriers on their capacity to work legally once their health stabilised, to visit or bring over family members and dependents.

Some described their situation as akin to 'captivity', as they had no control over their lives, could be relocated without notice to other geographical areas through the policy of dispersing asylum seekers. Others were using scarce income to paying solicitors to try to regularise their immigration status, as there is an increasing shortage of lawyers taking on immigration and asylum cases with legal aid. Moreover some had exhausted their claims and were resorting to expensive solicitors in the private sector.

Although most had planned to come to the UK simply to work temporarily, after falling ill, their illness itself and the lack of treatment at home contributed to the decision to stay on in the UK, a viewpoint that was often reached in discussion with relatives at home. After receiving the diagnosis, these women then had to make sense of the illness within the context of their transnational obligations, shaped by hyperinflation and hardships in Zimbabwe. For many, a primary concern was to find a means of reducing unrealistic financial expectations from children and others in Zimbabwe while at the same time getting relatives' support in the decision to stay on. The HIV positive women made full, or more commonly partial disclosures about their ill-health to family at home in this context. Women commonly described disclosing only to their children's female guardians, in most cases the participants' mothers (i.e. the children's grandmothers) that they were 'unwell' using the euphemisms described above to explain why they could not continue to send so much money. Mostly they did not explicitly reveal the nature of their illness, but the implications were generally understood, and relatives also reinforced the decision to stay on in the UK to receive treatment. One woman, for example, who had children back in Zimbabwe who had already lost their father, explained: 'Ahh! When I went to hospital I was very sick. I was planning to go back home but then I became very ill. I had promised people at home that I was coming but I was advised not to go because I may not have been able to access *mapiritsi* (pills) at home'. (Mother, age 45).

Such disclosures of HIV to those left behind, when they were understood as such, were also described as moral dilemmas, as relatives were said to be worried, and engaged in *kumbofamba famba* ['walking about' i.e. consulting traditional healers], which involved spending money, and costs tended to escalate if healers found out that the person being consulted for was in Britain. Yet many women also appreciated the concern, and had followed advice from home as to how to manage their condition, including taking such herbs, even as they also followed advice from support groups over nutrition and HAART. One woman explained: 'My mother is always looking for herbs. They are sending some to me [pause] mixed herbs. They are very, very bitter but they say they are working for people who are drinking them. They are working a lot. So I also go to the support group to get more information about the nutrition side of treatment and HIV tablets'. (Mother, age 41).

Many women reported gaining immeasurable emotional support from their kin back home. One elaborated: 'I think the gain from relatives in Zimbabwe is something you cannot measure. ... It's just something which you can't put in words. It's the association on that thing ... to say this is my family. This is my *mukoma* [brother or sister]. You know and knowing that you have a family lessens the suffering. It's just something good that comes out.' (Mother, age 50).

Yet many of those who had disclosed their HIV status through euphemisms also described very complicated exchanges over the phone, where both parties would be talking about the illness without mentioning it directly, or trying to explain it as something else, both trying to avoid shaming the other. One women described her conversations with her mother at home as follows:

> Sometimes *mai* [mother] will ask 'how are you feeling? Is everything OK? How is your body?' I will just say these days as I am coughing a little bit or I am developing pink lips. Mother says it's probably something else not '*izwozwo*' [those things]. Don't think about it [the illness] too much. It's probably something else and you think 'it' is responsible. Maybe you are not eating well or thinking too much.
>
> (Mother, age 30)

Strategies of euphemistic disclosure of illness often did not, however, stop relatives from continuing to ask for money. This was not surprising, as livelihoods in Zimbabwe have been so drastically undermined over the last decade, and the combination of hyperinflation and repression has affected everyone. But such demands were also a burden and source of great anxiety. As one mother described:

> People at home, after I had told them that I am sick and not well they still asked me to send money ... For them, I am sick but I am able to eat. But for them they are not sick but they are unable to eat. But they are also looking after [a] sick one or they are not sick but they are not able to feed the sick. So the situation is similar to the one of a person with the disease. They have hardships. You are troubled with sickness but you will see they are also troubled by the same situation. So if I have that '*ka*' [small] pound [money] to give, I give.
>
> (Mother, age 29)

Anxiety over responsibilities for dependents and a fall in income brought on by late clinical presentations and hospitalisation was a repeated theme in my interviews. The HIV positive Zimbabwean women described how the ongoing need to support children and others left behind compromised the quality of foods that they themselves could afford to eat. Most women continued to send money and goods home, even though most received less than £40 per week from NASS. One woman explained her budget for herself and children left behind:

I get £30 per week. The five pounds is for transport money. The doctors tell me I have to eat rice and vegetables, which are all expensive. The food for the week costs me £15 per week. I also need £3 per week for the tithe. The change I save to send home to my children and husband. I must also have money for the phone card.

(Mother, age 25)

The HIV positive women explained continuing to remit in terms of the hyperinflation and crisis back home, as well as being a reflection of 'love' and *'chivanhu'* [humanity], as well as in terms of the values of being African and the importance of extended family. Getting an HIV diagnosis did not award them a medically sanctioned 'excuse' for not sending money home. Exchanging and sharing resources was the basis family life, some explained, irrespective of the geographical location. It was also crucial to maintaining family honour and not giving others cause for derision at your expense: One young mother explained: 'I know from the time grandfather died saying "don't withhold help from someone amongst yourselves. Whosoever is able to give must give so that those outside may not laugh at you."' (Mother, age 22).

These women did not conceive of themselves as individuals, but as tied to other family members for whom they were responsible, and in turn the family was responsible for them, and not helping was perceived as acutely shameful: 'What will people say when they see my mother and the children I left with her starving and she has a daughter in London? They will laugh at her. So I have to give.' (Mother, age 42). This sense of shame was magnified when the women positioned themselves in relation to other Zimbabweans in the diaspora who had managed to send money home to build houses and buy taxis (Combis) to use for public transport, earning their families back home a some income. One Zimbabwean woman captured this, saying: 'You tell them you have no money they do not believe you. They ask you what about other people whose children are in the UK who have combis, houses and are sending money. Why don't you have those things too? We are suffering here and you are there.' (Woman, age 33).

Such communications increased the burden to remit. Many also embedded their sense of obligation to give in their Christian faith, and construed it in part as preparation for a peaceful death: 'Giving helps because you have always believed in God', one explained. 'You are no longer afraid. You have hope. The way you believe is that when I die I hope to die in right[eous]ness. So you stay in peace because most of the time you are sick you always think of death. Who will bury me?' (Mother, age 55).

Religious practices across national boundaries enabled these HIV positive women to reaffirm their sense of presence in Zimbabwe through transnational prayers, which were important in the way they managed their everyday lives. A wish to be remembered in prayers back home and redefine one's position as a member of that 'original' community often led to the disclosure of an illness (but not HIV) to relatives in Zimbabwe. Many women described how prayers from 'home' were helping them cope with the HIV diagnosis and their ill health. One mother narrated how she had disclosed that she was 'unwell' (rather than HIV positive) to her own mother in Zimbabwe, who had gone on to inform her prayer group (Prayer Warriors) that the daughter in England, was sick, and had engaged them in praying for her daughter for divine interventions in healing. She explained how this gave her hope:

> My mother and her Prayer Warriors in Zimbabwe are praying for me. They pray for me. This give me hope as the Bible tells you Jesus healed such and such a person so you are strengthened because you know you are saved, so the faith in me is what is at work. Because I believe I am healed even when I know I am on medication. My belief is that I am not sick even if I am sick. Prayers are getting through and there is a breakthrough as I feel much better.
>
> (Mother, age 27)

Others also described the immense support they found through prayers from Zimbabwe, in coping with their illness. One mother reported how her daughter in Zimbabwe had passed on the information of her illness to the local pastor back in Zimbabwe: 'My daughter found a preacher back home whom she told that I was not well. She told the preacher that my mum is ill in England. Because she is ill she can't come back soon. Please start praying for her'. (Mother, age 55).

These women also prayed for their families at home, and with compatriots in Zimbabwean church fellowships that meet in Britain, where the groups incorporate and remember kin at home. Such church groups are enormously important for those living with HIV (Ridge et al. 2008; Chinouya and O'Keefe 2004). Ridge et al. (2008) argue that prayers constituted a kind of dialogue with an absent counsellor and could promote positive thinking general wellbeing. While such prayer meetings can depend on physical contact, transnational prayers in physical absence of the beneficiary are also important, and are enabled by the telephone as it is used to convey information about health and mobilise resources for prayer.

These women's narratives of their communications with their own mothers at home add to our conceptual understanding of transnational exchanges amongst African migrants in the UK. As well as adding to the burgeoning literature on African remittances, particularly from a position of marginality (Stayn 2007; Boon 2006; Bloch 2005), I hope to have shown how women living with a chronic condition, namely HIV, and asylum-seekers make sense of transnational family lives, and gained care and support from relatives at home. This emotional care was translated in various ways – sending money back home, transnational prayers and use of language that 'normalised' HIV so as not to cause pain to the person in question and to whom partial disclosure has occurred. There was often reciprocity in flows not only of money and goods, but also emotional support and prayers. Such intangible 'goods' are often disregarded in discussions of remittances, including the satisfaction and moral value that the sender gets in sending the money. Despite this reciprocity, however, there were tensions and inequalities within transnational families, which were also structured by broader relations of power and unequal development. These inequalities emerge more clearly in patterns of disclosure to children back home. This requires some further discussion here, as it illuminates the strains of managing transnational family relationships, particularly with regard to children living in countries where access to treatment is limited.

Telling, or Not Telling Children About 'The Modern Illness'

We have seen how Zimbabwean HIV positive women in the UK disclosed or partially disclosed their illness first to adults left behind – particularly to their own mothers or siblings who had responsibility for the day-to-day care of their children in Zimbabwe. But the implications for an HIV positive diagnosis extended beyond the practicalities of remittances and strained capacity to send funds home. For women with children, an HIV positive diagnosis meant that their children too could have been at a high risk of being HIV positive, given the risks of transfer between mother and unborn child. Thus the HIV positive mothers in the UK had a dual dilemma, regarding whether or not to tell children of their own status, and whether to tell children that they too might be 'living with the modern disease'. The children that caused most anxieties to the women in this study were those born in Zimbabwe before the mothers migrated to the UK and who were also resident back home. There was uncertainty over these children's status as the mothers had not taken them for tests, mostly because the mothers themselves were not aware of their own HIV status before migrating to the UK. Young children were a particular worry, and the age of the child was important in considerations as to whether or not to tell children left behind that their mothers in the UK were living with HIV.

Children living in the UK would be in a position to go for tests and access treatment, but for the children left behind, where access to treatment is inadequate, the dilemmas of disclosure were different and many women reported not telling children, particularly if they were young, that they too might be HIV positive. As I have argued elsewhere, based on a different group of interviewees, African parents living with HIV in the UK generally think that children who might also be infected or affected by HIV have 'some sort of right' to know both that they or their parents were HIV positive, but it was difficult to help children promote their right to information (Chinouya 2006). The Zimbabwean mothers interviewed in this study echoed those findings. The factors that encouraged disclosure included the desire to educate children about the risks, plan for the children's welfare in the event of the parents' death, and discuss inheritance. But these were commonly outweighed by the factors that encouraged not disclosing, such as wanting to protect the children from the stigma attached to HIV, especially given that access to HAART treatment in Britain meant that parents would be in a position to continue to care for them. Some HIV positive mothers described how their children had 'witnessed too many deaths' in their families, including seeing the decline and loss of their fathers from suspected AIDS-related illnesses, making it highly problematic to tell children that the remaining parent was also living with HIV. As one mother noted: 'Ahh! My child is only 12 years old. She will think I am dying here in the UK. Maybe one day I will tell her but it's very hard' (Mother, age 34).

Although they were hiding their diagnosis from children, these mothers faced a dilemma that the children could find out on their own, especially given the partial disclosures they had usually passed on to their own mothers, the children's daily carers, described above. Some feared that not sharing knowledge of their illness would damage their relationship and trust with the children. There was also concern that younger children were unable to understand the significance of either a full or partial disclosure. The HIV positive mothers were also anxious that children might tell their friends, who may in turn tell others, resulting in subsequent stigmatisation of the children and the family. Not telling the children, in this light, was a means of protecting the children from shame.

The children based in the UK who were coresident with the HIV positive women interviewed in this study were mostly said to be aware to various degrees that there was 'something wrong with their blood' as well as with their mother's health. But those back home were less likely to know, or to have been subjected to HIV tests and their uncertain HIV status was a major concern for these mothers. By not disclosing their HIV status, mothers felt that they were protecting their children from the pain of knowing, as HIV is so closely associated with death in Zimbabwe. Indeed, as Niehaus has argued, the stigma attached to the disease cannot only be understood through the implication of sexual transmission, rather the fact that it kills slowly and painfully contributes to the stigma, as the sufferer goes through a period of 'living death' in which they are incapacitated and dependent (Niehaus 2007). Mothers reported that most of their children back in Zimbabwe had not been tested, as it was complicated to organise this at a distance, particularly if the guardians of the children had often not been told of the mothers' diagnosis, or had been told only ambiguously. As one HIV positive mother in Britain described:

> How do I begin to tell my mother to take my child for an HIV test when I have not even told my mother that I am living with HIV. She thinks I had the cough due to the cold weather ...! How can I begin this. If the child is positive my mother will know that I am too. She is my child and I am her child. So I am preparing but I am very afraid.
>
> (Mother, age 44)

The HIV positive mothers also felt that distance mattered, and that sensitive information needed to be discussed face to face, not on the telephone or via text messages. All the HIV positive mothers wanted medical help for their children, but questioned the benefit of disclosure to children in circumstances where they were unlikely to get access to antiretrovirals, and could not afford to sponsor treatment for children back in Zimbabwe when they were not working. There was also a lack of information about what was available in terms of treatment for children in Zimbabwe, although it was generally agreed that treatment back home was difficult to access, and if it was available it was sporadic. The issues surrounding disclosure to children were thus complex, and the general sentiment that children in Zimbabwe should know did not generally translate into actually telling them, because the mothers did not want to add to the burdens the children lived with and felt powerless in the face of so many constraints on their capacity to support the children in the Zimbabwean context.

Conclusion

These women's accounts of the anxiety and worry of managing their own ill-health and obligations to family can contribute in important ways to existing understandings of transnational families and the management of HIV positive status. They show how family lives are radically altered by the complex intersections of migration/asylum, HIV, and the north/south divide in the availability of HAART. This context affects the health of HIV positive women in the UK who delay seeking tests, as well as the health of the children left behind, who are more closely enmeshed in the epidemic, and are not given information about their mother's or their own potential HIV positive status. Children and the families left behind had different understandings of the illness, given the high death rates from HIV/AIDS in the absence of anti-retrovirals, which affected how HIV positive women decided to manage disclosure in a transnational context. The lack of disclosure to children within transnational families has implications for public health and the risk of onward transmission, but the concept of the 'best interest of the child' was complex in the Zimbabwean context, given the stigma around HIV, the potential for children and whole families to be stigmatised, and children to be emotionally disturbed by the prospect of their mothers', or their own, death. The women living with HIV/AIDS in Britain who were the subject of this study, were not in a position to secure access to or pay for HAART for their relatives back in Zimbabwe, given the decline in their own incomes following their own delayed diagnoses, hospitalisation and enforced unemployment. Their attitudes towards children's' 'right to know' were shaped within this context, as well as being influenced by the age of the child, and notions of authority within the family, as the idea of child rights was widely regarded as undermining parenting strategies, particularly for maintaining discipline (cf McGregor 2008).

Reducing the time between infection and clinical diagnosis of HIV is a key strategy aim (HPA 2006). But the factors that contribute to late presentations have been poorly understood, particularly in Western contexts, where treatment is available. Early HIV diagnoses could have averted the problems these Zimbabwean HIV positive women experienced as a result of delaying seeking help. Had their capacity to earn not been undermined so drastically by hospitalisation, they would have been in a better position to continue to help family at home, including to pay for antiretrovirals, which in turn would have altered the considerations related to disclosure to children. Yet strategy and policy documents targeting African communities in England do not pay attention to transnational obligations. This chapter has highlighted the ways in which these transnational obligations shaped the ways in which Zimbabwean women managed their own HIV positive status, and their patterns of disclosure. On the one hand, the incapacitation of these HIV positive women as a result of late diagnosis revealed the emotional and other support they received from home – as their own mothers sent prayers, encouragement and even traditional herbs to help them cope – flows that tend to be overlooked in the literature on transnational families. But at the same time, the inequalities within families, the developmental divide in access to treatment, and the constraints created by state immigration and asylum policies undermined the potential for disclosure to those at home. This chapter has argued that researchers investigating the effects and management of HIV/AIDS could learn from greater understanding of transnational family obligations, as these are shaped by a range of factors discussed here, including religious ideas. But there are also implications for policy makers responsible for HIV health promotion messages, as these messages could usefully highlight the negative economic impact of late clinical presentations on remittances and obligations within transnational households as a strategy for encouraging early disclosure.

Notes

1. The data drawn upon in this study was funded by the Nuffield Foundation collected under a broader study 'Zimbabweans Getting on with Life', involving interviews with sixty HIV positive Zimbabweans (both men and women), who were accessing support services in London and the Home Counties. As participants were assured anonymity, quotes in the text below show only age and date of interview, alongside other information about family circumstances where appropriate.

References

Baldassar, L., C. Baldock, and R. Wilding 2006. *Families Caring Across Borders: Aging, Migration and Transnational Caregiving.* London: Macmillan.

Bloch, A. 2005. 'The Development Potential of Zimbabweans in the Diaspora'. International Organisation for Migration No. 17. Geneva: Switzerland.

Boon, M. 2006. 'BME Remittance Survey'. London: ICM research. Retrieved 6 October 2008 from http://www.dfid.gov.uk/pubs/files/ukremittancessurvey.pdf.

Bracking, S. 2003. 'Sending Money Home: Are Remittances Always Beneficial to Those Who Stay Behind?' *Journal of international development,* 15, 5: 663–644.

Bracking, S. and L. Sachikonye. 2007. 'Remittances, Poverty Reduction and the Informalisation of Household Wellbeing in Zimbabwe'. Conference Paper, Living on the Margins, Stellenbosch 26–28 March.

Bryceson D. and U. Vuorela (eds). 2002. *The Transnational Family: New European Frontiers and the Global Network.* Oxford: Berg.

Cattell, M. 1997. 'The Discourse of Neglect: Family Support for the Elderly in Samia'. In C. Bradley, T. Weisner and P. Kilbride (eds). *African Families and the Crisis of Social Change.* London: Bergin and Garvey.

Chinouya, M. 2002. 'HIV Disclosure Patterns Amongst African Families Affected by HIV/AIDS in London', PhD Thesis. London Metroplitan University.

——. 2006. 'Telling Children About HIV in Transnational African Families: Tensions About Rights', *Diversity in Health and Social Care* 3: 7–17.

Cliggett, L. 2005. 'Remitting the Gift: Zambian Mobility and the Anthropological Insights for Migration Studies', *Population, Space and Place,* 11, 1: 35–48.

Department of Health. 2008. 'Table of Entitlement to NHS Treatment as of May 2008'. Retrieved on 7 October 2008 from http://www.dh.gov.uk/en/Healthcare/International/AsylumseekersAndrefugees/index.htm.

Finch, J. and J. Mason. 1993. *Negotiating Family Responsibilities.* London: Routledge

Gregson S., G.P. Garnett, C. Nyamukapa, T. Hallett, J. Lewis, P. Mason, S. Chandiwana and R. Anderson. 2006. 'HIV Decline Associated with Behaviour Change in Zimbabwe', *Science,* 311: 644–6

Health Protection Agency. 2006. 'A Complex Picture: HIV and Other Sexually Transmitted Infections in the United Kingdom, 2006'. London: Health Protection Agency.

Horst, H.A. 2006. 'The Blessings and Burdens of Communication: Cell Phones in Jamaican Transnational Social Fields', *Global Networks* 6, 2: 143–59.

ICAR. 2005. 'Statistical Snapshot Series: Zimbabwe Asylum Applications to the UK 1990–2005', London: ICAR. Retrieved on 7 October 2008 from http://www.icar.org.uk/?lid=2409.

International Labour Migration. 2006. 'HIV/AIDS: Global Estimates, Impact on Children and Youth, and Response'. ILO: Geneva.

Kane, A. 2002. 'Senegal's Village Diaspora and the People Left Ahead'. In D. Bryceson and U. Vuorela (eds). *The Transnational Family: New European Frontiers and the Global Network*. Oxford: Berg.

Levitt, P and B. Jaworsky. 2001. 'Transnational Migration Studies: Past Developments and Future Trends', *Annual Review of Sociology,* 33: 129–56.

Maimbo, S. M. and D. Ratha. 2005. 'Remittances: An Overview'. In S. Maimbo, D. Ratha (eds) *Remittances: Development Impact and Future prospects*. Washington: World Bank.

Maphosa, F. 2005. 'The Impact of Remittances from Zimbabweans Working in South Africa on Rural Livelihoods in Southern Districts of Zimbabwe'. Forced Migration Working Paper Series 14. Johannesburg: University of Witwatersrand.

McGregor, J. 2007. 'Joining the BBC (British Bottom Cleaners). Zimbabwe Migrants and the UK Care Industry'. *Journal of Ethnic and Migration Studies*, 33, 5: 801–24.

____. 2008. 'Children and 'African Values': Zimbabwean Professionals in Britain Reconfiguring Family Life', *Environment and Planning A,* 40, 3: 596–614.

Ncube, W., J. Stewart, J. Kazembe, M. Donzwa, E. Gwaunza, T. Nzira and K. Dengu-Zvobgo. 1997. *Continuity and Change: The Family in Zimbabwe*. Harare: Women and Law in Southern Africa Research Trust.

Niehaus, I. 2008. 'Death Before Dying: Understanding AIDS Stigma in the South African Lowveld', *Journal of Southern African Studies*, 33, 4: 845–60.

Parreñas, R. 2005. 'Long Distance Intimacy: Class, Gender and Intergenerational Relations Between Mothers and Children in Filipino Transnational Families', Global Networks, 5, 4 : 317–336.

Ridge, D., I. Williams, J. Anderson and J. Elford. 2008. 'Like a Prayer: The Role of Spirituality and Religion for People Living with HIV in the UK'. *Sociology of Health and Illness,* 30, 3: 413–28.

Styan, D. 2007. 'The Security of Africans Beyond Boarder: Migration, Remittances and London's Transnational Entrepreneurs'. *International Affairs* 83: 1170–91.

Ter Haar, G. 1998. *Half Way to Paradise: African Christians in Europe*. Cardiff: Academic Press.

Thomas, F. 2006. 'Stigma, Fatigue and Social Breakdown: Understanding the Impact of HIV/AIDS on Patient and Carer Well-Being in the Caprivi Region, Namibia', *Social Science and Medicine,* 63, 12: 3174–87.

Turner, S. 2008. 'Studying the Tensions of Transnational Engagement: From the Nuclear Family to the World-Wide Web', *Journal of Ethnic and Migration Studies*, 34, 7: 1049–56.

UNAIDS. 2008 'Country progress Report'. Retrieved on 8 October 2008 from http://data.unaids.org/pub/Report/2008/zimbabwe_2008_country_ progress_report_en.pdf.

Van Blerk, L. and N. Ansell. 2007. 'Alternative Caregiving in the Context of HIV/ AIDS in Southern Africa: Complex Strategies for Care', *Journal of International Development* 19, 7: 865–84.

Vertovec, S. 2004. 'Cheap Calls: The Social Glue of Migrant Transnationalism', *Global Networks*, 4, 2.

Weisner, T. 1997. 'Support for Children and the African Family Crisis'. In C. Bradley, T. Weisner and P. Kilbride (eds) *African Families and the Crisis of Social Change*. London: Bergin and Garvey.

Zinyama, L. 2002. 'International Migration and Zimbabwe: An Overview.' In D. Tevera and L. Zimyana (eds) *Zimbabweans Who Move: Perspectives on International Migration*. Migration Policy Series 25. CapeTown: Southern African Migration Project.

Zontini, E. 2004. 'Immigrant Women in Barcelona: Coping with the Consequence of Transnational Lives', *Journal of Ethnic Migration Studies,* 30, 6: 1113–44.

Diasporic Identities and
Transnational Media

8

Debating 'Zimbabweanness' in Diasporic Internet Forums: Technologies of Freedom?

Winston Mano and Wendy Willems

The protracted and multi-staged economic and political crises that visited Zimbabwe in the 2000s were accompanied by politically charged, narrowed-down definitions of national identity and citizenship. As many Zimbabweans left for Britain, the USA, South Africa and other destinations, so the internet became an important multi-platform medium for publishing and obtaining news about Zimbabwe. It could provide linkages between Zimbabweans in different parts of the diaspora and enabled them to debate political and economic change. The burgeoning diasporic Zimbabwean media have primarily served the growing population outside Zimbabwe but have also been accessible to some constituencies at home, and have provided alternatives to the shrinking state-controlled media space in Zimbabwe. Leading diaspora websites such as *SW Radio, Zimdaily* and *New Zimbabwe* have offered up-to-date news and provided critical reflection on Zimbabwe's demise.

The internet has often been celebrated as a medium which enables those subject to censorship to evade regimes of control. For example, de Sola Pool (1983: 5) argues that '[f]reedom is fostered when the means of communication are dispersed, decentralised, and easily available, as are printing presses or microcomputers. Central control is more likely when the means of communication are concentrated, monopolised, and scarce, as are great networks'. The internet has been described as making possible a new form of cyberdemocracy or as enabling a more inclusive public sphere

(Poster 1997; Tsagarousianou et al. 1998; Liberty 1999; Gimmler 2001; Papacharissi 2002; Dahlberg and Siapera 2007). Others have discussed the way in which the internet can threaten the power of authoritarian regimes (Kedzie 1997; Kalathil and Boas 2003). In the context of Zimbabwe, Peel (2008) has proposed that Zimbabwean internet fora constitute 'a microcosm of Zimbabwean diversity which deconstructs the authoritarian nationalism that has been a signature of Mugabe's 28–year rule'.[1] However, against these positive celebrations of the liberating potential of the internet, more sceptical observers have highlighted the way in which the internet can also give a voice to extremely reactionary perspectives such as those of the extreme right and neo-Nazi white supremacists (Brophy et al. 1999; Adams and Roscigno 2005; Atton 2006; Roversi and Smith 2008).

This chapter considers the way in which national identity and citizenship were debated within an online discussion forum on the diasporic website *NewZimbabwe*. It specifically focuses on discussions around the participation of a Zimbabwean nurse, Makosi Musambasi, in the British *Big Brother* series, broadcast on Channel Four in 2005. Via the 'Makosi case', the chapter examines how diasporic Zimbabweans defined themselves and how they imagined 'Zimbabweanness' in internet chatrooms. Through the case study, the article discusses the extent to which their imaginations can be seen as an alternative to the narrow and exclusionary nationalism articulated by the ruling ZANU PF government. The first part of this article provides a background to the authoritarian nationalism espoused by the Zimbabwean government in the 2000s. Subsequent sections address emerging diasporic Zimbabwean media and the specific case of *NewZimbabwe*, Makosi's entry into the *Big Brother* house and the final section discusses online discussion forum debates on 'Zimbabweanness'.

Nationalism and the Articulation of Authentic, Patriotic Citizenship

In the 2000s, national identity and citizenship in Zimbabwe became defined in increasingly restrictive terms (Alexander 2004; Muponde 2004; Muzondidya 2004, 2007; Alexander and Muzondidya 2005; Raftopoulos 2004; Ranger 2004). State nationalism excluded certain groups of Zimbabweans who were regarded as inauthentic and unpatriotic Zimbabweans and not considered to rightfully belong to the 'nation'. While at the eve of independence, President Robert Mugabe made a pledge for reconciliation to the white population and assured them that '[i]f yesterday I fought as an enemy, today you have become a friend and ally with the same national interest, loyalty, rights and duties as myself',[2] in the 2000s, white Zimbabweans were more and more categorised as aliens who did not have a lawful claim to Zimbabwean citizenship.

Coinciding with Mugabe's numerous insults against whites, the government also introduced the Citizenship Amendment Act in 2001 which denied citizenship to anyone whose parents were born outside Zimbabwe unless he/she would renounce their claim to a second citizenship. The act not only affected white Zimbabweans but also impacted on Zimbabwe's coloured and Indian community, as well as Zimbabweans of Malawian, Mozambican and Zambian descent whose ancestors had mostly migrated to Zimbabwe to work in mines and on farms.[3] As Muzondidya (2007: 334–5) has pointed out, the latter category has often been excluded from the 'Zimbabwe nation' in official discourses through derogatory names such as 'mabwidi emutaundi' (foolish people without rural homes) or 'manyasarandi,' or 'mabhurandaya' (Malawians), 'mamosikeni' or 'makarushi' (Mozambicans).

'True' Zimbabweans were not only those whose ancestors were born in Zimbabwe but also those who resided in or had strong links with the rural areas. Peasants toiling the land were seen as the authentic vanguard who had assisted in 'giving birth' to the Zimbabwean nation through their participation in the liberation struggle. While trade unions and urban workers played an important role in the emergence of African nationalism in the period between the 1940s and 1960s, government's narrow version of 'patriotic history' ignored their contribution and instead focused on the revolutionary role of peasants and emphasised their support for and assistance to the guerrilla fighters (Ranger 2004: 218).[4] Urban Zimbabweans were increasingly presented as not belonging to the 'nation'. For example, during an election campaign rally in Bindura in 2000, President Mugabe singled out residents of Harare's oldest township Mbare as 'undisciplined, totemless elements of alien origin'.[5] Mbare was established during the colonial period as a dormitory township and housed a significant number of migrant workers from the broader Southern African region.

The exclusion of urbanites was particularly expressed through the so-called Operation Murambatsvina/Restore Order (OM/RO) which began on 19 May 2005 and lasted for several months.[6] While OM sought to 'weed out criminals in the informal sector', RO aimed to demolish 'illegal' residential structures in the urban areas. The two operations resulted in many urban residents losing either their home or their livelihoods, or both. Around the time of OM/RO, a Deputy Minister defined 'Zimbabweanness' as follows during a debate in Parliament: 'the definition of an indigenous person is one who has a rural home allocated to him by virtue of being indigenous, and a home that one has acquired in an urban area because it has been bought or it has been allocated to him by the State'.[7] Not having access to a rural home was associated with not being 'indigenous' and 'un-Zimbabwean', and therefore as undeserving of a place in Zimbabwean society. OM/RO particularly affected Zimbabweans of Malawian, Zambian and Mozambican descent who either worked on farms or lived in urban areas and often did not have access to land in rural areas.

The attack on urban residents was primarily motivated by the fact that Zimbabwe's urban areas were the major support base of the opposition party, Movement for Democratic Change (MDC). In all elections between 2000 and 2005, MDC received the majority of votes in urban areas and ZANU PF's support remained confined to the rural areas.[8] Before the March 2005 parliamentary elections, President Mugabe addressed Harare residents as follows in a speech at a funeral of a government minister at the national burial ground Heroes Acre:

> You are Zimbabweans, you belong to Zimbabwe which was brought by the blood of our heroes lying here and others scattered throughout the country. Should we give it away to sellouts here in Harare? This is our capital city. You are sons and daughters of revolutionaries. What wrong have we done you? Harare: think again, think again, think again.[9]

Whereas Mugabe represented MDC voters as 'sell-outs', those voting for ZANU PF were portrayed as true, authentic and patriotic Zimbabweans. For government, the MDC posed a threat to national sovereignty and represented British, American and Rhodesian interests. While MDC was constructed as an alien party unconnected to Zimbabwe's history, ZANU PF's role in the liberation war served as a justification for its continued rule over Zimbabwe.

Apart from invoking binary oppositions such as black/white, indigene/ stranger, rural/urban and ZANU PF/MDC, President Mugabe also began to exclude the increasing number of Zimbabweans leaving the country for greener pastures in South Africa, the United Kingdom and the United States. For example, in his speech at Independence Day in April 2006, he blamed Zimbabweans for joining the diaspora in the United Kingdom:

> You might go to England, but you will be discriminated against there. You will be given menial jobs like looking after old people in their homes. If you flee then who will make the country better? Is it Mugabe alone? Did I fight for the country alone? The answer is no. It was a collective exercise [...]. We should remain united, love each other and help each other and know that we are all Zimbabweans especially in the face of the current challenges. Zimbabwe is one country and is the only country we have. If it's the only country we have, let's make it great because people fought for it [...]. You might flee and go to South Africa or the UK, but we will meet; *nyaya haiperi* [the crimes will not be forgiven].[10]

While the increasingly desperate economic situation forced many Zimbabweans to seek their fortunes elsewhere, Mugabe blamed them for not being committed to their country.[11] In another speech in 2006, he mocked the diaspora for returning back to Zimbabwe as 'retirees in wheelchairs'.[12] When South Africa saw a spate of xenophobic attacks targeting Zimbabweans and other foreigners in May 2008, he urged South Africa-based Zimbabweans to consider coming back to Zimbabwe and offered that '[w]e have land for our people in South Africa who may want to return home'.[13]

Therefore, in order to qualify as an authentic and patriotic Zimbabwean, one was expected to: be black; have ancestors who were born in Zimbabwe; live in rural areas or at least be entitled to land in the rural areas; and vote ZANU PF. The next sections discuss whether discussions on diasporic websites provided an alternative discourse to this increasingly narrow form of authoritarian nationalism.

Emerging Diasporic Media: The Case of *NewZimbabwe*

Coinciding with the increasing Zimbabwean diaspora, there was a corresponding rise in different types of media that began to cater for the growing numbers of Zimbabweans abroad. In December 2001, former journalists of the state broadcaster Zimbabwe Broadcasting Corporation (ZBC) set up a radio station *SW Radio Africa* which operates from a studio in northwest London and broadcasts on the shortwave in Zimbabwe as well as on the internet. In February 2005, a weekly newspaper, *The Zimbabwean*, was established which was produced and disseminated in the United Kingdom but also distributed in Zimbabwe and neighbouring countries.

Apart from these 'old' media, Zimbabweans increasingly began to profile themselves through a range of websites which were mostly set up by former journalists. Websites such as *The Zimbabwe Situation* (http://www1. zimbabwesituation.com), *Zimdaily* (http://zimdaily.com), *NewZimbabwe* (http://www.newzimbabwe.com), *ZWNews* (http://www.zwnews.com/ contact.cfm) and *ZimOnline* (http://www.zimonline.co.za) sought to keep Zimbabweans posted on developments back in their country. Most of these emerging media provided news, information, entertainment and advertisements, and offered discussion fora on current affairs and the challenges that were part of living in a foreign country. They covered topics of relevance to Zimbabweans in the diaspora, e.g. legal issues to do with asylum applications and carried political activism aimed at exposing the injustices perpetrated by the Zimbabwean government. However, they also aimed to provide critical perspectives on the crisis to Zimbabweans 'at home' in the context of the increasing repression of private media and the monopolisation of public debate by government. These newly emergent media therefore aimed to connect 'the homeland' and 'the diaspora' in multiple and imaginative ways.

The website *NewZimbabwe* is of particular interest because of the way in which it sought to imagine a 'New Zimbabwe' beyond the 'official' version of the Zimbabwean nation articulated by the ZANU PF government in its increasingly authoritarian nationalism. The website advertises itself through various slogans such as 'the Zimbabwe news you trust', 'the biggest name in Zimbabwe news' and 'breaking news as it happens'. The website features news items, both written in-house and compiled from other sources, as well as showbiz news, sports, columns and opinion articles. Prominent Zimbabweans have contributed pieces, including the previous Minister of Information, Jonathan Moyo, businessman Mutumwa Mawere, young academics, intellectuals and novelists such as Chenjerai Hove.

The website was set up by Mduduzi Mathuthu in June 2003.[14] Mathuthu is a Zimbabwean journalist who used to work for *The Daily News* as correspondent in Bulawayo, which is the second biggest town in Zimbabwe, located in the western part of the country. Like many other Zimbabwean journalists, Mathuthu came to the United Kingdom to embark on postgraduate education. He enrolled for an MA degree in Journalism at Cardiff University and started the website after he completed his degree. As one of his major sources of inspiration, Mathuthu names Piers Morgan, the previous editor of the British tabloid *The Daily Mirror*. In an article on the website, Mathuthu said to be 'drawn to editors with a sense of mischief, who want to make waves, and who take risks', even though these editors 'occasionally drop clangers – but that's the nature of taking risks: you have to push the envelope'.[15] The front-page of *NewZimbabwe* is indeed modelled along the lines of a British tabloid, with bold and provocative headlines in big capital letters. For example, when Makosi's application for asylum was accepted by the British Home Office, *NewZimbabwe*'s front page featured a close-up picture of Makosi's bare breasts, taken in the *Big Brother* house, and the headline read: 'They can stay'.[16]

NewZimbabwe is supported by a large number of advertisements and banners on the front page, addressing diasporic Zimbabweans, mainly those based in the United Kingdom. Money transfer companies present their services to transfer money to Zimbabwe against 'parallel' exchange rates. HIV/AIDS anti-retroviral medicines, groceries and fuel can be bought for relatives in Zimbabwe. Phone companies offer cheap calling rates to friends in Zimbabwe and other companies advertise affordable flights to Zimbabwe. Announcements of events featuring Zimbabwean musicians or DJs are made as well as notices of social gatherings in Luton, which are informally known in Zimbabwe as 'braai' or 'gochi gochi' (barbecues).

Apart from news articles and advertisements, visitors are strongly encouraged to join 'the debate' on the discussion forum section of the website, which has proven very popular with 8,152 members registered in May 2006.[17] New members can join by simply choosing a username and password which provides them access to the forums. The forum section has been divided into debates on different categories of topics: general discussion, high school reunions, audience with a politician, talking sport, hot gossip, humour, relationships, technology, music and entertainment, religious corner and health and lifestyle. The 'general discussion' and 'relationships' sections are the most popular with the highest number of postings. The discussion forums on *NewZimbabwe* particularly address what can be called the 'interpretive community of in-group members' (Mitra 1997), given that active participation in the chatrooms requires some knowledge of local languages in Zimbabwe. Discussions are mostly held in English and Shona, or Shonglish, which refers to the mixture of Shona and English that is common among Zimbabweans, and sometimes Ndebele is also used.

The issue of 'tribalism', as it is referred to in the chatrooms, is a popular discussion topic in the forums and moderator Mathuthu, a Ndebele-speaker, has occasionally been accused of stirring up 'tribal' divisions on the forum and for promoting tribalism and advocating 'Mthwakazi', which refers to the call for self-determination of the 'Ndebele nation'. One participant in the forum even suggested introducing a special section on the forum for discussions on tribalism in order 'to keep the main page "venom" free'.[18] As the same contributor argued: 'Those with an itch to post some tribally or racially stuff, would then simply click on that link and post their anger, frustration dreams hopes and lies. If you don't want to read the tribal crap then you will keep off that thread! Summarily let birds of the same feather fly together'.[19]

Although this would require further offline research, it appears likely that a significant number of participants in the *NewZimbabwe* forums are Zimbabweans based in the United Kingdom. This is demonstrated not only by the language that participants use but also by the topics they discuss in the chatrooms which strongly relate to everyday life situations of Zimbabweans in Britain. For example, in a thread entitled, 'Nzondoro [chicken feet] in the UK', participants discussed where to buy chicken feet, a Zimbabwean delicacy, and Palmers Butchery in Bletchley, Milton Keynes was recommended as the best place. According to one participant, queues at Palmers Butchery often resembled the '[a]gricultural show days with zimboz coming as far as Leicester etc for the meat'.[20] The question about 'why the fuss? Aren't there any other butchers which have right about the same quality of meat' was dismissed by those who appreciated the 'supreme taste' of meat from the 'famous Palmers Butchery'.[21] The participants were familiar with most places in the United Kingdom as shown by the way in which they tried to help each other in identifying the exact location of Palmers Butchery.

Both the front page of *NewZimbabwe* and the forum section often carried lively debates on a range of issues, and particularly on the crisis. While the front page mainly gave space to opinion pieces from Zimbabwean academics, intellectuals and politicians, the forum section was accessible to 'ordinary Zimbabweans', i.e. all members who had registered with the website. As the title of the website suggested, *NewZimbabwe* aimed to establish a new version of Zimbabwe with new possibilities and challenges. It sought to imagine a different country from beyond the physical borders of the nation. Mathuthu played a crucial role in triggering debates and provoking responses, in line with his motto to 'make waves' and 'to push the envelope'. As will be demonstrated in this article, a particularly interesting debate took place on *NewZimbabwe* around the participation of Makosi Musambasi, a migrant nurse from Zimbabwe, in the 2005 British *Big Brother* television show, broadcast on Channel Four.

Makosi Musambasi: A Zimbo in *Big Brother*

The 2005 *Big Brother* show that provoked such significant debate among diasporic Zimbabweans in Britain was the sixth edition in the United Kingdom. The show kicked off on Friday 27 May 2005 and drew thirteen contestants together for seventy-five days in the confinement of the *Big Brother* house. Makosi quickly drew the attention of Zimbabweans, both those based in Zimbabwe and those part of the diaspora. Bubbly, charismatic, confident and stunning, Makosi provided Zimbabweans with plenty of material to talk about. During her days in the *Big Brother* house, she confessed to being a virgin upon entering the house, went topless, controversially kissed female housemate Orlaith, allegedly engaged in unprotected sex in the pool with fellow housemate Anthony and claimed to be pregnant. As a prominent Zimbabwean in the United Kingdom commented: 'I have been to several Zimbabwean gatherings in the past few months and was surprised at the amount of time spent by people discussing the Makosi issue. We have to admit that Makosi has become a household name to many of us'.[22]

The website *NewZimbabwe* fulfilled an important role in providing space to diasporic Zimbabweans to discuss their recent move to the United Kingdom and to debate the antics of their fellow Zimbabwean in the *Big Brother* house. More generally, the internet played a key role in the lives of diasporic Zimbabweans. A study conducted by Bloch (2005: 72–3) for the International Organisation for Migration (IOM) concluded that participating in internet discussion groups was the most regular activity that diasporic Zimbabweans engaged in with other diasporic Zimbabweans (24.5 per cent). Although this could to some extent be explained by the fact that the IOM conducted part of its survey through internet questionnaires, it is significant that this activity was mentioned and recognised as an activity that kept them in touch with others, as a means to maintain a sense of community.

In line with Mathuthu's tabloid aspirations mentioned earlier, *NewZimbabwe* quickly set the stage for a lively debate through its announcement that '[e]very Zimbabwean should be ashamed' of Makosi in an article on its frontpage:

> The reality TV show *Big Brother* – a sad and pointless contest in which 13 participants compete for fame and £100 000 in the same house for nearly 2 months, trailed by television cameras – this year features a pathetic, self-obsessed Zimbabwean who claims to be a virgin! [...] Zimbabweans are generally cultured people, but not this chicken-brained sanctimonious squit. She has already started behaving like an Amazon squirrel, plunging the depths of iniquity to try and rile the other inhabitants of the jungle that is *Big Brother*.[23]

NewZimbabwe referred to Makosi as a 'foul mouthed weasel' who undermined fundamental Zimbabwean values. The provocative front page article quickly triggered a significant amount of debate in the forum section of *NewZimbabwe* and at least one hundred discussion threads in the forum section focused on Makosi. As chatroom participants noted, Makosi soon became a topic that could not really be avoided. For example, one participant remarked that 'the girl's antics have forced her into all the newspapers (for the wrong reasons) and you just cant help reading about it, its like trying to ignore the Iraqi war, its always in your face anyway'.[24] Another participant confessed to not normally watch the show but somehow felt obliged to engage with conversations about Makosi: 'I not a fan of *Big Brother* and I don't stay glued to the TV either. As a matter of fact I have not been watching *Big Brother* at all. Its just that all the white people at work been talking about her and her antics on a daily basis. I did not even witness the said incident but everyone is talking and there is no smoke without fire'.[25] The remainder of this article focuses on the way in which *NewZimbabwe* forum participants discussed Makosi's involvement in the *Big Brother* show.[26]

Defining the 'Nation' Through Makosi's Multiple Identities

Makosi's participation in the *Big Brother* show clearly brought to light the contested nature and often exclusionary definition of what forumites perceived as 'Zimbabweanness'. Initially, the arrival of Makosi in the *Big Brother* house generated huge excitement amongst diasporic Zimbabweans participating in the *NewZimbabwe* discussion forum. One participant had immediately identified Makosi as a Zimbabwean through the way in which she spoke English: 'I picked it up from her DISTINCT Zimbo accent before they said "She's originally from Zimbabwe". Our accent is unique and quite easy to pick!! Can't wait to hear her scream "MAIWEEEE" '.[27] 'Maiweee' literally is a call for one's 'mother' in Shona, Zimbabwe's major local language, and is an expression often used when facing danger or when calling out in disbelief.

Another *NewZimbabwe* member exlaimed 'We are on the map', hereby suggesting that Makosi's partaking in the show had made diasporic Zimbabweans visible in the United Kingdom.[28] It was felt that Channel Four's *Big Brother* show was meant to represent society, 'ratio in a way', and Makosi's participation therefore suggested that 'Zimbos are now getting the recognition'.[29] Forum participants felt that Channel Four had finally realised the presence of large numbers of Zimbabweans in Britain, hence the need to portray this minority through Makosi. But the recognition of Zimbabweans in Britain, through Makosi's participation in the *Big Brother* show, was felt not going to last for long. As a result of persistent forms of racism in British society, one chatroom participant expected Makosi to be voted out of the show fairly soon:

> HOW LONG DO YOU THINK SHE WILL LAST I GIVE HER 2 WEEKS OR LESS YOU KNOW THE BRITISH AINT GOING TO LET A BLACK PERSON WIN, LET ALONE A AFRICAN AND OHH SHIT EVEN WORSE SHE IS FROM ZIM, TONY BLAIR WILL HAVE THAT BITCH OUT OF THERE QUICK.[30]

The capital letters used by this chatroom participant serve to underline the urgency of the comment which was indirectly a comment on the broader diaspora experience of Zimbabweans in the United Kingdom. As Cunningham (2001: 136) notes: 'much diasporic cultural expression is a struggle for survival, identity and assertion, and it can be a struggle as much enforced by the necessities of coming to terms with the dominant culture as it is freely assumed. And the results may not be pretty'. The above posting shows the participant's disappointment about majority white 'British' attitudes towards 'a black person' and more particularly about Tony Blair's possible vindictiveness on a fellow Zimbabwean. This imagined power of the dominant white British hosts was an issue recurrent on the *NewZimbabwe* forum. Participants shared a number of fears and conspiracy theories on behalf of Makosi which ultimately connected to their own insecurities of being diasporic Zimbabweans in Britain, many of whom did not have a secure residence status or permit.

Another participant expected Makosi to be voted out because she indirectly represented Zimbabwe's regime with which the British government no longer had sound diplomatic relations. While the participant above emphasised Makosi's identity as a black person in Britain and more specifically as a Zimbabwean who by virtue of being Zimbabwean did not enjoy a secure residence status in Britain, participant 'Dr Chinoz' portrayed Makosi as a representative of the ruling party ZANU PF because of her alleged affair with Philip Chiyangwa, a prominent ZANU PF parliamentarian and businessman. Makosi, which literally means 'princess' in Ndebele, was in fact a 'Zanu princess':

> I got a feeling that Makosi has been lined up as the first candidate to be booted out next Friday not only because she is Zimbabwean, but because she has been a 'Zanu Princess'. How can they give her the tall order of having to receive the highest nominations from all the house's in mates within the first seven days?[31]

In these comments, diasporic Zimbabweans strongly identified with Makosi and in the process expressed their own views on their self-perceived roles and positions in British society. The hostile attitudes of British 'hosts', both in the house and more generally in British society, led participants to show their solidarity with Makosi.

However, debates did not always express a demarcation between 'us' (Zimbabweans) and 'them' (British). Makosi's participation did not necessarily strengthen collective identities but precisely brought to the fore the fragmented nature of the 'Zimbabwean nation'. Instead of identifying with Makosi as diasporic Zimbabweans based in the United Kingdom, some forum participants began to distance themselves from her in terms of both her class and ethnic background. They attempted to situate her back in her previous Zimbabwean context which was not shared by all chatroom participants. For example, one *NewZimbabwe* member mainly saw Makosi as a fairly well-off Zimbabwean, often expressed in the term 'musalad' ('salad-eater') which refers to young well-to-do urban residents of upmarket suburbs who dress in Western clothes and are often embarassed to speak in local Zimbabwean languages:

> Haaa!!! Wanditangira JoeDoe. Zi Accent racho. I told my young brother she was from Zim, before Davina said it. Gore rino tinoonerera. Accent yacho haiite kunge akakura achishoferwa tho. ndainonga chop chop. Makosi... Makosikhazi? [32]

English translation from Shona:

> Haaa!!! You beat me to it. It's a very Zimbabwean accent. I told my brother she was from Zim, before Davina [*Big Brother* presenter] said it. This year has plenty in store. She has a posh Zimbabwean accent, although she sounds as if she grew up being chauffeur driven. I quickly figured out the accent. Makosi [literally princess] ... Makosikhazi [literally queen]?

Makosi was thus represented as a relatively wealthier Zimbabwean which was expressed in her particular accent in English. Despite the likely class difference between Makosi and the chatroom participant, Makosi was still considered as a Zimbabwean. Another participant agreed that judging from the way Makosi speaks, she is a 'pure muZimba'.[33] But this was disputed by others on the forum who rejected that one could be identified as Zimbabwean simply through the way one speaks: 'So you're saying she's Zimbabwean because she has an accent? Under those qualifications I would be american because of my accent'.[34] The same chatroom participant stated:

> She [Makosi] only identifies herself with Zimbabwe because she grew up there. But in terms of the blood running in her very veins and even her genetic make up she is not Zimbabwean. The fact fact she has 0% = Zimbabwean blood. Scientifically speaking, culturally speaking you name it she is not Zimbabwean.[35]

So while most of the early forum postings celebrated the arrival of Makosi in the *Big Brother* house, subsequent contributions rated her 'Zimbabweanness' in a much more unfavourable light. Her ethnic background became a factor that was often drawn into this debate, particularly when *NewZimbabwe* members began to reflect on Makosi's roots. Some believed Makosi was born in Zimbabwe to a South African mother and a Mozambican father, and this suddenly made her Zimbabwean identity appear questionable:

> Can't vouch that a Mosken [derogatory term used for Zimbabweans of Mozambican origin] with a South African mother represents Zimbabwe in the true sense of the word, values, culture, the lot. Were they passing through Harare when she was born? She is quite a loud mouth, and not very likeable.[36]

Some considered her to be a 'muNyasarandi' which is a derogatory term referring to migrant workers of Malawian descent. Others pointed towards Makosi's surname which for them proved that she was no 'Zimbabwean': 'OK to end this argument is "Musambasi" a zimbabwean surname? – No its not! Just like surnames Liboma or Modimo its not a Zimbabwean. She just grew up in Zimbabwe but is not Zimbabwean'.[37]

Merely having been born in Zimbabwe was not sufficient for being 'Zimbabwean', and another participant drew parallels with his/her own British-born child: 'If she [Makosi] is Zimbabwean then my son is English'.[38] Others felt that 'Zimbabwean culture' should simply be defined in terms of a person, born and bred in Zimbabwe, someone who has solid 'roots' in the country.[39] One *NewZimbabwe* member even argued that it did not make sense to discuss 'foreigners' on a forum that was supposed to deal with 'Zimbabwean' issues: 'She is beautiful its a pity Zimbabweans argue about foreigners on a ZIMBABWEAN FORUM' and the participant acknowledged to be 'proud of ZIMBABWEANS that excel but I resent foreigners that masquerade as Zimbabweans, one's nationality is of paramount importance. Visiting a stable does not make you a horse'.[40]

However, calls for support to Makosi were made and justified particularly by referring to her position as an African and victim of racism in the *Big Brother* house. For example, one participant put it as follows: 'I read "pull her down" syndrome in the majority of contributions. Why not support a sister from mother Africa guys? If she does not get your support, who will give it?'[41] It was felt that Makosi could not count on votes from British viewers who were unlikely to support her. Fellow housemate Saskia's racist remarks were also mentioned as a reason for support to Makosi: 'Yeh, let's support her. We should nominate Saskia for eviction. She sez she hates immigrants!'[42] The mood thus shifted to 'she got my support' and to 'Guys we should stick together and prevent her from being voted out next week'.[43]

Other ways in which Makosi was discussed was through framings of gender. Several participants, most of whom seemed to be male, were not particularly concerned about Makosi's exact roots but primarily saw her as a 'hot chick'. When a picture of Makosi was posted on the forum, participants exclaimed: 'damn she looks quite nice, She has that Zimbabwean look, at least they found a descent girl to represent Zimba. I now might jus vote to keep her in'.[44] One member alerted the forum to the fact that Makosi was in a 'Bikini right now on E4. Wow nice to see a woman with hips for a change! Was tired of sticks with boobs!'.[45] The debate turned into adulation for black women: 'I love black women. Black women huchi [honey]!!'[46] The comments queried Makosi's claim that she was a virgin and became suggestive of her sexual potential with talk of thighs looking 'like they have never been stretched that much'.[47] Makosi was considered to be a 'proper' and 'voluptuous' Zimbabwean woman as compared to her 'thin' British housemates.

Conclusion

It is arguable that the growing numbers of Zimbabweans leaving their country for greener pastures, such as the United Kingdom, have set up a vibrant media culture that has catered for a wide audience. The above discussion has shown how diasporic Zimbabwean media culture incorporated and subverted mainstream representations in the British media. The intensity and scope of the debates around the participation of a Zimbabwean nurse, Makosi Musambasi, in the 2005 British television show *Big Brother* are a good example of the mobilising aspect of issues of national identity on the internet. As a nurse, Makosi was the archetype of the Zimbabwean diaspora experience in the United Kingdom.

Well-summarised by Taffy Nyamwanza, a UK-based lawyer, in the newspaper *The Zimbabwean*, Makosi 'brought to the fore some critical issues that Zimbabweans in the diaspora are all too familiar with: nursing as a platform to bigger things, AIDS and the rumours of AIDS, media xenophobia, and perhaps by far the most topical, a perilous immigration status accompanied by the constant fear of forced removal to Mugabeland by the real *Big Brother*, the Home Office'.[48] Zimbabweans could easily identify with Makosi's experience in Britain but also profoundly distanced themselves from her.

As a migrant to the United Kingdom, Makosi underwent training as a nurse upon arrival in the country. As Nyamwanza suggested, this was not because she was particularly interested in nursing but like many other Zimbabwean migrants, Makosi considered nursing as a 'stepping stone' to a more glamorous professional career. Another issue that enabled diasporic Zimbabweans to identify with Makosi was the amount of racism that both Makosi and other Zimbabweans were confronted with in their daily lives in the United Kingdom. The producers of *Big Brother* received a number of complaints from viewers about alleged racism when Makosi's fellow housemate Saskia told her 'You lot always have a chip on your shoulder' and made derogatory comments about her Afro-hairstyle: 'And you wear a fucking wig on your head'.[49] Furthermore, Makosi was also confronted with the same levels of insecurity surrounding her immigration status in Britain when she faced deportation two weeks after the show.

But most importantly, Makosi's television performance profoundly challenged and provoked ideas about what internet participants understood as 'Zimbabwean' identity, morality and womanhood. The 'Makosi case' triggered a more serious debate about what it means to be 'Zimbabwean'. This case has illustrated the ways in which diasporic Zimbabweans tried to fix identity, to provide an essence that could be seen as 'Zimbabweanness'. Participants attributed different identities to Makosi such as 'muZimbo', diasporic Zimbabwean in the United Kingdom, 'musalad', 'Mosken', 'muNyasarandi', foreigner, 'hot chick' and 'Zimbabwean woman'. While some identified with Makosi because she was 'a pure Zimbabwean', others explicitly denied that she was a Zimbabwean because her parents had not been born in Zimbabwe. These imaginations of the nation to some extent echoed the authoritarian nationalism espoused by ZANU PF in the 2000s. Although Makosi had lived her whole life in Zimbabwe, forum participants excluded her from the nation in similar ways as the Zimbabwean government sought to disenfranchise Zimbabweans of Malawian, Zambian and Mozambican descent from their citizenship. In this way, official highly exclusionary notions of the nation were thus reproduced on the *NewZimbabwe* forum. Hence, while it is tempting to consider the internet as a free counter-medium compared to controlled, monolithic and monopolised state media in Zimbabwe, internet debates among diasporic Zimbabweans about Makosi's participation in the *Big Brother* house often reflected state discourses and presented nativist conceptions of Zimbabwean citizenship instead of more cosmopolitan notions. The internet proved a forum that served to highlight and reinforce divisions among Zimbabweans instead of project a common understanding and identity. Divisions were not only along political lines but ethnicity proved a recurrent marker used by diasporic Zimbabweans on the internet to frame each other.

Notes

1. Peel, Clayton, 'An African Perspective; is Cyberdemocracy Possible?' In: *Pambazuka Newsletter*, 30 July 2008. Retrieved 12 October 2008 from: http://www.pambazuka.org/en/category/features/49780.
2. Available from Kubatana website. Retrieved 2 September 2007 from http://www.kubatana.net/html/archive/demgg/070221rm.asp?sector=OPIN&year=0&range_start=1.
3. However, in 2003, the act was amended in order to enable the following persons to retain dual citizenship and exempted them from having to renounce foreign citizenship or entitlement to foreign citizenship: (1) persons of SADC parentage who may be citizens of those countries; (2) persons born in a SADC country, whose parents were born in Zimbabwe and migrated to such country for the purposes of employment. The act then thus mainly affected white, coloured and Indian Zimbabweans. See Kubatana website for a copy of the act. Retrieved 10 November 2007 from http://kubatana.net/html/archive/legisl/030214citbill.asp?orgcode=par001.
4. See Raftopoulos and Yoshikuni (1999) for an urban historiography of Zimbabwe, and specific focus also on the role of urban associations in the resistance against colonialism.
5. 'Zanu PF Accused of Tribalism', *The Daily News*, 14 October 2002.
6. The Shona term '*murambatsvina*' literally means 'clear the dirt or filth'.
7. Statement made in Parliament, 23 June 2005, by Phineas Chihota, Deputy Minister of Industry and International Trade, 'Urban Dwellers not Zimbabwean – MP', *The Zimbabwe Independent*, 1 July 2005 (quoted in Muzondidya 2007: 334).
8. This refers to the following elections: June 2000 parliamentary elections; March 2002 presidential, mayoral and council elections; September 2002 local elections; August 2003 council and municipal elections and March 2005 parliamentary elections,
9. 'Harare, Think Again', *News24*, 2 March 2005. Retrieved 11 November 2005 from http://www.news24.com/News24/Africa/Zimbabwe/0,,2–11–1662_1670 235,00.html, quoted also in Kamete (2006: 263).
10. Quoted in: 'Come Home, Let's Rebuild Zimbabwe', *Association for Zimbabwe Journalists website*, 20 April 2006.

11. While President Mugabe mocked the diaspora for being 'unpatriotic', the governor of the Reserve Bank of Zimbabwe (RBZ), Gideon Gono, urged Zimbabweans to work abroad and to remit foreign currency back to Zimbabwe. As he said in June 2004, '[t]he country's foreign currency reserves would improve significantly if more people went to work abroad [...]. The exportation of labour has helped many countries in earning foreign currency as citizens use official channels to send money back to their families at home. I encourage Zimbabweans to seek jobs outside the country' (quoted in: Kahiya, Vincent, Mugabe's shadow dogs Gono in diaspora, *The Zimbabwe Independent*, 19 June 2004). In order to ensure that remittances from diasporic Zimbabweans would be channelled through official money transfer services, RBZ launched the HomeLink scheme in May 2004.

12. Nyamutata, Conrad, 'Don't Demonise the Diaspora', *The Zimbabwe Standard*, 27 August 2006.

13. 'Land for Zimbabweans who Return from South Africa – Mugabe', *Reuters*, 25 May 2008.

14. In mid-2007, *NewZimbabwe* also launched a tabloid newspaper which was circulated in branches of the Nandos restaurant chain and African shops across the United Kingdom. This article strictly focuses on the *NewZimbabwe* website.

15. Mathuthu to edit new Zimbabwe paper in UK, *NewZimbabwe*, 22 September 2004. Retrieved 21 February 2008 from http://www.newzimbabwe.com/pages/fusion3.11665.html.

16. *NewZimbabwe*, 'Makosi Update'. Retrieved 29 May 2006 from http://newzim.proboards29.com/index.cgi?board=zimele&action=display&thread=1118907878.

17. A count of members was conducted in the forum section on 29 May 2006. Retrieved 20 August 2008 from http://newzim.proboards29.com/index.cgi?action=members.

18. Post by nygent on 26 June 2006, 10.58am, part of thread 'Start a Tribalism Section'.

19. Post by nygent on 26 June 2006, 10.58am, part of thread 'Start a Tribalism Section'.

20. Post by Valerie on 12 May 2006, 09.09am, part of thread 'Nzondoro in UK'. The Agricultural Show is one of the most well attended annual events in Harare.

21. Post by Valerie on 12 May 2006, 09.09am, part of thread 'Nzondoro in UK'.

22. 'Chireka, Dr Brighton, Makosi's Case, as I See it', *The Zimbabwean*, 25 November 2005.

23. 'Every Zimbabwean Should be Ashamed', *NewZimbabwe*, 29 May 2005. Retrieved 26 June 2006 from available from: http://www.newzimbabwe.com/pages/fame4.12697.html.

24. Post by DRBOB on 8 June 2005, 11:23am, part of thread 'Makosi's Blow-job on National TV.'

25. Post by TSOTSI on 8 June 2005, 11:24am, part of thread 'Makosi's Blow-job on National TV.'

26. On 29 May 2006, an advanced Google search on Makosi was done on the forum section of *NewZimbabwe* (http://newzim.proboards29.com). This yielded

221 hits. Ultimately, nearly 100 threads were identified with the subject heading Makosi. These were ordered chronologically and analysed. In order to retain the character of the postings, none of the quotes from the chatrooms have been edited. All typing and grammar errors have been retained.

27. Post by jmcguire on 27 May 2005, 9:37pm, part of thread 'A Zimbo in *Big Brother*!!!!!!'.
28. Post by Bantuwarrior on 27 May 2005, 9:39pm, part of thread 'A Zimbo in *Big Brother*!!!!!!'.
29. Post by watisthis on 27 May 2005, 11:07pm, part of thread 'A Zimbo in *Big Brother*!!!!!!'.
30. Post by watisthis on 27 May 2005, 10:21pm, part of thread 'A Zimbo in *Big Brother*!!!!!!'.
31. Post by Dr CHINOZ on 28 May 2005, 11:29am, part of thread 'A Zimbo in *Big Brother*!!!!!!'.
32. Post by FullMassage on 27 May 2005, 9:44pm, part of thread 'A Zimbo in *Big Brother*!!!!!!'.
33. Post by watisthis on 27 May 2005, 11:04pm, part of thread 'A Zimbo in *Big Brother*!!!!!!'.
34. Post by spie on May 28, 2005, 7:39pm, part of thread 'A Zimbo in *Big Brother*!!!!!!'.
35. Post by spie on 28 May 2005, 8:12pm, part of thread 'A Zimbo in *Big Brother*!!!!!!'.
36. Post by munodawafa on 27 May 2005, 10:58pm, part of thread 'A Zimbo in *Big Brother*!!!!!!'.
37. Post by spie on 28 May 2005, 4:21pm, part of thread 'A Zimbo in *Big Brother*!!!!!!'.
38. Post by spie on May 28, 2005, 5:42pm, part of thread 'A Zimbo in *Big Brother*!!!!!!'.
39. Post by munodawafa on 27 May 2005, 11:21pm, part of thread 'A Zimbo in *Big Brother*!!!!!!'.
40. Post by vumani on 28 May 2005, 8:55pm, part of thread 'A Zimbo in *Big Brother*!!!!!!'.
41. Post by munodawafa on 28 May 2005, 12:22am, part of thread 'A Zimbo in *Big Brother*!!!!!!'.
42. Post by JonDoe on 28 May 2005, 12:39am, part of thread 'A Zimbo in *Big Brother*!!!!!!'.
43. Post by spie on 28 May 2005, 12:32am, part of thread 'A Zimbo in *Big Brother*!!!!!!'.
44. Post by watisthis on 27 May 2005, 10:50pm, part of thread 'A Zimbo in *Big Brother*!!!!!!'.
45. Post by JonDoe on 27 May 2005, 10:54pm, part of thread 'A Zimbo in *Big Brother*!!!!!!'.
46. Post by munodawafa on 28 May 2005, 12:58am, part of thread 'A Zimbo in *Big Brother*!!!!!!'.
47. Post by munodawafa on May 28, 2005, 1:08am, part of thread 'A Zimbo in *Big Brother*!!!!!!'.

48. 'Nyawanza, Taffy, Makosi and the Real *Big Brother*,' *The Zimbabwean*, 16 September 2005.
49. Makosi in *Big Brother* racism row, *NewZimbabwe*. Retrieved 21 February 2008 from http://www.newzimbabwe.com/pages/fame14.12816.html.

References

Adams, J. and V.J. Roscigno. 2005. 'White Supremacists, Oppositional Culture and the World Wide Web', *Social Forces*, 84, 2: 759–78.

Alexander, K. 2004. 'Orphans of the Empire: An Analysis of Elements of White Identity and Ideology Construction in Zimbabwe'. In B. Raftopoulos and T. Savage (eds) *Zimbabwe: Injustice and Political Reconciliation*. Cape Town: Institute for Justice and Reconciliation.

Alexander, K. and J. Muzondidya. 2005. 'The Ghost Voters, The Exiles, the Non-Citizens: an Election of Exclusion', *Cape Times*, 31 March 2005.

Atton, C. 2006. 'Far-right Media on the Internet: Culture, Discourse and Power', *New Media Society*, 8, 4: 573–87.

Bloch, A. 2005. *The Development Potential of Zimbabweans in the Diaspora: A Survey of Zimbabweans Living in the UK and South Africa*. Geneva: International Organisation for Migration.

Brophy, P., J. Craven and S. Fisher. 1999. *Extremism and the Internet. British Library Research and Innovation Report 145*. Manchester: Centre for Research in Library and Information Management (CERLIM).

Cunningham, S. 2001. 'Popular Media as Public "Sphericules" for Diasporic Communities'. *International Journal of Cultural Studies*, 4, 2: 131–47.

Dahlberg, L. and E. Siapera. 2007. *Radical Democracy and the Internet: Interrogating Theory and Practice*. Basingstoke: Palgrave Macmillan.

Gimmler, A. 2001. 'Deliberative Democracy, the Public Sphere and the Internet'. *Philosophy & Social Criticism*, 27, 4: 21–39.

Kalathil, S. and T.C. Boas. 2003. *Open Network, Closed Regimes: The Impact of the Internet on Authoritarian Rule*. Washington, D.C.: Carnegie Endowment for International Peace.

Kamete, A.Y. 2006. 'The Return of the Jettisoned: ZANU-PF's Crack at "Re-urbanising" in Harare'. *Journal of Southern African Studies*, 32, 2: 255–71.

Kedzie, C.R. 1997. *Communication and Democracy: Coincident Revolutions and the Emergent Dictator's Dilemma*. Santa Monica, CA: RAND.

Liberty. 1999. *Liberating Cyberspace: Civil Liberties, Human Rights, and the Internet*. London: Pluto Press.

Mitra, A. 1997. 'Diasporic Web Sites: Ingroup and Outgroup Discourse'. *Critical Studies in Mass Communication*, 14: 158–81.

Muponde, R. 2004. 'The Worm and the Hoe: Cultural Politics and Reconciliation After the Third Chimurenga'. In B. Raftopoulos and T. Savage (eds) *Zimbabwe: Injustice and Political Reconciliation*. Cape Town: Institute for Justice and Reconciliation.

Muzondidya, J. 2004. '"Zimbabwe for Zimbabweans": Invisible Subject Minorities and the Quest for Justice and Reconciliation in Post-colonial Zimbabwe'. In B.

Raftopoulos and T. Savage (eds) *Zimbabwe: Injustice and Political Reconciliation.* Cape Town: Institute for Justice and Reconciliation.

———. 2007. 'Jambanja: Ideological Ambiguities in the Politics of Land and Resource Ownership in Zimbabwe', *Journal of Southern African Studies,* 33, 2: 325–41.

Papacharissi, Z. 2002. 'The Virtual Sphere: The Internet as a Public Sphere'. *New Media & Society,* 4, 1: 9–27.

Poster, M. 1997. 'Cyberdemocracy: The Internet and the Public Sphere'. In D. Holmes (ed.) *Virtual Politics: Identity and Community in Cyberspace.* London: Sage Publications.

Raftopoulos, B. 2004. 'Nation, Race and History in Zimbabwean Politics.' In B. Raftopoulos & T. Savage (eds) *Zimbabwe: Injustice and Political Reconciliation.* Cape Town: Institute for Justice and Reconciliation.

Raftopoulos, B. and T. Yoshikuni (eds). 1999. *Sites of Struggle: Essays in Zimbabwe's Urban History.* Harare: Weaver Press.

Ranger, T. 2004. 'Nationalist Historiography, Patriotic History and the History of the Nation' *Journal of Southern African Studies,* 30, 2: 215–34.

Roversi, A. and L. Smith 2008. *Hate on the Net: Extremist Sites, Neo-fascism On-line, Electronic Jihad.* Aldershot: Ashgate Publishing.

Sola Pool, I de. 1983. *Technologies of Freedom.* Cambridge, Mass.: Belknap Press.

Tsagarousianou, R., D. Tambini and C. Bryan. 1998. *Cyberdemocracy: Technology, Cities and Civic Networks.* London: Routledge.

Internet Chatroom Thread References

NewZimbabwe, 'Start a Tribalism Section'. Retrieved 26 June from http://newzim. proboards29.com/index.cgi?board=zimele&action=display&thread=1151315 932.

NewZimbabwe, 'Nzondoro in Uk'. Retrieved 26 May 2006 from http://newzim. proboards29.com/index.cgi?board=hotgossip&action=display&thread=1147 377775.

NewZimbabwe, 'A Zimbo in *Big Brother*!!!!!!'. Retrieved 29 May from http://newzim. proboards29.com/index.cgi?board=zimele&action=display&thread=111722 6092.

NewZimbabwe, 'Makosi's Blow-job on National T.V.'. Retrieved 29 May from http:// newzim.proboards29.com/index.cgi?board=zimele&action=display&thread =1118191997.

NewZimbabwe, 'makosi update'. Retrieved 29 May from http://newzim.proboards29. com/index.cgi?board=zimele&action=display&thread=1118907878.

9

Rhodesians Never Die?
The Zimbabwean Crisis and the
Revival of Rhodesian Discourse

Ranka Primorac

In 1979, on the eve of independence, Zimbabwean settler novelist Peter Armstrong published a science-fiction adventure novel entitled *Hawks of Peace* (1979a). Set in an imaginary independent Zimbabwe of the future, the novel imagines the country engulfed by widespread hunger and violence (brought on by a misguided black nationalist president and his party), which the idealistic, nature-loving male settler hero is powerless to prevent. Clearly aimed at gratifying the sentiments of a colonially-minded settler readership at the end of an exhausting internal war, *Hawks of Peace* did not accurately predict the causes of the social crisis which engulfed Zimbabwe at the last turn of the century. It did, however, feed into a long tradition of fictional narratives in which lone settler heroes are the only obstacle that stands in the path of large-scale destruction and disorder. (A more widely known and influential text that belongs to this tradition is John Buchan's 1915 thriller classic, *The Thirty-Nine Steps*.)

This chapter explores how twenty-first century narratives by displaced descendants of a colonial diaspora – that is to say, multiply culturally displaced subjects, or exiled white Zimbabweans – have modified and reproduced this narrative tradition, using it as a tool of political critique aimed at Robert Mugabe's regime. In order to question the effectiveness of such critique, the chapter traces the post-independence genealogy of the narrative genre to which *Hawks of Peace* belongs. It will be seen that, even as it strives to adapt its sense of home and belonging to conditions of crisis and multiple exile in the twenty-first century, a certain formation of white writing that identifies itself as 'Zimbabwean' continues to reproduce a deep and colonially-rooted ambivalence towards notions of Africa, home and belonging.

The ideology[1] in which Armstrong's plot (and the plots of his other novels – see Armstrong 1978, 1979b, 1980, 1981 and 1983) is grounded has as its cornerstones a series of colonial suppositions about the essential and radical otherness of Africans – their infantility, laziness, weakness and potential bestiality – that have by now been thoroughly unmasked and discredited. (In colonial Zimbabwe, such systems of suppositions – and the corresponding assumptions regarding the innate rationality, leadership capacity, bravery and nobility of Europeans – assumed a particularly virulent local form, the 'Rhodesian discourse' of my title.) Nevertheless, the violent, lawless and racist manner in which white-owned agricultural land was taken over in Zimbabwe at the beginning of twenty-first century summons a memory of the worst settler fears from the war-torn 1970s, which *Hawks of Peace* was deliberately stoking, and which were, at the time, spurned on by the demonisation of Mugabe in particular (on this, see for example Chan 1985 and Burns 2002).

Paradoxically, this is so (at least in part) because the current official version of Zimbabwean nationalism – the 'patriotic' narrative of the black nation's progress instigated concurrently with the land takeovers in order to both inspire and justify them – pointedly represents the post 2000 land redistribution as the closing stage of the 1970s liberation war that was waged against the settler-nationalist government of Ian Smith (Ranger 2004). In so doing, the Mugabeist 'patriotic' nationalist narrative has foregrounded precisely the discourse which it purports to be battling against, and which was itself propelled by a fear of advancing pan-African nationalism: 'No to Rhodesia and Rhodesians', read a placard held by a Zimbabwean 'war veteran' at a demonstration held in 2001 (Dondo 2003). In that sense, the twenty-first century Zimbabwean 'patriotic' discourse is both polemical and parasitic, and it is arguable that texts such as *Hawks of Peace* may have helped to put in place a self-fulfilling prophecy. In the novel, the imaginary leader of the Zimbabwean nation asserts, for example, that 'the resources of Zimbabwe belong to Zimbabweans and that they must be allowed to decide the destiny of their national heritage' (Armstrong 1979a: 49). This would not be out of place in a Mugabe speech of today (see Mugabe 2001).

This chapter is particularly interested in the ways in which diaspora-related written narratives manufacture, codify and help to reproduce group identities related to race and nation. Recent work by Louise White (2004a, 2004b) illustrates the cultural role performed in 1970s Rhodesia by settler-authored novels and autobiographies, in disseminating and sharing 'sentiments and memories' (White 2004a: 108) through which settler nationalism contested and sought to marginalise African nationalist claims and aspirations. White points out the high level of intertextuality involved in such cultural transactions, so that the tropes and meanings appearing in one book, 'which were presumably commonplace before the book was written' (Ibid.), frequently reappear in several other texts. Analogous linkages can be found among the cultural expressions of rival African nationalism[2]: the two sets of nationalist cultural practices have always been locked in mutual contestation, so that 'Africans necessarily became part and parcel of white Rhodesian identity' (Shutt and King 2005: 262), and vice versa.

During the first two decades of independence, a whole new range of cultural symbols and modes of expression came into being – and it may have seemed to some that the old identity binaries were becoming a thing of the past (Kaarsholm 2005). However, since the onset in 2000 of the 'fast-track' land reallocation and the attendant violence, the nationalist cultural repertoires have been reworked and redeployed. As official narrative renderings of African nationalism have become increasingly streamlined in order to accommodate and counteract the threats to those in power posed by a variety of agents and alliances (see Sylvester 2003; Mugabe 2005), the now-marginalised Rhodesian discourse has also been revisited and revived – in this case, by white-authored texts written in opposition to the violent social practices of the Mugabe regime, which I will call 'neo-Rhodesian', and which are often articulated from a position of exile. Cultural expressions of the two opposing nationalisms may thus be seen to be locked in the kind of mutually-perpetuating series of mirrorings and distortions referred to by Achille Mbembe when he describes colonialism as: 'a refracted and endlessly reconstituted fabric of fictions, [which] generated mutual utopias - hallucinations shared by the colonisers and the colonised' (Mbembe 2002: 263).[3]

A key aim of this chapter is to show how recent texts by displaced authors who claim white Zimbabwean identities – most prominently, in recent years, Peter Godwin and Alexandra Fuller – may be related to (gendered) blueprints for the performance of 'white African' identities reminiscent of the colonial era. In order to do so, however, the chapter must first sketch the outline of a textual history spanning the publication of Armstrong's *Hawks of Peace* and the present historical moment, and give some indication of the extensions and permutations of 'Rhodesian' discourse itself since 1980. (This digression is necessary since, to the best of my knowledge, no survey of this kind has been attempted since independence – and yet, without it, it would be difficult to properly historically contextualise the narratives of present-day displaced writers such as Godwin and Fuller.) In briefly analysing a series of autobiographical and fictional narratives, authored by both women and men and published both inside and outside Zimbabwe, I hope to show that, despite the changes and modifications, present-day 'neo-Rhodesian' narratives by displaced writers such Godwin, Fuller and others continue to draw on a common repository of images and a shared narrative grammar.

Narrating a Settler Nation

The participation of fictional and autobiographical narratives in Rhodesian discourses has been studied since the 1970s by Antony Chennells (Chennells 1977, 1979a, 1979b, 1982, 1984, 1995, 2002, 2005, 2007). He has found that the body of colonial narrative texts which may be termed 'Rhodesian' is not homogenous, nor is the texts' own understanding of Zimbabwean colonial identities fixed and static.[4] Nevertheless, from his work and that of others (Kaarsholm 1991, Godwin and Hancock 1993) - and, of course, the texts themselves – it is possible to extrapolate a model of what might be called the Rhodesian master code or master fiction.

The terms 'master code' and 'master fiction' are used by Achille Mbembe (1991, 2001) in the context of writing about the African postcolony. Discussing political environments where state power inscribes itself as a world order, Mbembe describes master fictions as discursive blueprints which aspire to generate and underlie all socially produced meanings. Such master fictions seek to govern those who are exposed to them, and to become a new form of 'common sense'. They generate their own jargons and fulfil their own needs; and although they are fictions – that is to say, fantastical – they are also coherent and self-perpetuating. When he writes that the rulers of an African postcolony seek to dominate their subjects through the production of 'a local, coherent and codified genre which *strings facts and events together* in a fantastical way in order to produce the incredible' (Mbembe 1991: 173, emphasis added), Mbembe is stressing the master fictions' narrativity. Furthermore, in describing the rhetorical devices employed in transmitting such narrative blueprints, he compares them to 'those of communist regimes – to the extent, that is, that both are actual regimes given to the production of lies and double-speak' (Mbembe 2001: 118). In the Zimbabwean context, this statement is also applicable to the colonial period: indeed, in his analyses of Rhodesian fictional narratives, Chennells makes a comparable claim, when he speaks of the inability of the Rhodesian master-discourse 'to account for the events in which everyone in Rhodesia was caught up' (Chennells 1995: 128). To the extent that they generated untruths which sought to pass themselves off as 'common sense', Rhodesians – the 'spokespeople of the discourse of empire [...] also naming their own identity' (Chennells 1995: 103) – generated a local version of the larger imperial master fiction, based on a set of three interlocking sets of assumptions about space, human agency and time. The presence of these assumptions may be traced (in varying forms and degrees) in the 'neo-Rhodesian' narratives of the twenty-first century, and also – as I explain elsewhere (Primorac 2007 b) – in the current Zimbabwean 'patriotic' master narrative.

By the 1970s (when it was threatened by means of sustained physical violence), settler discourse had come to be based on the assumption of the discreteness of Rhodesian colonial space. In a book-length study of settler fiction, Chennells (1982) writes about the Rhodesian discursive search for a mythical location of origin (usually located in the Great Zimbabwe ruins, which were taken to mean that the settlers were engaged in re-civilising the region), and the search for a discrete Rhodesian national identity (which caused even the early autobiographical accounts by imperial explorers to be appropriated into local white nationalist narratives – see Chennells 2005). After the Unilateral Declaration of Independence (UDI) in 1965, Rhodesian discourse placed Rhodesian space and identities in firm opposition to the outside world, including – or especially – Britain. Donal Lowry (2005) has shown how post-UDI Rhodesians came to regard themselves as the true inheritors of the spirit of the Empire, in opposition to the decadence and faint-heartedness emanating from the metropole. Within Rhodesia's boundaries, it was the non-urban spaces of the unspoilt, 'empty' bush that were seen as the location of authentic settler identities, free from the restraint and conventionality associated with towns and cities. Preben Kaarsholm points at a key spatial component of the Rhodesian master fiction when he emphasizes how the Rhodesian 'colonial pastoral' was centred on the notion of 'the organic closeness to nature of settler life, its immediacy, authenticity, vitality and practical roughness as opposed to the verbose abstractness and idealism of metropolitan imperialism'(Kaarsholm 1991: 37).

Circumscribed by such a representation of space, the Rhodesian master fiction firmly specifies the kind of agents that it allows to function as its subjects. Although it is structured around the opposition between settler and native, a typical colonial-era Rhodesian narrative has only a certain kind of settler – male, white and British by origin (yet local by choice) – as its hero.[5] Chennells shows how female authors undermine the dominant notion of Rhodesian agency, but not such Rhodesian notions of space-time, by regarding white women as the bearers of civilised domesticity who are able to moderate the essentially male violence involved in the relationship between settler and nature (see Chennells 1982 and Ranger 1994). Such settlers (the heirs to the Rhodesian pioneers) arrive at self-knowledge and demonstrate their mastery of space through the ability/ease with which they cross boundaries, and through the hardiness, bravery and resourcefulness they demonstrate by surviving in and conquering the 'excitement and terror' (Hulley 1969: 28) of the African bush. This typically includes an intimate understanding of plant and animal life (and, in a certain group of texts, 'terrorist' insurgents), a concern for the preservation of natural resources, an ability to improvise, a handiness with weapons and (often) a physicality that involves a cartoonish, anti-intellectual sense of humour. The Rhodesian master fiction does not assign independent agency to Africans. They are reduced to the stereotypes of the happy, grateful native and the bloodthirsty savage, and are denied both creativity and individuality, except (to a limited extent) in the case of exceptional male helpers – for example, the trusted Ndebele servants. In the narratives of war, native insurgents are no more than puppets animated by agents located outside, in non-Rhodesian spaces.

In terms of attitude towards time, the Rhodesian master fiction is characterised by what may be termed a longing for stasis. Although the validating force behind it was the idea of the settlers' civilising mission (which, in theory, implied a commitment to a changed future), and although a typical Rhodesian narrative is constructed around a belief in the possibility of overcoming any obstacle, Chennells points out a seemingly contradictory orientation towards the past when he describes Rhodesian writing as a 'literature of nostalgia' (Chennells 1982: 214). From very early on, Rhodesian narratives encapsulated a desire to *defer change*. Even an early settler text such as Crosbie Garstin's *The Sunshine Settlers* (first published in 1918, when settlers' loyalty to Britain was still free of post-UDI complications) is, despite its humour, tinged with the knowledge that the idyllic bush life it describes must come to an end. (In this case, the end is brought on by the outbreak of World War One). Later texts, especially those dealing with the guerrilla war of the 1970s, are a more explicit expression of the Rhodesian master fiction's fear of the non-Rhodesian future. In that sense, the master fiction may be seen as an expression of a colonial settler longing for a temporal, as well as spatial, discreteness.

With the arrival of independence, this longing was proved to be fruitless. But the hope that majority rule would cause Rhodesian discourse to disappear was equally unfounded. In the early 1980s, Chennells wrote that, with Mugabe's first victory at the polls, both Rhodesia and Rhodesian discourse 'were simultaneiously swept away' (Chennells 1995: 129). This hope turned out to be premature.

Postcolonial Entanglements

After 1980, the hermeneutic framework for reading Zimbabwean texts changed dramatically, as 'minor and major histories … swapped places' (Chennells 2005: 136) and the formerly proscribed African nationalist discourse became dominant inside the country. The 'non-Rhodesian time' had arrived, and, with the ascent of black Zimbabweans to positions of political power, the openly racist aspects of Rhodesian discourse were sent into exile. Outside Zimbabwe's physical borders, texts perpetuating the Rhodesian master fiction survived in specialist and internet publications, in which a sense of nostalgic longing for lost pasts (and with it, an ambivalence towards the notion of 'home') became multiplied.[6] In 1997, Rhodesia's last Prime Minsiter, Ian Smith, published an autobiography in London entitled *The Great Betrayal*, in which he 'insists that justice and pure rationality were inherent in Rhodesian nationalist ideology'(Chennells 2005: 136). (Betrayals, great and small, have of course featured prominently in Rhodesians' sense of self since 1965: see, for example, Skimin 1977). In that sense, Smith's memoir finds its most fitting antithetical counterpart in Judith Todd's recent *Through The Darkness* (2007).) Inside Zimbabwe, however, this could not be done openly. In particular, Rhodesia's guerrilla war could no longer be represented from the white supremacist viewpoint implicit in the Rhodesian master fiction.

On the other hand, white writers wishing to be critical of Rhodesian discourse could now, unprecedentedly, do so in public. Bruce Moore King (1987), Angus Shaw (1993), Tim Mc Loughlin (1985) and Nancy Partridge (1986) all published war-related narratives which, like Doris Lessing's before independence, exposed the untruths contained in the key assumptions of the Rhodesian master fiction.[7] But, although their texts could now be published inside the country, white-authored writing was stripped of canonical status in independent Zimbabwe, and since 1980, it has never been fully integrated into the literary mainstream (white Zimbabwean-authored texts, for example, have never been part of the Zimbabwean school syllabi). At the same time, alongside a proliferation of complex and/ or artistically ambitious narrative accounts of the past[8], a more diverse market opened up for popular and 'light-hearted' narratives of all kinds, and it was in some of those narratives that the key aspects of the Rhodesian master fiction survived and continued to be reproduced (and satirised – as in the work of John Eppel (for example 2001, 2002)) after independence.

In 1983, former policeman David Lemon published a thriller entitled *Ivory Madness*, which returns to the theme of the liberation war indirectly, by staging its post-independence reenactment (and in doing so, prefigures in several ways the work of Godwin and Fuller, as I hope to show below). The novel's hero is an idealistic and noble former Selous Scout (elite Rhodesian soldier), who fights for the preservation of Zimbabwe's natural resources (here represented by an ancient bull elephant) against an alliance of corrupt black officials, army members and poachers. There is a face-off in the bush, in which the corrupt former guerrilla, Major Nduna, reveals the extent of his irrationality and superstition, while the white hero, Lew Davies, shows his superior knowledge of the wilderness. (Africans, including his trusted servant, refer to him as *Ishe ingwe*, the lord leopard, 'the man who never missed with a rifle' – Lemon 1994: 137). Davies refuses to acknowledge that the guerrilla forces have liberated Zimbabwe, and reverts to Rhodesian war-time vocabulary while trying to save the elephant. In a pre-1980 novel, a character such as this would have triumphed. In *Ivory Madness*, Davies dies – but his funeral is well attended, mostly by former soldiers and 'simple tribesmen' (Lemon 1994: 142). As it celebrates the beauty and national importance of wildlife and the wildlife industry, *Ivory Madness* mourns the passing of old Rhodesia.[9]

Peter Armstrong's *Tobacco Spiced with Ginger* is written in the same spirit – except that here, wildlife is replaced by tobacco. Published in 1987, following three popular novels written in the wake of *Hawks of Peace*,[10] *Tobacco Spiced with Ginger* is a biography of Ginger Freeman, an early Rhodesian settler who became a tobacco executive and sanctions buster in Rhodesia after UDI. Using a form of expression similar to Lemon's,[11] Armstrong charts Freeman's rise from the early days in the bush and on tobacco farms, and revives the notion of Rhodesia's opposition to the spaces outside it by describing the means through which Freeman bypassed the trade embargo imposed on his country and reproduces, as part of the text's centrepiece, the entire text of UDI. Although it ostensibly represents Freeman's contribution to the tobacco industry as a contribution made to independent Zimbabwe, *Tobacco Spiced with Ginger* implies that the black inheritors of political power (whose actions were in direct opposition to those of Freeman) have made no such contributions, and have thus in no way earned their positions. In the forward, Armstrong underscores a colonial brand of defiance when he openly admits that he knows his book might offend (Armstrong 1987: 2). To the best of my knowledge, however, neither this nor any other texts mentioned here were ever banned by the Zimbabwean state censor.

Some – such as Peter Rimmer's voluminous *Cry of the Fish Eagle* (1993), and Keith Meadows' equally ambitious *Sand in the Wind* (1996) could still be found in Harare's depleted bookshops two and a half decades after independence. Both novels resemble Wilbur Smith's 'Ballantyne quartet' (Smith 1980, 1981, 1982 and 1984; for an analysis, see Chennells 1984) in that they combine the genres of adventure fiction, historical novel and family saga in order to create broad-sweep, quasi-historical narratives that extol settler heroism and represent colonial Rhodesia as a lost Eden. Both Rimmer's and Meadows' texts replicate, with little variation, key stereotypes generated by the Rhodesian master fiction. In both, the meaning of independence is pre-given. 'Tragedy is, they are only politically free' – says a character in *Cry of the Fish Eagle*. 'Not free of poverty. Now the rich exploit them from afar by paying as little as possible for minerals, coffee, cocoa, tobacco. You see, if the blacks starve under their own government it doesn't prick the First World's conscience. Everyone is happy' (Rimmer 1992: 544). The hero of Meadows' *Sand in the Wind* also seeks to protect Africa from unwelcome intrusion after independence; for him, however, the focus is on the continent's wildlife (threatened by poachers), nationalist guerrillas, the Rhodesian army and the forces of transnational capital alike. Its hero, the martyr-like game warden Harry Kenyon, sums up his motivation (and that of generations of Rhodesian fictional heroes) with the words: 'Me? I'll be here. In the bush. Looking after the animals ... Whether it's Rhodesia, Zimbabwe or Noddyland, it's the country I love. The valley. And whatever happens, the wildlife will need to be protected. Properly. And I will do that, Garnet. Absolutely' (Meadows 1996: 359).

Other 'neo-Rhodesian' texts continue the master fiction by operating with the pointedly less 'grand' notion of the African bush as a place in which it is possible to cultivate a conflict-free family, rather than individual, life. C. E. Dibb's memoirs *Ivory, Apes and Peacocks* and *The Conundrum Trees* (published in Zimbabwe in 1981 and 1989 respectively) are both organised around a series of sketches of animals, plants, landscape and episodes from a timeless wilderness, focused in each case through a female narrator who has experienced them alongside her family.[12] Maureen de La Harpe's *Msasa Morning* (1992) records the 1950s and 1960s memories of a tobacco farmer's wife; David Lemon's *Hobo Rows Kariba* [n.d.] is a memoir of a lakeside adventure in which conquering the forces of nature results in the kind of self-knowledge that leads the narrator away from the wilderness and towards a better understanding of his relationship with his family, while Roland Hill's popular romance-inflected *Burnt Toast on Sundays* (1995) is a fictional narrative that foregrounds the kind of plot formerly relegated to secondary or tertiary sub-plot status in settler fiction, and tells of a rich white rancher's efforts to find a wife. While none of these texts are overtly racist, all represent the Zimbabwean countryside (the only space they depict) as an essentially white space, in which Africans feature only peripherally, or as intruders. Dibb speaks of a 'primordial' link between herself and the African earth (1989: 17), De la Harpe is able to distinguish between the 'good' and 'bad' kinds of 'African magic' (the latter is represented by the liberation war guerrillas), Lemon writes of getting unused to 'civilisation', while the British bride of Hill's hero must undergo a radical change of identity if she is to live with him on a cattle ranch. Dibb's and de la Harpe's texts are awash with nostalgia, Lemon's is past-oriented in the sense that it represents its author's adventures as non-repeatable, and Hill's narrative is able to open itself up to the future only by constructing the possibility of overcoming the inherent difference between the spaces of Zimbabwe and Britain – that is to say, of envisaging a fresh influx of newcomers into the white Zimbabwean space it represents.

By the late 1990s, however, there were signs that white-authored popular literature might join canonical texts in interrogating the key tenets of the Rhodesian master fiction. David Lemon's *Killer Cat* (1998) and Paul

Freeman's *Rumours of Ophir* (1998) resemble the pre-1980 settler fiction in that they feature tough white male policemen (aided by a seasoned hunter and an old-time miner respectively) who seek to avenge the brutal killings of their wives. But in Lemon's and Freeman's thrillers, neither wife is white – and their respective heroes' principal helpers are black women: a glamorous game ranger and tough young former prostitute. This would have been unthinkable before independence. In addition to that, outside the country, Peter Godwin (a former policeman, like Armstrong and Lemon) and Alexandra Fuller (a daughter of Rhodesian farmers) published autobiographical narratives (Godwin 1996, Fuller 2001) which bore traces of the master fiction, but related to it in complex and ambivalent ways.

Both authors insert themselves into colonial-era ideologies by writing about 'African' childhoods with a mixture of nostalgia and anxiety, and both evoked, at best, an uneasy sense of belonging. But while both of their narratives may be linked to imperial romance (with its spatial rhythm of journey, illumination and return) and the Rhodesian pastoral, both may also be read as parodies of those genres. While Caroline Rooney (2001: 175) detects a hint of the saviour complex in Godwin's attitude towards Africa (as a journalist, he witnessed and exposed the post-independence massacres of civilians in south-western Zimbabwe), Chennells (2005) points out his welcome refusal to attach a simple complex of meanings to the place of his birth. Fuller's story is reminiscent of the post-independence neo-Rhodesian texts in that it tells an all-white narrative, and locates a sense of belonging in white settlers' hard work, resilience, solidarity and sense of humor. Fuller also (pointedly?) refuses to apologise for the stark racism of the settler milieu she describes – even though most of her story takes place after independence. But *Don't let's Go to the Dogs Tonight* also evokes Doris Lessing's *The Grass is Singing* in that its ruthless description of 'poor white' life on the land demolishes the myths of the African pastoral and of 'land' or 'nature' as a source of stable identities or harmonious domesticity.[13] And so it may have seemed that the process of the reproduction of the Rhodesian master fiction was finally coming to an end – had Godwin's and Fuller's narratives not made it clear that strategic permutations of this fiction (no matter how ambivalent) could be put to a new use, which surpassed mere nostalgia.

In both *Mukiwa* and *Don't Let's Go to the Dogs Tonight*, narratives of personal memory are used as a means of critiquing the dominant version of Zimbabwean nationalism. Godwin exposes the failures and hypocrisies of Zimbabwe's 1980s policy of reconciliation: his sense of Zimbabwe as 'home' is finally shattered by the atrocities he witnesses in Matabeleland, which points at the fact that non-Shonas (the Ndebeles and the whites alike) are not likely to be admitted into the new nation on an equal footing. (In the preface, Godwin stresses that all the politicians and public figures mentioned in the story are accurately identified.) Fuller's story was published after the beginning of the controversial land redistribution programme in Zimbabwe, and there is a strong sense in her text that the injustice of this process gave her license to tell a story which could not previously be told, because the story itself contains a similar injustice: '[The Fullers' farm] Robandi is put up for mandatory auction under the new land distribution program' (Fuller 2001: 160). It is as if the 'obviousness' of this injustice removes the previously assumed political incorectness of a neo-Rhodesian story.

In the following sections, I look at a group texts written since the beginning of the Zimbabwean 'crisis' in which the Rhodesian master fiction is revived and used as a platform for a (more or less explicit) critique of Mugabe's regime. Because they revitalise aspects of a colonial discourse, the critique these narrative perform must be perceived as retroactive. This is to say that it relativises and undermines the value of the very concept of independence – not only for Zimbabwe, but, by implication, for Africa as a whole. The texts fall into two categories: John Osborne's *The Guiding Son* (2004), David Lemon's *Never Quite a Soldier* (2000) and Derek Huggins' *Stained Earth* (2004) are aimed at, and have been able to reach a relatively narrow range of readers (Osborne and Lemon's texts are self-published, while the book of short stories by Huggins – not an internationally-known author – is difficult to obtain outside Zimbabwe). By contrast, Alexandra Fuller's second book, *Scribbling the Cat* (2004) and Peter Godwin's recent *When a Crocodile Eats the Sun* (2006) have reached global audiences.

Rhodesian Discourse and the Zimbabwean Crisis: Stained Truths

John Osborne's *The Guiding Son* is a self-published series of reminiscences about outdoor life not unlike those by Dibb and Lemon. But it also amounts to an autobiography, because it covers the lifespan of its author (a former professional hunting guide) from young manhood to retirement, and firmly fixes his chosen identity as a man of the bush, dedicated to 'the hard work of improving my little bit of Africa' (Osborne 2004: 68) – which, throughout the text, he routinely refers to as 'the dark continent'.

Osborne's narrative starts with an account of how he and his young family cleared and tamed a wild natural space in order to start a cattle ranch (a beginning common in Rhodesian narratives), and ends with his retirement from professional hunting, after a series of only vaguely explained personal betrayals. Throughout this time, the text represents its author as hardworking and courageous, but simple and honest to the point of gullibility. The narrating voice professes a lasting aversion to city people and intellectuals such as bankers, lawyers, 'shrinks' and the kind of ruthless businessman who 'disguised himself as a gentleman' (Osborne 2004: 6); in this, his text closely follows the work of Armstrong.

On a visit to America, in order to attend an international game conservation convention, he refers to himself as 'naïve and fresh from the bush', and is daunted by the 'concrete jungle' and 'experienced and shrewd New York traders' (Osborne 2004: 73, 76). However, when he is hunting in the African bush, in all-male company (his wife and are family away on a distant ranch, and the text makes it clear that sex and hunting do not mix), the narrator performs feats of bravery and endurance. He faces and kills charging elephants and rhinos, braves the dangers of snakes and battles with a crocodile with his bare hands, and is able to laugh at foreign clients whose inappropriate dress and conduct in the wild reveals an inferior kind of white masculinity. Africans, on the other hand, are consigned to the roles of trackers and servants, and are represented as lazy, docile, happy, feeble-minded, cowardly and essentially savage: a celebration by the local 'Batonka' people is centred on the 'gyrating half naked bodies leap and dance to the rhythm of pulsating tom-toms' (Osborne 2004: 64).

Although some of Osborne's chapters refer to pre-independence, and others to post-independence time, he notes no essential change in the world he describes: when, after 1980, his servant Hlupo becomes Chairman of the Worker's Committee ('Commy thinking I'd reckon' – Osborne 2004: 85), this simply 'gave Hlupo many devious opportunities to shack-up with other staff members' wives'(Osborne 2004: 86). The implication regarding Africans' ability to govern themselves is clear – and it is made against the background of indirect references to the present political situation in Zimbabwe. The book's introduction points out that 'we live in difficult times', and hopes that the text which follows will 'help mask the sharp thorns of the scrubby bush that surrounds us'. The narrative's closing paragraphs ponder the nature's cycles, where every stage of life must pass and give way to a new one: 'Every species is made safe and secure because in time the young ram challenges the more mature but ageing bull', and 'seeing the young bull displacing his sire, is most satisfying' (Osborne 2004: 194). These phrases were written amid intense speculation about the retirement and displacement of the ageing Mugabe, who has, after supplanting Joshua Nkomo as the seniormost post-independence nationalist leader, been referred to as *karigamombe*, one who knocks down or gelds a bull. But they criticise Mugabe from a neo-colonial standpoint, and are therefore capable of contributing to his own simplified critique of neo-colonialism.

Osborne's attitude is replicated and made explicit in David Lemon's autobiographical *Never Quite a Soldier*. Lemon's narrative charts his experiences in the British South Africa Police in the war-torn period between 1971 and 1983, when he had a variety of postings across the country and progressed to the rank of Company Commander in a fighting support unit – the Black Boots. Despite its horrors, Lemon claims to have enjoyed some aspects of the war. However, although in the 'Author's Note' Lemon insists that his account is the 'unvarnished truth', his understanding of the social causes of the fighting bears a striking resemblance to that of the Rhodesian war novels of the 1970s.

When UDI was declared in 1965, Lemon was a policeman in England, and the first part of his narrative claims both British and Rhodesian identities for its narrator, who uses the phrase 'my country' to refer to both spaces. In the end, however, he makes a firm choice. He relates an episode from the early days of his police life, when he witnessed a white instructor striking a black policeman. After he expresses shock at this behaviour, the instructor reproaches him for applying British criteria to the situation, and failing to adapt to the 'African way of life'. He later concludes that the officer was right (Lemon 2000: 67). *Never Quite a Soldier* spends several chapters instructing its readers in what Lemon considers to be the basic assumptions of this way of life.

Readers thus learn that Rhodesian Africans were essentially cheerful, tactile and possessed of a 'herding instinct', and that their 'tribal culture' was based on immediate satisfaction of bodily needs (Lemon 2000: 22, 33, 34, 38). Although Lemon admits that there were problems inherent in the 1931 Land Apportionment Act, he speculates that 'the problem actually had its roots in African culture', and thinks that 'traditional farming methods would have to change before the situation could possibly be resolved'(Lemon 2000: 29, 28).

In the very first chapter, readers are informed that 'Rhodesia's fight was not against her own black citizens but against communism itself,' and later they learn that the 'abandonment of Rhodesia was the real obscenity of colonialism' (Lemon 2000: 14, 237) and that 'This is Africa and *any vote* here hinges on threats and intimidation' (Lemon 2000: 55, emphasis added). It is from this perspective that *Never Quite a Soldier* narrates the key war-time events, and expresses Lemon's mistrust of Mugabe, his lack of faith in the policy of reconciliation and his outrage with the post-independence war in Matabeleland (some of which he witnessed). But the culmination of Lemon's narrative is the last chapter, where he condemns the methods and outcomes of the recent land redistribution. Here he reveals the reason for recalling the liberation war in the first place, when he makes a direct link between what he calls the 'mounting savagery' (Lemon 2000: 313) in Zimbabwe and the coming of independence: '*any* elections held in Zimbabwe will be as free and fair as they were in Rhodesia of 1980'(Lemon 2000: 314). The implication here is that the present-day 'mounting savagery' is merely a replica of the unmotivated savagery involved in the war of liberation, and that most black Rhodesians did not really object to the condition of being colonised. So when, towards the very end of the text, Lemon asks: 'why on earth are my countrymen still being killed?' (Lemon 2000: 314), the question is, in fact, rhetorical.

Derek Huggins is, like Lemon, of British origin and a former policeman. In the introduction to the thirteen short stories collected as *Stained Earth*, he expresses a hope that the stories will provide 'a guide to the past and a clue to the greater picture of the way it was' (Huggins 2004: xi). Most of the stories deal with the experiences of a character called Greg Stanyon, a white policeman in Rhodesia during the nationalist struggle of the 1960s and 1970s. Several focus on nature and wildlife; all are about men.

Like Osborne (who also published his text inside Zimbabwe), and unlike Lemon and Fuller, Huggins is able to refer to the present Zimbabwean crisis only indirectly. The introduction to the story entitled 'Sent to Coventry' uses a colonial turn of phrase, yet makes the link the contemporary violence in Zimbabwe to the wrongs of colonialism. The narrator says:

> The grains of truth related here cannot hurt the white man in Africa any more than he has been hurt already; it does not alter what occurred, but it may help to explain the way it was and why. In the end there is always retribution, and atonement, but seldom by those who instigated the suffering and incurred the wrath. *The retribution falls on their children and their children's children. There is yet another cycle of violence and suffering and again the need for change, retribution and atonement* (Huggins 2004: 6, emphasis added).

This is the crucial link that Lemon fails to make. *Stained Earth* sees the colonial project as doomed from the start. But it also implies that this was so only because of the manner in which it was executed. It questions and undermines the Rhodesian master fiction; in the end, however, it leaves its central premise intact.

'Sent to Coventry' is about a Rhodesian policeman of English origin ostracised by fellow white policemen for treating an African fairly, during the rise in Matabeleland of black nationalism and its leader, 'The Bull, The Father of the People' (Joshua Nkomo), who in his own turn, is described by one of his own followers as someone who 'never works and he gets paid' (Huggins 2004: 8). Social justice in a colony, the story implies, is not racialised: that is merely a construction imposed on events by both black and white extremists. The story entitled 'The Sell-Out' makes this proposition explicit. It tells of a successful black farmer who owns a farm in a 'native purchase area'. The farmer confesses to Greg Stanyon that he is being intimidated by African nationalists. 'I owe much to the government. It has helped me become independent and self-sufficient,' he tells the policeman. 'Yet I am a nationalist. I love my country. I love the land. I would like to see the country become become independent under the right leadership. But I am not an extremist. I do not follow the nationalist party meetings, or their politics or their violent ways' (Huggins 2004: 26).

The complexity of the farmer's dilemma undermines the clear-cut Rhodesian assumptions about agency, and so does the white policeman's response: Stanyon advises the man to join the extremists in order to survive. The story entitled 'A Tribute to Magadza' relates in the same way to the assumption of white mastery over non-urban space. It features a widowed, old and tired white man stumbling through the bush in pursuit of a leopard, guided and rescued by a black servant without whom he would not be able to survive – a far cry from David Lemon's *Ishe ingwe*. But despite the complexities of colonial life that it foregrounds, the notion that only the white man can bring order to Africa manages to find its way into *Stained Earth*.

In all of the Stories, Stanyon is represented as a fair and honest policeman. At the end of 'The Sell-Out', despite all the odds, he manages to protect the black farmer from nationalist intimidation through clever detective work. In the story entitled 'Sacrificial Son of the Soil,' he advises the father of a young man who was coerced into joining the guerrillas to forgive him. (He refuses, and the guerrillas kill him.) In 'Night Hunting', in a conversation with a younger colleague who fears the coming of independence because 'the blacks want everything', Stanyon says:

> There's nothing much we or anybody can do about that. Somebody is going to stand here under the moon. There's not much difference who stands here. (...) The only difference between them and us is that they're more hungry than we are. *And they're more greedy, and will kill everything that moves until there's nothing left* (Huggins 2004: 71, emphasis added).

The contradiction between the last two sentences points at the difference between *Stained Earth* and *Never Quite a Soldier*: unlike Lemon, Huggins does not regard the coming of independence as something that could have been prevented, and understands that the African nationalist demands for freedom were rooted in the colonial system of injustice. Yet the trace of an essential difference between 'us' and 'them' remains: 'they' are not only more hungry, but also more violent and greedy than 'us' – and this has, presumably, had an impact on the current stage of the 'cycle of violence and retribution' in Zimbabwe.

Rhodesian Discourse and the Zimbabwean Crisis: Exiles and Returns

Allexandra Fuller's *Scribbling the Cat* – a sequel to *Don't let's Go to the Dogs Tonight* – resembles *Stained Earth* in that it does not leave the Rhodesian master fiction un-eroded. In the Authors' note, Fuller (like the male authors considered in this section) emphasises the truth of the story she tells – but also that it is the story of another: a man who resembles Huggins' hero and Lemon's narrator in having participated in Zimbabwe's war of independence on the side of white Rhodesia.

Fuller's initial description of K, the former Rhodesian soldier with whom she travelled from Zambia into Zimbabwe and Mozambique in order to recall the time he spent in the Rhodesian army, emphasises his mastery of the African space that surrounds him. He looked 'as if he owned the ground beneath his feet, and as if the sky balanced with ease on his shoulders,' and walked barefoot 'as if defying Africa to rear back and bite him' (Fuller 2004: 20). Later, after seeing K on a farm in Zambia, the narrator describes him as organically connected to the land: 'Seeing him on his farm, I couldn't decide if the man had shaped the land of the other way around' (Fuller 2004: 56). (The textual importance of this organic connection is something that a recent, otherwise valuable, academic analysis of *Scribbling the Cat* misses: in the course of interpreting Fuller's insistence on the flimsiness of 'white' African dwellings as a (welcome) sign of dissociating Southern African whiteness from its colonialist heritage, Antje M. Rauwerda (2009) neglects to notice that K himself takes on some of the components of the meaning of 'home' normally associated with physical structures: in an early chapter he is described with the sentences 'He looked bulletproof' and – unusually yet strikingly: 'He looked cathedral.' (20))

Later still, Fuller's narrator shows K moving effortlessly in the Mozambican bush, killing a crocodile (in a manner not unlike Osborne's – see Fuller 2004: 54–55) and attacking a lion bare-handed:

> Suddenly a lion, who had been crouching behind a stand of lemongrass, came barrelling out from his cover, ducked behind Mapenga's legs, and made straight for me, pouncing from a flat-out run into a soaring attack. I was aware only of something massive and tawny spread-eagled in flight behind me. Before the lion could land on my back, K had caught him with a block to the throat (Fuller 2004: 191).

Despite thus establishing a link with the key tropes of the Rhodesian master fiction, Fuller's narrative also makes a conscious attempt to distance itself from it and to subvert it. In the early chapters, she explains (for the benefit of her Western readers) that the 'black guerrillas were fighting for their freedom – the freedom to vote, to own land, to receive a good and equitable education, and to walk the streets of their own country without fear' (Fuller 2004: 38). And yet, on meeting K in the early 2000s, Fuller's narrator feels that some part of the truth about the war, and about her own Rhodesian identity, has remained unarticulated. This is partly to do with the Zimbabwean crisis: she invites K to undertake the journey after struggling to write a newspaper article in which she tries 'to make sense of the mess in Zimbabwe'(Fuller 2004: 81).

The histories and emotions she encounters turn out to be painful and complex. K emerges as a broken, traumatised man who has been brutalised by circumstances beyond his control, but who has also, as a soldier, committed unspeakable atrocities. Fuller recognises that there is a real sense in which K may be seen as a victim:

> K was what happened when you grew a child from the African soil, taught him an attitude of superiority, persecution, and paranoia, and then gave him a gun and sent him to war in a world he thought of as his own to defend
> (Fuller 2004: 219).

She also accepts that she and her family were complicit in the atrocities he was to commit (and which her text describes in detail) when, in the 1970s, they encouraged the Rhodesian troops and sang the nationalist songs about the undying Rhodesian spirit.

> And I thought, I *own* this now. This was *my* war too. I had been a small, smug white girl shouting 'We are all Rhodesians and we'll fight through *thickanthin*' ... I said, 'I had no idea ...' But I did. I know, without really being told out loud, what happened in the war and I knew it was as brutal and indefensible as what I had just heard from K. I just hadn't wanted to know
> (Fuller 2004: 152; emphasis in the original).

This is laudably complex writing, which goes a long way towards demolishing the Rhodesian master fiction. Where *Scribbling the Cat* falls in line with this fiction, however, is when it describes K and other former soldiers and mercenaries (whom, as I tried to show above, Fuller does not entirely deglamourise despite their racist vocabularies and manners) as the only sources of order in the chaos that is post-independence Africa. Fuller describes K's farm with the words:

> There was no garbage lying about, and the yards in front of the staff houses were swept clean. It was as if the Africa I knew, with its assault of smells and its flotsam of debris and its inevitable chickens and goats and carelessly strewn life, had been pressed and contained beyond the borders of the electric fence. This farm was a model of industry and discipline (Fuller 2004: 121).

When she asks the workers on K's farm what it is like working for him, they grin and tell her that 'working for Bwana K is very good'; K, in turn, praises his farm manager by saying he is a 'good gondie' and 'willing to learn', and only exempt from the supposed sexual insatiability of Africans (and therefore a certain death from AIDS) through being impotent(Fuller 2004: 123, 124; for a description of K himself risking AIDS in order to help Africans, see Fuller 2004: 124 – 125). All these are colonial clichés, and so it the stereotype of Africans' cunning and resourcefulness that Fuller evokes when she encounters hunger and poverty in rural Zimbabwe ('Dad once said to me, 'When the world goes tits up and we're back to square one [when independence comes], I'd bet my money on these buggars surviving'. Fuller 2004: 245).

In Zambia, former Rhodesian soldiers tell Fuller that the guerrilla war was preferable to the present state of Africa, while in Zimbabwe other ex-soldiers join an impoverished road-side hawker (whom K helps) in criticizing Mugabe's government (Fuller 2004: 141, 133). *Scribbling the Cat* tries hard to disengage itself from the Rhodesian master fiction. But because it contains an explicit critique (Fuller 2004: 77–78) of the social effects of the Zimbabwean crisis; because this critique is mouthed by, or juxtaposed with the standpoint of those who fought to prevent independent Zimbabwe from coming into being, and because it represents former colonial soldiers as the only antidote to the wider African social crisis in Africa as a whole, echoes and reverberations of the Rhodesian discourse continues to resonate in the text of *Scribbling the Cat*. In this narrative, male, white former Rhodesians – no matter how compromised – still hold the key to the possibility of seeing the precious, nearly-vanished quasi-Edenic aspects of Africa and its landscape: '"There, lovely creature", said Mapenga, kissing my hand. "I've shown you heaven and earth"'(Fuller 2004: 231). It is no wonder that a sense of unease runs through some early, positive reviews of this text (Longworth 2004; Rosenthal 2004).

Among the persons to whom Fuller dedicates *Scribbling the Cat* is the Zimbabwean novelist Alexander Kanengoni, and Part One starts with a long quote from his 1997 novel *Echoing Silences*. Kanengoni's writing, Fuller states, 'stared war in the face and chose not to look the other way'. It is true that *Echoing Silences* contains an unflinching and poignant analysis of the cruelty, incompetence and corruption that plagued the field operations of ZANLA (Mugabe's nationalist liberation army) throughout the 1970s – and the implication is that Fuller's text is doing something similar for 'the other side'. Yet there is nothing in Kanengoni's text that exonerates Rhodesia and Rhodesians, and his text is in no way ambivalent as to the relative morality of the causes which the warring sides in the Rhodesian conflict represented (see, for example, Kanengoni 1997: 7–17). The work of the Rhodesian novelist C. Emily Dibb, on the other hand, belongs more obviously among the literary antecedents of *Scribbling the Cat*.

It is true that the 'magical days' (Dibb 1981: 2) of the idealised white Rhodesian childhoods evoked by Dibb in *Ivory, Apes and Peacocks* and *The Conundrum Trees* bear little resemblance to the kind of settler family life represented in *Don't Let's Go to the Dogs Tonight* and *Scribbling the Cat*. But Dibb was also the author of adventure novels, and her 1978 novel *The Bite* centres on a young white Rhodesian woman who leaves colonial Salisbury (the place of 'civilisation') in order to embark, alone, on an adventure in newly-independent Mozambique. Carol Innes, Dibb's fictional narrator, soon realises that she may have 'bitten off more than [she] can chew' (Dibb 1987b: 55). In this she resembles the narrator of *Scribbling the Cat* – and the two texts also share an underlying view of the position of whites in independent African countries ('Just *being* here is a risk, isn't it?' (Dibb 1978b: 59, emphasis in the original)). Where the two texts differ significantly, however, is in their constructions of gender difference: while Dibb's heroine accepts (and could not do without) the protection a white male figure whose strength and resourcefulness obviously surpass her own, Fuller's narrator is unwilling to make any such concessions. In the end, she rejects the former soldier not because of his attitude towards Africa and the Africans, but because of his attempts to claim ownership of her body (Fuller 2004: 236–240). It is only as an extension of this claim that K's mastery over the African landscape and African natives is also refuted: 'I'm not a banana field, or your wife, or your servant' (Fuller 2004: 245).

Like *Scribbling the Cat*, Peter Godwin's *When a Crocodile Eats the Sun* – another sequel – is refracted through the perspective of a Rhodesia-born narrator, now permanently based in America but constantly consumed with longing for Africa as home. Godwin's book further resembles Fuller's in having attracted positive reviews tinged with a certain amount of scepticism in the global media (Cowley 2007; Gevisser 2007; Kakutami 2007; and Mazanenhamo 2007). *Crocodile* narrates the final years in the life of Godwin's father, blighted by the violence and economic hardship in crisis-ridden Zimbabwe, and in the process of doing so articulates the thought (voiced by the father, after a lifetime of concealing his Jewish identity) that '[b]eing a white here is starting to feel a bit like being a Jew in Poland in 1939 – an endangered minority – the target of ethnic cleansing' (Godwin 2006: 175). The narrator does not qualify this thought, and reviewers Kakutani and Muzanenhamo have rightly pointed out that the rash parallel ignores the horrors of colonialism. But this is not the only way in which Godwin's memoir is compromised by the discursive angle from which its approaches its denunciation of Robert Mugabe and his government.

The book's very title is an act of political criticism: the crocodile (Shona: *garwe*) is Mugabe's family totem, and the eclipse of the sun (which, unusually, occurs twice in the course of the seven year time period spanned by the memoir's narrative present) is regarded as an ill omen by several Southern African ethnic groups. As a newspaper reporter, Godwin witnessed the tragic outcomes of the violent commercial farm appropriations of the 2000s, and he describes them in detail with a sense of outrage which is appropriate, but is not – as Mark Gevisser (2007) points out – sufficiently historicised. Both colonial depredation and postcolonial white racism – the isolationist stance of Zimbabwe's white community eloquently described by the Zimbabwean author Chenjerai Hove in a recent interview (Primorac 2007a) as well as his own and much other black Zimbabwean fiction (see

Hove 1988 and Primorac 2006) – are absent from Godwin's text. Instead, he constructs an image of a multi-racial, tolerant society (exemplified in the main by his liberal sister and parents), riven by a sudden outburst of violence whose source is repeatedly designated as both primordial and irreducibly 'African'. After a particularly fraught moment with his parents in a car late at night, when a fear that they would be attacked by carjackers suddenly dissolves, the narrator feels 'like weeping. Weeping at the way Africa does this to you' (Godwin 2006: 298). And although he routinely tells his young sons, based in New York, that he is going home 'to Africa', the memoir constantly also refers to the entire African continent (rather than pointing specifically at crisis-stricken Zimbabwe) as the seat of irrationality and chaos. During an aeroplane trip in 2003, the narrator contemplates 'a continent of catastrophe' in his flight path (Godwin 2006: 202). Elsewhere, he writes of an aid workers' 'faith [being] eroded by the vagaries of Africa' (Godwin 2006: 286), and of aid-related projects being moved from Zimbabwe to 'other African countries, ones where things are a little less crazy' (Godwin 2006: 287).

In temporal terms, African 'craziness' articulates itself as a propensity towards regression – another familiar colonial-era trope: 'I realize that maybe not so much has changed as we all thought, that maybe the whole idea of progress is a paradox, a rocking horse that goes forward and back, forward and back, but stays in the same place, giving only the comforting illusion of motion' (Godwin 2006: 49). This is a notion of time unmistakeably linked to Rhodesian discourse – and it therefore seems fitting that Godwin employs an image from an iconic text of the empire, Conrad's *Heart of Darkness*, on the very next page. The pre-independence Rhodesian texts (as analysed by Chennells) resembled Conrad's in that they assigned to 'the white man' the thankless task of trying to move the intransigent 'rocking horse' of African history forward, and so does Godwin. His gendering of the notion of 'white settler' is routinely male throughout ('Bougainvillea is exotic to Africa, just like the white man' – Godwin 2006: 63), and his own ceaseless crossing and re-crossing between 'the First World' and 'Africa' in order to bring some comfort and solace to his parents (who see themselves as resembling the cultured but disempowered 'Greek slaves in Rome' – Godwin 2006: 295) resonates with the spatial mobility of earlier neo-Rhodesian heroes (Armstrong's idealistic but helpless Rhodesian environmentalist in *Hawks of Peace* or the unyielding wildlife enthusiasts in texts by Meadows and Rimmer), whose dogged determination is to keep struggling against encroaching chaos until the bitter end, and against impossible odds.

The generic affinity of *When a Crocodile Eats the Sun* with the Rhodesian master narrative (albeit distant, and multiply refracted) explains how it is possible for Godwin to articulate genuine sympathy with *all* victims of Zimbabwe's decline, but then also to refer, without apparent irony, to his own 'sacrifice' (Godwin 2006: 233), or to the 'sad' event of his sister's Shona servant leaving her employment and striking out on her own once they have both emigrated to London, or to the neo-colonial cliché about the evils of colonisation being matched only by the comparable evils of decolonisation (Godwin 2006: 153). In keeping with this ambivalence is the fluidity with the narrator's subject position as constructed by the text: not unlike David Lemon's memoir, which refers to both England and Zimbabwe as it's narrator's home country, *Crocodile* uses the personal pronoun 'we' to strategically designate either all the suffering Zimbabweans, or the dispossessed white Zimbabweans, or (frequently), a metonymic slide between the two, through which a sense of 'African' belonging can be both asserted and denied as needed: when the narrator states, for example, that '*we* are now a people cowed and fearful, vulnerable, disposable' (Godwin 2006: 292; emphasis added), the referentiality of the personal pronoun is unclear. At the memoir's end (where, in a sequence repeated verbatim, the body of the narrator's father is engulfed by flames whose symbolism is not hard to decode), the narrator's insistence that Mugabe's oppressive rule has wrought a 'real racial unity' (Godwin 2006: 320) between his family and the majority of Zimbabweans remains uncomfortably close to Fuller's assertion of her own African belonging: belied by its own generic affinity, and under-girded by decades of textual ambivalence.

Instead of Conclusions: Unmasking Textual History

By way of concluding and as a counter-example, another cluster of narratives by white Zimbabwean authors should briefly be mentioned. Catherine Buckle was one of the first white farmers to be violently displaced by the 'war veterans', in the early stages of Zimbabwe's land occupations in 2000. She relates her experience in minute detail in a memoir entitled *African Tears* (2001), and its sequel, *Beyond Tears* (2002). Despite her title (which summons echoes of easy colonial essentialisms), Buckle refrains from insisting that there is anything peculiarly 'African' in her misfortune. Instead, she presents a complex and specific account of the struggles over space, agency and future identities that were involved in the farm takeovers. She speaks of those who occupied her farm as individuals with names and agencies of their own, and shows (in Contrast to Godwin) that the process of land occupations was disorderly and violent, but far from chaotic. It was, instead, spurred on by a careful inversion of the key characteristics of the Rhodesian master fiction, the outline of which may be gleaned through her story. (She cites government pronouncements which declare that white Zimbabweans are in fact foreigners and therefore the enemy, that outside spaces were essentially different from, and hostile to, the national one, and that in the future, Zimbabwe must be saved from regressing to colonial status. Buckle's memoirs show that it is in this form – transmute into Mugabeist versions of 'patriotic history' – that the neo-Rhodesian master fiction is currently most malignantly alive.

Several years after Buckle's second memoir, Harare schoolteacher Ian Holding published a novel entitled *Unfeeling* (2005) and dedicated simply to 'the victims' of Zimbabwe crisis-related violence. Focused through the character of a white teenager seeking to avenge the brutal murder of his farm-owning parents, the novel can be read as both mourning the decline of Zimbabwean white rural lifestyle and exposing the racism and patriarchy on which this lifestyle was based. Despite a seeming closeness to it, *Unfeeling* rejects the key tenets of the Rhodesian master fiction through two carefully articulated narrative devices. Firstly, the novel includes an extended description of black farm workers' suffering at the hand of government-sponsored attackers as one of the central aspects of the present-day Zimbabwean tragedy, to which the abuse of white farmers must unavoidably be linked. And secondly, it stresses that many white farmers cultivated a sense of entitlement based on a wilful act of forgetting: as the youthful hero enjoys a typical day in the countryside – hunting, fishing and dreaming of the day when he will become a farmer, like his father – he keeps postponing the writing of a school history essay asking him to outline the history of his family's arrival on Zimbabwean soil.

No such forgetfulness is possible in *The Voluptuous Delights of Peanut Butter and Jam* (2008) by displaced Zimbabwean Lauren Liebenberg. A central section in this account of farm girlhoods tells the life story of the family's black servant, once a miner in South Africa, with whom readers are asked to both identify and sympathise. The novel is set in the dying days of colonial Rhodesia, and it transmutes what Emily Dibb, Maureen de la Harpe and Alexandra Fuller represent as the 'primordial magic' of the African bush into an all-pervading sense of evil and foreboding. Central to the story is the figure of Ronin, a white male teenager whose chivalrous manner is no more than a mask hiding a disturbing, cowardly brutality. Ronin's unmasking, which unfolds in parallel to a family tragedy, the abandoning of the farm and the end of war, is an apt metaphor for this novel's treatment of its own generic predecessors – and for the only desirable fate of the discursive convention on which they are based.

Notes

1. I here understand 'ideology' in the Bakhtinian sense, as a pattern of evaluative accents configuring the combination of discourses that make up a novel.

2. For an exploration of the parallels between African and settler political discourses in the 1960s and 1970s, see Day 1975. For an analysis of the 'marco-genre' of the Zimbabwean war novel, see Primorac 2006.
3. I have written elsewhere on how fictional narratives have bolstered and reproduced the contemporary version of Zimbabwean black 'patriotism', which has, in turn, re-trenched binary modes of thinking characteristic of colonial-era settler discourses (Primorac 2007b). Since both of these discursive formations are referential only in as much as they contest the validity of their shadowing doubles, it goes without saying that neither nationalist discourse represents a valid form of social critique. And as both facilitate violent exclusions, together they highlight the urgent need for a movement away from oppositional and towards pluralistic modes of thinking about the contemporary Zimbabwean nation.
4. For a problematisation of his definition, see Primorac 2003.
5. For a discussion of 'degrees' of Zimbabwean colonial whiteness, see Mlambo 2000.
6. In an unpublished exchange about white Zimbabwean autobiographical writing, Chennells (2002) has written that 'perhaps [there exist] gender differences in recalling the past: women remember a more private past while the men are actors on the public stage (...) In fact I would argue that the private is never private in a colonial context and the white woman was always a public person in being required to bear little Rhodesians for a future nation.' (Chennells, chapter proposal for Muponde and Primorac, *Versions of Zimbabwe,* 2002).
7. See, for example, *Rhodesian.Net,*__http://rhodesian.server101.com/ and *Rhodesians Worldwide – contact site for folk from Rhodesia,* http://www.rhodesia.com/. A paper edition of *Rhodesians Worldwide* was published in Britain until the late 1990s.
8. Partridge's text identifies itself as fiction, Moore King's is an eyewitness account, and McLoughlin's is a fictionalised account of real events, while Shaw's claims to represent a 'true life situation that involved hundreds of people and a broad timespan,' with changes made, nevertheless, for the sake of clarity. Partridge's text resembles other Zimbabwean women's war narratives in that it refrains from representing armed combat.
9. '[The elephant] Chikuru is almost a national monument and it would be terrible to lose him after all we have done so far.' Lemon 1994: 44.
10. Zimbabwean themes do not feature centrally in *Cataclysm* (1980), *The Last Movie* (1981) and *The Pegasus Man* (1983).
11. 'There were a few darkies, but not what I thought. Didn't look like Africa at all.' Armstrong 1987: 22.
12. For an analysis of her wartime adventure/romance *Spotted Soldiers* (1978a), see Chennells 1979b, 1982 and 1995.
13. For a full-length analysis of *Don't Let's Go to the Dogs* and *Mukiwa,* see Harris 2005.

References

Armstrong, P. 1978. *The Iron Trek.* Salisbury: Welston Press.
——. 1979a. *Hawks of Peace.* Borrowdale [Salisbury]: Welston Press.
——. 1979b. *Operation Zambezi – The Raid into Zambia.* Salisbury: Welston Press.
——. 1980. *Cataclysm.* Borrowdale [Harare]: Welston Press.
——. 1981. *The Last Movie.* Borrowdale [Harare]: Welston Press.
——. 1983. *The Pegasus Man.* Borrowdale [Harare]: Welston Press.
——. 1987. *Tobacco Spiced with Ginger: The Life of Ginger Freeman* Borowdale [Harare]: Welston Press.
Buchan, J. 2008 [1915]. *The Thirty-Nine Steps.* London: Collector's Library.
Buckle, C. 2001. *African Tears* Johannesburg: Jonathan Bull.
——. 2002. *Beyond Tears.* Johannesburg: Jonathan Bull.
Burns, J. M. 2002. *Flickering Shadows: Cinema and Identity in Colonial Zimbabwe.* Athens, Ohio: Ohio University Press.
Chan, S. 1985. *The Commonwealth Observer Group in Zimbabwe: A Personal Memoir.* Gweru: Mambo Press.
——. 2005. *Citizen of Africa: Conversations with Morgan Tsvangirai.* Cape Town: Fingerprint, 2005.
Chennells, A. 1977. 'The Treatment of the Rhodesian War in Recent Rhodesian Novels', *Zambezia* 5, 2: 177–202.
——. 1979a. 'The White Rhodesian Novel', *New Statesman*, 90, 7: 872–874.
——. 1979b. Review of *The Yellow Mountain* by L. Burton, *Spotted Soldiers* by C.E. Dibb and *Operation Zambezi: The Raid Into Zambia* by P. Armstrong, *Zambezia* 7, 1: 121–124.
——. 1982. *Settler Myths and the Southern Rhodesian Novel.* PhD thesis, University of Zimbabwe.
——. 1984. 'Just a Story: Wilbur Smith's Ballantyne Trilogy and the Problem of a Rhodesian Historical Romance', *Social Dynamics* 10, 1: 38–45.
——. 1995. 'Rhodesian Discourse, Rhodesian Novels and the Zimbabwe Liberation War,' in N. Bhebhe and T. Ranger (eds) *Society in Zimbabwe's Liberation War.* Harare: University of Zimbabwe Publications, 102–129.
——. 2002. Chapter proposal for Muponde and Primorac, *Versions of Zimbabwe.*
——. 2005. 'Self-Representation and National Memory: White Autobiographies in Zimbabwe,' in Muponde and Primorac, *Versions of Zimbabwe*, 131–141.
——. 2007. 'Great Zimbabwe in Rhodesian Fiction', in M. Z. Malaba and G. V. Davies (eds), *Zimbabwean Transitions: Essays on Zimbabwean Literature in English, Ndebele and Shona.* Amsterdam: Rodopi, 1–24.
Cowley, J. 2007. Review of *When a Crocodile Eats the Sun. The Observer*, 4 March. www.guardian.co.uk/theobserver/2007/mar/04/society.politics. Accessed 14 Dec 2008.
Day, J. 1975. 'The Creation of Political Myths: African Nationalism in Southern Rhodesia', *Journal of Southern African Studies* 2, 1: 52–65.
de la Harpe, M. 1992. *Msasa Morning.* Harare: Roblaw Publishers.
Dibb, C.E. 1978a. *Spotted Soldiers.* Salisbury: Leo Publications.

——. 1978b. *The Bite*. London: Robert Hale.
——. 1981. *Ivory, Apes and Peacocks*. Bulawayo: Books of Zimbabwe.
——. 1989. *The Conundrum Trees*. Harare: Modus Publications.
Dondo, C. 2003. 'War Veterans' (2001), photograph exhibited at the *Artists for Zimbabwe* exhibition, Gallery 27, Cork Street, London W1, 3–8 March.
Eppel, J. 2001. *The Curse of the Ripe Tomato*. Bulawayo: amaBooks.
——. 2002. *The Holy Innocents*. Bulawayo: amaBooks.
Freeman, P. 1998. *Rumours of Ophir*. Harare: College Press.
Fuller, A. 2001. *Don't Let's Go to the Dogs Tonight*. New York: Random House.
Fuller, A. 2004. *Scribbling the Cat: Travels with an African Soldier*. London: Picador.
Garstin, C. 1971. *The Sunshine Settlers*. Bulawayo: Books of Rhodesia.
Gevisser, M. 2007. 'The Dispossessed'. *The New York Times*, 14 June. http://www.nytimes.com/2007/06/17/books/review/Gevisser-t.thml? Accessed 10 Dec 2008.
Godwin, P. 1996. *Mukiwa: A White Boy in Africa*. London: Picador.
——. 2006. *When a Crocodile Eats the Sun: A Memoir*. Johannesburg: Picador Africa.
Godwin, P. and I. Hancock. 1993. *Rhodesians Never Die: The Impact of War and Political Change on White Rhodesia c. 1970–1980*. Harare: Baobab Press.
Harris, A. 2005. 'Writing Home: Inscriptions of Whiteness/Descriptions of Belonging in White Zimbabwean Memori-Autobiography', in Muponde and Primorac, *Versions of Zimbabwe*, 103–117.
Haw, R.C. 1966. *Rhodesia – The Jewel of Africa*. Salisbury: Flame Lily Books.
Hill, R.K. 1995. *Burnt Toast on Sundays*. Harare: HarperCollins.
Holding, I. 2005. *Unfeeling*. London: Pocket Books.
Huggins, D. 2004. *Stained Earth* Harare: Weaver Press.
Hulley, C.M. 1969. *Where Lions Once Roamed*. Salisbury: The Pioneer Head.
Kaarsholm, P. 1991. 'From Decadence to Authenticity and Beyond: Fantasies and Mythologies of War in Rhodesia and Zimbabwe, 1965–1985,' in P. Kaarsholm, (ed.) *Cultural Development and Struggle in Southern Africa*. Harare: Baobab Books, 33–60.
——. 2005. 'Coming to Terms with Violence: Literature and the Development of a public sphere in Zimbabwe', in Muponde and Primorac, *Versions of Zimbabwe*, 3–23.
Kanengoni, A. 1997. *Echoing Silences*. Harare: Baobab Books.
Kakutani, M. 2007. Review of *When a Crocodile Eats the Sun*. *The New York Times*, 18 May. http://www.nytimes.com/2007/05/18/books/18book/html? Accessed 14 Dec 2008.
Lemon, D. 1994 [1983]. *Ivory Madness*. Harare: College Press.
——. 1998. *Killer Cat*. Harare: College Press Publishers.
——. 2000. *Never Quite a Soldier*. Stroud: Albida Books.
——. n. d. *Hobo Rows Kariba*. Harare: African Publishing Group.
Liebengerg, L. 2008. *The Voluptuous Delights of Peanut Butter and Jam*. London: Virago.
Longworth, P. 2004. 'Dark Hearts', *The Guardian* (UK), 11 September.
Lowry, D. 2005. 'Queen's Rebels: Rhodesia's UDI and the Colonial Tradition of Conditional Loyalty'. Paper delivered at *UDI 40 Years On: A Conference to Mark*

the *40th Anniversary of the Rhodesian Declaration of Independence*, University of Cambridge, 21–22 September.

Mbembe, A. 1991. 'Power and Obscenity in the Post-Colonial Period: The Case of Cameroon,' in J. Manor (ed.) *Rethinking Third World Politics*. London: Longman, 166–182.

——. 2001. 'The Aesthetics of Vulgarity,' in *On the Postcolony*. Berkeley: University of California Press, 102–141.

——. 2002. 'African Modes of Self-Writing,' *Public Culture* 14, 1: 239–273.

McLoughlin, T. 1985. *Karima*. Gweru: Mambo Press.

Meadows, K. 1996. *Sand in the Wind*. Bulawayo: Thorntree Press.

Mlambo, A.S. 2000. '"Some are More White than Others": Racial Chauvinism as a Factor in Rhodesian Immigration Policy', *Zambezia* 27, 2: 139–160.

Moore King, B. 1987. *White Man Black War*. Harare: Baobab Books.

Mugabe, R. 2005. 'We won't go back to the Commonwealth', *New African* 441: 6–12.

Mugabe, R.G. 2001. *Inside the Third Chimurenga*. Harare: Department of Information and Publicity, Office of the President and Cabinet.

Muponde, R. and R. Primorac 2005. *Versions of Zimbabwe: New Approaches to Literature and Culture*. Harare: Weaver Press.

Muzanenhamo, T. 2007. 'Another Eclipse of the Son'. *Guardian* 31 March. http: www.guardian.co.uk/books/2007/mar/31/featursereview.guardianreview36/ Accessed 10 Dec 2008.

Osborne, J. 2004. *A Guiding Son*. Bulawayo: John Osborne.

Partridge, N. 1986. *To Breathe and Wait*. Gweru: Mambo Press.

Pichanick, J., A.J. Chennells and L.B. Rix. 1977. *Rhodesian Literature in English – A Bibliography (1890–1974/5)*. Salisbury: Mambo Press.

Primorac, R. 2003. 'The Novel in a House of Stone: Re-Categorising Zimbabwean Fiction', *Journal of Southern African Studies* 29,1: 49–62.

——. 2006. *The Place of Tears: The Novel and Politics in Modern Zimbabwe*. London: I.B. Tauris.

——. 2007a. '"Dictatorships are Transient": Chenjerai Hove Interviewed by Ranka Primorac'. *The Journal of Commonwealth Literature* 43, 1: 135–146.

——. 2007b. 'The Poetics of State Terror in Twenty-First Century Zimbabwe'. *Interventions* 9, 3: 434–450.

Ranger, T. 1994. 'Landscape Gardening in Zimbabwe', *Southern African Review of Books* 6, 2: 7–8.

——. 2004. 'Nationalist Historiography, Patriotic History and the History of the Nation: the Struggle over the Past in Zimbabwe', *Journal of Southern African Studies* 30, 2: 215–234.

Rauwerda, Antje M. 2009. 'Exile Encampments: Whiteness in Alexandra Fuller's *Scribbling the Cat: Travels with an African Soldier*', *The Journal of Commonwealth Literature* 44, 2: 51–64.

Rimmer, P. 1993, *Cry of the Fish Eagle*. Harare: HarperCollins Publishers.

Rooney, C. 2001. *African Literature, Animism and Politics*. London: Routledge.

Rosenthal, J. 2004. 'Scribbling the Rhodesian Past', *Mail & Guardian* (SA), 24–30 September.

Shaw, A. 1993. *Kandaya*. Harare: Baobab Books.

Shutt, A. K. and T. King, 2005. 'Imperial Rhodesians: The 1953 Rhodes Centenary Exhibition in Southern Rhodesia', *Journal of Southern African Studies* 31, 2: 357–79.

Skimin, R. 1977. *The Rhodesian Sellout.* New York: Libra Publishers.

Smith, I. D. 1997. *The Great Betrayal: The Memoirs of Ian Douglas Smith.* London: Blake.

Smith, W. 1980. *A Falcon Flies.* London: Heinemann.

——. 1981. *Men of Men.* London: Heinemann.

——. 1982. *The Angels Weep.* London: Heinemann.

——. 1984. *The Leopard Hunts in Darkness.* London: Heinemann.

Sylvester, C. 2003. 'Remembering and Forgetting "Zimbabwe": Towards a Third Transition', in P. Gready (ed.) *Political Transition: Politics and Cultures.* London: Pluto Press, 29–52.

Todd, J.G. 2007. *Through the Darkness: A Life in Zimbabwe.* Cape Town: Zebra Press.

White, L. 2004a. 'Civic Virtue, Young Men and the Family: Conscription in Rhodesia, 1974–1980', *International Journal of African Historical Studies* 37, 1: 103–21.

——. 2004b. 'Precarious Conditions: A Note on Counter-Insurgency in Africa after 1945', *Gender & History* 16, 3: 603–25.

10

Exile and the Internet: Ndebele and Mixed-race Online Diaspora 'Homes'

Clayton Peel

Since the mid-1990s, diaspora groupings formed in the UK by Zimbabwean migrants have flourished on the web, taking advantage of increased access to the internet through new technology. These online communities inform, affirm and help to reproduce their different constituencies. Zimbabweans who produce and participate in these online fora join a global interactive phenomenon that challenges previous communication practices and cultural conventions. This article aims to explore the role of the internet in the formation of diasporic identities through an examination of the experiences of transnational Zimbabweans in Britain, whose interaction through new technologies is attracting a growing body of research. It contributes to an understanding of how the cultural capital and agency of transnational Zimbabweans in Britain is put to effect as they interrogate their own identities, their citizenship and sense of belonging, their politics, and their transnational aspirations.

The existing literature on Zimbabwean diaspora websites (Pasura 2006a; Mano and Willems 2008 and this volume) has focused on some of the best known internet news sites, such as www.newzimbabwe.com and www. zwnews.com, but has overlooked other sites that bring together sub-national collectivities and serve particular sectional interests among Zimbabweans abroad. Consequently, their research carries with it a (possibly unintended) implication of Zimbabwean diaspora internet communities as homogenous wholes. By contrast, the discussion in this chapter focuses on two websites with openly ethnic and racial content and constituencies. The sites are www.inkundla.net and www.goffal.com[1], which bring together diasporic Zimbabweans who identify respectively as Ndebele (one of Zimbabwe's two major ethnic groups, which comprises about fifteen per cent of the population in comparison to the majority who identify as Shona) and Coloured (i.e. mixed-race). The names of these websites are meaningful: 'Inkundla' is the Ndebele word for a pre-colonial consensus-seeking court where community elders discussed important matters, while 'goffal' is a Zimbabwean slang word for a mixed-race person.

Informed by Habermasian concepts of public discourse, the chapter tracks evidence of identity re/production on the websites' online message boards, and aims to demonstrate a 'degree of salience' (Burnett and Marshall 2003: 8) for individuals whose purposes are served by the two websites. The chapter argues that the online communities' focus on ethnicity and race represents free (i.e. uncensored) public speech, and that the websites therefore have the potential to become one facet of a pluralised media, which can help democratise the Zimbabwean public sphere. The 'inkundla' and 'goffal' communities go some way towards demonstrating how the internet has revolutionised media use by expanding the possibilities for 'lay' speakers – the 'public' – to actively create and engage with media content by generating immediate dialogue and debate. It is therefore arguable that these websites have become an integral part of what media scholars have described as 'citizens' media', 'participatory media', 'alternative media' or even 'radical media' (Rodriguez 2004).

In connection with these arguments, I hope to show how the reach of discourses generated on the two websites transcends the virtual domain of the internet and may affect material transactions and social formations. There is evidence of political/social action emanating from the two websites, as, for example, through an online consultative process on inkundla. net and a web-generated charitable trust providing relief of basic needs to members of Zimbabwe's mixed-race communities on goffal.com. The social interventions resulting from online communication may be seen as part of a re-enfranchisement of the websites' constituencies, both inside and outside Zimbabwe, which has been influenced by the internet.

This research on which this chapter is based was conducted as part of a larger project seeking to test the assumption that Zimbabwe-related websites run from Britain are a key source of interaction and information for Zimbabweans resident in the UK. Between 2003 and 2008, I have followed debates on selected websites, interviewed key individuals and tracked website through questionnaires, which were distributed and filled in online as well as in face to face interactions. All in all, I solicited responses from over 1,500 respondents.[2] These questionnaires can shed light on the importance of internet sites for Zimbabweans based in Britain. In response to a multiple-choice question regarding the favoured source of

Zimbabwe-related news, seventy-six per cent of the respondents prioritised the use of internet websites (forty-seven per cent favoured British-based Zimbabwe-related websites while only twenty-nine per cent preferred websites generated from within Zimbabwe). This suggests the British-based websites are more attuned to the communication, information and societal needs of Zimbabweans in the UK than those based in Zimbabwe. None of the alternative sources of information (reading British newspapers, text messages and word of mouth) rivalled the internet as a primary source of data or medium of interaction. The 12.5 per cent of respondents who said they relied primarily on 'word of mouth' to update themselves on Zimbabwe suggest that written-language media are still in part a powerful authenticator of informal oral communication, while the 8.5 per cent who said that they primarily use British newspapers for information on Zimbabwe reinforce the view that a Zimbabwean perspective is more important to the majority of Zimbabweans in UK than the reporting and discussing of events inside Zimbabwe by non-Zimbabwean sources. The 2.8 per cent of the respondents who chiefly use text messaging point to the importance of this mode of communication, although this figure does suggest that mobile phone texts are neither the main source of information nor the foremost way of Zimbabweans getting in touch with one another.

In 2003, a representative of inkundla.net, which is one of the earliest Zimbabwean website communities, described how the arrival of the internet in the 1990s was something of a godsend to Zimbabwe's expatriate communities because it created a public domain to which they could have free, direct and uncensored access.[3] In that sense, inkundla.net and goffal. com represent 'homes' for Zimbabwe's minority ethnic/racial communities. The sites enunciate some of the values, prejudices and fears shared by their constituent communities in the diaspora. They also connect the respective diaspora and homeland communities through homeland focused initiatives, which are funded through the overseas members who have the capacity to provide financial support and to realise ideas frequently expressed on the website fora. Below, I analyse key excerpts from internet debates on the two websites that discuss the possibility of organised intervention (i.e. public action). These discussions provide insight into the ways Zimbabweans in Britain have aimed to alter the material situation in Zimbabwe itself, and I use them to draw some preliminary conclusions regarding the relationship between internet debates and identity construction in the diaspora.

'Our Land, Our Heritage': Inkundla.net

The Ndebele-speaking expatriate internet community in the UK have the oldest Zimbabwe-diaspora online presence, having started out in 1996. The first site (www.mthwakazi.org)[4] was created to assist activism in favour of Ndebele minority rights and political autonomy. This later evolved into inkundla.net, which has an embedded radio station, Shaya FM, in 2001. Rolinhlanhla Masiane, the inkundla.net founder-member who addressed the Britain Zimbabwe Society in 2003, made it clear that while the immediate motivation behind the creation of the website was community support and cultural solidarity, gradually longer-term practical objectives began to take shape. It was, he said, that time when 'ideas flow into reality; when we see happen what all along we thought was possible' (Masiane 2003). After 2005, those who met on the site took substantial steps towards strengthening Ndebele economic, political and social life by investing in Matabeleland. These initiatives emerged from an inkundla.net discussion over how the Matabeleland region could be saved from two perceived ills: the 'invasion' by Shona-speaking households who were now populating not just Bulawayo, but the rural heartland of Matabeleland, and the dearth of economic and cultural vibrancy in the region resulting from alleged neglect by the central Zimbabwean government.

Inkundla.net participants reflected on the ZANU PF-led land redistribution programme, criticising the way it had worked out in Matabeleland. Instead of local traditional leaders being given control over the allocation so that deserving locals get a fair share, the inkundla community complained (citing news reports from other media), Shona-speaking businessmen and farmers from outside Matabeleland were being given vast tracts of land. The aim was clearly to transform the Ndebele base of rural Matabeleland and dilute, once and for all, Ndebele ethno-political space. Their fears appeared to be confirmed through a series of radio interviews with angry local villagers in Matabeleland protesting the 'invasion' of the Shona-speakers, which was broadcast by the Zimbabwe diaspora radio station SW Radio Africa in 2004.[5] This sparked a series of emotional exchanges on inkundla.net, and led to action in the form of an engagement by the expatriate inkundla community with the officials of Bulawayo's Housing Department and a provincial agricultural officer in Matabeleland. They aimed to get information on the housing plots in Bulawayo and rural agricultural land that was becoming available. The exiles' intention was to use their resources to purchase as much urban and rural land as possible and to settle the stands with Ndebele-speakers.

In view of the ethno-nationalist slant of these debates and interventions, it seems fitting that it was a web-board diaspora contributor using the name of the nineteenth century Ndebele king, Mzilikazi, who first challenged expatriate Ndebele to invest their capital in Matabeleland, and to give support to elected Zimbabwean institutions such as the Bulawayo City Council. The latter was, at the time, operating under difficult conditions because it was controlled by the political opposition, the Movement for Democratic Change (MDC) and was harassed by the central government.

An excerpt from the initial posting by 'King Mzilikazi' entitled 'Regaining Lost Ground' that spurred this action can provide some insight into the emotional, and rousing tone of the debate:[6]

> Mthwakazi. Matabeleland North province, Matabeleland South province and the Midlands is our land, our heritage which we were left by our forefathers. Bulawayo is the nerve centre of what defines uMthwakazi [the land of Mthwakazi] in general. It is the cultural spirit of those who have gone before us.
>
> We therefore have a responsibility to ensure it remains so. We have seen the efforts of the enemy to change our region, our city from what our forefathers wanted it to be. Yes circumstances beyond our control have led us to abandon our lands, our towns and cities in a bid to survive. Now that we are abroad, it is important for us to remember home. As we all leave in search of greener pastures, we must remember that we have left behind even fewer people to make up the Mthwakazi population. In the process we open up space for more Shona invasion and if this is not reversed our talk of Mthwakazi will remain an academic exercise. Every Mthwakazian has to see to it that he prepares to return home, once the political situation has changed. We know that where we are now is a temporary sojourn. I know that there are Shonas who, even when they have the citizenship of other countries, do not neglect their homeland.
>
> Yes, they are many, and indeed they have developed the knowledge economy to maximise their foreign earnings and invest in Zimbabwe. But we, whatever it takes, have to go back to preserve what our forefathers left behind.
>
> We must make sure that with the foreign currency we are generating we buy houses in Bulawayo, Gwanda, Vic falls etc
>
> We start ibizinisi [businesses]
>
> We seek out and exploit every opportunity that arises in our region - don't worry about Harare etc. The whole idea is to shut out the marauding and invading Shona tribesmen from our region.
>
> I am impressed with the way some of our guys in Mzansi [South Africa] have changed the face of iKhezi [Khezi district] and its surrounding areas. Unfortunately iBulawayo [Bulawayo city] has already has been taken over by Shonas. We need to regain lost ground. You see, when people vote in local govt elections, they must own property in that local area. Now if iBulawayo ends up dominated by Shona-speaking people, I foresee a situation where the future Council, councillors and Mayors will all be Shona. Remember your home!

In this rhetorically skillful call to action, 'King Mzilikazi' evokes the pre-colonial era (in the reference to the 'marauding and invading Shona tribesmen') and establishes the gender (male) as well as the ethnicity (Shona) of the website users' perceived 'enemy'. This online monologue stresses the inkundla community's diaspora residence as a 'temporary sojourn' and stresses the speaker's own testimony of having bought property in an upmarket Bulawayo estate, whose symbolic value is increased by the fact that it is formerly owned by the late Ndebele nationalist leader Joshua Nkomo. It continues:

> Most of the plots in Burnside left behind by ubaba [father] Joshua Nkomo, now under uThandiwe [Nkomo's eldest daughter] were bought by amaShona mostly from Harare. I know this for a fact because I bought one, but all my neighbour are Shona. Where are we, people of Mthwakazi? This is our city and we should not be allowing this.

> Nowadays houses new and old are bought in foreign currency – we are many 'Mthwakazians' in the Diaspora. Buy these properties and let's not allow outsiders to do as they wish. It's up to us to resolve this!

It is clear that the changing demographics of Bulawayo and rural Matabeleland as these have been shaped by Ndebele emigration to South Africa, Botswana and Britain and the resettlement of people from Shona-speaking provinces presents a challenge for the Mthwakazi project.[7]

Following Mzilikazi's intervention, a number of the forum members came out in favour of development-oriented interventions that would assist Bulawayo and institutions in 'Mthwakazi' more broadly. Acquisition of properties, urban and rural, by amaNdebele continues to feature in the threads that address this. Another contributor (going by the name of Mzilikazi's son and heir Lobengula), took the project further:[8]

> Folks,

> Currently there is the on-going Homelink Scheme being aggressively marketed by the Reserve Bank of Zimbabwe which is targeted exclusively to people in the diaspora or those working outside the country.

> I recently (after Xmas) went to the Bulawayo City Council housing department (where I also met one of the leading members of our forum Hlathi hk hk), and specifically asked them about their experiences of the Homelink Scheme and how our people can utilise it. The grim answer I got was that currently there are 1 Acre x 1 Acre stands available in Khumalo/Parklands areas. Similar stands exist in Mahatshula/Selborne Park areas. Stands are also availble in Mganwini and Pumula South near the Mbonqane area.

> The council housing staff expressed discomfort with the fact that the only people who keep enquiring about stands or property were people from the East (Mashonaland) who are based in foreign countries. The question they asked me was where are our own people, the Khumalos, the Ndlovus, the Ncubes, Dubes, Nkalas, Moyos (not Jones), the Mlotshwas etc etc??????. It would seem that the Tshabi [derogatory term for 'Shona'] bloc is trying

to use the Homelink scheme to monopolise Bulawayo!!!. But as a patriotic organisation, the BCC [Bulawayo City Council] has tactfully delayed the use of the Home Link scheme thereby deliberately giving us the time to make a decision whether or not we want to acquire property using this scheme. The fact of the matter is that whilst we are still undecided and dilly-dallying, the Tshabis are waiting on the fence to sneak in should we delay even further. The next thing we will be kicking ourselves in the back crying foul when all our suburbs have been colonised by these people with the consequent that our sisters will unwittingly fall victim to the economic power of these monsters.

So the question is what should our policy be regarding these Homelink schemes? Some might want to know how the whole Homelink scheme functions?, we can address this if needs be. Will the acquisition of a property by any <u>Mthwakazian</u> in Byo be equated to being a turncoat? I think we need to pronounce on this issue so that we approach it from a concerted and collective viewpoint. If we pronounce on whether or not Mthwakazians can buy property using such schemes, it will open new opportunities whereby we keep updating each other on new opportunities without fear of being labelled or branded with predictable ugly names.

So members of this forum must express their opinions on this issue because further delay will only disadvantage us as a people. It is useless for Lobengula or Gazlam to acquire a stand or house in Khumalo or Parklands when the whole area is swamped by the Tshabis, but it is good if we can acquire these stands and properties en masse as Mthwakazians.

After echoing the sentiments of 'Mzilikazi' (in part through the suggestive pile-up of Ndebele family names and the ominous reference to the possibility that Ndebele-speaking women will be lured into partnerships with prosperous local Shona-speaking men), 'Lobengula' reveals that he has been in personal contact with a member of Bulawayo City Council. (The council is referred to as 'patriotic' – i.e. loyal to the 'Mthwakazi' cause for apparently delaying the acquisition of properties by Shona-speaking transnationals.) Concomitant with this activism that engages officials within urban Bulawayo's Housing Department was a significant development in rural Matabeleland that the inkundla community had become aware of and exploited, for the purposes of monitoring land redistribution patterns and lobbying the responsible agency at provincial-regional level: 'Lobengula' (whose initial suggestion was taken up by other speakers) asked the Ndebele in the diaspora to take advantage of a recent appointment of an Ndebele to the position of government resettlement officer in Matabeleland, an appointment 'Lobengula' insisted had helped 'keep these Shona vultures out of our provinces'. Other contributors to the forum were skeptical that the new appointment will have had much effect, but 'Lobengula' was adamant that already, the appointment had resulted in locals being given priority for land as the new officer 'wants amajaha eSindebeleni [Ndebele-speaking young men] to come in their thousands to get their potions (sic) of the land in their respective provinces'.[9] The challenge, according to 'Lobengula' was for Ndebele in the Diaspora to stop philosophising about an immediate political solution, and to move by stealth towards empowering and working with agencies 'on the ground' that shared the inkundla agenda.

It has been difficult to get information from the Bulawayo City Council on the Ndebele diaspora's success in turning around the alleged rush by Shona-speaking transnationals to acquire housing stands and units in Bulawayo. An official in the Housing Department told this researcher that all interested buyers were required to register with the department; that this required filling out a form, providing proof of funds, and the down-payment of a deposit.[10] Payment of the deposit secured the prospective buyer a place on the waiting lists for either housing units or undeveloped stands, and there were separate lists for stands and houses in the low and high density suburbs. There was no provision in this process for discrimination on ethnic grounds and while it was true that an increasing number of expatriate Zimbabweans were purchasing properties, the municipality neither encouraged, nor kept a record of, ethnically-linked purchases and settlement. Similarly, the government resettlement officer identified on inkundla.net referred the researcher to official government policy regarding the Model A resettlement schemes (sub-division and resettlement of formerly white-owned large scale commercial farms), which was where much of the focus of the current redistribution lay. The criteria targeted 'indigenous persons [black Zimbabweans] with agricultural production potential' and did not discriminate among black Zimbabweans, he said. Only beneficiaries resident in Zimbabwe could benefit from the scheme and so there could be no 'collusion' with externally-based agencies, including Zimbabweans in the diaspora, to influence land redistribution trends.[11]

Nevertheless, the revelation by 'Lobengula' in message 11699 of direct contact between inkundla.net members and the Bulawayo Housing Department, and the apparent empathy in those quarters seems significant, for it is not difficult to see how this might have taken place (see, for example, Lobengula's reference to meeting a 'leading member[...] of our forum' in Bulawayo itself). Nor should Lobengula's other entry (message #7591), suggesting a new agricultural officer's appointment in Matabeleland as an opportunity for Ndebele abroad, be discounted as insignificant. The possibility that an element of collusion between council personnel and the Ndebele diaspora to ensure more housing is accessed by Ndebele-speakers had been sparked by the sentiments expressed online remains. As the title of the discussion thread cited ('Regaining Lost Ground') suggests, this was perceived as the epoch-making reversal of historical wrongs, in which the internet was seen (and may have been used) as an indispensable tool.[12]

'Count on us': Goffal.com

This website grew out of Zimbabwean exile Andrew Longworth's 1999 online guestbook, hosted on a Bravenet server. It was at first a 'forum for visitors, mostly friends but also other Zimbabweans, to leave their comments, ideas, or just praise of some of the issues I was raising for discussion', Longworth has said.[13] Born in Arcadia, Harare, of mixed black and white parentage, he described himself as an 'average IT enthusiast' who was hoping the guest book would keep him in contact with family and friends. Longworth's webpage was soon inundated with messages from 'coloured' Zimbabweans seeking to make contact with others, as Longworth himself explained:

> It [the website] became a means of communication, a venue for discussions, and a source of information at the same time. I used to get messages asking for news from home, like I was a news agency with a staffer in Harare. Eventually I had to arrange for updated news feeds to my home page to satisfy the demand for news. This stimulated more interest and even more discussion, and the number of visitors to the guestbook grew.[14]

Around the turn of the millennium, as the trickle of messages increased in volume and the posts became more varied, Longworth began to detect growing evidence that mixed-race Zimbabweans were discovering the internet as a resource for mobilising among themselves in Britain – to stave off homesickness, to win solidarity and advice from others on issues like immigration, job-hunting and social concerns, or to express anguish at the slide of the political and socio-economic situation in Zimbabwe. In December 2001, goffal.com was registered through Bravenet, the webpage builder and website host. Two years later, protracted online discussions gave birth to the website's 'Count on Us' project, a UK-registered charity seeking to raise resources in Britain to support areas of need in 'coloured' communities in Zimbabwe.

> 'Count on Us' was born on goffal.com. A few of us mooted the idea of organising ourselves to support causes at home, if not from our own pockets, then through fundraising and specific public events that would attract website users to a day of live entertainment, sport, the opportunity to meet with other 'coloureds' in the UK and re-establish that kindred spirit, and the chance to socialise as individuals who may or may not be familiar with each other, but certainly share a common use of the www.goffal.com website. All the proceeds from these 'fun days' would go towards identified projects in Zimbabwe. The first such event – in Lower Sydenham in 2002 – was such a huge success, both in terms of the proceeds and the ability to bring Zimbabwean 'coloured' people together in the UK, that it rapidly became a twice-yearly event.[15]

'Count on Us' was registered as a charity in June 2003 and now has an organisational structure and website of its own (http://www.cou.org.uk). Longworth is not among the trustees and has taken a back seat. Nevertheless a strong link between the charity and goffal.com continues and the charity continues to advertise events and report back on its achievements through goffal.com as well as on its own website.

While discussions on inkundla.net anchored its notion of users' identity in 'traditionally' understood ethnicity, goffal.com links it to the Southern African notion of an 'in-between' ('coloured') race. The users of both websites rely on these Zimbabwe-originated identity categories to help launch specifically-targeted social interventions inside Zimbabwe itself. In July 2002, a goffal.com user going by the name 'Another Goffal' emphasised the notion of racially-defined communities in floating the idea of a diaspora-led charity initiative targeting mixed-race Zimbabwe residents: [16]

Goffals,

2 QUESTIONS

Why is it that other communities (races) much larger than ours can love and support one another and yet ours so small, lives so divided by hate and gossip?

Why cant we love one another, give each other good advice, give support to those who need it, uplight each others spirits by positive messages? Yes our country has fallen apart but should our community do the same.

Why goffals, why? Other people are organising themselves, arranging support structures for people arriving in UK. The blacks take care of the blacks, the whites take care of the whites. But goffals pretend they don't know you, even if they see you sleeping on the street. Right now black Zimbabweans are sending money back home to support their relatives and their s.chools. How many of us are doing something for our communities back home?

All we can do is come on this website and talk kak [nonsense] about each other. Why?

A few days later, the board administrator (Longworth himself) supported the idea and reinforced the notion of identity it entailed by describing it as a 'goffal initiative', and referring to 'raising funds as goffals':[17]

I am glad to see that people are discussing something more constructive. The trading of insults that had become routine on this message board was an embarrassment. This is what we should be talking about: Helping ourselves, and helping others. A number of us have been talking about setting up a charity to help both the people at home, and those who live here in the UK but who may not have status or who may be in distress. We can raise funds as goffals.

Look how many successful fun days we've had? If we can run those every so often for deserving causes – take away a few hundred pounds for administration and rentals – we could make a good start. We would be supporting our own, instead of the local pub, and all for a deserving cause.

As I say, let's think about this. Let's make it a goffal initiative, not one in which a few do all the work. We can all be involved. I look forward to more constructive comments.

After some practical deliberations, however, and in contrast to the fixity of the 'Mthwakazian' identity in debates on inkundla.net, several web-board contributors initiated an interrogation of the very category of 'goffal' in the context of Britain. A contributor using the name 'Fire Lion' wondered whether Zimbabwean assistance should be extended to members of the other Zimbabwean racial groups, while 'Low Down' pointed at the racist connotations attached to the very term 'goffal' in contexts where it has not been reclaimed by mixed-race speakers themselves:

(Fire Lion) I'm a bit concerned at the racist nature of this website. First you have all the hate messages against blacks on the messageboard. Now there's talk of setting up a charity to help Coloured people. So, if I may ask, what will you do if approached by a poor widow whose children need school fees, and who happen to be black? Or a white family in desparate circumstances, like been thrown out on the street for debts, etc. How will your charity respond to that? [18]

(Low Down) I wish to agree with Fire lion this website is very biased as calling it 'goffal.com' is not very nice we live in an age of equal rights so please consider those who's [sic] feelings are being hurt[19]

In answer, 'G-Dep' evokes a mix of racially-defined media outlets in Britain, America and Zimbabwe, seemingly unaware that understandings of 'blackness' and 'whiteness' they imply do not overlap neatly. This inconsistency is, however, pointed out in the reply posted by a speaker called 'Maputi':

(G-Dep) Fire Lion and Low Down, you need to Lay Low. How can you say goffal.com is racist? Could you please give clear, precise and detailed evidence as to why you think it is racist.

In the UK, they have B.E.N television (black entertainment network,) B.E.T (black entertainment television), the Voice and New Nation papers who both use the headline 'Britain's best black newspaper'.

In America, you have Jet magazine, Mahogany and Ebony magazines, all black only magazines. We have goffal.com where we can come and chill out with goffals from our communities. If you don't like what you see here, Chirundu.

com and bottomhalf.com await you. Bear in mind that both sites are for white Zimbabweans. If you still feel lost there, you can go to zvakapressa.com or inkundla.net where they cater for black Zimbabweans.

Don't come here and try to stir up shit [cause trouble]. Hater. [20]

In response, 'Maputi' points out that the dominant understanding of 'blackness' in Britain relegates Zimbabwean 'goffals' to the very racial category ('black') that they (following the colonial-era Southern African racial hierarchy) seek to distance themselves from. (The phrasing of this message, with its reference to 'persons' rather than 'men' highlights the contrast between the implied gender inclusivity of goffal.com, and the patriarchal implications of masculine pronoun usage on inkundla.net.)

> (Maputi) Its strange how us goffals are quick to accuse someone of being racial towards us but we are even quicker to insult a black person.
>
> Those that live in london [sic] and the uk [sic], I know about 75% of us have said these vit mensa [white people] are racial. I heard a few guys taking this weekend and they comments were along the lines of ' These vit mensa are racial bus#'#ds they think we are chorkies [blacks]'
>
> Now how the hell do you say you have experienced racial abouse coz they called you a chorkie????? by using that word, you are being racial aswell [sic].
>
> Please correct me if im [sic] wrong but that is really stupid.
>
> Im a pure goffal and YES I have used those words but I have stopped and I think its about time us as goffals stop being so silly
>
> PLEASE[21]

Although 'Maputi' does not say so directly, the parallel drawn by this message – between racist Southern African whites, designated by a slang phrase derived from Afrikaans, and anti-black prejudice of Zimbabwean 'goffals' themselves – implies the possibility of Zimbabwean 'coloured' identities being reimagined or 'translated' in the diaspora (as, say, 'black British' or merely 'Zimbabwean'). But 'Maputi's' own reference to being 'pure goffal' forecloses this possibility, and the online debate that followed his intervention did not take up or extend this line of thinking. A few days later, Longworth was putting into place concrete arrangements that were to culminate in the formation of 'Count on Us'. In contrast to the uncertain outcome of the inkundla.net housing initiative, the 'coloured' Britain-based diaspora's material initiative has had long-lasting and tangible results:

> Further to my email last week, a committee of volunteers has been set up to launch the fund, open a bank account and co-ordinate fundraising activities.

We appointed a co-ordinator to look into the logistics and report back to the community, through this website, since this is where the idea was conceived. Watch this space for more details.[22]

The Internet and Diaspora Public Action

As examples of debates conducted on the two internet websites show, both 'inkundla' and 'goffal' online networks have worked on implementing their social initiatives around understandings of ethnic and racial affinities dominant in Zimbabwe itself. The key difference between the two online communities (the contrast between a deterritorialised Ndebele nationalist community that reveals itself as obsessed with land, and the 'in-between' coloured community that remains unable to do so) serves to highlight the fact that in the diaspora, both communities articulate an inward-looking focus as imperative. This seems especially important as both the 'goffal' and 'inkundla' constituencies consider themselves marginalised inside Zimbabwe (National Association for the Advancement of Coloureds [NAAC] 2003). For goffal.com users, the downside of such understandings of identity (as articulated by 'Fire Lion' in the webboard contribution cited above) is that the racial exclusivity implied in the term 'goffal' has both affirmative and malevolent aspects: the 'goffals' have, as 'Fire Lion' warns, adopted a discriminatory approach to social action. Likewise, the 'Mthwakazi'-centred rhetoric of inkundla.net has the potential to create forms of marginalisation for ethnic and linguistic minorities in the Ndebele-speaking heartland, replicating the ills suffered by the Ndebele themselves in Zimbabwe as a whole.

However much this might be blamed on the divisive policies of pre-Independence Rhodesia the examples of the two websites discussed in this chapter indicate that many Zimbabweans in the British diaspora remain committed to preserving Zimbabwe-established understandings of regional, ethnic and racial differences and disparaging the backgrounds some of their compatriots in the diaspora. Nevertheless, I would argue that the plural articulation of Zimbabwean cultural and ideological practices provided by the juxtaposition of the two websites discussed in the chapter (and others) is a measure of the democratic potential of the internet as a transnational mode of communication. As engines of public action, the diaspora websites may be related to Giddens' idea of 'social movements' that attempt collectively to 'further a common interest or secure a common goal through action outside the sphere of established institutions' (2001: 439).

Web theorists Burnett and Marshall point out that web-centred sources of information such as the web-boards on inkundla.net and goffal.com shift the production of information away from the more constructed quality of the web site into the interpersonal correspondence register of gossip and expressions of emotional investment' (2003: 34). In the case of Zimbabwe-related discourses, this means that the post-1980 Zimbabwean National Unity Project, and more recently the extreme form of nationalism known as Mugabeism (Raftopolous 2004; Ranger 2005, 2002) may be subjected to the kind of examination unparalleled by other media, whether inside or outside Zimbabwe. The consultative processes constantly underway in the 'inkundla' and 'goffal' virtual communities may, in fact, be regarded as contemporary rearticulations of the oral Zimbabwean public spheres of pre-colonial origin (called 'inkundla' in Ndebele and 'padare' in Shona), where issues are engaged and resolved communally and dialogically. By whatever name it is called, in whichever language, the public discourse generated by these 'traditional' public spheres is representative of all the participants and takes into account the views of all who have contributed, even those whose views do not carry. The translocation and translation of the inkundla/padare ethos from the deliberative forum of village elders into a trans-national, virtual medium of the internet points at the possibility of giving media representation to all Zimbabwean constituencies. This resonates with Habermas' expectations that '[a] legitimate decision does not represent the will of all, but is one that results from the deliberation of all. It is the process by which everyone's will is formed that confers it legitimacy on the outcome, rather than the sum of already formed wills' (1989: 446).

In online debates such as the ones excerpted in this chapter, meaning is constantly evaluated and re-interpreted, with peer review and interrogation subjecting online data to constant scrutiny. When they engage in online debates, Zimbabweans in the diaspora trade 'validity claims' (Habermas 1989: 2) in a public sphere that constantly exposes the contestability of all world views. One can only hope that its dynamism and elasticity will one day be echoed in a new, pluralist Zimbabwe of the future.

Notes

1. In November 2008 the webmaster of Goffal.com decided to change its name to Mr Zims.net – an acronym of sorts for 'Mixed Race Zimbabweans Network'. The website can still be accessed using the www.goffal.com url. As the name change came at the end of my research, and certainly long after the extraction of data from its message boards, the chapter will continue referring to 'goffal.com' for the sake of clarity and continuity.

2. The constituencies of inkundla.net and goffal.com were accessed in person at two public events, advertised on the websites in advance: an anti-Mugabe demonstration at Westminster seeking to attract the attention of South Africa's

Minister of Foreign Affairs, Nkosazana Dlamini-Zuma on 25 October 2003 and a fund-raising 'fun day' at Footsie Sports Club in Lower Syndenham on 10 July 2004. On these two occasions, 120 Ndebele speakers and 165 mixed-race Zimbabweans answered a questionnaire that explored use of the web and identity issues.

3. Pers. comm., Britain Zimbabwe Society Research Day, June 2003.
4. 'Mthwakazi' (the land of the 'baThwa' or 'bushmen') was the first name given to territories in what is now Zimbabwe by their Ndebele conqueror, king Mzilikazi Khumalo. Today, it is sometimes used to refer to Zimbabwe's Ndebele-speaking communities.
5. 'Row Over Land Takeovers in Matabeleland', 'News Hour', 7–8pm. Print version retrieved 30 September 2004 from http://www.swradioafrica.com.
6. Thread 'Regaining Lost Ground', initiated by Inkosi uMzilikazi ka Mashobane. Note no. 34019 – 06/13/07 04:52 pm. Retrieved 12 December 2007 from inkundla.net.
7. The demographic fears of 'King Mzilikazi' are is not merely the product of overheated imaginations on the tribalist fringe: in 2005, a report from the Central Statistical Office in Harare projected decrease in Matabeleland's population as a result, in part, of high emigration levels to South Africa. Projections in a 2005 bulletin suggested that, based on abnormally high migration levels from especially rural Matabeleland to South Africa, the Ndebele population resident in Zimbabwe could fall to between eight and ten per cent, from about fourteen to sixteen per cent of the population recorded during the previous national census in 2002. Telephone interview, CSO official 2 June 2005.
8. Thread 'Mthwakazeans in Diaspora Urged to Supply Council with Equipment', initiated by 'Lobengula' 30 September 2004. Note no 11699 – 05/21/06 08:46 pm. Retrieved 30 September from inkundla.net.
9. Thread 'Mthwakazians in Diaspora', started by 'Lobengula', 30 September 2004.
10. Telephone interview, Bulawayo Housing Department, 22 September 2007.
11. Telephone interview, regional office, Ministry of Lands, Resettlement and Rural Development, 22 September 2007.
12. http://www.inkundla.net/ubbthreads7olde/ubbthreads.php/ubb/showflat/Number/34019
13. Andrew Longworth, interview, 10 May 2003.
14. Longworth, interview, 10 May 2003.
15. Longworth, interview, 10 May 2003.
16. Another Goffal, Note No: 3032 from 2002–07–23 12:56:00. Retrieved 20 September 2002 from goffal.com.
17. Admin, Note No. 3062 from 2002 – 07–30 06:56:49. Retrieved 20 September 2002 from goffal.com.
18. Fire Lion, Note No. 3076 from 2002–07–31 08:05:56. Retrieved 20 September 2002 from goffal.com.
19. Low Down, Note No. 3091 from 2002–08–04 12:40:17. Retrieved 20 September 2002 from goffal.com.
20. G-Dep, Note No. 3105 from 2002–08–04 17:59:28. Retrieved 20 September 2002 from goffal.com.

21. Maputi, Note No 3112 from 2002–08–04 18:56:11. Retrieved 20 September 2002 from goffal.com.
22. Admin, Note No. 3153 from 2002–08–09 17:09:46. Retrieved 20 September 2002 from goffal.com.

References

Bloch, A. 2005. *The Development Potential of Zimbabweans in the Diaspora*. London: IOM.

Boyd-Barrett, O. and C. Newbold. 1995. *Approaches to Media – A Reader*. Oxford: Oxford University Press.

Burnett, R. and P. D. Marshall. 2003. *Web Theory: An Introduction*. London: Routledge.

Carey, J. W. 1989. *Communication as Culture: Essays on Media and Society*. London: Routledge.

Ebo, B. 1998. *Cyberghetto or Cybertopia? Race, Class and Gender on the Internet*. Westport: Praeger.

Giddens, A. 2001. Sociology. Cambridge: Polity.

Habermas, J. 1989. *The Structural Transformation of the Public Sphere* trans. Thomas Burger Cambridge, Mass.: MIT Press (first ed. 1962).

——. 1992. Moral Consciousness and Communicative Action trans. Christian Lenhardt and Shierry Weber-Nicholson. Cambridge, Mass: MIT Press.

Mano W. and W. Willems. 2008. 'Emerging Communities, Emerging Media: The Case of a Zimbabwean Nurse in the British Big Brother Show', *Critical Arts* 22, 1: 101–128.

McQuail, D. 1992. *Media Performance: Mass Communications and the Public Interest*, Chicago: University of Illinois Press.

Masiane, R. 2003. 'Media and the Zimbabwean Diaspora', Paper presented at the Britain- Zimbabwe Society Research Day, Oxford, 14 June 2003.

Nyamnjoh, F.B. 2006. *Insiders and Outsiders: Citizenship and Xenophobia in Contemporary Southern Africa*. London: Zed Books.

Pasura, D. 2006a. *Mapping Exercise Zimbabwe*. London: IOM

——. 2006b. 'Towards a Multi-Sited Ethnography of Diaspora Communities in Britain', Paper presented at the Britain Zimbabwe Society Research Day, Oxford, 17 June.

Peel, A.C. 2003. 'The Internet and the Zimbabwean Diaspora', Paper presented at the Britain-Zimbabwe Research Day, Oxford, 14 June 2003.

Raftopolous, B. 2004. Plenary Address to the BZS Research Day, Oxford, 12–13 June 2004

Raftopolous, B. and T. Savage, eds. 2004. *Zimbabwe: Injustice and Political Reconciliation*, Cape Town: Institute for Justice and Reconciliation.

Ranger, T.O. 2002. *The Historical Dimensions of Democracy and Human Rights in Zimbabwe Vol. 2*. Harare: University of Zimbabwe Press.

——. 2004. 'The Uses and Abuses of History in Zimbabwe'. In *Skinning the Skunk – Facing Zimbabwean Futures*. M. Palmberg and R. Primorac (eds.) Uppsala: Nordiska Africa Institute, pp. 7–15.

Rodriguez, C. 2004. 'The Renaissance of Citizens' Media' in *Citizenship, Identity, Media: Media Development* 2.

Zaffiro, J. 2002. *Media and Democracy in Zimbabwe, 1931–2002* Colorado Springs: International Academic Publishers.

Web-based Threads

Mthwakazeans in Diaspora urged to supply council with equipment'. Thread started by Lobengula', 30 September 2004. Retrieved 30 September 2004 from: http://www.inkundla.net/ubbthreads7olde/ubbthreads.php/ubb/showflat/Number/7484/fpart/5

Regaining Lost Ground'. Thread started by 'Inkosi uMzilikazi', 13 June 2007. Retrieved 15 December 2007 from http://www.inkundla.net/ubbthreads7olde/ubbthreads.php/ubb/showflat/Number/34019#Post34019.

Untitled thread started by 'Another Goffal', 23 July 2002. Note No. 3032. Retrieved 20 December 2002 from www.goffal.com. (NB. The web link to this thread is no longer available)

11

One Dandelion Seed-head

Brian Chikwava, introduced by Ranka Pimorac

Introduction

The very existence of today's Zimbabwean literary canon in English is predicated on displacement. In late 1960s and 1970s, following the Unilateral Declaration of Independence and as the guerrilla war in Rhodesia intensified, a group of black male authors (the best-known are Stanlake Samkange, Charles Mungoshi, Dambudzo Marechera and Stanley Nyamfukudza) published eleven novels in English outside the country. (They could not do so at home because their texts were critical of settler colonialism and would not have passed muster with the Rhodesian censors.) After 1980, most of these texts were republished at home, those authors who had been in exile returned too (Wilson Katiyo and Dambudzo Marechera), and many of their texts entered the syllabi of Zimbabwean schools and universities. It was as if these authors' pre-independence faith that their texts *will* one day find wide Zimbabwean readerships was instrumental in bringing those readerships about (Primorac 2006).

As the wide availability of public education and the scope of the publishing industry expanded after independence, locally-published written literature (in the three main Zimbabwean languages) participated in the vibrant and plural Zimbabwean public sphere (Kaarsholm 2005). In the late 1980s and 1990s, the male-dominated canon was diversified and enriched with the return home of the novelists Tsitsi Dangarembga and Yvonne Vera, whose personal displacement and overseas climb to literary prominence was both reminiscent of and counter-posed to their male counterparts' trajectories. In the 2000s, following the onset of 'the crisis' and as freedom of expression inside Zimbabwe became increasingly curtailed, several aspiring writers joined the swelling wave of Zimbabwean migrants, and found themselves thinking and writing about their home country from a position outside its borders. During the 2005 Britain Zimbabwe Society (BZS) Research Day in Oxford (entitled 'Zimbabwe, Africa and the World'), a literary round table (comprised of diaspora-based Zimbabwean researchers Maurice Vambe and Drew Shaw, and myself) discussed the possibility that the next phase of Zimbabwe-related literary creativity in English would be led by writers in exile.

Already, back then, it seemed clear that Caine Prize winner Brian Chikwava would be something of a generational leader – although others (for example his Switzerland-based colleague Petina Gappah, who participated in the BZS Research Day in 2007 and whose collection of short stories, *An Elegy for Eastery*, was published in 2009) were not far behind. These young authors model themselves in part on their internationally-acclaimed Zimbabwean predecessors: there are echoes of Marechera's playfulness in Chikwava's work and of Dangarembga's gift for social analysis in Gappah's, and both eschew the somewhat stilted idealism that marked the UK-set fiction of someone like Wilson Katiyo (1979). But there are also significant divergences. Chikwava's first novel, *Harare North* (2009), forges a new, strikingly powerful linguistic mode of expression which melds together elements taken from Zimbabwean, British and Caribbean English, as well as Shona and Ndebele. In Chikwava's stories in particular, post-modernist layered ironies steer clear of the depths and rawness of Marechera-style angst (Viet-Wild and Chennells 1999), and are, instead, often accompanied by gentle humour and warmth. In the interview that follows his short story 'One Dandelion Seed-head' (published here for the first time), Chikwava appears both inspired and bemused by the idea of Marechera as a cultural predecessor, and this seems in keeping with his fluid sense of self which combines a national rootedness with an easy-going cosmopolitanism (similar to that discussed by Appiah in 1998) and a refusal of identity labels. Like many transnational intellectuals of his generation, Chikwava is both sensitive to social injustice and well aware how difficult it is to publicly denounce what JoAnn McGregor (in the introduction to this volume) calls 'the cultural politics of vulnerability', without simultaneously participating in it in some way (in the case of writers and intellectuals, by converting it into textual commodities).

Brian Chikwava was born in 1971 in Zimbabwe and has lived in London since 2002. In 2004, he was awarded the Caine Prize for African Writing for his short story 'Seventh Street Alchemy'; in 2009, his first novel *Harare North* was published to critical acclaim. Brian was Charles Pick Fellow at the

University of East Anglia in 2005; he is also a musician and a journalist, and has worked as a consultant in construction engineering. Brian Chikwava and Ranka Primorac (both self-exiled from their countries of birth) talked about writing, notions of 'home' and life in the diaspora in London on 27 August 2007, 29 November 2008 and 8 July 2009.

References

Appiah, K.A. 1998. 'Cosmopolitan Patriots', in P. Cheah and B. Robbins (eds), *Cosmopolitics: Thinking and Feeling Beyond the Nation.* Minneapolis: University of Minnesota Press, pp. 91–114.

Chikwava, B. 2004. 'Seventh Street Alchemy', in I. Staunton (ed.), *Writing Still: New Stories from Zimbabwe.* Harare: Weaver Press, pp. 17–30.

———. 2009. *Harare North.* London: Jonathan Cape.

Gappah, P. 2009. *An Elegy for Easterly.* London: Faber and Faber.

Kaarsholm. P. 2005. 'Coming to Terms with Violence: Literature and the Development of a Public Sphere in Zimbabwe', in R. Muponde and R. Primorac (eds), *Versions of Zimbabwe: New Approaches to Literature and Culture.* Harare: Weaver Press, pp. 3–23.

Katiyo, W. 1979. *Going to Heaven.* Harlow: Longman.

Marechera, D. 1978. *House of Hunger: Short Stories.* London: Heinemann.

Primorac, R. 2006. *A Place of Tears: The Novel and Politics in Modern Zimbabwe.* London: I.B. Tauris.

Viet-Wild, F. and A. Chennells (eds). 1999. *Emerging Perspectives on Dambudzo Marechera.* Trenton, NJ: Africa World Press.

One Dandelion Seed-head
Brian Chikwava

Dad,

I'm putting this down by dictaphone, that old thing that belonged to grandpa. That was long back, when everything was alright; when mum was still around and you were still at the embassy. You will struggle to find a way of listening to this tape, I know; the machines to play this kind of tape on aren't used much any more, which is maybe why I'm sending it to you. But then I see you have succeeded, seeing as you are listening to me right now, dad. Or is this a nosey stranger who has stumbled upon the tape?

London is hot, the streets full of knives and the park near here is crawling with squirrels. The grey ones. The foreign ones like you. I was born here so I'm no foreigner, ha!

Until about a couple of hours ago I had a boyfriend, Ali, who didn't mind my stammer. He has mosquito-leg like hairs sticking out of his nose. Just like you. But my demons came again. I kicked him out. He made fun of Jay. Jay is dead, dad.

It's way past midnight dad – or stranger – and I will tell you about this evening if you still care. To listen.

Every city must have this kind of corner in one form or another, I mean this corner where I was living when I recorded this. When I was still around.

This evening was Jay's send-off. Ali and I joined the neighbours who congregated by the front garden wall. Wine was poured and soon everyone was sipping from paper cups.

I'll take you through the evening because tonight might be the night. Is that squeaky old armchair still there? You will need to be seated, dad.

Our garden wall was Jay's favourite spot. That's where you normally saw him trying to engage anyone who happened to be passing by. I didn't mind him hanging outside my lounge window like that. He was 19, black and homeless but he was alright.

Ali, he's from somewhere in Africa and also seemed to get on well with Jay. Or maybe not, I don't know.

A small heap of flowers and cards had accumulated on the pavement by the wall.

Close your eyes and listen dad.

That heap of flowers – see it? – flapping about. Forlornly.

Margaret picked one of the cards and read it aloud.

'Dear Jay, I love you. I miss you. Sarah.'

Sarah is maybe 8 and lives three doors from me. I kind of liked her card: an old Christmas card recycled into... well it had big-eyed crayon stick-figures and a big green heart, all but buried under a splurge of glitter. That's what I want.

And then the conversation.

'Was he really 19?'

'No, 18.'

'Not 20?'

You see, once you are dead it doesn't take long before your age is undergoing revision, I already knew before recording this. That's what happened to Jay's age this evening.

It was also a somewhat wooden conversation, but that's how neighbourly strangers talk while clearing space to cart in heaps of opinion. Care is needed. Especially if last year someone got hurt at another's BBQ. That's probably why Jo was not there to begin with. Last summer Ed had the whole block fluttering in gales of rumour and scandal when he implied that Jo was more upset by Jay going missing than by her husband's death – words fly-tipped onto the street after Jo had kept Jay in her house all day and before he, in his homeless ways, disappeared without trace. Ed can still walk with his head held up high, having at least admitted to putting his foot wrong. He tried to apologise but Jo wasn't having any of it. She has not wanted to talk to him ever since. A simple slap on the back is all what was needed to put all this right but this is Jo we are talking about. What does she do instead? Spends the whole week sulking, at the end of which, attempting to loosen up, she goes to the Prince Albert, and ends up hauling back home this man-thing that's rough as a badger's arse, runs it ragged all night and at five in the morning it's seen staggering away in the direction of the council estate. Next thing her house has been burgled and all attention is on her for another week.

Croydon behaviour and all that - you can almost hear the words from the sneering twist on Geoff's nose whenever he talks about Jo. He lives next door.

Keep your eyes shut. You are doing well dad.

Sue found Jay comatose in her lounge, two apologetic deposits of poop on the carpet. She lives in the basement flat below me.

I have seen Jay charm one neighbour after another right by the garden wall. Pensioners, Guardian-reading mothers and their kids during the day, and the distressed suited-and-booted returning in the evening. But these are also people that can be busy with their lives. Too busy to even know what to do when Jay turned up at their doorsteps, except parcel out some of their guilt with a token food handout. I've seen it with my own eyes. Even that time when Jay was in a bad state - one eye weeping a flood, full of gunk and in clear need of medical attention, all they could do was to give him food. But then again who can blame them really? It's the ways of the city, as Ali likes to say. Liked to say.

The conversation this evening, again:

'He is going to be terribly missed,' Sophie trills. Unconvincingly. Looking at another card. From Ali's face I know what he was thinking. Ali is still new and yet to have any meaningful observations of his own about people here. That's why he sometimes still takes people at face value.

Sophie says that last summer Jay came to their house while she was in the garden, demanded nothing except to sit in the sun at the corner of the garden, quietly watching her weed. A robin landed on his shoulder and he could not have been more indifferent.

'Yes, he is going to be missed.'

'Oh he knew everyone.'

'Oh, everyone knew him.'

'Everyone!'

'Him?'

And so on and so on until someone yanks the conversation in the direction of their pet subject: '...and little Emily made a good Grandma Koala's clock at school this year.'

Again?

Yes, that's right dad, again!

How, even after alcohol has sunk in, this kind of conversation manages to snake its way back to the original subject, I don't know.

Margaret, she began to tell the story all over again, this time adding the little detail that she had left out earlier: how Jay was found sprawled across Sue's couch and so on. It was the first time Jay had ever gone into Sue's flat, apparently.

Margaret is head-honcho at some real estate company and is supposed to be a tough cookie, hard-nosed and all. She lives with her sister Elina in the flat above us and wept openly when Jay was found in Sue's flat. She, Elina and Catherine, from across the road, ran around doing all the emergency stuff - making phone calls and transporting Jay.

Elina reckons Jay got enough affection without it tipping into the ridiculous. She can be bolshy at times and teaches at St. Antony's College in Oxford. She's good for those times when Some Jehovah's Witness is wearing out the door-bell button: just ignore them until they start getting medieval on every button they can lay their finger on and Elina has to get off her desk and come down to the front door. Ha!

Jay. He was just like those who die homeless. It's only when they are gone that the scale of their friendships in the neighbourhood becomes apparent. Ron joined us later in the evening. Apparently conversation at the Prince Albert was all about Jay and that's not the first time this has happened. Jay was also favourite topic last year when he briefly disappeared and started all those small dramas in Jo's life.

'What a shame.' That's what Ron said about Jay, hoping that he had managed to pull off an air of genuine sympathy. He's now eligible for a bus-pass, Ron, and is badly hen-pecked; all manner of shenanigans have been going down at his house since he left the keys in the ignition of his wife's old car while washing it and was astonished to find it gone half an hour later. Most unexpectedly, he has taken to unburdening himself on me whenever we bump into each other. Not real conversation there but those self-talk therapy monologues that work better if you can find a figurehead to throw words at. It's the curse of this stammer dad; it's a sin and attracts this kind of casual but full-on abuse. Qualifies one for a fit-for-all-purposes self-talk aid object: incapable of speech and unable to comprehend (at least that's the thinking as far as I can tell). You want to say 'bus stop' but 'bus station' somehow drops off your lips, you want to say 'laptop' but only gasp '..ptop'. That kind of thing; that's the thing that leads people in positions of authority here to suspect that behind an untidy tongue lies an untidy tangle of thoughts; the thing that frightens these people into thinking that, somewhere along the way you will get things all tangled up if we give you responsibilities that require clear thinking. Soon you learn to be silent and invisible: a sinner.

Anyway - Ron, I don't mind. I'm kind of getting used to him now. Never mind that in the beginning, with every one of our chance encounters, I would stagger away with a peculiar feeling that I had just polished off the entire cheeseboard at the local deli and gone to sleep. Pinch pinch, ouch!

But he's ok, Ron.

'Ow, my missus,' that's how he always starts. He has the rare gift of being able to be bang out of order, making the most shockingly un-PC remarks without losing the old pitiable face. It's always meant with plenty of goodwill.

You have not dozed off, I hope? Are you still with me; can you still see us? Dad?

Picture this: now, while talking about Jay, Ron has just dropped another clanger and everyone is pretending they did not hear him. Elina has turned away to start a new conversation with Catherine to her right. Ed - he is normally the yellful, portly type of bloke who can play swamp football and talk the hind leg off a donkey all at the same time. Here he is, frozen in a gasp of horror, staring motionlessly into the middle distance. Margaret is whirling her wine around inside the paper cup and, for this elastic moment, trying to see how close to the rim she can take it without spilling any. Ron is not sure what kind of face to put on now but flashes of a little boy genuinely puzzled are noticeable.

On the opposite pavement Jo floats by in a bright-yellow ra ra dress. Doesn't acknowledge any of us.

'She won't be in a rush to join us,' says Ed resurrecting and limbering up to the garden wall to tie a shoe lace, if I remember correctly.'

'Here,' someone, whose name I've already forgotten, hands me Margaret's Blackberry which has been going round. I flip through the pictures of Jay, grin and pass the phone on.

And there in that corner there, Margaret is now talking about her family. How she got washed up on the shores of that topic I have no idea. But it turns out she and Elina are Norwegian by descent. Their family settled here when they were toddlers. Norwegian; don't know how I missed that. As often happens, the conversation sucks in more people and a familiar past-time gathers momentum. Whereas migrants usually put tons of effort into repressing cultural baggage so they can blend into the local order of things, here, with nothing at stake, it's the other way round - reclaiming a lost exoticism, in whatever shape or form. Ed – he's Turkish? Amhed, that's his full name. I missed that one too. Catherine – she's half French but doesn't say what the other half is. And old Ron – he is still too startled to be able to claim or disown anything. Sophie? Irish. By that logic I'm Zimbabwean then, ha! Somehow feels desperate, that.

'Hi.' That's Geoff's voice dad. He's just joined us. Now there's a real possibility that the conversation will lurch towards Croydon or the Ivy Restaurant - how last night Geoff was again rubbing shoulders with this or that celebrity. It's always those two with him. Except for Elina, Geoff doesn't think much of everyone here and has made it clear in the past but he doesn't even have a clue how clear he made it. He's an ex-student of Elina's. She found out he had moved into the flat next door one weekend when they bumped into each other while throwing rubbish away. He's since been fawning over her. But she is not thrilled to have an ex-student living next door. Now - are you still awake? - Elina has just blanked him completely, which is alright by me. Never thought much of his face; he's not yet worth getting excited about seeing in the crosshairs of this previously deactivated weapon in front of me right now. My sin count says he's not much of a sinner as far as I can see, Unlike me – syntax-wrecking deviant, thief, bi-polar lover, lost child, unable to belong neither here nor there, cherry flavoured happy-pill eater, fucked up as they say … and so on and so on; ticking all boxes that mark out me as a sinner, among these people or the ones that you call your people, dad.

And Jo. Now, as I recall, she is on her way back from the shops, carrying a full Sainsbury bag. This time she has Ron's missus in tow and both are rabbiting on in the middle of the road and edging towards us. Ed is decidedly sheepish, his eyes are all over the pavement.

In this evening's brass-sunlight, in this corner of the city dad, Jay's food bowl struck a desolate note on the garden wall. On our window ledge – another of Jay's favourite spots, and onto where bits of his fur can still be found – yet another black cat from across the road eerily rolled himself, and having claimed territory gave me a sharp quizzical look. A white patch of fur on his chest, just like Jay, except smaller.

Well, this is it dad. This end of this recording nicely takes me up to the ultimate sin. When you finally decide to leave this country and stagger back to where you call home to rest your bones, tell the cousins that I did say goodbye: a wind of a kind blew and dispersed one dandelion seed-head way up into the blue sky.

With love,

Sam

12

'Making New Connections': Interview with Brian Chikwava

Ranka Primorac

RP: When we last spoke, you said that Zimbabwe feels less and less like home as time goes by. Can you say more about that?

BC: Bulawayo, where I grew up and where my family still lives, now feels like a dying city ... There was a time, in the 1970s and early 1980s, when Bulawayo had this kind of self-confidence, which you could almost feel. It probably came out of ... I don't know, my father and his brothers are from Mashonaland, but they all ended up in Bulawayo. Bulawayo was attracting people in a strange way, probably because of its proximity to South Africa. When there was a new tune or something coming from South Africa, you'd hear it in Bulawayo before you'd hear it anywhere else. So it was like a kind of a 'happening' place. And then gradually, by the mid-1990s, young people didn't want to stay in Bulawayo any more. It's almost like they wanted to escape; most of Bulawayo's youth is now probably in South Africa. Harare, where I lived after finishing university, has also changed because there has also been a huge outflow of people. I have been going back to Zimbabwe for visits fairly frequently and it just feels so different ... It's another place now, in a lot of ways. You know how it is when you're living in a place – you basically know how to find your way; you have friends, connections, a whole life-support system of networks and acquaintances and people who can help you to get things done. And when all those people disappear and you come to that same place, you feel like you're not connected to it any more. You don't know anyone. You almost don't know how to go about your way; you feel like an outsider. You have to start making new connections, and people look at you differently: it's like 'oh, it's that guy who lives in the UK', and things become different. It's another world altogether … And then when you meet your old friends in London it's often also like something has changed. You may have been friends back home and you are still the same people but you project [yourselves] very differently and it becomes a different relationship.

RP: Do you try to find old acquaintances through the internet? Diaspora communities have been organising online …

BC: I've been to a few websites, but after the initial novelty, you stop following it.

RP: On a site called 'inkundla.net', there was this drive to try and use diaspora influence to help revitalise Bulawayo … to stop Shona speakers from invading the 'Mthwakazian' territory.[1]

BC: [Laughs] Yeah, I remember inkundla … You come across some really crusty hard-core Ndebele guys out there, who see the world as very, very narrow. That makes me feel uncomfortable. You also get the opposite of the 'Mthwakazi' guys, the hard-core Shona tribalists. It is also very discomforting.

RP: They're hanging onto the old identities … How about you, how do you see yourself, as a Zimbabwean writer, or an African writer, or? I remember you once got upset when somebody called you a Black British writer.

BC: I don't know if I could claim that identity … I don't feel I am that, or that I belong there.

RP: You mean here [in the UK]?

BC: Yeah.

RP: So Zimbabwe no longer feels so much like home anymore, but here doesn't feel so much like home yet?

BC: I don't know what it is … I do not mind using the label 'African writer', although I would not go about advertising myself as that. To say I am a Zimbabwean writer feels a lot more genuine.

RP: What is the first thing that comes to your mind when somebody says 'Bulawayo'?

BC: Blue skies![2] This is almost a cliché but a lot of the times when I think about Bulawayo I also call it *Kontuthu ziyathunga* – the place of pluming smoke – which is what everyone from Bulawayo associates with home. Or *Kontonga ziyaduma* – thundering knobkerries. This is something that you'll hear said by a Highlanders Football Club supporter – the 'traditional' Ndebele guy who you see cycling on his elaborate metal bike with two rear-view mirrors and a cow's tail at the rear mud-guard.

The macho guy who really believes in the Highlanders Football Club: what they call *i-Highlander ngenkani* [laughs].

RP: The 'Mthwakazian' guys! The decorated bike, is this a Bulawayo thing? I've never seen one in Harare.

BC: This is a pure Bulawayo thing; they don't do it in Harare. It probably started as a kind of working-class aspiration towards a car or something. A bicycle with two rear-view mirrors probably feels like … and then you put on a centre light, and then just some traditional thing – remove the rubber flap from the rear mud-guard and put a white cow's tail. It has to be white! And it will be shifting along the mud-guard as he rides [laughs].

RP: How about London, do you like living here?

BC: I've got a whole mixture of feelings about living in London. I like it because there is so much in one place you can do; you've got access to a lot of things that you would not have anywhere else. But at the same time, it's a hard place to live in, because … well, it's a big city, and you really have to work hard to be able to focus, and do what you want to do without any distractions. Also, it's a difficult environment because it doesn't have any kind of sense of [over-arching] community, and that makes it quite bleak.

RP: A little like in your short story 'One Dandelion Seed-head'?

BC: Yeah. It's almost like … I remember talking to you a while ago about this guy from Zimbabwe who had come here - this tough karate[-practicing] guy from Mbare[3] who came here, and it's almost as if he had to learn a new kind of toughness. His old kind of strength and resourcefulness did not matter anymore, and he had to learn this strange new kind of toughness, interesting in itself. It's the toughness you see sometimes in fragile-looking, delicate-looking little girls in London – and they are not really fragile at all, but there is a kind of toughness in them that they use to get through this environment [laughs]. It's a mental thing!

RP: Your novel *Harare North*[4] is about a 'green bomber'[5] who enters UK by applying for asylum. He is not a sympathetic character, but there is a kind of humour attached to his interpretation of London and his world-view. Do you think it's a story that will be controversial inside Zimbabwe?

BC: No. I can't see it offending anyone. Everybody knows that not everyone who is applying for asylum here is genuine.

RP: You sound very sure of that – yet your book contains sharp social critique.

BC: Why I say that is because – the way the [literary] establishment in Zimbabwe works is … There may be some review in *The Herald*[6] – but I can't imagine that happening because the way that the [social] critique works in my book is not very straightforward. It would be hard to call it colonialist literature or similar.

RP: But it's a very clever critique of the idea of cultural authenticity. The way you use the word 'native' for example – it's so ironic!

BC: I might be wrong, but for the regime establishment in Zimbabwe – they like things that are simplistic, and then they pull them apart.

RP: So you think they won't 'get it'?

BC: A lot of them won't get it. Some will – maybe those working at *The Herald*. But I think it's one of those books that they won't know what to say about. I might get criticised by some Pan-Africanist readers out there, but that is likely to happen over a drawn-out period of time so it probably won't have much effect. The humour of it will probably help: I suppose I was inspired by ... Do you remember when you took me to those Žižek lectures,[7] and he was talking about his student days [in Slovenia] when they were publishing this student magazine in which they were not supposed to criticise the Communist Party. So they praised the Party to such a ridiculous extent that the authorities called them in, and they were told they had to stop this thing. When they asked why they had to stop, the officials couldn't explain what they were not happy about. They could see it was a satirical kind of exaggeration but they did not want to have to explain it! There are a lot of situations like that. The best way is not to go head to head with [what you are critiquing], but make [your work] a little bit absurd, and suddenly you have a much more interesting thing – a lot more effective.

RP: Are you saying you were influenced by Slavoj Žižek in writing *Harare North*?

BC: I think that aspect of it – that approach – I did kind of go with that!

RP: The book is about the diaspora: people living in squats and difficult circumstances, under pressure from home to send money. Did you model that aspect of the book on actual encounters?

BC: Yes. In the Zimbabwean community here, that really is the story. A lot of people are repatriating money to Zimbabwe; the only source of income for many in Zimbabwe now is the hard currency from the diaspora. And you hear that kind of story in the Zimbabwean community everywhere. People get tired and angry because the demands from relatives back home can be almost endless – completely ridiculous and out of proportion sometimes.

RP: Tell me more about your main character in *Harare North*: an 'Afrocentrist' critic might condemn his lack of community spirit and the book's 'postmodernist' bleakness.

BC: But in a way he gets these characteristics from Mugabe himself! In the whole book, there is in him a certain kind of denial of the way things are, and also a determination to continue and refuse to acknowledge that maybe he was wrong in the first place because he would have to repudiate the whole past, and he is not prepared to do that.

RP: There is also a great deal of ignorance there ...

BC: ... and he is cold-hearted. There is a determination to be hard-hearted. In Zimbabwean politics at the moment, there is that refusal to acknowledge that maybe we've got it wrong, maybe things have gone too far. [The ruling elite] can't afford to do that anymore, so they will just have to plough all the way through, until things come to a standstill. Which is what has happened in Zimbabwe – almost like a dead end, a refusal to reflect genuinely about what has gone on in the past.

RP: Do you think that [literary] writing by Zimbabweans in the diaspora will be different from the work produced in the 1980s and 1990s, when authors were able to live and publish in their home country more easily?

BC: It would be good if we could hear more from the Zimbabwean writers who are still there. Their perspective is important. Outside, the world feels different ... and we are also open to a wider range of influences.

RP: Like Dambudzo Marechera two generations ago. Is he a role model?

BC: He is. His work has a nice spirit about it. On the other hand, his whole tragic life story ... it's a little too tragic!

RP: The phrase 'mental backstreets' recurs in *Harare North*. Is that taken from Marechera's work?

BC: No. I think I got that from some magazine – can't remember – probably *The Big Issue* or something – some article talking about how the back streets can be 'mental'. When saw it I was really attracted [to that phrase] – I liked that idea and then played with it. It appealed to me as a piece of ambiguity, where it can be a backstreet that's in your head, or a backstreet that is really out there, and mental – crazy – things can happen. I wanted to link the real world and what is going on in his mind.

RP: And the character of Shingi [in *Harare North*] – you were not consciously influenced by Edmund in [Marechera's] *The House of Hunger*?

BC: No, it was not a conscious influence. I hadn't thought of that. Interestingly, Shingi came into my mind first as an image of broken glasses – the cracked glasses stuck in my mind before the person came.

RP: But that in itself is a Marechera-like image?[8]

BC: I didn't know that!

RP: Can you comment on the language of your narrator in *Harare North*? It is not really Zimbabwean English and it's not standard British English either.

BC: Yes – I arrived at that style after a hard search – in Nigeria, there is this kind of pidgin English but I could not use that, and in Zimbabwe the only thing I could think of is this thing called *Chilapalapa*[9] – but the problem with that is that it has really negative connotations, so it would not really work (although you could try to re-invent it and I thought maybe I could do that, but it just wasn't working). So I had to come up with a colloquial language made up of common phrases from urban slang and then fuse them into Caribbean *patois* – a very natural relative of a lot of African speech. What can I say? Who was it, Ngugi or Achebe, who talked about inflecting the English language to carry the weight of African experience?[10] I thought this was the only language that could carry that.

RP: And you used Shona and Ndebele words as well.

BC: Yes.

RP: Are you familiar with the work of any white Zimbabwean writers?

BC: I've read some Alexandra Fuller. She is quite an intense writer, and a really honest writer, which I admire.

RP: Do you think you'll ever live in Zimbabwe again?

BC: Maybe; I don't know yet. Right now, it's very hard to decide.

Notes

1. See Clayton Peel's chapter in this volume.
2. 'Skies' is a Zimbabwean slang word for Bulawayo.
3. Mbare is the oldest 'high-density' area (colonial-era black ghetto) in Harare; its inhabitants have a reputation for toughness.
4. 'Harare North' is a Zimbabwean colloquial designation for Britain.
5. 'The green bombers' are a violent Zimbabwean pro-Mugabe youth militia.
6. The government-sponsored daily newspaper in Zimbabwe.
7. The philosopher and cultural theorist Slavoj Žižek, himself a trans-national intellectual, held a series of public lectures at Birkbeck college in London in the summer of 2006.
8. See, for example, the facial asymmetry in the description of Cicero in Dambudzo Marechera's *The Black Insider* (Harare: Baobab, 1990), p. 45, or the photograph of Marechera himself in Flora Veit-Wild and Ernst Schade's, *Dambudzo Marechera 1952–1987* (Harare: Baobab, 1988), p. 17.
9. A colonial-era pidgin spoken in Zimbawe and Zambia.
10. See Achebe, C. 1975. 'The African Writer and the English Language' in *Morning Yet on Creation Day*. London: Heinemann, pp. 55–162.

Notes on Contributors

Martha Chinouya is Lecturer in Social Anthropology at the London School of Hygiene and Tropical Medicine. She completed her doctoral thesis on HIV/AIDS among Africans in Britain, and has published widely in health policy and social science journals on HIV/AIDS in Britain and Zimbabwe.

Brian Chikwava is a writer, musician and journalist, who has lived in London since 2002. In 2004, he was awarded the Caine Prize for African Writing for his short story 'Seventh Street Alchemy'. He was Charles Pick Fellow at the University of East Anglia in 2005 and *Harare North*, his first novel, was published by Jonathan Cape in 2009.

Norma Kriger is an independent consultant and a visiting fellow at Cornell University's Institute for African Development. She has published widely on politics in Zimbabwe, including elections, land, human rights, the liberation struggle, and war veterans' 'integration'. She is author of *Zimbabwe's Guerrilla War: Peasant Voices* and *Guerrilla Veterans in Postwar Zimbabwe* (both published by Cambridge University Press).

Winston Mano is Senior Lecturer and Course Leader in the School of Media, Arts and Design, University of Westminster, UK. He edited 'The Media and Zimbabwe', a Special Issue of *Westminster Papers in Communication and Culture* (2005) and is a founding editor of the *Journal of African Media Studies* published by Intellect. His areas of research include: audiences, media, democracy and development in Africa.

Beacon Mbiba is Senior Lecturer at Oxford Brookes University and served on the Commission for Africa. He has published widely on development and planning issues in Zimbabwe and other parts of Africa, including in the journals *Africa* and *Progress in Development Studies*. His recent research has focused on Zimbabweans in Britain.

JoAnn McGregor is Lecturer in Geography at University College London. She is co-author (with Jocelyn Alexander and Terence Ranger) of *Violence and Memory: One Hundred Years in the 'Dark Forests' of Matabeleland* (James Currey 2000), and author of *Crossing the Zambezi: The Politics of Landscape on a Central African Frontier* (James Currey 2009).

James Muzondidya is a Zimbabwean academic and policy analyst currently working at the Human Sciences Research Council, Pretoria. His main area of research interest is in migration, citizenship and identity in postcolonial Africa. He is the author of *Walking a Tightrope: Towards a Social History of the Coloured People of Zimbabwe* (Africa World Press 2005).

Dominic Pasura holds a Postdoctoral Fellowship at University College London. His doctoral thesis 'A Fractured Diaspora: Strategies and Identities Among Zimbabweans in Britain' (University of Warwick, 2008) has formed the basis of recent publications in *African Diasporas, Global Networks* and the *Journal of Ethnic and Migration Studies*.

Clayton Peel gained his PhD from the University of Wales through the Oxford Centre for Mission Studies. A journalist by profession, he is a former Deputy Editor of *The Chronicle* newspaper in Bulawayo. He is vice-chairman of the Britain Zimbabwe Society and a member of the Association of Zimbabwean Journalists in the UK.

Ranka Primorac is Teaching Fellow at the University of Southampton. She has written widely on Zimbabwean literatures and cultures, and is the author of *The Place of Tears: The Novel and Politics in Modern Zimbabwe* (2006) and co-editor of *Versions of Zimbabwe* (2005) and *Zimbabwe in Crisis* (2007). Her edited collection *African City Textualities* is published with Routledge in 2010.

Blair Rutherford is Associate Professor in the Department of Sociology & Anthropology and the Institute of Political Economy at Carleton University in Ottawa, Canada. Since 1992, he has carried out research on the politics of land, labour, and citizenship in Zimbabwe and South Africa. He is the author of *Working on the Margins* (Zed Books, 2001) and has published widely in academic and popular journals.

Wendy Willems is Lecturer in Media Studies at the University of Witwatersrand in Johannesburg, South Africa. Her PhD, completed in 2009 at SOAS, focused on global media, nationalism and popular culure in the context of the Zimbabwe crisis (2000–2007). She is Associate Editor of the *Journal of African Media Studies* and Book Review Editor of *Ecquid Novi – African Journalism Studies*.

Index

inflation in 129
injiva (young single male migrants
to South Africa) in 39, 40
Interception of Communications
Act (2006) 107
maguma-guma, muggings by 65–6
marginalisation inside 241
Masvingo, access to *musha* in 64–5
National Army 2, 151
National Association for the
Advancement of Coloureds (NAAC)
241
National Unity Project 242
political repression in 8
public sphere, vibrancy and
plurality in 246–7
reciprocity, history with South
Africa of 17
Reserve Bank of 82, 116
South Africa-Zimbabwe Joint
Permanent Commission on
Defence and Security 88–9
violence in, elevation of 7–8
vulnerability, cultural politics of 17,
247
Zimbabwe Action Support Group
(MDC) 52
Zimbabwe African National Liberation
Army (ZANLA) 219
Zimbabwe Association (ZA) 9, 122,
125–7, 135, 138
Zimbabwe Broadcasting Corporation
(ZBC) 187
Zimbabwe Community Campaign to
Defend Asylum Seekers (UK) 136

Zimbabwe Community in Leeds 135
Zimbabwe Diaspora Development
Interface (UK) 20
Zimbabwe Exiles Forum 8, 90
Zimbabwe Gentlemen's Club (UK) 20
Zimbabwe Health Training Support
(UK) 136
Zimbabwe Institute of Engineers (UK)
20
Zimbabwe Open Forum, London
(2005) 136
Zimbabwe Political Victims'
Association 9
Zimbabwe Times 90
Zimbabwe Vigil 104, 106, 108–11, 115,
117–18, 119, 120n5, 134
Zimbabwe Women's Network (UK) 137
The Zimbabwean 110, 187, 196
Zimbabwean website communities
229–31
'Zimbabweanness' in South Africa 37
Zimbabwejournalists.com 23, 187
Zimbwa, Eladino 153
ZimCare 131
Zimdaily.com 23, 106, 107, 183, 187
Zimonline.co.za 23, 187
Zinyama, L. 63
Zuma, Jacob 89
Zvishavane Burial Society,
Johannesburg 50–51, 147
zwnews.com 187, 229
Zylinska, J. 128